Faith in Action

Religion, Race, and Democratic Organizing
in America

Richard L. Wood

The University of Chicago Press
Chicago and London

The University of Chicago Press, Chicago 60637
The University of Chicago Press, Ltd., London
© 2002 by The University of Chicago
All rights reserved. Published 2002
Printed in the United States of America
11 10 09 08 07 06 05 04   2 3 4 5

ISBN: 0-226-90595-0 (cloth)
ISBN: 0-226-90596-9 (paper)

Library of Congress Cataloging-in-Publication Data

Wood, Richard L.
    Faith in action : religion, race, and democratic organizing in
America / Richard L. Wood.
        p.   cm.—(Morality and society series)
    Includes bibliographical references and index.
    ISBN 0-226-90595-0 (alk. paper)—ISBN 0-226-90596-9 (pbk. :
alk. paper)
    1. Christianity and politics—United States. 2. Community
organization—United States. 3. PICO (Organization). I. Title.
II. Morality and society.

    BR526 .W658 2002
    261.7'0973—dc21

                                                    2002001049

for Dana
for Ella and Adam
for the coming of a more democratic future

Contents

Tables and Figures

Acknowledgments

In the research and writing that led to this book, I have incurred more debts to friends, colleagues, sponsors, and loved ones than I will be able to acknowledge here. It is with deep gratitude that I name at least a few of them. To Bob Bellah I owe the aspiration to do "public sociology" that combines critical analysis and social commitment; he also helped cultivate in an often recalcitrant man the patience and discipline to do so. To Ann Swidler I owe much more than the title of this book, a play on the title of a seminal article by her; she also instilled in me the habits of mind to combine intellectual rigor and empirical research. It is a joy today to call them both mentors and friends.

Other faculty members at the University of California at Berkeley and the Graduate Theological Union (GTU) were crucial influences in my development as a writer, ethnographer, and sociologist. Don Gelpi S.J., Bill Spohn, Barry Stenger, Marty Stortz, Mike Hout, John Coleman S.J., Kim Voss, Martín Sanchez-Jankowski, Bob Cole, Michael Burawoy, and Alan Pred played important roles in this regard. Judy Haier and Elsa Tranter facilitated this research in innumerable ways, far beyond their official duties.

I have learned much from colleagues on the journey. Jerome Baggett, Jim Ron, Dan Dohan, Chris Rhomberg, Phil Gorski, Paul Lichterman, Nina Eliasoph, Ricky Bluthenthal, Carolyn Chen, Rod Benson, Mark Chmiel, Margarita DeCierdo, Patricia Chang, Michael Emerson, Si Hendry S.J., and Eric Klinenberg all taught me much, and helped make the light and dark sides of academic life more fun.

At the University of New Mexico, Felipe Gonzales, Bert Useem, and Richard Coughlin provided helpful comments on earlier drafts of some chapters. They and other colleagues have welcomed me into their midst and made UNM a comfortable intellectual home for the writing of this book. Staff members Karen Majors, Jennifer Marshall, Rose Muller, and Judith Bernhard likewise aided this writing in many ways.

More distant colleagues at universities and other institutions have at various points read portions of this book and provided valuable feedback. These include Elisabeth Wood, Alan Wolfe (as series editor), Michelle Dillon, Nancy Ammerman, Chris Smith, Rhys Williams, Kelly Moore, David Yamane, Robert Wuthnow, Craig McGarvey, Jeannie Appleman, Don Miller, Jim Ron, Mike Miller, Neil Fligstein, Craig Calhoun, Mark Warren, Steve Hart, Omar McRoberts, Joe Palacios S.J., Michael Foley, Bob Edwards, Clark Roof, Joe Szazos, Bill Mirola, Sue Monohan, and anonymous reviewers along the way.

Financial support for this project's fieldwork and writing came from a variety of sources, all of whom I gratefully acknowledge. Through fellowship support, the University of California at Berkeley funded the majority of the fieldwork in Oakland. The shorter fieldwork in a half dozen cities around the country was made possible by funding from the Lilly Endowment, via a project at the GTU Center for Ethics and Social Policy on which John Coleman served as principal investigator. During recent years of writing, support of various forms has come from Pew Charitable Trusts, the College of Arts and Science at UNM, and Interfaith Funders; the latter also collected the data and sponsored the analysis for the national survey of faith-based organizing.

My respect and gratitude go to multiple people in the Pacific Institute for Community Organization and the Center for Third World Organizing. Though I cannot name all the leaders, activists, pastors, and staff who shared with me their work, insight, and passion for politics rightly understood, I am grateful to all. In CTWO, these particularly include Dan HoSang, Rinku Sen, Frances Calpotura, Rita Cotton, Margarita Sanchez, Gwen Hardy, and María Leal. In PICO, they include John Baumann S.J.,

Scott Reed, Jim Keddy, José Carrasco, Stephanie Gut, Denise Collazo, Joe Givens, Mike Kromrey, Bill Masterson, Ron Snyder, David Mann, Judy Reyes, Peter Phillips, Art Rose, and Jocelyn Coogler.

Father Paul Vassar, Father Ignatius de Groot, the men who appear here as Pastor Ron Owens and Karl Morrison, and numerous other pastors provided access to their faith communities and insight into their faith traditions.

The photographs at the start of each chapter are the work of a variety of people, both in taking photos and in making them available to me. These include Michelle Longosz, Claudine Niski, Sean Masterson, Dan HoSang, Kathleen Murphy, Don Buckholz, Glen Korengold, Stephanie Gut, and Don Stahlhut.

It has been a delight to work with Doug Mitchell, Robert Devens, Leslie Keros, and the rest of the editorial team at the University of Chicago Press, along with copyeditor Michael Koplow. A writer can do no better than to work with them. Alan Wolfe as series editor was his always-incisive and insightful self; he and the academic reviewers helped improve this book greatly.

Yet all would be for naught without those who form the very fabric of my life: family, friends, a faith community, loved ones. Many are named above, others already know who they are. My parents, Bill and B. J. Wood; my siblings and extended family; friends Maija & Jim, Chón y Juanita, Miguel y Marielena, Angela & Ken, Jerome & Sherry, Gerardo y Irene; the pastors and congregations of Aquinas Catholic Newman Center and Saint Andrew Presbyterian Church; and the witness of the Catholic martyrs of El Salvador are all central to that weave. Dana Bell is my life's companion, wife, mother to my kids, and (along with Libby) my best critic. She, Ella, and Adam bring unbelievable joy and love to this life. I am eternally grateful to all of you.

Democratic Renewal in America

On May 2, 2000, three thousand people converged on the State Capitol in Sacramento, California. But these were not the usual well-heeled lobbyists serving the interests of the well-off. Rather, these were working poor, working-class, and lower-middle-income folks lately referred to as "working families," who went to Sacramento because they were tired of living on the verge of financial ruin or physical debility. They went to demand adequate health coverage for Californians left out by our for-profit medical system—and they were angry about that, at a time when remarkable wealth was being accumulated all around them and California was running a $10 billion budget surplus.

They came for an "action" called "Healthcare for All: Reweaving the Fabric of American Communities," sponsored by the Pacific Institute for Community Organization (PICO). During the day's event, they drew on recent academic research showing that 7.3 million Californians held

Community leaders Cesar Portillo *(left)* and the Rev. Ken Chambers address the May 2000 statewide action on health care for working families, organized by the PICO California Project. Photograph by Glen Korengold.

no health insurance, including 1.5 million children eligible for subsidized coverage but still uninsured due to onerous inscription procedures. Most relied on community clinics or emergency rooms for their medical care— or did without.[1]

They packed the huge Sacramento Community Center Theater plus a nearby hall linked via television monitors with a crowd approximately 40 percent Latino, 40 percent white, and 20 percent combined African American and Hmong. And they were loud, as they believed they had to be to turn around a state government that had so far refused to address the health care crisis. More than a few leading California politicians and political aides reportedly did double-takes as they entered the largest and most multiracial political gathering in Sacramento in years.[2]

The event began with a reading from the Book of Amos, the Hebrew prophet who denounced an earlier society in which the wealthy violated God's covenant by turning their backs on the poor:

> I hate, I despise your feasts
> I take no pleasure in your solemn festivals.
> When you offer me holocausts [sacrifices] and grain offerings
> I will not accept them . . .
> Take away from me the noise of your songs;
> I will not listen to the melody of your harps.
> But let justice roll down like waters,
> and righteousness like an overflowing stream.[3]
>
> Amos 5:21–24

The event continued with a prayer by a San Francisco pastor, Bill Knezovich:

> Holy God, be here with us. At the beginning of our work, send upon us the spirit of Amos, so that we may go forward knowing that change will only be done by ourselves, advocating for our families and for all those not here with us. Hold before us all those old people forced to choose between food and medicine; all those couples ruined by medical diseases; all our own children whose health is neglected because we cannot afford to pay for medicine. Hold them before us so that we might fight with a righteous anger, as Amos did.[4]

There was much more, including testimony by a woman traumatized by her husband's suicide: he preferred to kill himself rather than ruin his family financially through a long illness. There were reports in English,

Spanish, and Hmong from families suffering the gnawing anxiety of living without medical coverage. There were demands that part of California's surplus be used to alleviate the health care crisis, a specific proposal to better fund community health clinics, and talk of a legislative bill to expand the "Healthy Families" medical insurance program in California.

PICO leaders then challenged a series of state political figures to commit themselves to work with PICO on this agenda. Among others, the president pro tempore of the California senate, John Burton, stepped to the microphone saying, "First of all, I'm overwhelmed at this magnificent turnout." He then committed himself to working with PICO to expand health coverage in California for the working poor.

More followed, but the flavor of the evening is perhaps best captured by two phrases. The first was repeated by a number of PICO leaders: "Health care now, for *all* God's people! Alleluia! Amen." The other was invoked repeatedly by leaders calling out "Se puede?" (Spanish for "Can it be done?"), in response to the political mantra of "no new entitlements" common in American politics today. Each time, the crowd thundered back, "Sí, se puede!," with the English-language speakers gradually adopting the chant.

This event and related work by PICO and its allies during the ensuing months dramatically shifted the political dynamics surrounding health policy in California. Within months, it led to $50 million in additional funding for community health clinics and the easing of bureaucratic requirements that kept many eligible immigrant families uninsured—and came within a hair's breadth of winning $130 million in new state money to provide health coverage for working families. Though they lost the latter in a legislative fiasco on the last day of the 2000 state legislative session, less than a year later they would win it back—despite a dramatic worsening of the state's financial position.

I will return to this story in chapter 2. For now, I note only that this is a story of grassroots work successfully reshaping public policy around a prominent issue (health care) in one of the largest political arenas in the United States (the state of California), pursuing the interests of those families at the lower rungs of the American social ladder. Furthermore, it is a story of using the language of religious faith—and, in a parallel analysis, the language of racial/ethnic identity—in the public arena to promote the interests of low-income Americans. This book is written for all those who want to build a more democratic future in America, as well as for scholars and students seeking insight into the intersection of religion, race, and democracy.

Our national political life has been saturated with religious language in recent years; the rise of the Christian Coalition and other elements of the religious right has made family values, issues of sexual morality, and (in a theological stretch) income and corporate tax reduction salient issues of "religious politics." More recently, the Bush administration's "faith-based initiative" has pushed to facilitate provision of government-funded social services by religious institutions. The faith-based organizations studied here also represent the intersection of religion, politics, and social issues, but how they draw on religious commitment—and the goals they pursue in doing so—differ quite dramatically from these models for linking religion and politics. In contrast to President Bush's faith-based initiative, these organizations work through religious institutions to reshape government policy via the exercise of democratic power. Religious institutions thus become sociopolitical critics of government and social policy rather than channels for government-funded social services. As we shall see, the tension between these two understandings of the role of religion vis-à-vis government raises important questions about the faith-based initiative. In contrast to the religious right's emphasis on individual and legislative moral change, these organizations struggle to improve the socioeconomic lot of poor, working-class, and middle-income Americans.

So this book is fundamentally about democratic renewal. The last thirty years have produced deep tears in our social fabric: real family incomes have declined steadily since the early 1970s, with only a marginal recovery in recent years. The gap between the well-off and the working class has become a chasm; apathy and cynicism—or perhaps just honest recognition that standard forms of participation make little difference—lead to rampant refusal to participate in political life. Families confront ever-mounting financial and cultural pressures. Though until recently masked by the longest peacetime expansion of our economy in memory, these trends cannot bode well for the future of America. Democratic life has a hard time flourishing in the hard soil of a society deeply divided between haves and have-nots.[5]

But this book carries a more analytic focus as well. It is about the underpinnings of democracy in the cultural dynamics, social capital, and institutions of American society. It is about politics—but politics in the broad sense of our shared life as a nation. I approach this by conceptualizing political culture in a way that takes politics seriously:[6] How do those excluded from the full benefits of societal life organize themselves to project political power in defense of their interests and as a voice for the common good? When they do so, how do they build an organizational culture to sustain their political engagement? I argue that we can adequately understand the struggles, successes, and failures of this kind of democratic organizing only if we look carefully at the *cultural dynamics* within their work. That is, strategies, political opportunities, and financial resources alone do not determine the outcomes of these struggles. Alternative cultural strategies for building political power give different organizations quite differing access to community ties and social capital, and at the same time deeply shape the flow of internal cultural resources within those organizations. I will show how both these culturally rooted factors impact the organizing process and its political outcomes.

The increased inequality of American society provides concrete evidence that the fruits of democratic life are not being distributed to all. The popular perception of politics as a degrading vocation, unworthy of people of integrity, suggests that many Americans recognize this democratic failure (even if they misdirect the blame for it). At the same time, there are promising signs from some of the deepest wellsprings of American democracy. As has occurred throughout our history, twin traditions of democratic activism and religious commitment are producing new forms of civic engagement. The embers of the democratic fire are being stirred by new efforts to hold our economic and political systems accountable to our common interests, and to the needs of poor, working, and middle-class families. So I write with a sense of hope in our future, a faith that our democratic yearnings may help us confront the challenges and embrace the opportunities of the new global economy and of ethnic and religious diversity in American life.

Two presuppositions lie behind my focus on those at the lower end of American society, their allies in more advantaged positions, and their joint efforts to build a more democratic society. First, to live up to its promise, democracy must be constantly renewed and perpetually deepened to include groups heretofore denied the full fruits of democracy. When American society succeeds in that democratic renewal, it rescues whole segments of its populace from being condemned to economic, political, and cultural marginalization—and replenishes its own democratic wellsprings. Second, if we fail in this democratic calling in our time, future generations will be haunted by that failure.

I do not argue that grassroots organizations or movements alone can renew American democracy, but rather that they are one crucial source for such renewal. They will require collaboration from allies in the political world, foundations, academic and cultural institutions, the media, labor and the corporate world, and from ordinary citizens. Their story is a challenge and invitation to such potential allies.

Models for Renewal: Faith-Based and Race-Based Organizing in Multiracial Communities

The two models of grassroots political participation examined here both fall under the rubric of "community organizing." Both often work in highly multiracial settings, but one pursues an explicitly faith-based model of such organizing, while the other pursues a secular model.

The term "community organizing" typically describes work inspired or influenced by the dean of community organizers in the United States, Saul Alinsky, whose work spanned four decades and deeply shaped subsequent grassroots organizing throughout urban America.[7] Both models of community organizing analyzed here incorporate certain techniques of organizing promulgated by Alinsky, but they also transcend his legacy in important ways.

I primarily focus on the style of organizing practiced by PICO and other organizations, known as "faith-based," "congregation-based," "broad-based," or "institutional" community organizing. Faith-based organizing roots itself institutionally in religious congregations, and culturally in the diverse religious practices and worldviews of participants—their religious culture. Though linked to religious congregations, such efforts occur in organizations independent of any specific congregation or denomination and incorporated separately as tax exempt, nonpartisan organizations (typically as 501c[3] organizations under the Internal Revenue Code).[8]

Although faith-based organizing remains rather unknown in academic circles, the first nationwide study of the field shows it to be second in size only to the labor movement among drives for social justice among low-income Americans today.[9] With 133 local or metropolitan-area federations linking some 3,500 congregations plus some 500 public schools, labor union locals, and other institutions, faith-based organizing can plausibly claim to touch the lives of some two million members of these institutions in all the major urban areas and many secondary cities around the United States.[10] These federations operate in thirty-three states and the District of Columbia, with strong concentrations in California, Texas, New York, Illinois, and Florida.[11] Their median budget is $150,000 per year; the vast majority of federations are affiliated with one of four major faith-based organizing networks (IAF, PICO, Gamaliel, and DART; see chapter 1).

Much of this book focuses on this broad field of faith-based community organizing, using PICO as a case study to understand the organizing techniques that have allowed it to build so broad a movement and gain the level of success exemplified in the PICO California Project, other statewide and regional efforts, and a host of local organizing projects. This focus will also allow us to understand how faith-based organizing bridges the divide between the faith lives of congregations and the social and political world around them, as well as the lessons this may hold for our democratic life.

This book also analyzes a second influential model of community organizing, known as "race-based" or "multiracial" organizing. Multiracial organizing roots itself culturally in the racial identities of participants, appealing to potential participants as "people of color." Here, the title *Faith in Action* applies in a rather different sense: participants in this kind of organizing place a great deal of their political faith in the power of "direct action" to change institutionalized power relations. They devote a significant portion of their energy to changing society and public policy by revealing the ways that current political and economic institutions exclude large numbers of people—particularly people of color. The organizing techniques used in doing so are quite similar to those used in faith-based organizing, but they appeal to cultural elements identified with participants' racial, ethnic, or national traditions, rather than those identified with religious traditions.[12] Likewise, multiracial organizing works through local institutions, but of a different kind: instead of religious congregations, it is rooted institutionally in social service agencies serving low-income urban residents— but only in a limited way, in order to remain institutionally autonomous.

Nationally, race-based organizing operates on a smaller scale than faith-based organizing, but it can be found in metropolitan areas and some rural areas throughout the country. Its local proponents sponsor "accountability sessions" similar to the Healthcare for All Californians action, albeit on a somewhat smaller scale. One of its leading institutional proponents is the Center for Third World Organizing (CTWO). Like faith-based organizing, race-based organizing is an influential movement for social justice in America. It has gained particular influence in urban settings with populations of high racial diversity and is important here due to its local influence, its focus on building a multiracial political culture, and the comparative light it sheds on the broader cultural and institutional dynamics of community organizing.[13]

So two models of community organizing lie at the center of this story of democratic life in low- and middle-income America today. Both sponsor high-profile public events to force political institutions to better serve the interests of low-income residents. These events are typically led by local organizations affiliated with faith-based organizing networks or with CTWO, the Southwest Network for Environmental and Economic Justice, or myriad local and regional groups; less often, they are led by independent local groups. Both models organize in highly multiracial settings, but each adopts a quite different cultural strategy for doing so—a different approach for appealing to the identities, beliefs, and commitments of potential participants in order to engage them in the work of nonpartisan political organizing. I focus on the institutional and cultural dynamics arising from their cultural strategies. By institutional and cultural dynamics, I mean the ways their appeals to religious culture or to being people of color shape the internal political culture of each group, its ability to collaborate with other institutions, and ultimately how these factors affect its ability to project democratic power. I draw on concepts from political sociology and recent studies of social movements and at the same time move beyond those concepts to address broader questions regarding the political culture of American democracy—including the way culture (whether linked to religious or racial/ethnic identity) enables and constrains democratic action.[14]

Why PICO and CTWO?

Both faith-based and race-based community organizing work to reshape local politics (and increasingly state-level politics as well) toward the needs of low-income communities. In the language of democratic theory, each organization strives to empower its constituents to articulate their public concerns in the political arena in order to redirect governmental policy to better meet the needs of less privileged members of society. In the process, they seek to transform the relationship between citizens and public institutions.

I analyze faith-based and race-based organizing by looking in detail at two of their most successful sponsors. The PICO/CTWO comparison makes it possible to hold constant a number of factors that otherwise would confound the analysis of their institutional and cultural dynamics. These factors include locale, political opportunities, resources, issues, organizing techniques, and demographics.

Locale

Rather than abstractly comparing the overall organizing efforts of CTWO and PICO in differing local contexts, I look at their respective projects in one city: Oakland, California. This allows me to focus on specific cultural and institutional dynamics of interest here and to hold constant the wider social environment faced by the two organizations.

As important as their location in the same city, PICO and CTWO organize within essentially identical neighborhoods in East and West Oakland. CTWO targets particular sections of those neighborhoods, notably the poorer sections and those where incidents (such as police abuse) may have generated particular discontent related to their organizing. PICO's church-affiliated organizing committees typically include members from within such sections but also incorporate broad swaths of low- and moderate-income inner-city neighborhoods and a few somewhat more affluent neighborhoods.

Political Opportunities

Closely related to the organizations' locale is the set of political opportunities faced by each organization. Scholars call this the political opportunity structure that an organization faces—a structure because it is a product of the specific setting and historical moment in which a political movement exists, both of which lie beyond an organization's control.[15] Political opportunity structure includes such factors as the relative openness of political institutions to influence by new political actors; the stability or state of flux of governing political alignments; and the presence or absence of possible allies within governing elites. The first two features are essentially identical for CTWO and PICO in Oakland, since they operate in the same political environment; the third feature differs due to differing possible allies available to CTWO and PICO by virtue of their cultural strategies and organizational cultures—precisely the factors explored here.

Resources

The financial resources on which CTWO's and PICO's efforts in Oakland draw are quite similar. During the course of my primary fieldwork, PICO's organizing budget in Oakland remained relatively stable around $180,000 per year, and CTWO's organizing budget in Oakland declined slightly, from $150,000 per year for several years to just below $130,000 per year.[16] Out of this budget, each pays rent for office space that includes a meeting room and several small offices and supports professional organizers (during most of this study, two full-time and one part-time at CTWO; three full-time at PICO). Primary funding for both organizations comes from foundation grants.

Finally, both organizations draw on the expertise regarding organizing, fund-raising, media work, and staff development of their central organizations. That is, the home offices of CTWO and PICO (both located in Oakland and thus equally available) provide significant input in these areas. It is difficult to measure the actual value of the services rendered, but they appear to be similar, as both PICO and CTWO hold strong reputations among community organizers nationally.

Issues

Despite superficial differences, the issues addressed by CTWO's and PICO's organizing efforts in Oakland were structurally quite similar. In the period prior to my fieldwork, CTWO had successfully pursued a comprehensive children's immunization program, testing for lead contamination, improved translation services at the local public hospital serving most indigent patients, morning "nutrition breaks" at public schools, and distribution to social service agencies of drug-connected assets seized by the Oakland Police Department. PICO had successfully pushed the city to improve parks, recreation services, and street lighting in flatland neighborhoods; convinced the public schools to improve learning conditions and programs in classroom and strengthen the reporting of public school attendance; and convinced the Oakland Police Department to institute a "Beat Health" unit that uses violations of public health and zoning laws to shut down crack houses, and later launch a citywide community policing program.[17]

Simply listing these issues creates an illusion of dramatically different organizing efforts, but this masks significant underlying similarities. Through these issues, both organizations have targeted city and county governments and the Oakland public schools to extract improved services for low-income areas under their jurisdictions. Both have included social services, educational conditions, and changes in police practices within their demands. Neither set is discernibly more liberal or conservative than the other.[18]

During my fieldwork, CTWO and PICO both succeeded on a set of higher-level issues—that is, issues they considered more challenging because they required the organization to enter a broader political arena (e.g., citywide politics instead of one city councilperson), entailed overcoming greater political opposition, or involved forming broader coalitions. For PICO, these include economic development in East and West Oakland, conversion of a traditional public school to a teacher- and parent-run (but still publicly funded) charter school, and (in a partnership with the local teachers union) redirection of public school funding priorities to reduce the number of children in each teacher's classroom and increase teachers' salaries. It was also part of a successful statewide PICO effort to reform secondary education to provide more effective preparation for college and the "school-to-work transition," and for more extensive after-school programs funded with public dollars. CTWO successfully promoted a campaign to guarantee funding for public schools in Oakland and redistribute drug seizure money from law enforcement to social service agencies, and it continues to seek greater civilian oversight of police operations. It has collaborated in statewide efforts to organize immigrant women workers and an effort to increase police accountability in several cities nationwide.

Again, though superficially different, these issues are structurally similar; thus, the issue areas pursued by the two organizations before and during my fieldwork are reasonably parallel: Both had a history of extensive success with lower-level issues, both successfully pursued more challenging issues during the course of this study, and both came to dedicate significant organizational effort to statewide or multicity initiatives (with differing success, as we shall see).

Organizing Techniques

The core organizing techniques of the two organizations are remarkably similar, many having a common source in the Alinsky community organizing tradition. These include an emphasis on organizing through person-to-person meetings, the strategic use of conflict and tension within the organizing process, evaluation sessions after meetings, a focus on "challenging" and "holding accountable" other participants in the organizing process, and an effort to have nonprofessional participants, rather than paid staff, take all public leadership roles—all practices to which we will pay some detailed attention later. Even where the organizations' terminology diverges, substantial overlap of organizing techniques exists: "political actions" in PICO and other faith-based organizing networks are in nearly all respects structurally identical to CTWO's "accountability sessions"; the role of "political education" in CTWO is discernibly different from the role of "training" and "reflection" in PICO—but only marginally so. As will become clear, these organizations have different emphases and styles of work, but they are not separate species; their actual practices of organizing make them siblings in the work of democracy—or at least close cousins.

Demographics

The racial and ethnic demographics of the two organizations differ, but not radically: PICO in Oakland primarily draws African American and Latino participants (in approximately equal numbers), plus 20 percent non-Hispanic whites and a handful of Asian-Americans and Asian immigrants. CTWO in Oakland primarily draws African American and Latino residents, plus 10–20 percent Asian-Americans and Asian immigrants and a handful of non-Hispanic whites. Both can be fairly described as multiracial organizations, assuming that term includes white participation. Also, although demographics of the organizations vary from one local neighborhood to another, African American and Latino participation divides roughly equally in each organization taken as a citywide whole. Gender demographics diverged more strongly: CTWO's leaders were predominantly women, and PICO's leaders divided quite evenly between men and women.[19]

The socioeconomic status of participants tells a more complex story. PICO's constituency reflects church membership in East and West Oakland: some quite impoverished, periodically unemployed, or supported by welfare; many working-class laborers or low-level office workers; many struggling to stay within the lower middle class, the older ones homeowners and the younger ones renting and with little prospect of purchasing a home; and a few members of comfortable, two-income households. The primary constituency for CTWO's organizing effort in Oakland covers only the lower part of this spectrum: the working poor, lower-middle-class non-homeowners, and those supported by welfare (formerly mostly AFDC, now TANF).

CTWO thus primarily represents a highly marginalized constituency, whereas PICO's constituency includes both the highly marginalized and those with more significant though limited economic, political, and cultural resources. This clearly gives CTWO a certain affinity for a more anti-institutional political tenor and PICO some greater access to certain kinds of cultural skills. But the overlap is substantial, and the socioeconomic differences do not appear to predominate in determining the organizations' political development.

Other than their divergent cultural strategies, PICO and CTWO thus display significant similarities: they use similar organizing techniques to organize in essentially identical neighborhoods of Oakland; face very similar political opportunities; address similar but not identical issues; have access to comparable financial, in-kind, and strategic support; and display overlapping demographic profiles whose differences are rooted in their contrasting cultural and institutional bases of appeal. By analyzing the internal dynamics and political experience of the two organizations, we will gain insight into the implications of two key cultural strategies for pursuing greater democracy in American life.

How I Studied PICO and CTWO

To study the process of community organizing, I carried out what sociologists call participant observation of both organizations. I spent three years systematically observing the organizing process in PICO's Oakland project, two years in CTWO's Oakland project, and subsequently tracked events in both organizations via interviews and newsletters. In both organizations, I regularly attended monthly meetings of the core citywide leadership and often attended weekly meetings of smaller subcommittees in CTWO and organizing committees at individual churches in PICO. As part of my role in both organizations, I periodically provided Spanish translation of public actions or written documents. I also acted as one of five key "leaders" of the PICO organizing committee in my own local congregation. I thus became at least a low-level participant in both organizations; this helped me gain far greater insight into the experience of other participants. It also gave me greater entree to the inner workings of CTWO and PICO; I was able to attend internal agenda-setting meetings of the core leadership in each organization, watch evaluation discussion to which outsiders are not normally invited, and have very frank conversations with participants at all levels. But of course this role also challenged me to maintain a critical distance from their work; scholars, friends, and other organizational outsiders played crucial roles in helping me gain perspective on what I was seeing.[20]

I also observed both organizations' political events, cultural celebrations or prayer vigils, and fund-raising events, as well as their background research meetings with political officials, academics, and corporate leaders and their participation at public hearings. I attended training workshops led by PICO organizers, political education and study groups led by CTWO organizers, the five-day "national training" run by PICO, and some parts of the summer-long training institute for minority organizers run by CTWO. Finally, in order to more fully understand the cultural underpinnings of faith-based organizing, I attended worship services at all the churches that were members of PICO in Oakland, then selected the key cases discussed in the second half of this book and attended worship in those churches multiple times.

I conducted seventy formal interviews with participants, in addition to scores of informal interviews before or after the meetings I attended. Some thirty-five of the formal interviews were in Oakland and in Denver, the only other city in which both CTWO and PICO sponsor organizing efforts. These interviews lasted from forty-five minutes to two hours and included organizing staff, local leaders, and pastors, as well as political leaders the organizations have targeted.[21] Wood 1995 provides further information on my interviewing method and questions.[22] I learned more about faith-based organizing through forty additional formal interviews in PICO federations in five cities nationwide. The strategy of concentrating on Oakland while doing brief research in other cities (and more recently in other networks, research not reported here) allows me to take advantage of the rich ethnographic data possible through in-depth case studies while also assessing and highlighting those patterns that are typical of faith-based and race-based organizing rather than idiosyncratic to Oakland.

Sometimes trying and often exhausting, this research was also a great deal of fun, due to the generous spirits of the people involved and the joys of sharing in their idealistic yet pragmatic political work to deepen democracy. I hope that the insights gained through this research will provide the reader with some taste of this democratic work; offer its practitioners some guideposts for their own reflection and praxis; and invite all of us to more thoughtful engagement in overcoming the dilemmas of market-based democracy.

Structure of the Book

The chapters ahead integrate narrative and analytic modes to draw an account of contemporary democratic organizing in America. The narrative sections focus on how these movements promote democratic participation and egalitarian social policies, while the analytic sections explore the longer-term significance of these movements by examining how they confront the institutional and cultural dilemmas of modern democracy. Chapters 1 and 2 focus on faith-based organizing at the local, metropolitan, and statewide levels. Chapter 3 focuses on race-based organizing as practiced by

CTWO in order to highlight its contrasting cultural strategy and resulting political experience. Chapter 4 comprises the analytic heart of the first half of the book. It draws on the concepts of social capital, civil society, and the public realm to analyze and compare how faith-based and race-based organizing confront two key institutional dilemmas of modern democracy: the weakening of social capital in low-income urban communities and the gulf between those communities and our political institutions. This analysis highlights how differing cultural strategies lead to differential access to social capital, with important political consequences.

These early chapters leave unanswered a series of questions concerning the place of cultural factors in sustaining and strengthening democratic life: Beyond the access it provides to social capital, does culture also matter directly *as culture*? In particular, does that form of cultural life we call religion matter *as religion*? Or does religion perhaps just provide a perception of legitimacy, access to social capital, and some organizational and financial resources to sustain political engagement?

The second half of the book examines these questions through a much more explicit cultural analysis of the organizing process in CTWO and PICO. Chapter 5 explores the cultural dynamics within faith-based organizing, particularly how the intersection of practices and beliefs rooted in democratic or religious cultural strands of American life together shape an organizational ethos I term "ethical democracy." Chapter 6 draws on recent studies of political culture, social movements, congregations, and the sociology of organizations to highlight the cultural dilemmas of modern democracy and outlines a framework for examining how democratic movements resolve those dilemmas. The closing part of that chapter and all of chapter 7 apply this framework to three different congregational settings to show that asking how "religious culture" affects political organizing is much too broad a question. By examining the impact of three distinct religious cultures on faith-based organizing, these chapters show that much depends on the particular forms of religious culture. The book concludes with chapter 8, which again places race-based and faith-based organizing in comparative perspective, now in light of how they overcome or are undermined by the cultural and institutional dilemmas of democracy; the chapter reflects on the implications of this analysis for the future of American democracy. Appendix 1 provides a list of faith-based organizing and CTWO-affiliated organizations nationwide; appendix 2 gives a fuller account of the development of PICO over the past twenty-five years.

Diagnosing Democracy and Democratic Movements

Democratic theorists and other social scientists have diagnosed the short-comings of contemporary democracy and civic life under several rubrics, most prominently as a matter of declining social capital, the distortion of communicative dynamics in the public sphere, weakened political institutions, and the inculcation of democratic skills in ways skewed by socioeconomic inequality, racial/ethnic identity, and gender.[23] Chapter 4 will draw on these diagnoses to argue that a key institutional dilemma of democracy lies in the *structural fragmentation of the public sphere* and to analyze the potential for faith-based and race-based organizing to overcome this fragmentation. Here, I note briefly how other scholars have assessed the democratic potential of similar movements, using two exemplars of such assessments.

In *The City and the Grassroots,* his now-classic study of urban social movements in Europe, the United States, and Latin America, Manuel Castells highlighted the democratic aspirations of such movements, but ultimately came to believe them incapable of overcoming the weakness of their structural position. In the final analysis, these movements try to change cities too beholden to international capital flows and elite political power to meet democratic and egalitarian demands. Castells closes the book with great sympathy for such movements, but profound pessimism regarding their democratic potential.

In contrast, in a series of books about citizen democracy in the United States, Harry Boyte and his coauthors argue for "the democratic promise" of citizens' participatory movements, including the kinds of organizations studied here. The title of one book (1996) gives a flavor of this literature: *Building America: The Democratic Promise of Public Work.* These books tout the accomplishments of such organizations and are optimistic about their potential for transforming American life.

How are we to understand this contrast? Is Castells too pessimistic to see the democratic implications of modern social movements? Is Boyte too optimistic in his reading of their potential impact? Or has the strategic ability of urban movements changed enough in the last twenty years to justify an optimistic stance where only pessimism made sense previously? *Faith in Action* suggests a cautiously hopeful answer: partly due to their sophistication in working with grassroots institutions and drawing on the social capital embedded there (analyzed in chapters 1–4), and partly due to having recently developed a more sophisticated political culture (analyzed in chapters 5–7), some versions of contemporary urban organizing have indeed transcended the limits that Castells saw in the late 1970s. At the same time, this hopefulness is tempered by the overwhelming social fact of our time: a global economy unaccountable to democratic pressures or the needs of local communities. Whatever its costs and benefits—and there clearly are many of both—the global economy clearly transcends the abilities of traditional democratic institutions to regulate it. I thus strive to present the difficulties and ambiguities inherent in new forms of organizing as they face the obstacles of the new global economy.

Early in the twenty-first century, formal democratic governance is widespread, but there is cause for real concern about the *substance* of democracy in America. Never perfect, yet ever challenged by marginalized groups and prophetic leaders to live up to its democratic ideals, American democracy today faces new temptations and confronts new social dynamics that threaten to undermine its foundations. The vast wealth accumulated by a new elite in American society tempts them to ignore the struggles and anxieties of those at the bottom of the economic pyramid. The nation's status as the only "hyperpower" and the locus of global financial capital bring new temptations to abuse our global power. Our situation also opens up new windows of opportunity to address national and global inequities, but only democratic pressure from below and visionary leadership from above will lead us to take advantage of those opportunities. Meanwhile, under the surface of American society, powerful dynamics may be eroding our ability to generate effective democratic pressure and elect visionary leadership. If money continues to dominate our politics, if working-class folk have unequal opportunities to learn civic skills, and if social capital in middle-class and marginalized communities continues to erode, these citizens will find it impossible to shape the political and economic decisions that affect their lives. The organizations studied here provide no panacea for these challenges, but understanding their achievements and dilemmas may help us all build a more democratic future.

Part I   Dynamics of Contention in Faith-Based and Multiracial Organizing

Generating effective democratic power from below is in part a matter of building networks of solidarity within society. This includes solidarity among those who least enjoy the benefits of contemporary affluence, as well as solidarity between them and democratically inclined people holding positions of influence in more elite institutions. But how are such networks of solidarity built? Part 1 explores this question by looking in detail at how effective efforts at democratic work go about the organizing process—and by comparatively analyzing the fruits of faith-based and race-based efforts.

A vast body of scholarly and popular literature has examined how subaltern groups strive to gain a more equal footing in society. The classic case for many of these studies has been the movement for the civil rights of African Americans in the 1950s and 1960s (McAdam 1982, 1988; Morris 1984). But a much broader series of studies looks at similar questions in myriad other settings, typically under the analytic rubrics of resource mobilization, political opportunities, identity formation, mobilizing structures, democratization, and consciousness raising. These studies have provided significant insight into these movements and important new knowledge about political contestation throughout the world. But more recently, three of the leading figures in this line of inquiry have questioned whether this analytic framework really tells us what we need to know about the "dynamics of contention" (McAdam, Tarrow, and Tilly 2001). They suggest that these analytic labels have directed our attention to key factors influencing the outcomes of movements, but in the process have distracted our attention from the *relational processes* that lie at the heart not only of social movements, but also of democratization efforts, revolutions, and other cases in which institutional power is contested.

Part 1 of *Faith in Action*—written in response to the same dissatisfaction with the social movement analytic framework that appears to have beset McAdam, Tarrow, and Tilly, but quite independently of their efforts—at least partially takes up their challenge to rethink how we understand the dynamics of political contention.[1] It examines those dynamics by beginning within the organizing process, with an eye to understanding how participants build networks of solidarity that allow them to enter into contention with political elites. Later, we will consider the ways that this contention sometimes becomes the basis for constructive collaboration with political or economic elites. Where sufficient solidarity can be built, either on the basis of previously existing social capital or of new relational networks built within the organizing process, these movements can gain a powerful voice in the political arena.

A pleasant irony underlies the new scholarly attention to relational processes. Professional organizers in both of these models have long resisted one of the standard labels given them in academic studies: social movement entrepreneurs. They have therefore also resisted having their organizations described as social movements, insisting instead that their work is "relational organizing." Thus, scholarly analytic categories may have finally caught up with the better instincts of sophisticated democratic practitioners "on the ground."

Chapter 1

Faith-Based Organizing in Action: The Local Organizing Committee at Saint Elizabeth Catholic Church

From 1985 to 2000, the Pacific Institute for Community Organization grew from four federations in California to a network of twenty-eight federations in metropolitan areas around the country (see appendix 2). Paralleled by growth in other faith-based organizing networks, this has placed faith-based organizing among the most influential movements for social justice among low-income residents of urban America today.

Faith-based organizing begins in local organizing committees, most of which are associated with individual religious congregations. These committees make decisions about what issues to address, run the political actions sponsored by their congregation, build the networks of relationships through which congregation members are invited to those actions, and link these local efforts to broader citywide organizing projects. Through such

Top: Oakland Community Organization members march down East Fourteenth Street, February 1998. In English the sign reads, "We want a school on the Montgomery Ward site." Photograph by Michelle Longosz. Courtesy Oakland Community Organization. *Bottom:* Crane demolishes the Montgomery Ward building in Oakland, California, February 2001. Photograph by Don Buckholz.

efforts, religious culture and religious institutions—along with political strategy and organizing techniques—help generate the political dynamism and ethical leverage needed to reorient public life toward more human and democratic ends. Later chapters will consider how such congregation-based efforts are coordinated and multiplied to produce the citywide political power exerted in larger public actions. During the research for this book, such larger actions included twenty-five hundred leaders from around California urging a Republican governor to fund after-school programs; five thousand Louisiana residents gathering to urge gubernatorial candidates to support a diverse agenda regarding schools, police corruption, and other issues; fifteen hundred Denver residents pushing for greater and more equitable funding for public schools; and eighteen hundred San Diegans working in coordination with the local teachers union to reduce class sizes in public elementary schools. Through such gatherings and the gradual organizing work leading up to them, faith-based organizing strives to exert sufficient leverage to influence public policy in a world of distant government and unfettered corporate capital flows. Faith-based organizing has generated its greatest successes through these kinds of metropolitan (as well as statewide) organizing efforts, which will be the focus of chapter 2. But gaining this degree of political clout depends greatly on the organizing dynamics within individual congregations.

So we first explore faith-based organizing by describing PICO's work in its fundamental building block: the "local organizing committee" within a sponsoring religious congregation. This chapter focuses on a strong example of a local organizing committee: Saint Elizabeth Catholic Church, of the PICO-affiliated Oakland Community Organizations (OCO). While OCO participants overall are evenly divided among African American, Latino, and white residents, with a smattering of southeast Asian immigrants, Saint Elizabeth is heavily Latino. It incorporates Mexican-Americans, immigrants from Mexico and Central America, and smaller numbers of white non-Latinos. The chapter shows religious culture in action by following local PICO participants through the organizing process.[1] The following extended narrative typifies the organizing dynamics through which PICO has gained high-profile political leverage: the incorporation of religious cultural elements within the organizing process; the role of professional organizers; a focus on developing participants' democratic skills; and the flow of respect and conflict between elected officials and the faith-based organizing participants.

The Organizing Process: Politics on the Ground, Religion in the World

Saint Elizabeth Catholic Church lies a block off East Fourteenth Street, the main thoroughfare through a crowded, low-income, largely Latino district of Oakland, California. By the 1990s, this part of the city had been hard hit by fifteen years of global economic restructuring and the disappearance of unionized blue-collar jobs that once provided stable incomes for thousands of Oakland workers. The street's lively but grim commercial district held a multitude of small retail stores, fast-food chains, and family-owned taco-and-burrito restaurants, outnumbered only by run-down and boarded-up storefronts. The skyline of the area was dominated by the huge hulk of the former Montgomery Ward retail outlet. That building, abandoned for over ten years, occupied a full block along East Fourteenth, casting a visual and economic shadow over the whole area.

On an October evening in 1994, members of the Saint Elizabeth organizing committee of PICO's Oakland federation met at the church to do something about the abandoned building. They had been working on the Montgomery Ward issue for several months, after extensive one-to-one meetings with church members and neighbors had revealed that lack of job opportunities and Fourteenth Street's run-down atmosphere were among residents' prime concerns. The initiative was also informed by a broader PICO campaign focused on generating jobs and economic development in Oakland and other cities.[2]

For this meeting, seven lay leaders from Saint Elizabeth gathered in a meeting room at the parish school. Three were men, four were women, and six were Latino.[3] Two spoke primarily English, two were bilingual, and three were immigrants from Mexico who spoke primarily Spanish. Also present were a female PICO organizer working with this committee and a woman representing a local developer seeking to redevelop the Montgomery Ward site. The meeting began with a prayer, led by lay leader Lucy Nevarez:[4]

> Lord, we gather in your name as friends, as family, as concerned citizens. We ask you to help us continue your work, to build a better city, to transform this place that has been so abandoned. We know that you never abandon us, that you walk with us as we do your will.

The first part of the evening was designated a research meeting: the developer's representative updated the group on the state of plans to redevelop the abandoned building site. Following some questions and discussion, the focus shifted to the other key players in the redevelopment effort: city government and the local city council representative, Ignacio De la Fuente. He had been spearheading this issue within the city government, but a leader who had tried to set up a meeting with him reported that he was unwilling to meet personally and wanted instead to send an aide, yet appeared to want to take all the credit for the redevelopment effort. In the ensuing discussion, some leaders were angry at being snubbed, others wanted to "just go with it." The organizer (Denise Collazo, then new to PICO, today the director of its San Francisco Organizing Project), stepped in, speaking both Spanish and English:

> Do you think it will help us move this forward to just meet with an aide? [Discussion: "not really."] How many people have you met with one-to-one about this issue just in the last couple months? ["Altogether, more than fifty, and lots more before that."] So you've put a lot of work into this already; all that to end up not even meeting with him? ["De la Fuente promised to support this, but now he's going backwards."] Well, he's done some work, but not as much as he has for Kmart [another redevelopment project]. The question here is, does he have the right to refuse to meet with the people he represents?

With this discussion framing the issue, the group soon agreed to pursue a meeting with De la Fuente himself. Roberto Montalvo summarized the group's sentiment: "Let's get a meeting with him to make sure this project happens. I don't care *who* runs it or gets the credit for it, as long as it gets done." They agreed to write a letter to De la Fuente, with their own signatures and that of the parish priest, who had strongly supported OCO's organizing.[5]

The last part of the meeting was dedicated to a group discussion of a significant problem: they felt that the pastor of Saint Elizabeth, Father Ignatius de Groot, had become less supportive of their work than in the past. Though his credentials in social action were strong, after years of involvement with the farmworkers' movement and more recently strong advocacy of faith-based organizing, he had not attended recent meetings and was resisting the group's desire to do a written congregational survey during masses.

Some leaders expressed frustration with the priest and wanted to confront him on these issues; others urged patience and "understanding his position." Collazo moved the group toward a decision by simply asking,

"So shall we wait for next week? Or meet with Father Ignatius about this now?" Manuel Arias initiated the group's final position: "I think we should meet with him now. It's a problem. We're fighting De la Fuente *and* Father Ignatius. We can't do that, we *need* the pastor's support and can't work around him."[6] This persuaded the group, and Arias was asked to set up the meeting and act as chairperson, but his respect for religious authority made this assignment difficult. Ultimately—and it appeared reluctantly—he accepted both roles.

Before ending the meeting, the group pieced together an agenda for the meeting with de Groot. Collazo asked, "What do we want to get out of this meeting?," to which leader Lucy Nevarez responded: "What we'd like is a commitment to back us up"—clarified to mean a willingness to write the letter to De la Fuente, freedom to make announcements at Mass, and preferably to do the Mass survey. Estela Cerda, a Spanish-speaking immigrant woman and the one person who had not previously spoken during the meeting, noted: "We need to understand *why* he's opposed to this. He never used to be. He's always supported us before." The organizer encouraged her to ask this question "directly to the padre" at the coming meeting. The meeting concluded with a short prayer led in Spanish by one of the lay leaders: "Lord, be with us as we go out tonight. Help us to have courage, to have faith as we work together to make our city a better place for everyone. May we not be afraid, but trust that you work through us if we work for what is right." They then prayed together the traditional Lord's Prayer in both languages and exited into the night air, set to confront two significant authority figures in different ways: a fairly assertive challenge to a political leader from their community who had been a valuable ally but now seemed to be shunning them, and a more gentle but still heartfelt challenge to a respected and supportive religious leader whose support now appeared to be wavering.

The denouement of the latter challenge was somewhat anticlimactic: the group met with de Groot and expressed their concerns; he reiterated his full support for their work and willingness to give them access to make announcements and survey parish members, but insisted that this happen in a way that would not take too long or disrupt the worship experience of the community. He also began to attend meetings more often, while making clear he would not always be present for what he said should always be "a lay-led ministry." Thus, some mild conflict led to a recommitment on the part of the religious authority in this congregation. A letter signed by him was sent to initiate the group's challenge to De la Fuente:

> I am writing on behalf of the Saint Elizabeth parish and the Oakland Com-
> munity Organizations to express my concern that you have been unwill-
> ing to meet with us regarding our work on the K-Mart and Montgomery
> Ward's projects. Our parish has done hundreds of 1-1s [one-to-one meet-
> ings] with families throughout the district about these two projects and
> we would like to meet with you to tell you what we have learned. . . .
> [W]e feel it is urgent that we meet with you, Councilman De la Fuente, as
> soon as possible. Please contact me in order to set up a meeting with us.

At the next meeting, de Groot was present and reported that De la Fuente had contacted him saying he was willing to meet. Three dynamics were evident in the ensuing dialogue. First, the organizer worked hard to develop the group's interpretive resources, the "lens" through which they observe the political world. She pushed the participants to be aware of how the councilman might have been manipulating them politically; invited them to return constantly to "what we know" rather than speculation and hearsay; and encouraged them to be flexible regarding minor issues, not to stake out unbending positions on details like dates for meetings. Second, the pastor urged the group to understand the complexities of an elected official's role, and thus not to caricature the councilman's position. Third, the more experienced Saint Elizabeth lay leaders drew on this political and ethical input as they positioned themselves pragmatically "to make sure De la Fuente's accountable even while we collaborate with him." Longtime leader Fran Matarrese articulated the group's final position:

> You're right, Father Ignatius, we should work with De la Fuente and un-
> derstand his position. But we don't want to kowtow to him either. We
> want him to *prioritize* his time, make time for us if he wants our support.
> . . . This is about accountability. We want a representative who shares our
> priorities, who isn't too busy to meet with us.

This meeting concluded with the group setting a time line for the next four months.

These ensuing months of the nuts-and-bolts of community organizing were quite eventful. The group continued to wrestle with the nature of its collaboration with De la Fuente. Being a nonpartisan community group working in partnership with an ambitious political leader raised a host of issues, around which the group gradually defined the limits as well as the possibilities of the collaboration. At different points, the organizer, the pas-tor, and the more experienced leaders sometimes pushed the group forward into confrontation with a recalcitrant political system and sometimes encouraged the group to pursue constructive collaboration with that system. Within a few months, De la Fuente committed himself explicitly to working with the Saint Elizabeth OCO group "to make the Montgomery Ward project work." He also tried to convince the group to be part of an employment service he was establishing. The group refused to participate in selecting individual candidates; they later described this as "patronage politics."

Significant tensions arose at a meeting in January 1995 as OCO and De la Fuente negotiated their roles in the Montgomery Ward project, a potential apprenticeship program in local labor unions, and several other projects. Ultimately, however, the meeting ended on quite amicable terms: the council member asked OCO's help in pushing forward several initiatives, and OCO elicited his commitment to having a senior staff member meet with them monthly for several months. Before leaving, in response to the latter request, De la Fuente noted: "Yes, we need communication, but we also need the confidence to disagree sometimes. We won't agree on everything—but I'll tell you, when I commit to something, I'll do it. I did not back off on street lighting for this part of town like some council members did."[7]

In preparation for the planned action, the leaders met with a variety of groups within Saint Elizabeth to outline the potential issues for the action and solicit their input. These groups included choirs, charismatic prayer groups, a youth group, liturgical readers, ushers, women's groups, and others. This recruitment via preexisting associational ties is a standard key to social movement success.[8] Three factors at Saint Elizabeth allowed this to be pursued especially successfully there: the dense network of such ties, the strategic outreach to literally all parish groups by the organizing committee, and the level of trust provided by shared membership in the worship community of this church. These complemented and reinforced another approach used by the committee for larger actions, asking the pastor to invite people to attend. As one leader noted, "We know from experience that everyone listens to Father Ignatius." Saint Elizabeth has been especially effective because it combined strong commitment to lay organizing with strong pastoral support.

A small crisis developed in mid-February 1995, when it became clear that many of the planned meetings with parish groups had not yet occurred, although leaders had pledged to do them by this date. The PICO organizer turned up the heat, noting the failure and asking, "Given the [lack of] work you all have done, do you think it's realistic to be planning an action for next month?" An awkward silence followed. Finally, a response from Lucy Nevarez reasserted the organization's commitment to informed participation and moved the discussion forward: "No, we won't have our people aware of what we're doing. We'd just turn them out to the meeting, not aware of what is really going on. We either have to do the work of informing people now, or move the action back." More silence followed; morale was low. Collazo then focused the group's attention on "what we have already." The group together listed information gleaned over several months of research interviews with key players in any potential project at the Montgomery Ward site: the site was available; the city was committing $2.3 million in loans; the community had "lots of anger at the current situation"; and an estimated annual outlay of $25 million in groceries could be spent there. De la Fuente saw this as an issue that could potentially secure his reelection; he was the most influential city council member and might be able to channel reinvestment capital from labor union investment funds. In addition, major retailers had expressed significant interest in the site. In the midst of the depressed Oakland economy and high local unemployment (in the mid-1990s), being reminded of this set of advances already achieved galvanized the group. Suddenly there was renewed enthusiasm in the room: "We have lots going for us," "there's no reason not to have a March action; we'll just move it back a little," and, from Collazo, "I've never seen a church with this much on its side going into an action." These comments set the group in motion planning to make more contacts with parish groups. After that planning, the meeting ended with a prayer, this time thanking "the Holy Spirit, who calls us to action."

The group had moderate success in a new effort to draw the small but growing Filipino community at the parish into the organizing effort. They did so by using the shared religious symbols and shared recognition of pastoral authority to gain entree to the extended family and business ties among Filipinos; simply saying they were members of the parish or that de Groot had suggested they meet was always enough to set up a meeting.

Over the coming weeks, gradually escalating numbers of participants attended the organizing committee meetings. From a core of ten or twelve people, numbers rose to sixteen and then forty leaders actively engaged in preparing for the action. The goal of the action was defined as asking de la Fuente and the city's director of economic development to spearhead the drive to convince Montgomery Ward to redevelop its land for productive use under the theme "develop it or tear it down."

In mid-March, four days before the action had been scheduled, a crisis erupted: De la Fuente had notified one of the leaders that he would not be attending the action, in spite of having agreed to do so several weeks previously. After a brief prayer led by the priest ("We ask for you to give us your power and your Spirit, that we may work for your reign"), the meeting immediately became quite animated as leaders expressed their outrage and drafted a letter to their council member saying they would not cancel the meeting and telling him, "[I]t will look very bad for you unless a very valid explanation can be given." When the letter was delivered, De la Fuente arranged to attend the meeting as planned.

Three days later, during rush hour on East Fourteenth Street, two dozen parish leaders held a prayer vigil on the street in the shadows of the Montgomery Ward building, "asking God to bless the community in its efforts to transform the building from a symbol of despair to one of hope." It included a biblical reflection based on a passage from the Book of Nehemiah: "Remember the Lord, who is great and awesome, and fight for your brothers, your sons and your daughters, your wives and your homes." The vigil served to advertise the next day's public action, and the biblical reflection encouraged the leaders to fight for their community but also to treat elected leaders with respect "when they truly serve the community."

Political Action: Public Ritual and Political Power in Community Organizing

The action took place on a rainy March evening, a slow drizzle falling on the abandoned factories, boarded-up storefronts, and dilapidated houses of East Oakland. Despite the rain, people congregated at the Saint Elizabeth's school meeting hall.

By 7:30 P.M., the meeting was overflowing, perhaps 350 people crowding into the hall. Some 90 percent were Latino, including both native Hispanics and immigrants from Mexico. Other participants included African Americans and descendants of Portuguese, Irish, and Italian immigrants. At the front of the room a large banner read "Oakland Community Organizations," and under the banner stood a podium, with two tables on either side. At one were the OCO members leading this action, along with a translator (participants spoke in whichever language they felt more comfortable, and summary translations into Spanish or English were provided). At the other table were the "targets" of the action: the local city council member and the head of the city's Office of Economic Development and Employment. At the back of the cafeteria were reporters for a local television station and the local newspaper: in an age of widespread political apathy and nonparticipation in civic life, a meeting with several hundred people makes news—and, as we shall see, brings political clout. The meeting began with a Latina woman leading a prayer-reflection drawing on the legacy of the great nineteenth-century African American inventor-scientist George Washington Carver to invoke the audience toward work for the common good:

> [Carver] used what God gave him, he took initiative. We must use our re-sources for the development of all. Those with more responsibility must work for all, by increasing their responsibility and labor, like George Wash-ington Carver. . . . We can do many things, as long as we always trust in God. . . . How beautiful it is to meet here, unified and working together as a community. In preparing this reflection, I thought about how we must have faith, a faith that leads to action. God has given us a place, and asks us what we are going to do with it. . . . Part of the place God has given us is this street and that huge building that has been unused for ten years. We want to make this place something to serve everyone, something for the community. . . . So we pray: God, we want to revolutionize the city of Oakland . . .

Another Latino leader then outlined the purpose of the meeting:

> We are bringing together the community to do something about the Montgomery Ward building. . . . Developers have not done anything. It's an urgent issue, and we're tired of promises. None have been fulfilled. We want action and progress. We ask city officials to work with us to put pres-sure on the Montgomery Ward corporation to develop it or tear it down. . . . We have faith that we can make this happen—and there are more than four hundred of us here.

The meeting continued with testimony from local residents regarding the lack of jobs paying decent wages, followed by a research report by Lupe Soltero and Estela Cerdas detailing the history of the site and the possibili-ties for redeveloping it, as projected slides showed the abandoned building and its surrounding area:

> This building is a symbol of blight and neglect that plague our neighbor-hood. . . . But let's not concentrate on the negative: let's use our imagina-tions. What could be here? Food stores, a job training center, a police sub-station. . . . We could have these things, but Montgomery Ward refuses to sell the property and is not willing to invest in it. [They went on to de-

scribe various potential uses of the site and the city's ability to use eminent domain laws to take over abandoned property.] We have done our homework. Given all these interested parties and the city's leverage over Montgomery Ward, we have faith that we can turn this dream into a reality: that's why we're here. . . . Montgomery Ward, let's do it *now!* [Applause.]

Next came the heart of the meeting: direct challenges to the city officials to take action for this redevelopment. These came in the form of "pinning questions," in response to which city officials committed to a specific time line for putting the building to productive use, to be met by pressuring Montgomery Ward to either redevelop the site or donate it for public development efforts. Officials also committed to working with OCO to make this happen. De Groot summarized the meeting in a way that implicitly credited the officials as well as the community organization—and promised continued vigilance to assure momentum: "I think we're moving! [Applause.] I have been here six years, and the only change I have seen has been more graffiti on that building. Now I feel a sense of going forward, of movement. And we will see to it that this continues!" The action closed with a prayer led by a nun on the staff of Saint Elizabeth:

Lord, I feel energy and excitement here I have not felt before. . . . You are not a god of emptiness, not a god of waste, not a god of irresponsibility. . . . You want us to have life, to have life to the full. Strengthen our energy, strengthen us, to bring life to what is dead, to fill what is empty, for our children and for the children of the future.

As a result of this action, the demolition of the old building initially moved forward quite quickly, but seeing the project through to completion would require several more years of political work. The effort had to overcome the indictment of the proposed developer, reluctance on the part of the company to develop or donate the abandoned building, constraints on government funding, and delays occasioned when a local group filed suit against the demolition. In response, the Saint Elizabeth OCO leaders continued their two-pronged approach: organizing in the local community to generate pressure on both corporate and political players in the development process, and working with De la Fuente to help make the political decisions fall into place. In a confrontational move, they distributed fliers at regional Montgomery Ward stores critical of the company's stance. This tactic infuriated OCO's partners in city government—but also may have contributed to pushing the company toward a final resolution. For their part, De la Fuente and the city's Office of Economic Development fulfilled the commitments made at the OCO action: they met regularly with the group, and aggressively pursued a "develop it or demolish it" strategy.

Ultimately, this coalition of players was successful: demolition began in February 2001, accompanied by a large celebration sponsored by OCO. By this time, local priorities had shifted toward better public education rather than private-sector jobs at the old Montgomery Ward site. Saint Elizabeth's OCO worked with the city of Oakland and the school district to plan for two new public schools to be built on the site in order to ease severe overcrowding at a local elementary school. These schools opened in September 2001, part of a wider OCO initiative to improve public education by creating smaller schools throughout the city.

The political action described above was a critical juncture in forging the coalition that ultimately saw the redevelopment process through to completion. It was typical of such events in that its key dynamic lay in the interplay of conflict, compromise, and (sometimes) mutual support between the "guests" and the organized leadership. Here, the tensions underlying the organizing process were contained within the negotiations leading up to the political action; the latter came off in a way that allowed all parties involved to claim credit for some forward movement. Managing the complex political relationships needed to sustain simultaneous conflict *and* collaboration demanded sophisticated work behind the scenes by the staff organizer, political savvy and pragmatic calculation on the part of the public official involved, and significant democratic skills embedded within a relatively mature community organization. Understanding how faith-based organizing cultivates leadership skills and uses conflict to forge public collaboration—and what happens when conflict breaks out into the public arena—requires paying attention to the typical practices that constitute the field.

The Practices of Faith-Based Organizing

The description above illustrates many of the core practices of faith-based organizing as developed by PICO and other federations. "Practices" here means simply the things these groups do regularly—that is, the standard techniques used to advance the work of organizing committees within member congregations like Saint Elizabeth, which provide PICO's crucial links to local communities. The same practices—albeit with slightly different emphases—are central to citywide, regional, and state-level organizing efforts within PICO and other faith-based organizing efforts. The most important such practices are one-to-ones, prayer, research, actions, "challenging" and "holding accountable," evaluations, and the public use of conflict.

One-to-Ones: Building Solidarity

The crucial work of the organizing committees occurs through a process of face-to-face meetings between one committee member or staff organizer and an individual member of a congregation or other institution (or at times a neighbor). Such one-to-one meetings typically last about a half hour, and are simply conversations—but conversations rather different than most Americans are used to, in that participants are encouraged to seek what really motivates the other person, what they care deeply about, and thus establish a relationship built on more than casual chat. They are designed to activate preexisting networks within the congregations, to extend those networks more broadly by reaching out to new people, and to cross-link preexisting networks more densely. Social scientists have recently come to speak of such work as "building social capital," but its centrality to community organizing long predates the current social capital fashion. In any case, this is social capital with a twist: these relational networks are built with an explicit moral-political *content*—that is, these ties are important to people because they are laden with political and ethical meaning, not seen as ends in themselves.

The ultimate goal of one-to-one work is to increase the capacity of the congregation to act in unison around issues affecting its members. But one-to-ones are also used to identify those issues, to invite people to reflect together on the challenges facing their communities, to identify potential future leaders, and to probe how people are affected by a given issue. Professional organizers see these one-to-ones as the critical building block of everything their organizations do.[9]

One of the key sessions at an annual PICO national training retreat for leaders and pastors focused on doing initial one-to-ones with potential participants.[10] PICO training staff listed three goals for such one-to-one meetings. The first was to "identify their self-interest" by looking for intense *feeling* within answers to questions such as "How are things in your neighborhood?" The second was to look for any leadership qualities in the other person: "look for 'public ability' in them, ability to implement a plan, whether they can help move other people into action, whether they appear dependable and consistent." Even if these qualities were present only in inchoate form, they could be developed later during the organizing process

itself and through PICO's formal leadership training program. The third
was to use one-to-ones to identify other possible leaders, by asking with
whom else to talk about the organizing, with an emphasis on finding leaders "who reflect the diversity of the community."

Throughout the training, leaders were encouraged to look for ways the
other person was "coping" instead of trying to change things in their community—and to invite them into to a more assertive role in such change.
In this and other ways, leaders are encouraged to act authoritatively within
the organizing process: to know what they want, to seek conversations that
contribute to the community organizing process, and to structure their conversations to further that objective. In contemporary America with its therapeutic culture, this often feels instrumentalizing or manipulative to new
leaders. In the culture of organizing, in which participants assume that others carry an interest in public life, such authoritative roles are legitimated.
In discussing this, one participant asked, "How do we avoid the one-to-one
degenerating into a therapeutic relationship, one based just on sympathy?"
The PICO staff person leading the discussion suggested:

> The key thing is to get into the *values* behind the people's problems . . .
> invite them to be involved in their church's efforts to address problems
> . . . point out they can't possibly address the problems on their own—
> that they have to organize with others to change things . . . generate
> some vision with them, or see if they have some vision of their own
> about how to change things.

PICO staff strongly pushed the centrality of this practice of one-to-one
meetings within the PICO organizing model, through such phrases as "to
PICO, community organizing is an art, and the one-to-one is the process"
and "building power means building relationships." The critical role of the
church context in all of this emerged once again when the PICO staff person
noted that "the pastor has to sanction this whole process, or it goes nowhere."

Mary Ellen Burton-Christie, a long-time PICO leader in California,
clearly articulated the central role of one-to-ones in this kind of organizing:

> The model of the one-to-ones is really basic, and unless the one-to-one
> work is happening, the organizing will not work. It won't have the solid
> foundations that I feel we have to have when we are doing this work. If
> you end up with a bunch of pastors getting together, making decisions
> and telling their flocks to come to these meetings, it wouldn't have the

same effect in developing leaders—the same empowering effect that it does when leaders have all made this decision together.[11]

Credential: Building Organizational Identity

Among the practices most consistently included in PICO meetings and actions is the "credential." This ritualized assertion of the organization's identity, purpose, and strength occurs at the start of virtually every meeting, whether attended by a few members of a local organizing committee or by two thousand citywide supporters meeting with political officials. The credential typically includes several elements: it identifies the organization as separate from but rooted in religious congregations; it expansively asserts the numerical and institutional strength of the organization; and it outlines the general purpose of the organization in civic and/or religious terms that are broad enough to command broad assent as legitimate.

A strong credential might look something like the following, printed in the program for a citywide action in 1994:

> Oakland Community Organizations is a federation of eighteen church
> and community organizations representing 25,000 families in East, West,
> and North Oakland. The purpose of our organization is to improve the
> quality of life for families through putting our faith into action. . . . Our
> organization is a member of the Pacific Institute for Community Organiza-
> tion. PICO is a national network of faith-based community organizations.
> We have sister organizations in 42 cities across the country. Our goal is to
> be able to act at the local, regional, and state levels. . . . We believe that
> because each of us is a child of God we deserve to live with dignity. We
> work together to change those conditions in our neighborhoods which
> threaten our dignity.

Clearly, this robust credential serves a public function. But what of the rather formulaic credentials like the following, typical at small meetings of single-church organizing committees:

> St. _____'s Organizing Committee is the social action arm of our
> parish. We represent over 1,500 families from throughout this area of the
> city, working to improve conditions for ourselves, our community, and
> the city. Through a process of one-to-one contacts, we build our power to
> hold our elected officials accountable.

This brief statement seems almost vestigial, but serves two important purposes. "Doing the credential" is often the first public leadership role for new leaders, their first chance to have a public voice. It also gives the organization a forum for asserting its strength by noting its ties to far more people than are actually in the room for a given event. Of course, the claim to "represent" tens of thousands of people in a city—or even fifteen hundred families in a given neighborhood—cannot be taken at face value. Yet it is not purely rhetorical posturing; for a given church to be involved, legitimate authority within that church must have agreed to participate and support the effort. More importantly for the political calculus of elected officials, significant social ties connect those present with other members of their church, other family members, neighbors, acquaintances, etc. Even in an age of media-driven politics, local candidates must take these flesh-and-blood ties seriously since they can exercise considerable influence on voting patterns. Even a few hundred votes can swing a local election—or razor-thin state and national elections, as shown by the 2000 presidential race.

Prayer: Invoking Divine Power

Recall the prayer that started PICO's statewide Healthcare for All Californians action (see introduction):

> Holy God, be here with us. At the beginning of our work, send upon us
> the spirit of Amos. . . . Hold before us all those old people forced to
> choose between food and medicine; all those couples ruined by medical
> diseases; all our own children whose health is neglected because we can-
> not afford to pay for medicine. Hold them before us so that we might
> fight with a righteous anger.

To recognize the centrality of this kind of public prayer in contemporary faith-based organizing, it is helpful to contrast it with past practice. Before its turn to a more explicitly faith-based model of organizing, PICO often incorporated prayer only superficially or not at all. As PICO director John Baumann recalls, "In Chicago in the 1970s, I suggested we pray before a meeting once, and someone said, 'We're not here to pray, we're here to get things *done,* not to pray.' And I agreed, went on with the agenda." When prayer was included, it was often done in quite pro forma ways that often served to dress in religious garb the political agenda being pursued, but did not much influence the tenor of the overall organizing effort. In this way, organizing largely adopted the assumptions of the "culture of disbelief" about which Stephen Carter has written (1993). In thus marginalizing religious faith from the public realm, old-style Alinsky organizing unwittingly fell into the evisceration of both religious commitment and vigorous public life that Carter diagnoses.

In contrast, prayer occupies a central place in some—though not all—contemporary federations.[12] During my research, virtually every congregation-sponsored local organizing committee under OCO's auspices opened with prayer; the same is true in some PICO groups in other cities. Within the more evangelically inclined congregations, one-to-ones sometimes began with prayer, though this was left up to local leaders. In addition to brief prayers at the start of large public actions, small gatherings of the onstage leaders immediately prior to facing the public often ended with prayers for confidence, power, and inspiration. Many leaders reported that they often prayed privately before actions or meetings, especially when they were anxious about taking highly public roles.

These prayers take many forms, depending both on the religious or civic setting and the particular moment within the organizing process in which they occur. In internal meetings involving a *single* religious congregation, prayers reflect that tradition's religious style: more emotionally fervent and Jesus-centered in the black evangelical congregations; Mary- or Father-centered in Hispanic Catholic congregations; more staid and abstract, using a language focused on "God" or "Lord" rather than Jesus in mainline Protestant and middle-class Catholic congregations, whether black or white. In internal meetings involving congregations from *different* denominations, prayers tended to focus on elements shared across traditions (Jesus, the Spirit, the Kingdom of God) and avoid elements controversial in one tradition or another, such as the most highly emotional prayer forms of Pentecostalism or very Mary-centered Catholic prayers. Federations with greater internal religious diversity, with Islamic, Jewish, Unitarian, or other congregations as members, face a greater challenge in incorporating this diversity into their public prayer. An organizer noted this difficulty and suggested one way of overcoming it:

> It takes two or three years to build trust, overcome the distrust across interfaith lines. Evangelicals and Pentecostals have lots of distrust about interfaith work, and about the word "interfaith." Jewish congregations have distrust of being involved in anything that seems Christian dominated. They have lots of sensitivity to the language that's used, to the religious cultural stuff that's used. Our approach in board meetings, task forces,

committee meetings has been to invite people to reflect and pray in their own faith traditions, and over time everybody gets exposed to a little bit of various traditions.

In *public meetings* such as political actions, three strategies are evident for handling religious diversity. The most common in American politics (at least outside the religious right) is to avoid religious language altogether. But this approach is rarely adopted in faith-based organizing, which instead typically follows either of two strategies summed up by one organizer: "In public actions, we ask people to use more universal language, or we'll have three or four different faith traditions pray at the same action."

Thus, one strategy encourages participants to speak strongly from their own traditions, praying explicitly to Adonai or God or Allah or Jesus or the Holy Spirit, with other participants translating these expressions into their own faith languages. But this approach demands significant trust across religious traditions, confidence that one view of God is not being imposed on all. Another strategy is to ask all participants to pray in neutral terms that seek to avoid any language that is not acceptable in other traditions, for example by using "God" instead of "Jesus," or "God's will" instead of "the Kingdom of God." The former strategy places a burden on everyone to learn something about others' religious traditions; the latter strategy runs the risk of so diluting faith language that it no longer "moves" participants. Deciding when to adopt which strategy represents an important area of continuing experimentation, discernment, and strategic choice in faith-based organizing. The choices made matter; expanding beyond the black Protestant/mainline Protestant/Roman Catholic core of traditional organizing culture may bring new constituencies, greater diversity, wider credibility, and deeper ethical insight into the organizing world—but may also weaken the organization's ability to elicit deep commitment from participants. The challenge lies in broadening this work while sustaining the flow of commitment and motivation that underlie its dynamism.

Research: Power in Information

Once an issue has been tentatively identified through one-to-ones and discussions between the organizing committee and staff, two processes move forward simultaneously. First, a series of "research meetings" are held with persons deemed to hold the information needed to develop a response to the issue. This research may involve elected officials, city staff, other parties interested in this issue, academic experts, union leaders, school officials, key players in the local economy, etc. The goal here is to learn more about the issue, possible ways to address it, obstacles to doing so, and ultimately to "cut the issue" by generating a concrete proposal and identifying who holds the authority to put this proposal into practice. Second, a further round of one-to-ones among congregation members communicates to them the issue the organizing committee is working on and checks their willingness to participate. This last round of one-to-ones is also used to identify people who have been negatively affected by the current state of affairs, and who are particularly passionate or eloquent spokespersons; these are invited to provide the "testimony" at actions, thus making information more meaningful by presenting it as part of a deeply charged human affair.

The background research provides much of the information that shapes decisions on how to coordinate the coming action: who the targeted guests will be, what commitments they will be asked to make, what concrete proposals will be put forward. In this way research—often research done by university-based scholars, public policy institutes, or city or state agencies, to which these organizations gain access via research reports or in-person meetings—becomes a central way for faith-based organizing to reorient government or corporate policy. Note also how the information gleaned through research is not neutral: the "research report" at the Saint Elizabeth action serves both to claim the moral high ground surrounding the future of the Montgomery Ward site and to show that the organization has sufficient knowledge to be a credible voice in planning that future.

Action: Power in Numbers

Once the organization identifies a person with decision-making authority over the chosen issue, that person becomes the "target" for the kind of "action" we saw in the introduction and earlier in this chapter: a public meeting at which the target is asked to commit to specific proposals put forward by the organization to address the issue. The term "target," implying someone to be shot at, is partly a holdover from Alinsky-era organizing, much more one-dimensionally conflictive than faith-based organizing is today. For example, Councilman De la Fuente was brought into the Saint Elizabeth action precisely as a potential partner in the redevelopment effort at Montgomery Ward, not as an enemy. But the term "target" continues to be used, and accurately describes some actions: if public conflict is to occur, it usually occurs during these public actions. More typically, however, since targets are usually told ahead of time what commitments they will be asked to make, they contain some tension but little overt conflict.

These actions are best understood as "public dramas," a term used by organizers in training core leaders. That is, actions are designed with a dramaturgical emphasis on drawing participants into the political tension of public life, and using the resulting energy of the crowd to push the drama—i.e., public decision making—in democratic directions. Actions thus appear rather scripted at times (and indeed are scripted) because much of the negotiation, development of strategy, and training of leaders for specific roles occurs in the weeks leading up to the action. I never saw leaders encouraged to distort the truth, only to package that truth in more rhetorically effective ways. For example, Lupe Soltero and Estela Cerdas had carefully crafted their research report with input from a staff organizer, the reflection had been through several revisions, those giving testimonies told of real experiences in their families but had been coached in how best to tell those stories, and De la Fuente knew what questions he would be asked.

Yet actions do carry real dramatic tension. In the fifteen actions that I observed,[13] the sponsoring organizations generally strove to push officials onto new terrain—i.e., toward new public commitments that would improve the quality of life in urban neighborhoods, either through new services or policy changes. Organizers always strove to maximize the likelihood that the target would support the organization's initiative, but there was often a real possibility that the target would refuse to do so. Ideally, then, organizers want to "win" on the given issue. But they consistently taught leaders that if the target refused to commit to the issue, it was far better to push the target to a "clear no" than to leave things unclear.

Actions vary in precisely how they are structured, but the overall dramatic flow always parallels that shown in the actions depicted here; great attention is given to maximizing turnout, and music often greets entering attendees in order to maximize the energy and enthusiasm in the meeting room. An opening prayer invokes God's presence on the gathering; it and a credential serve to legitimate the organization and set it apart from other organizations deemed to be pursuing more narrow interests. A series of leaders—selected for having invested themselves in the organizing work and in order to reflect the racial/ethnic makeup of the community—play significant roles, though one or two serve as chairpersons of the action. Organizers, though very visible in training the leaders prior to the action, *never* appear onstage. A series of dramatic testimonies seek to highlight the issue and show the human cost of doing nothing. A research report provides background on the issue, framing it as a problem affecting enough people that it demands a solution. A formal proposal suggests one best way forward, or it may ask elected officials to commit to negotiating with the organization in developing future policy or budget proposals. At this point, the target is given a limited time (typically two to seven minutes) in which to respond. The climax of the action comes in the "pinning questions," during which leaders pin the target to a clear yes or no answer. Finally, a closing summary, a prayer, and applause provide the emotional denouement to the dramatic tension.

"Disciplined" events are seen as crucial. To maximize the attention of participants, and thus the future political leverage of the organization, actions are limited to about an hour and a half. Actions are thus a technique for the exertion of power; in no sense are they occasions for deliberation regarding alternative policies or discernment around complex political or economic issues. For better or worse, deliberation and discernment are excluded from these large-scale venues. Faith-based federations either pursue them in other organizing settings, draw on the deliberative processes in academic institutions and political think tanks that shape the policy ideas they use, or forgo reflective deliberation entirely. Which option predominates appears to depend largely on the skills and inclinations of organizers.

Challenging and Holding Accountable

Professional staff and more experienced leaders quite self-consciously engage in a specific set of practices intended to strengthen the quality of organizing work. Termed "challenging" and "holding ourselves accountable," these practices are designed to foster leadership development and instill discipline within the organizing process.

Challenging a staff person, leader, pastor, or potential participant means inviting him or her to take a role within the organizing work that stretches his or her limitations of ability or confidence. Thus, though a new leader may be wary of speaking in public, an experienced leader will often challenge her to accept a public leadership role at an action. Likewise, if a pastor or leader seems strongly supportive of the goals of the organization but drags his feet due to what an organizer perceives to be a psychologically rooted aversion to conflict, the latter may challenge him to reflect on this aversion, whether God really wants people to avoid conflict at all cost.[14]

In some cases, challenging leads to significant ethical dialogue, as in the last example; the pastor ultimately acknowledged he should stand behind the organizing effort more fully and "had trouble with conflict," but also insisted that he would "not stand for people assuming the worst about politicians." Though it sometimes leads to conflict within the organizing process, organizers promote mutual challenge among participants. As PICO organizer Jim Keddy noted, "You never know until you challenge somebody how they'll respond. If you don't ask, some will just stay stuck in isolation, never get involved. And it's amazing how excited people are sometimes when you challenge them. . . . It opens up a whole new world to them."

The term holding accountable denotes fostering discipline. *Internal accountability* involves organizational discipline to keep participants focused on shared commitments and tasks, rather than individual agendas. While challenging emphasizes personal growth for the sake of more effective organizing, holding accountable emphasizes group discipline. It is essentially the expectation that when anyone (staff, leaders, or pastors) commits to a given task, he or she will fulfill it.

External accountability refers to the organization's relationships with elected officials, city staff, and business leaders. When asked to identify the fundamental task of their work, "holding officials accountable" was the most common response among leaders and the second most common (after "developing leaders") among professional organizers. Some elected officials I interviewed, all of whom had been targeted during political actions, found this disciplinary stance objectionable or insulting, calling it "unnecessarily confrontational" or "pretty one-dimensional" or offering some similar critique. But external accountability can also mean constructive and realistic relations with officials, in which the latter are kept accountable to their constituents. Most elected officials interviewed—unsurprisingly, particularly those who had developed collaborative relationships with local federations over several years—spoke of these organizations in very positive terms, for example as "the most important community partners I have, even if they push me sometimes."

Negotiations: Power in Policy Formulation

The more successful faith-based federations have parlayed the political power generated through actions into considerable influence throughout the process of policy formulation in local government. The public projection of power in actions thus leads to considerable backstage exertion of power through negotiations with political leaders. Where combined most effectively, these two forms of organizational power allow faith-based organizing to move beyond its historic role in extracting additional services from local government to a more substantial role in helping define the priorities and policies that elected leaders pursue.

Examples abound: PICO leaders at Saint Elizabeth engaged in extensive negotiations not only with De la Fuente but also with the mayor and with corporate leaders at Montgomery Ward; PICO leaders in West Oakland negotiated extensively with the mayor and the economic development office to shape city policies to attract investment into their community. Citywide leaders in San Diego, Denver, San Jose, and other cities have negotiated extensive reforms of public education, most successfully in San Diego, where class size reductions were instituted in part through PICO's work. Similarly, the citywide Oakland federation worked with the local teacher's union to negotiate class size reductions with the public school district. In recent years, strong PICO federations in New Orleans and Oakland have met extensively with incoming mayors to define a shared agenda for city government, *prior to* those mayors taking office. The stronger federations in the other faith-based organizing networks have adopted similar roles in political negotiation (e.g., BUILD in Baltimore, COPS and EPISO in Texas, GBIO in Boston, MICAH in Milwaukee, HOPE in Tampa). Perhaps most significantly, statewide and regional efforts have begun to play a role in negotiating power in high-level political arenas; the PICO California Project, the Texas IAF Network and Arizona IAF, regional efforts in the Midwest by Gamaliel and in Florida by DART, and PICO's LIFT project in Louisiana all represent examples of this kind of influence. The power possible through negotiations was well expressed in an interview with Cyprian DeVold, pastor of an African American Catholic parish in New Orleans:

> We don't just go to people and ask for something once. We create an ongoing relationship. So much so with this government [under Mayor Marc Morial] that nothing happens now that PICO is not sought out for advice. Any major decision by the mayor that affects the city, he will consult.

DeVold continued by noting that at times Morial seemed to push him too hard to get into a partisan stance "and I had to tell him, 'I don't work for city hall.'"

It is in backstage prepublic settings that lobbyists and political action committees exert their most powerful influence on the legislative process (West and Loomis 1998). To the extent that this influence is rooted primarily in campaign donations and expert knowledge purchased by private interests, democracy is deeply distorted. If faith-based organizing can consolidate a voice in this arena, it may help to bring democratic pressure to bear in what is today a site of elite maneuvering at the heart of our democratic institutions.

Evaluations: Developing Leaders through Critical Reflection

Most local and citywide organizing committee meetings and all the actions were followed by postmeeting evaluation sessions. Evaluations are in-house affairs; on several occasions—including the one following the Saint Elizabeth action—political officials or their aides had to be ushered out of the room before the evaluation began. In evaluations, organizers take center stage, eliciting comment and offering feedback. Some evaluations are quite pro forma, with participants simply asked how they felt about the meeting. The most effective organizers use evaluations as opportunities for group reflection and organizational learning. As we shall see, evaluations following unsuccessful or conflictive actions can lead to serious discussion of events or particular roles of individuals.

Public Conflict: The Constructive Uses of Political Tension

If the combination of practices discussed here fails to produce relations of accountability and respect with public officials, conflict may become a very public aspect of the organizing process. Such was the case in a different action in a different part of Oakland. Working with PICO, several churches had come together to gain city hall's support for attracting new economic development into severely depressed West Oakland. Six months of organizing had yielded little progress, and they felt that then-mayor Elihu Harris had failed to work constructively with them to provide leadership on this issue. Furthermore, they felt insulted when he consistently arrived late to meetings.

These underlying tensions led to public conflict at a political action when Harris notified them a few hours before the action that, though he was the featured guest, he would once again arrive late. The organization notified the mayor's office that it was not acceptable for him to be late. At the appointed time, some 250 African American, Latino, white, southeast Asian, and Filipino participants were present—and the mayor was indeed at the seat reserved for him. But the leaders of the action had previously discussed the mayor's "foot-dragging," "disrespect," and "failure to lead"—and how they would prevent it from continuing by "raising the tension level" during tonight's action.

Other than drawing strongly on the social Christianity of African American religious traditions, the action was similar to that described above. The opening prayer, gospel music, and initial greeting all invoked God's blessing on the gathering, generating a feeling of moral consensus on the need for action and leadership. They also created an ambience of ethical grounding in the Christian tradition, an inoculation against any perception of unfairness that might arise from the coming conflict.

Following a research report that detailed the organization's knowledge of what it would take to attract investment into West Oakland and what the city could do to facilitate this, Father Charles Burns set the stage for that conflict. He stepped to the podium with a copy of the Bible in his hand and waved it, crying out, "This is a book of *liberation!*" He cited President Aristide of Haiti as one who "stand[s] up in the power of Jesus Christ, work[s] with the poor as they move into their dignity. Where are the Jean Bertrand Aristides among us? Where is leadership in our own city? The call to leadership lies partly with Mayor Harris, and so we ask him to lead." In conclusion, he put the mayor squarely in the spotlight by quoting the poet Langston Hughes:

> We need leadership from our top politicians, especially Mayor Harris. We have a potential site and possible funding to subsidize the costs. . . . Langston Hughes wrote: "What happens to a dream deferred? Does it sigh, or does it explode?" We do not want this dream deferred, brothers and sisters, and we do not want it to explode. And we know that we as a community need *power* to make this dream a reality. But power has to be taken, it is not given.

In his response, Mayor Harris spoke vaguely of the "large-scale economic dislocations which have hurt West Oakland" and of city-sponsored efforts to "seek consensus about what we will do, and commitment to do it." The leaders later said that they found this whole speech evasive and self-serving, given the mayor's prior lack of commitment to this project and failure to focus on working with them. So when, in response to a series of pointed questions designed to pin down his commitment, the mayor answered in vague generalities and tried to remain on the podium to extend his speech, he was cut off pointedly by Father Burns. The mayor protested, tried to continue, but sat down when the priest said, "I am so angry that you suggest that we settle for [this response]. That is an insult. This book [raising the Bible] is a book of liberation from everything that oppresses us, from poverty but also from leaders who refuse to lead." As reported to me later, this confrontation left some in the room energized, others bewildered.

Such conflict can be invigorating, but sits uneasily for those who believe that the Christian faith teaches them to avoid conflict, especially with figures of authority.

The meeting closed with another leader summarizing the evening's events, reiterating the commitments made by the mayor and the organization, and announcing a much larger event being organized a month later by the whole citywide OCO federation, saying:

> The mayor *will* be present on May 16, he *will* hear the cries of the poor—otherwise, they will not be sighs, but an explosion. And the mayor does not want that. Power is in the people, working for quality of life and living as Jesus lived out his life. We began in Jesus' name, and we now go out in his name, knowing that God goes with us as we work to improve our city.

After the mayor and his aides departed and the crowd began to disperse, some twenty-five key leaders met for the evaluation. When asked broadly what they thought of the action, people were tentative, appearing uncertain how to interpret the conflictive events of the evening. One pastor noted, "We're going to need to go back and talk to our people, help them understand what went on tonight." One of the organizers noted, "That's right, people who haven't been involved will feel like we treated the mayor unfairly." A leader said he was representing his pastor, and that both had been involved in the Montgomery bus boycott. He offered a different point of view:

> This tension tonight was exactly what we needed. I am very excited and supportive about what happened tonight. In the last few months, I've been in on twelve different meetings at which the mayor was present. The last one was with the Oakland Black Pastor's Alliance. The mayor was there for a total of four minutes. At the other eleven meetings, he was never there for more than five minutes. Tonight, he stayed the whole time, sat through a whole meeting. That says something. That's about *respect*.

The priest, Charles Burns, then spoke:

> I want to explain why I did what I did, why the tension and conflict was necessary. . . . He had called us this afternoon to tell us that he was going to be forty-five minutes late. . . . What you saw tonight was the product

of that. I called his staff in our name and told the mayor that was an insult to us and to our people here. He came earlier than he expected and stayed the whole time because of that. [But] he treated us with disrespect, so I cut him off when he tried to take over the agenda. This is our meeting and our agenda; politicians want to make it their meeting and their agenda, and you can't let them do that. That's why we needed the conflict tonight, and why the tension was a good thing.

Further discussion followed, and the facilitator encouraged people to talk to others who had been present, "to get their reactions, see how they felt about the meeting." When asked to lead a final prayer, Pastor James Abner noted, "I know this was a tough meeting. And we do have to be careful to treat elected officials with respect. But I am completely behind the action, putting the mayor on the spot." His prayer sent people out into the evening:

> We thank you, God, for being with us tonight, for sending your Spirit
> here among us to be witnesses to you. We thank you that we did not
> allow these pharaonic tendencies to go unchecked, but worked for your
> Kingdom of righteousness, where we all are equal and worthy of respect.

Thus, the organization used public conflict to raise the tension level with a key city official when it felt that accountability and respect had not been forthcoming. And the participants drew on their religious traditions—interpreted in ways counter to dominant strands of American therapeutic culture—to understand and embrace that conflict.

Though it would require several more years of work, this effort ultimately proved successful. Gateway Foods opened in January 2000, the product of an OCO-catalyzed public-private partnership for economic development. It brought new jobs to West Oakland, as well as the first full-scale grocery store in many years.

Transforming the City or Sowing Seeds in the Public Realm?

The very local neighborhood-level organizing work examined in this chapter represents only one facet of contemporary faith-based organizing, which has now extended up into higher-level political arenas—very commonly in large metropolitan areas, in a few places at the statewide level. Such local efforts are key building blocks in constructing higher-profile actions like the statewide Healthcare for All event described in the introduction;

through local work, leaders gain confidence and political experience for subsequent higher-profile actions. Organizers who neglect such local efforts sometimes find themselves with collapsing organizations, bereft of new cohorts of emerging leaders.[15]

Analytically, these local actions already show many of the fundamental dynamics, relationships, and strategies involved in faith-based organizing. In beginning with them, we must not lose sight of the national political and global economic forces that have eroded the living standards of low- and middle-income Americans, and which neighborhood-focused efforts cannot begin to address. But we can best understand the democratic promise and current dilemmas of these efforts—and thus their possibilities for addressing these national and global factors—by paying attention to this local level of organizing.

At this local level, the balance of forces between local lay leaders, pastors, and staff organizers constructs a civic organization that no single group unilaterally controls. Much of the dynamism of faith-based organizing results from the playing out of the complex relations between these three groups, which creates a kind of miniature public square within PICO and the churches. Leaders are formed within this *internal public square* in ways that make them capable actors vis-à-vis decision makers in the wider society and in the church; PICO's fundamental role lies in linking such actors, as representatives of their communities, to institutional leaders in the wider public realm. But this does not amount simply to engaging in institutional politics. Rather, it involves forcing institutional politics to open up to new voices previously marginalized, and then using negotiations and public action to work for concrete policy changes within the institutionalized political system.

Even at the neighborhood level, these actions represent a step beyond the standard capabilities of traditional community organizing efforts, which were often able to initiate minor improvements in city services but found it difficult to push beyond this into "bigger" issues.[16] Both the coalition of West Oakland congregations and especially the Saint Elizabeth group used their influence with city officials to generate leverage on private business regarding the economic development issues that often lie beyond the reach of such local groups. These leaders were simultaneously working on citywide educational reform as part of a larger OCO effort; later, some were key players in successful statewide PICO efforts to strengthen public education, health care, and after-school programs in California. Such efforts suggest that, at least in some instances, faith-based organizing has transcended the parochial limitations of its earlier history, and learned to project democratic power into higher-level arenas.

The Saint Elizabeth story testifies to that congregation's long experience and prominence within PICO as a strong exemplar of contemporary church-based organizing. Not all local church affiliates are as successful, as we shall see. But when faith-based organizing is successful, many factors contribute simultaneously to that success. Such factors include trained leaders, astute strategy, professional staff organizing, the legitimacy accorded by church affiliation and clear pastoral support, the cultural resources of church life and of American traditions of grassroots democracy (such as populism and local unionism), the social networks rooted in churches, newly emerging political opportunities, sufficient financial resources, and adept collaborators in government and business.[17]

Subsequent chapters strive to do justice to these diverse influences, while focusing primarily on the institutional and cultural factors that make faith-based organizing unique. One focus of attention will be the place of conflict and compromise in this work, and the role of religion in sustaining the tension between them. The constructive use of political conflict to promote democratic engagement underlies much of the dynamism of faith-based organizing, and we cannot really understand the organizing process without recognizing this dramaturgical use of conflict. But it is not the one-dimensional, mechanical use of conflict that became common in the later years of Alinsky-inspired community organizing.[18] Today, the best faith-based organizing federations have matured organizationally to the point that they can sustain collaborative partnerships with elected officials while simultaneously using conflict constructively. The organizing narratives told here show the resulting tension: the leaders had to transcend any knee-jerk reflex toward automatic support based on religious authority or shared racial identity, in order to ask hard questions about whether their interests were being served or the common good promoted by their collaborative relationships with officials.

The faith-based organizing efforts examined here thus succeeded at something beyond the minor improvement in city services that community organizations have more commonly gained from city government. They accumulated sufficient power to transform their previously marginalized members into credible collaborators in the public realm, and then to translate this public influence into effective leverage on decision makers in private business. Such efforts offer real democratic promise as we enter a new millennium, in which it is not clear how low-income people will protect their interests in the new global economy.

Yet these are still very local efforts, gaining power at the margins of the huge capital flows and political power dynamics that determine the life chances of the working and middle classes. Such local efforts cannot shelter low-income residents from the long-term consequences of large-scale political and economic forces. We can respect those who successfully fought these battles while also acknowledging that they represent limited victories over forces that vastly transcend any single city. The significance of these efforts lies only partly in such victories; at least equally important are the organizational skills and taste for public life they acquire, and the way their efforts begin to reconstitute a democratic public sphere from the ground up. These are the seeds that, as they mature, allow faith-based organizing to address higher-level political issues in broader political arenas. The following chapters strive to assess these higher-arena efforts, compare them with similar organizing efforts based on an appeal to racial identity, and explore whether these models will be able to project power in ways that offer greater democratic promise.

Chapter 2

Higher Power: The Symbiosis of Religion and Politics

> When people find themselves unable to control the world, they
> simply shrink the world down to the size of their community. Thus,
> urban movements do address the real issues of our time, although
> neither on the scale nor terms that are adequate to the task.
>
> —Manuel Castells, *The City and the Grassroots*

Twenty years ago, in a now-classic study, Manuel Castells argued that contemporary urban social movements—though important for sustaining utopian visions of the city and for criticizing current power relations—were "reactive utopias" incapable of fundamentally reshaping the cityscape. In his analysis, the movements of the 1970s and early 1980s were too constrained by the fluidity of modern capital and the power of macrogovernmental institutions to successfully reform our cities. Though his writing remained empathetic with the goals of progressive urban movements, in the end he was pessimistic regarding their prospects. This chapter argues that

Oakland Community Organization leaders at a political action in 1998.
Photograph by Michelle Longosz. Courtesy Oakland Community Organization.

the institutional strength of the faith-based organizing model now provides grounds for partially revising Castells's conclusion.

National Profile of Faith-Based Organizing

The first national survey of faith-based organizing provides a first glimpse of this institutional strength.[1] The organizational base of the field, defined as organizations with an office and at least one professional organizer consists of 133 local federations spread across thirty-three states and the District of Columbia; this includes every major metropolitan area and many secondary cities in the United States. The vast majority of these organizations are affiliated with one of four organizing networks that provide much of the structure of the field. The most widely publicized of these is the Industrial Areas Foundation (IAF). In the minds of casual observers faith-based organizing is often synonymous with the IAF, but in fact this network represents about 36 percent of the 133 identified federations. The Pacific Institute for Community Organization (PICO) and the Gamaliel Network are the next largest networks, representing 23 percent and 20 percent, respectively, of the federations. Direct Action, Research, and Training (DART) represents about 9 percent of the federations. The remaining faith-based organizing efforts, which make up about 12 percent of the total, are independent federations or members of much smaller networks in a single metropolitan area.[2] Although each network carries a distinctive organizational emphasis that colors its work, all adopt a very similar organizing model utilizing the kinds of practices outlined in chapter 1. Thus, no one network dominates or defines faith-based organizing; rather, the field is constituted by a set of isomorphic (and often competitive) networks and local organizations.

Each federation organizes in a particular city or metropolitan area via interfaith teams of leaders representing from ten to sixty or more institutions, mostly religious congregations. These *institutions* form the membership base of the federations, which are not based upon memberships of individuals. The median budget for a federation is $150,000 per year, raised mostly from denominational agencies or other religiously based funders, secular foundations, and institutional membership dues. Nationally, of the approximately four thousand institutions that are formal members, 87 percent are religious congregations and 13 percent are public schools, labor unions, neighborhood associations, and a diverse array of other community organizations. Teams of leaders from these institutions organize other institutional members, do research on an issue selected in dialogue with them, and negotiate with political and economic elites. They gain a place at the negotiating table by mobilizing from a few hundred to five thousand or more participants in the nonpartisan political actions described in the previous chapter. In this way, these federations have come to influence government policy on housing, economic development, public schools, policing, working-class wages, recreational programs for youth, medical coverage, and other issues.

The first fruits of significant structural reform catalyzed by faith-based organizing can be seen in cities such as Oakland, New Orleans, and San Diego, where PICO's most successful federations have developed, in cities where the other faith-based organizing networks sponsor especially strong federations, and in recent efforts to project power in regional and state-level political arenas (analyzed later in this chapter). Subsequent chapters trace this institutional strength to the dynamics of social capital formation and organizational culture made possible by linking religious faith and political engagement in particular ways. This chapter focuses on the organizational roots of that linkage; how it can lead to a symbiotic relationship between PICO and religious congregations (and can also degenerate into a parasitic relationship); and how this organizational symbiosis serves as the foundation for transforming city politics. But before we can gain a clear view of the higher-level political leverage and democratic potential of faith-based organizing, we must see how the very local organizing like that at Saint Elizabeth is aggregated up to project power in citywide politics and in higher-level political arenas.

All Power Is Local: Overview of a Citywide Organizing Federation

In 1995, twenty-one of the twenty-three member organizations in Oakland Community Organizations (OCO), the PICO federation in Oakland, California, were churches of various kinds.[3] All of the most heavily involved and effective local organizing committees were sponsored by church congregations, each of which had decided (through whatever mechanism was appropriate for their particular denomination) to join OCO as an institution. The organization expanded considerably in ensuing years, but held to the pattern of primary sponsorship by religious congregations typical of faith-based organizing (though some federations have a quite substantial minority of non-faith-based institutional members).

Table 2.1 Racial and Institutional Composition of PICO's Oakland Federation (1995)

	Roman Catholic	Historic Black Protestant	"Mainline" Protestant[2]	Pentecostal[3]	Neighborhood Association[4]
Latino[1]	3	0	0	0	0
African American	2	5	2	1	1
White/Anglo	2	0	1	0	0
Multiracial	2	1	1	1	1

1. The "Latino" category here includes both U.S.-born Hispanics and recent immigrants from Latin America, mostly Mexico and Central America.
2. "Mainline" here refers to theologically moderate-to-liberal Protestants, once the dominant tradition of American Protestantism. Two of these four congregations were no longer active by 2000.
3. "Pentecostal" refers to a century-old Christian evangelical movement emphasizing the "gifts of the Spirit" such as praying in tongues and spiritual healing (see Cox 1995).
4. The most substantial "neighborhood association" participation came from a mixed-class, largely African-American neighborhood that sent a handful of members to OCO citywide events.

Table 2.1 shows the range of institutions involved in OCO at the time of this study. As we shall see in chapter 4, OCO's membership base was typical of faith-based organizing federations: First, predominantly Roman Catholic, historic black, and mainline Protestant, with a small contingent of other religious or non-faith-based institutions (in the case of OCO, no Jewish or Unitarian Universalist congregations were active). Second, it had strong representation from African American, white, and Latino communities (though this varies widely, and OCO included more "multiracial" institutions than most federations).

The local organizing committees based in these member institutions provided the foundation for OCO's work, defined in an annual report as follows:

Mission: OCO develops strong leaders and organizes diverse communities in East, West, and North Oakland to make Oakland a better place to live for families. We re-create hope and re-build communities. Using our faith values to unite around common concerns, we re-involve people from our neighborhoods in our public, democratic institutions to push for systemic change.

Building Community: We build the structure for people who trust and respect one another to organize and work together. OCO leaders build relationships through one-to-one, face-to-face conversations with congregation and community members.

Putting Faith into Action: Leaders share common values from our faith and
democratic traditions. We bring these values into the public arena
through action on concrete issues. Through relationships, research and
action, OCO leaders live out the call to serve one another and to seek
justice.

Empowering People: We believe that every person has a God-given dignity,
and collectively we have the right and responsibility to shape a common
future. OCO leaders are people closest to the problems who play key roles
in the solutions.

Developing Leaders: We provide experience-based, relevant leadership training and organization development for member organizations and their
constituents. We use the PICO model for congregation-based community
organizations. Our Executive Board consists of leaders elected from our
member organizations.[4]

When two or three dozen religious congregations coordinate their work
within the faith-based organizing process described here, the results can be
dramatic. Such "federated" actions have repeatedly mobilized between one
and two thousand residents in cities from Oakland to San Diego, from San
Francisco and San Jose to Denver and Camden, New Jersey; similar actions
occur in the other faith-based organizing networks. The New Orleans PICO
federation has drawn more than five thousand members to a public action,
coordinating the efforts of some sixty congregations. At a time when local
political parties often have trouble gathering more than a hundred or so
citizens for local political events, and community mobilizations may gather
large numbers in response to sudden crises but quickly lose steam, repeatedly gathering a thousand or more motivated participants quickly gains the
attention of elected officials, and (as we shall see) can exert real leverage
on the political system.

Religious Roots Flourishing in the Public Arena: A Citywide Action

On a typical early summer evening in downtown Oakland, the stragglers
from the departing business crowd enjoy spectacular weather as the city
streets empty. These relatively affluent members of the Oakland community—predominantly white or African American, secondarily Asian, with
only a few Hispanics and Native Americans among them—share the dress,
the hurried walk, and the purposeful look of office employees across the

country. But as they depart for homes in the East Bay hills and the suburbs beyond, they give up these downtown streets to a different mix of city residents with a different look. Most are African American or Hispanic, with a few whites and some southeast Asians among them. These are low-level office employees, still waiting for buses to their homes in the flatlands. This later crowd lacks the elegance of the more elite Oaklanders, their shoes more frayed, their clothes less fashionable. Soon they too will disappear from the streets, leaving the late office stragglers walking among the night-time population of the homeless and unemployed or working poor. This evening scene will be repeated in central cities throughout America, albeit with other racial mixes.

But on a Monday evening in May 1994 a different urban drama played out in downtown Oakland. As the usual crowds began to thin, new throngs entered the downtown streets. Small groups of poor and middle-class residents of flatland neighborhoods in West and East Oakland were arriving at the local convention center, and gospel music stirred the crowd, led by choirs from two local multiracial congregations emphasizing worship within African American forms of religious expression.[5] They sang three songs speaking of bearing God's light in the world, having courage, and treasuring God's grace:

> This little light of mine, I'm going to let it shine. . . . Everywhere I go, I'm gonna let it shine. . . .

> You shall be a witness, you shall be a witness . . . go and testify in my name. You shall be raised to be a witness for the Lord. . . . Don't be afraid, don't be afraid, to be a witness for the Lord. . . .

> Amazing grace, how sweet the sound, that saved a wretch like me. I once was lost, but now am found, was blind but now I see. . . .

By 7:00 P.M., more than fourteen hundred Oakland residents filled the hall, singing or speaking in English or Spanish; about half were African American, a third were Latino, a sixth were white, and a scattering of southeast Asian immigrants completed the mosaic. As the choirs concluded, the choir director said, "We are delighted to be here in this unity tonight, to be bound up in love together with all of you."

This evening's event launched OCO's HOPE Campaign, which focused on "improving the situations faced by young people growing up in Oakland." The biblical theme "Hope deferred makes the heart sick; a wish come true is the tree of life" (Proverbs 13:12) appeared on banners and the official agenda for this action. Tonight, the mayor and school board president would be asked to commit themselves to a set of school reform initiatives developed by OCO involving safety, job training, and attendance.

The OCO staff had structured a yearlong process building up to this event through the kind of organizing work we saw at Saint Elizabeth's, now multiplied across two dozen congregations. But tonight, organizers would remain in the background, taking no public role and doing no visible coaching; local leaders from religious congregations and neighborhoods carried the entire drama, centered on their relationship with their representatives in city government.

As the gospel music faded, a prayer was offered by Reverend James Abner, a black Baptist minister (with summary translation into Spanish, like all the meeting's speeches):

> Eternal and almighty God . . . we come on this mission of mercy, mindful of the fate of our children. In the holy writ, those persons who are not sympathetic with the children attempt to send them away, but our Lord says, "Suffer the little children to come to me, for of such is the kingdom of heaven." . . . Tonight we come bringing our children to you. There are many conditions in our environment that are not conducive to good role models for our children. . . . We come tonight asking for your Holy Ghost power. Allow the Holy Spirit to direct this meeting, allow the Holy Spirit to take full control. In the name of Jesus we pray. Amen.

Reverend Charles Burns then read a statement developed for this event and approved by consensus of the pastors involved in OCO:

> In the scriptures the justice of a society is measured by the treatment of the orphan and the widow (Deuteronomy 24:19–21). The Book of Proverbs calls upon us to "train up our children in the way they should go" (Proverbs 22:6). Christ in the Gospel of Matthew states: "Whoever shall offend one of these little ones . . . it were better for him that a millstone were hanged about his neck, and that he were drowned in the depth of the sea" (Matthew 18:6). In the spirit of the Scriptures, moved by the Word of God, we the Oakland Community Organizations come to express our concern about the well-being of the young people and children of our community.

The president of OCO, Henry Hemphill—an elder at a local African American Community Reformed church—then "credentialed" the organization as representing twenty-five thousand Oakland families, and as affiliated with sister PICO organizations across the country. He added, "We believe that because each of us is a child of God, we deserve to live with dignity. We work together to change those conditions in our neighborhoods which threaten our dignity."

After visiting political figures were introduced, Mary Ellen Burton-Christie, a white woman active in a local Hispanic Catholic church, and Marie Lee, a black woman from another local church, reported on the research done by OCO leaders:

> I'm here to tell you that our children are falling through the cracks. . . . Tonight, we begin our HOPE campaign. . . . *H* is for healthy and safe schools. *O* is for opportunities for employment. *P* is for students being present in school, rather than absent. And *E* is for creating enrichment programs during class and after school.
>
> We call this a campaign because we are in this for the long haul, because all of the OCO churches and neighborhoods are pulling in the same direction. We believe what we read in Proverbs: "Hope deferred makes the heart sick; a wish come true is a tree of life." We are starting the campaign to make our wish come true. Are you with us? [Loud applause, shouts of "yes!"]
>
> Tonight we are addressing the most basic needs of our children.

Lee went on to outline OCO's demands:

- Safe passage to and from school for all of the children in the city. Two OCO churches had started a pilot safe passage program at schools in their areas. OCO wanted this successful program at every school that needed it.
- A truancy program that alerts parents as soon as a student misses one class, as well as a stay-in-school program to encourage attendance. "The price our community pays for high truancy rates is a very high one," Lee noted. "Our children are wasting their days on street corners and are not prepared for jobs when they leave school."
- School-to-work transition programs, "to keep so many of our children from falling through the cracks of society."

Several adolescents from the OCO Youth Committee set the stage for the political leaders' responses by offering testimony about the negative effects of poor schools, violence, and absenteeism on their lives and studies.

Reverend Burns then invited responses from school board president Sylvester Hodges and Mayor Elihu Harris. Both politicians' answers extended beyond the three-minute limit they had been given, and they were cut off— in Hodges's case, by the moderator; in Harris's case, by an audience member, who was then himself cut off by the moderator. This is typical of actions under the faith-based organizing model: organizational discipline is used to prevent both manipulation by ambitious officials and spontaneous disruption by the audience.

Up to now, the politicians had been asked to hear OCO's initiatives and allowed to respond to them with generalities. Next, in the key moment of the action, they were asked to directly answer several questions presented for OCO by Judy Reyes and Reverend Stephen Brown:[6]

Reyes: Mr. Hodges, do you commit yourself to developing a comprehensive program to promote school attendance to begin in September of this year?

Hodges: Yes, I commit myself to that.

Reyes: Mr. Hodges, do you commit to convening a meeting before the end of June between representatives of OCO and school district officials in order to develop that program?

Hodges: Yes, I do.

Reyes: Mr. Hodges, do you commit the schools to fully implement the Aviation Academy program at Castlemont High School by the time school starts in the fall?

Hodges: No, I do not.

Reyes: Are you saying you are unwilling to make this happen?

Hodges: I cannot assure that it will happen by then.

This impasse was left on the table, to be resolved during subsequent meetings.

Brown: Mayor Harris, do you commit yourself to implementing the Safe Passage program in time for the coming school year?

Harris: Yes, I do.

Brown: Do you promise to make the safety of children a priority for your administration?

Harris:	Yes, I do.
Brown:	Mr. Harris, do you commit to convening a meeting with us and with representatives of the city of Oakland to shape this program?
Harris:	I already answered your question. Yes.

Burns summarized the commitments made by the school president and mayor, saying:

> We have received "yes" answers to five of our six questions, with a commitment to working with OCO to make concrete plans for improving safety and attendance in our schools. We still have some uncertainty about the future of Castlemont High School's aviation program, but we will be addressing that. We have asked for our elected leaders to be accountable to this community, and they have committed themselves to doing that. With God's strength among us, we shall hold them to that commitment! To our political leaders, I would say: This body *can* be an ally for you. And personally, I would not want OCO as other than an ally.

The meeting concluded with a prayer attributed to Jean-Bertrand Aristide, the president of Haiti:

> With God on our side, who can be against us? We thank you, Lord, for being with us tonight, for giving us perseverance that we might keep on pushing until we achieve that for which we strive. . . . We thank you for the Holy Spirit, who leads us and guides us in all we do. And with the disciple Paul we say "neither height nor depth, neither principalities nor powers shall separate us from the love of God." And God said, "Let all the people say Amen."

The audience responded to this with a loud "Amen!"

As the audience dispersed, filtering out into the night air an hour and a half after the action started, they encountered the same depressing scene found on urban streets throughout America: deserted storefronts, homeless families, the drug addicted and the desperate. They had won commitments for better communication from school personnel to parents regarding their children's school attendance, increased police presence at school closing times, and ongoing collaboration with elected officials—limited gains, to be sure, but significant for those raising children in Oakland. Perhaps as importantly, they confronted their difficult social reality with a new sense of engagement between their lives—for some, deeply rooted in religious faith—and the political and economic decision making processes that determine much about their quality of life.

Citywide Organizing: Process, Issues, Outcomes

Though these OCO leaders won potentially significant gains for young people in Oakland, those gains are also quite modest in the larger scheme of poverty in American society. They take on greater significance when placed in the context of the cumulative organizing work by OCO, and the wider organizing done throughout California and nationwide by PICO. At the time of this action in 1994, OCO claimed the following recent successes:[7]

Neighborhood and School Safety:
— developed the Police Beat Health Unit, a national model for community/police work.
— won $4 million to double the amount of street lighting in high crime areas.
— created "safe passage" zones for children walking home from school around four East Oakland schools.
— worked with Mayor Harris to establish the first police substation in Oakland.

Youth Training and Employment:
— worked in partnership with the Port of Oakland, United Airlines and the school district to establish Aviation Academy, a training program in aviation mechanics at Castlemont High School.
— initiated planning for the Coliseum Redevelopment Area, which promises to retain and increase jobs for East Oakland.

Neighborhood Revitalization:
— initiated a 53 unit first-time home-buyer housing project in the Jingletown neighborhood.
— closed several bars, motels, and liquor stores which were centers of drug and prostitution activity.

Schools:
— established a district wide truancy reduction program.
— helped create the first charter middle school in Northern California.[8]

This overall listing does not make clear the pattern of issue engagement characteristic throughout the PICO network. PICO strives to build citywide federations from the ground up by dedicating early organizational efforts to very locally rooted efforts of concern to individual congregations, identified through one-on-one meetings. These early efforts usually focus on issues seen as winnable. Two factors make an issue winnable at this early stage: a highly visible and relatively noncontroversial local problem, and a government official with authority over resources to address the problem. This combination makes the official vulnerable to public pressure. So a congregation new to the community organizing effort typically works on issues such as city funding for services in their local area, neighborhood crime, or safety for local schoolchildren. Some of the "safe passage" zones around schools and some of the closures of the "centers of drug and prostitution activity" in the above list occurred as part of such early efforts.

Beginning in the early 1990s, OCO moved to focus its activity on making a greater impact on issues affecting residents throughout Oakland (while continuing to foster local efforts by individual churches as well); the street lighting and employment initiatives above were part of this effort. Since 1996, much of this higher-level activity has revolved around reforming and strengthening public education in Oakland and in California as a whole. This primarily involved citywide organizing to push for changes in how the Oakland schools are run. Among the most important campaigns was one jointly led by OCO and the Oakland Educators Association, the local teachers' union. This labor-community collaboration was formed around one shared objective: to redirect school funding priorities in order to reduce class sizes from kindergarten through the third grade from over thirty to twenty-one students per class. Despite a great deal of opposition from school authorities (the initiative meant moving money from systemwide administrative budgets into classroom teacher salaries), this coalition ultimately was successful, in part due to OCO-organized community support during a teachers' strike.

Ultimately, this successful labor-community collaboration soured as a result of diverging perspectives on another school reform effort: charter schools. Some OCO local organizing committees were heavily involved in founding charter schools, whose autonomy is seen as a threat by the teachers union. This conflict, along with diverging styles of organization and different priorities rooted in their organizing models, led the organizations to part ways by 1997. Nonetheless, such efforts at labor-community collaboration represent an important future arena of growth for organizing within both the faith-based and labor-based models.[9]

Meanwhile, OCO's attention shifted to both smaller and larger arenas of action to strengthen public education for Oakland's children. Initially, OCO won funding from the city and the school district for thirty-five homework centers, organized sites for students to do homework and receive tutoring, and other after-school programs throughout Oakland. In 1996, OCO began a push to break down the huge multitrack public schools that had become the norm in Oakland and most American cities, in favor of smaller, more autonomous schools of 250 to 300 kids, modeled after alternative public schools in New York City. Some of these would be public charter schools, others would be small learning academies within the public school system. Three of these small charter schools opened in 1999, and as we have seen, two more in 2001 on the old Montgomery Ward site—"the first new schools built in Oakland in 30 years" (*Oakland Tribune*, March 5, 2001). Working in collaboration with the Bay Area Coalition of Essential Schools, OCO helped moved the school district to embrace a policy to establish ten new small schools over a three-year period (2000–2002) and provided prominent political support for passage of a $300 million bond issue for new school facilities.[10]

Other OCO initiatives during this period included establishment of new senior and low-income housing in the Bay Area's expensive housing market; neighborhood safety programs; and allocation of all funds available to the county through the state's settlement of litigation against tobacco companies (approximately fifteen million dollars per year) to pay for health care access for low-income residents.

A citywide action in 2000 gained the school district's commitment to open five new schools per year for the next five years—partly through money leveraged from the state through the work of the PICO California Project. As the oldest PICO federation, OCO played a crucial role in the statewide effort, including its work on health care and on public school funding (see below).

The strategy of fostering both very local actions and actions at the metropolitan and statewide level has three results. First, it gives new leaders an early taste of victory and of the power possible when they come together to work to improve their community. By developing the capacity of leaders at this grassroots level, PICO assures a steady supply of future leaders of higher-level actions, contributes to congregational development, and grounds the organizing process in strong local roots. Second, when grassroots leaders have gained experience and the organization believes itself to hold sufficient power, it mobilizes these local networks to tackle more difficult issues, such as economic development, school reform, or state-level social programs. Third, the state-level work sometimes leads to state budgetary decisions that create political opportunities at the local level, as in the new school money or the health care funding discussed below.

This focus on constantly combining local action with higher-level action appears to distinguish PICO's work from that of some other community organizing efforts, which focus on generating high-level action early on in order to heighten the sponsoring organization's profile.[11] PICO organizers—and supporters of this approach in the other faith-based organizing networks—suggest that high-profile work on big issues must be complemented by the slow work of locally rooted organizing and that over the long term only the *combination* can sustain democratic participation. They argue that jump-starting the process in order to immediately pursue the high-level issues sacrifices the future development of strong grassroots leaders and thus inhibits the development of stronger congregations and their own organizations.

PICO's Local Structure: The Strengths and Risks of Structural Dualism

PICO's organizational structure must be understood in relation to the church structure alongside which it works. Together, they represent two civic structures: PICO's civic (and political in the broad sense) structure for democratic organizing, and the churches' structures for generating a moral community and celebrating a transcendent realm of religious experience.

The formal structure of faith-based organizing federations is simple enough. The typical structure of a PICO federation involves a membership made up of institutions, not individuals. Somewhere between fifteen and forty member institutions make up a typical federation, though federations exist with as few as ten or as many as sixty. As in OCO, the bulk of those institutions are religious congregations, though neighborhood associations, public schools, labor unions, and other organizations are also occasionally members; in all cases, in order for the institution to become a member, its official decision-making body must choose to join. The federation is formally controlled by an executive board, with each member naming a fixed number of representatives (usually from one to three) to the board, and officers elected annually at a convention. The larger federations often have a small "action team" selected from leaders within the board, which serves to guide the organization between board meetings.

The staff of the federation (usually a director and from one to four organizers) formally report to the board. The board hires and can fire the director, who in turn controls the hiring of organizers. In practice, the fact that they oversee the day-to-day organizing process gives the professional staff significant informal power to shape the direction of the federation—most subtly but powerfully through their long-term formation of leaders, more directly through their role in establishing priorities, suggesting new ideas, "cutting issues," and leading internal meetings.

The strong links between faith-based organizing federations and religious congregations give a third group considerable power in the organizing process: pastors of member congregations. In one sense, pastors are no more powerful than lay leaders—indeed, they function as peers with lay leaders and are influential only to the extent they meet the same criteria as lay leaders (their dedication to the process, their skills, and the time they invest). The fact that many pastors hold institutional authority and possess strong communications skills means that they may gain positions of influence, such as moderating public actions or leading public prayers. But those positions may also be, and often are, held by lay leaders. In a second sense, however, pastors hold a separate power all their own: Ultimately, they control the federations' access to members of their congregations. This power is rarely invoked, at least where skilled organizers lead federation staffs. Only once during my study did I witness a pastor exert a veto by denying OCO access to his congregation, but that veto power remains always potentially available.[12] Organizers and leaders must therefore constantly calculate what is acceptable to the influential pastors in their federations, and either operate accordingly or work to broaden pastors' boundaries of what is acceptable.

Thus, on the PICO side of the organizational structure, the basic thrust of organizing lies in the dynamic interplay between organizers, lay leaders, and pastors as they engage in democratic political tasks: defining issues with potential to improve the "voice" and "equality" of poor and middle-income folk, establishing the ethical high ground on these issues, organizing communal power, and projecting this power into the public realm in order to influence these issues.

On the church side of the organizational structure, the basic thrust of congregational life is different: the fundamental dynamic of religious congregations in American life revolves around the construction and affirmation (through liturgy, preaching, prayer, and ritual) of a realm of spiritual experience, and through this experience the shaping of "communities of memory and hope"—that is, moral communities that transcend individualism.[13] Here, religiously rooted identities are constructed, the human search for meaning and commitment takes center stage, and particular religious understandings of the human condition thrive, wither, or are transformed as they come into contact with the very human drama of life in primary

communities of family and congregation. These particular religious understandings come packaged with particular worldviews, particular forms of
organization, particular models of gender roles, and particular views of conflict—which vary widely across congregations.[14] Here, the dynamism or las-
situde of congregational life lies in the interplay among religious leaders,
congregation members, and authoritative traditions (whether carried in
church teachings, ritual practices, scriptural texts, or oral preaching). Sometimes congregational "moral community" coexists uneasily with the conflict inherent in community organizing. But as I argue in chapter 5, community organizing's ability to bring ethical leverage to bear in politics—its
ability to claim the ethical high ground on issues—depends precisely on
its link to such moral communities and their ethical teachings.

This connection to religious and ethical traditions is one of the
strengths of the faith-based organizing model and offers another crucial
kind of power to pastors. As professional interpreters of their traditions,
pastors, priests, rabbis, imams, and other religious leaders can mediate into
the organizing process the best ethical insight those traditions have to offer.
This involves helping congregation members and faith-based organizing
participants more broadly to reflect on their political experience in light of
the moral-political teachings rooted in religious faith; guiding, illuminating, and criticizing the faith-based organizing process in light of those
teachings; and reformulating, reworking, and criticizing religious teachings
in light of democratic experience. All these are crucial roles within the faith-
based organizing process and within faith communities themselves, and no
one is as well positioned to carry them out as are the religious leaders of
sponsoring congregations. This power of cultural and ethical interpretation
is often neglected—and in any case is credible only if pastors are sufficiently
involved in the organizing process that they can understand it. But the status of pastors as gatekeepers to congregations does give them the ability to
exert this power if they so choose; if done well, it can strengthen faith-based
organizing.

Thus, understanding faith-based organizing requires looking not just at
the federation structure, but at the dual structure of church and federation.
This dual structure allows a division of labor between each citywide PICO
federation and the institutional structure of the local congregations. The
federation provides a unifying structure for focusing efforts at political dialogue and action, while the local congregations provide moral-political vision consonant with the pluralism of worldviews present within American
life.[15] Indeed, out of these various religious settings come leaders with quite
different understandings of how—and whether—their religious faith can

or should motivate their civic engagement. Judging from interviews with leaders, the spectrum includes those whose religious identity represents a vibrant core that radiates to all aspects of their experience (including their political engagement), and through which God touches and integrates their whole sense of self under the identity of "Christian," "Jew," or "believer"; to those who hold their faith as a central piece of what is important to them but experience it as segmented from other aspects of their lives; to those for whom faith and God's presence feel more tenuous, less vibrantly experienced, less core to their experience, but nonetheless meaningful to them; and, indeed, leaders who are not religious believers at all, who enter either from the margins of church life or through church members' ties to the neighborhood. But across this spectrum, the vast majority of leaders enter PICO through congregations.

At its best the faith-based organizing structure provides local leaders with the tools they need in order to influence city priorities and reshape their own neighborhoods, while allowing leaders to interpret this civic engagement in terms appropriate to their own traditions and biographies. In interviews, leaders expressed all these and more as the primary motivations for being involved: as "following Jesus" in "holding the authorities accountable and forming his disciples"; as "answering God's call to build the Kingdom"; as "taking the city for Jesus"; as "walking the walk just like we talk the talk" (i.e., as doing in our daily lives what we talk about in church on Sunday morning); as "helping my church be responsible for this world here and now, not just for the sweet bye-and-bye"; as "working with my neighbors to build a better community"; as "repairing the world" or "doing mitzvot"; or as "making city officials respond to the needs of poor neighborhoods with people of color, not just to rich neighborhoods where white people live."

The presence of this rich diversity of motivations, both religious and civic, allows leaders of many different kinds to feel at home within the faith-based organizing effort. Structural dualism allows these diverse motivations to thrive and be felt as legitimate within the umbrella organization: Since the communal settings for elaborating and celebrating the varying religious cultures are autonomous from the PICO structure, the contrasts between them are perceived as relatively unthreatening. They thus coexist successfully alongside one another and collaborate in pursuing mutual interests in greater political voice and equality in members' lives.

This is not to imply that conflict among different religious expressions does not occur within PICO organizations. It occasionally does, and chapter 7 will briefly examine the roots and consequences of such conflicts. But by and large, successful organizing federations mesh elements from these diverse traditions by structuring organizational life so that each tradition can thrive on its own congregational turf. The federation then provides a separate organizational structure in which these diverse traditions can be integrated in ways that promote political engagement.

From the perspective of a religious congregation, this allows the religious community actively to pursue reform in the social world while protecting its core practice—religious worship—from being swallowed up in the political demands of organizing, and thus being instrumentalized. This strategy parallels an organizational strategy familiar in business, referred to as "buffering of the technical core," in which a company shields its most crucial processes from distortion by external pressures (Thompson 1967). In this case, we might refer to *buffering of the sacred core:* the worship life of the community remains sacred ground, related to but autonomous from the pressures of engagement in the political system. Given the strong societal and political implications of these religious traditions, and in order for the relationship of the spiritual to the sociopolitical to be experienced by members, the worship life of the community must address and bear witness to wider social realities—but can do so *on its own terms* rather than losing its character in the search for immediate political relevance. When asked how his church combined political confrontation with the worship life of the community, Thomas Howe, a Methodist pastor in Louisiana, responded:

> It's because we're not confrontational in the worship setting. We separate the two in terms of carrying it out. Obviously the worship has to deal with it at some level, but it's a very subtle level except for a few times a year. But then we assign to committees certain responsibilities. . . . We don't let them off the hook, because if you come here to worship and are a part of this, you're immediately involved in a lifestyle. But secondly, in our worship services at the announcement time these programs are shared. We set up tables outside so that opportunity is there for them. In addition to that, everyone gets called when we do the one-to-one meetings. Everyone is called and involved in that. When we need people there, we will call and ask them specifically to be there.

Joseph Justice, a Catholic pastor in Southern California, saw his parish's worship life contributing directly to the organizing work: "I think the stronger the parish is as a Catholic community, in their Catholic identity, the more the rest of this works too."

From the point of view of the community-organizing federation, this unburdens the organization from generating a political culture from scratch and seeking to immerse participants in it. Instead, the organization can draw on religious symbols and meanings to which members are already committed, drawing out and emphasizing their socially relevant aspects.[16]

When this occurs successfully, the organizing federation and its member religious institutions both benefit substantially: each is freed to focus on pursuing its primary mission while drawing benefits from the primary mission of the other. The community organizing effort focuses on effective intervention in the public realm, while drawing on the ethical insight, social networks, and cultural resources of religious congregations. The congregations, in turn, focus on constructing a shared worship experience, while drawing on the PICO network's expertise in carrying the pressure for ethical-political reform into the public arena. I term this relationship *structural symbiosis,* to highlight its parallel in mutually beneficial association between symbiotic plant species—some of which indeed cannot survive without one another.[17] It is the antithesis of a parasitic relationship, such as that between a tapeworm and its human host, in which one organism draws sustenance from the other but contributes nothing in return—and often weakens or damages it.

So structural symbiosis contrasts sharply with what might be called *structural parasitism:* forms of community organizing that only exploit religious congregations without contributing to or respecting their legitimately different function. Some organizers are well aware of the need to sustain the symbiosis. Stephanie Gut, a leading PICO organizer and director of its San Diego project, says, "In the long run, I think the healthier the church the better for the organizing effort."

At its strongest, structural symbiosis gives faith-based organizing a highly adaptive organizational apparatus. This allows exemplary faith-based organizing efforts to effectively combine two sets of practices that are often kept in debilitating isolation or combined in highly reactionary forms: deeply rooted religious commitment and energetic engagement in the democratic public realm. The fact that faith-based organizing efforts must pay careful attention to both sides this dual structure results in a dilemma.

On one hand, faith-based organizing must keep its own structure vibrant, autonomous, and diversified enough that it can resist being captured by the political agenda of any one powerful congregation, denomination, or religious leader. This autonomy allows the federation to remain an attractive route of public engagement for diverse congregations and thus sustain its growth and legitimacy in increasingly diverse cultural settings. Several elected officials noted in interviews that as long as the local federation remained broadly ecumenical or interfaith, they would be willing to work with it—but if it became more narrowly sectarian, they would become very nervous.

On the other hand, faith-based organizing must sustain vibrant roots in local church congregations and its overall embeddedness in particular religious cultural traditions—as opposed to "thin" engagement in a plethora of traditions, each only superficially engaged. If pastors or church-sponsored funding agencies perceive a given federation or network as having little real religio-ethical vision or as simply instrumentally exploiting religion, they can be expected to sever their support. Given the reliance by individual federations and the organizing networks on financial backing from denominations, and the pastoral veto on congregational access discussed above, such a turn of events would be disastrous.

Several factors heighten the importance of cultivating close ties to religious congregations. The Bush administration's "faith-based initiative" may well create financial incentives for religious congregations to shift their focus toward social service provision instead of the more political ministry associated with faith-based organizing. Only close ties to congregations will give organizers the opportunity to remind clergy and lay religious leaders alike that their vocations include prophetic challenge to public policy regarding poverty and inequality. Without such reminders, the lure of federal dollars may entice congregations away from this more prophetic role. Likewise, faith-based organizing will have to defend its privileged ties to congregations as more political and para-denominational groups compete to mobilize people via religious congregations.[18] Thus, religious leaders may be expected to become wary of providing congregational access to any organizations seen as exploiting the resources of church life for their own ends—especially as churches of all stripes further recognize the ecclesial costs associated with those instances (especially in Latin America and Eastern Europe) in which a partisan political group captured denominational structures.

Recent work in the sociology of religion (Ammerman and Farnsley 1997; Becker 1999) suggests a final rationale for strong ties to local congregations. Individual congregations adopt varying institutional models of what life as a local religious community entails, which in turn profoundly shape the congregation's sense of its mission, how it approaches authority, what issues are likely to lead to conflict, and how that conflict is handled once it arises. Given the centrality of authority, constructive conflict, and a public mission for faith-based organizing, understanding the institutional model at work within participating congregations is crucial for effectively sustaining their public engagement.

As a result of all these factors, the faith-based organizing networks continually need to prove themselves as preferred channels for religious institutions to engage in the public realm, in ways consonant with democratic pluralism and each congregation's ethical traditions. Simply being ardent suitors for access to church resources, membership, and legitimacy will not suffice. How they structure the respective roles of clergy and professional organizers, how respectfully or cynically they handle the ethical resources of religious traditions, and whether constructive conflict effectively invigorates church life rather than undermining it will shape whether the dual structure of organizing grows symbiotically or withers parasitically.

An example of the kind of complex issues likely to arise continually within the dual structure arose in New Orleans in 1994. Riverboat gambling was coming to Louisiana, and All Congregations Together, the local PICO federation, was divided regarding how to respond. The split fell partly between pastors in denominations with divergent moral teachings regarding gambling, and partly between organizers and some pastors. Certain clergy members saw gambling as a bedrock moral issue, with the only possible moral position being to fight it; organizers saw it as an opportunity to negotiate for jobs and economic development in poor communities. The issue threatened to undermine a strong local federation, as neither side fully understood the position of the other, why it was deeply held, or the reasons behind what they saw as simple intractability on the other side. The federation was sufficiently powerful in the state political arena that it might well have been able to extract significant concessions in return for supporting the gaming initiative. The initial instinct of organizers was to settle both splits through democratic consultation with leaders, assuming positions to be negotiable if various economic self-interests could be addressed. But pastors' bedrock ethical commitments, rooted in very specific moral injunctions understood within particular religious traditions, proved nonnegotiable. Ultimately, organizers had sufficient ties to local congregations and were sufficiently adept professionally to recognize this. In the end, they backed down, and no federationwide initiative was launched on this issue.

Given the divergent core commitments on each side of the structural dualism of faith-based organizing, such tensions will inevitably arise. Indeed, the *differences* between organizing federations as democratic political bodies and churches as moral communities are precisely what make their relationship complementary, mutually enriching, and potentially powerful. Keeping those differences in creative tension involves the work of professional staff as the most stable presence within organizing federations, clergy as the institutional heads of congregations, and lay leaders as the key bridges across this dual organizational structure.

Sustaining Symbiosis: Power in the Roles of Pastors, Professional Organizers, and Leaders

Complex power dynamics arise among the three core internal constituencies within faith-based organizing because no one of them holds ultimate authority. Rather, pastors, professional organizers, and lay leaders each bring their own grounds for authority and power to bear within the organization.

The role of a congregation's pastor is crucial. He or she may or may not take part in the day-to-day organizing process; organizers typically prefer strong pastoral involvement, but cannot always get it. In any case, they must keep pastors aware of their work, since the pastor can immobilize the organizer and the local committee in myriad ways: by rejecting initial entrance into the federation, by refusing to identify potential leaders, by denying time during services to make announcements, by withholding public legitimation of its efforts, or by publicly delegitimizing them. In addition, pastors are often asked to take leadership roles during actions by leading prayers, moderating the meeting, or asking the questions that pin the target to a specific response—and may refuse to do so. When they agree to adopt these roles, pastors provide models of civic involvement for their congregation members, often bring highly developed public skills to that involvement, and provide moral legitimation to the action—each of which is vital for inspiring and sustaining lay involvement.

For their part, organizers bring several sources of authority to their work. They hold knowledge of effective organizing techniques and how to apply these within a congregation. They hold analytical skills for strategizing vis-à-vis the political world. In addition, they bring the direction and focus arising from the fact that they dedicate themselves full-time to this work— a direction and focus often missing among pastors, whose work commitments pull them in multiple directions. New ideas, possible policy alternatives, and expert contacts beyond the local area are often introduced to the organizing process by organizers, who have access to information through their ties to the faith-based organizing networks and because the best of them read more widely than most other participants.

Finally, lay leaders carry significant political authority within faith-based organizing. This authority comes partly from the way that one-to-ones lie at the heart of the organizing process; since lay leaders do most of these, they carry significant influence whenever the question of "what are our people out there saying?" comes to bear in decision making. In mature federations, long-term decisions ultimately are made by a more or less formally constituted board or strategic leadership group controlled by leaders. In newer federations, in which leaders are deemed to have less political formation and experience, pastors and particularly organizers often carry greater authority relative to lay leaders.[19]

This tripartite structure does not imply equal authority, for it functions only at the pleasure of the pastor as final arbiter in the religious sphere of the congregation. Woe to the organizer who overplays his hand and is perceived as inappropriately challenging the authority of the pastor. In principle, the trump cards always remain in the hands of local pastors, though they can be called to accountability through leaders in their member congregations.

But in practice something akin to equal authority often develops in the day-to-day process of organizing, particularly in the strongest federations. Many pastors see a crying need for civic engagement by their congregations, but have no expertise in how to promote it effectively; many lay leaders work passionately to strengthen their communities, but need expert help in doing so successfully. Thus, though organizers typically downplay the extent of their influence, it is substantial, exercised in myriad informal ways that shape the direction of organizational life. Ultimately, the degree of influence by organizers varies, from essentially controlling the organization to acting as a partner to congregation members advancing the public face of religion.

In all of this, the clergy-organizer relationship is crucial. PICO organizer Peter Phillips, who works in Alabama and Florida, describes the relationship this way:

> You don't want one to dominate, you want balance. Organizers and pastors have different functions. The role of the [organizer] is be able to teach the process, but also to be able to bring the principles of the work to people . . . to be objective about that. And to raise questions. The clergy leadership has some of those functions, but they also provide more of the long-term vision and guidance and stability to the organizations because the congregations are much more stable than these organizations are. So they have different functions. One doesn't dominate the other.

Father Joseph Justice from Santa Ana, California, saw it this way:

> I look for certain things in it. Are the organizers coming in with an
> agenda or are they looking for what are the needs? PICO certainly was
> looking for what are the needs here. And they have fulfilled what they
> said they would do, which is build relationships and develop lay leaders.
> And if you stay in dialogue with the organizers, in contact with what's go-
> ing on, then there aren't going to be any surprises or off-the-wall things.

In these and other interviews, organizers tended to emphasize those aspects of the clergy-organizer relationship that support vigorous political organizing. Clergy—who are responsible for the broader care of their congregations—tended to emphasize those aspects of the relationship that
contribute to the development of lay leaders and keep the organizing in
proper relationship to other aspects of church life.[20] The ultimate task for
both lies in using the moral-political traditions of religion to guide immediate political efficacy and congregational development, in order to generate
dynamic, ethically rooted democratic engagement over the long term.

From Symbiosis to Local Power

In its more sophisticated embodiments, where talented organizers and
strong pastoral support together foster lay initiative and responsibility, this
structural symbiosis has led to considerable power for previously marginalized constituencies in local political arenas. Some initial understanding
of the scale of that local power comes from the Interfaith Funders' national
study of faith-based organizing (Warren and Wood 2001). Over an eigh-
teen-month period, the field as a whole drew some 24,000 people into a
sufficient leadership role to be defined as "core leaders" by the federation
directors who responded to the survey. Some 2,700 of these people were
sufficiently involved in high-level leadership and decision making for respondents to identify them as "board members"—itself designating a variety of roles, but usually involving some degree of long-term strategic
planning for their organizations. In addition, 1,600 leaders attended the
multiple-day national training events that provide the core introduction to
and socialization into the faith-based organizing models as practiced within
each network. Finally, the field employs some 460 full-time professional
organizers.

These numbers suggest at least some *potential* for faith-based organizing
to play a significant role in the public sphere. But that potential is only

Table 2.2 Projecting Power: Highest Attendance at Local Political Actions

Maximum Reported Attendance at a Local Political Action	Number of FBCO Organizations
1,000 or more (max = 10,000; mean = 1,807)	27
400–900	36
120–350	28
less than 100	9

Source: Wood and Warren forthcoming.

realized to the extent a specific organization gains a significant role within a local political arena. One assessment of that role comes from how many people a local organization can gather to meet with local political officials. Table 2.2 shows the size of largest action gathering for each of the one hundred respondent organizations. Though raw numbers such as these do not directly measure these organizations' political capacities, they are a rough gauge of one key determinant: their ability to *mobilize*. In virtually any city in the country, an organization that can mobilize more than a thousand people to a public action with a focused agenda and reasonably skilled leadership can be expected to have powerful influence upon local political decision making at least on some issues; about a quarter of these organizations report this level of political capacity. Organizations able to mobilize many hundreds supporters around a focused policy agenda can likewise be expected to exert significant influence upon local political decision making; more than a third of these organizations report this level of political capacity. The political influence of groups mobilizing up to a few hundred supporters vary greatly depending on other factors, most notably the solidity or fractured quality of local governing coalitions, the organization's ability to garner support from other organizations, skillful organizational leadership, and other facets of political opportunity. It also presumably depends simply on the size of the local polity; in a small city, mobilizing two hundred supporters may give an organization significant local political influence. Just over one-third of faith-based community organizing groups have this more conditional political power.

Table 2.3 presents some issues that faith-based organizing has successfully addressed. It may provide a further sense of such organizing's local political power. By far the most common issues cited by interviewees (Warren and Wood 2001) were those involving public schools and the economy, with criminal justice and housing issues the next most common. What

Table 2.3 Issues Successfully Addressed by Faith-Based Organizing around the Country

Public School Reform:	Smaller public schools, smaller class sizes, site-based management, increased teacher salaries
Other School Issues:	After-school programs, teacher home visits, reading in schools, in-school suspension policy, tutoring, charter schools, safe school campaigns
Economy:	Public-private partnerships for local economic development, living wages, human development tax, worker rights, workforce development, immigrant rights, first-source hiring, sweatshop campaigns, minority hiring
Housing:	Low-income housing, senior housing, *colonia* infrastructure (mostly work on deed conversion, water access, sewage systems, street improvement, and waste removal in poverty subdivisions along border states)
Policing:	Community policing, gun control, improved community-police relations, more police presence, restorative justice, gun control; opposition to gang violence, drugs and crime, police abuse
Medical Care:	Expansion of state-funded health insurance, clinic infrastructure for low-income care, translation services at hospitals; campaigns against emergency room closures
Race Relations:	Interracial understanding, support for hate crime legislation; campaigns against racism
Public Finances:	Bond issues (public school support, *colonia* infrastructure), banking issues (mostly community reinvestment act), tax-based sharing, equalization
Environment:	Environmental cleanup, antinuclear work
Social Services:	Access to health care, long-term care for seniors, welfare rights, senior services
Miscellaneous:	Eyesore removal, public transport, early childhood intervention to combat infant mortality, lifeguard training; campaigns against political corruption

Source: Adapted from Warren and Wood 2001, 40.

table 2.3 does not communicate is the scale on which faith-based organizing addresses these issues, which vary from small improvements to local neighborhoods to major initiatives like PICO's California Project and Louisiana Interfaith Together, the Alliance Schools project of the Texas IAF Network, the Nehemiah owner-occupied low-income housing project of the New York IAF, and similar efforts elsewhere. A typical midrange initiative sponsored by a faith-based organizing project might move several hundred thousand dollars (or several million in a larger city) to address one of the issues. Thus, these organizations no longer engage only easy-to-win neighborhood-based issues that may help a group feel successful but do little or nothing to address the policies that determine the quality of life for working families—the charge often made by competing organizations. Though many federations follow Alinsky's counsel to engage initially in such issues in order to foster a sense of effectiveness and empowerment among leaders, many of them also have far transcended such low-level (albeit important) issues.

As impressive as the list may be, however, we must also recognize the limitations implied in it. First, many important issues—such as the civil and human rights of gay and lesbian Americans, protection of international human rights, antimilitarism—appear nowhere on the list. Such issues are seen as simply too divisive, controversial, or distant from the immediate experience of local congregations to be addressed by most faith-based organizing federations (and other potentially divisive issues that the federations do confront, such as directly challenging police brutality or racism, have only rarely been central issues in these federations). Second, there is an acute limitation of scale reflected in the list; faith-based organizing successfully addresses a number of areas critical to the quality of life of poor, working-class, and middle-class families, but nowhere does so at a scale sufficient to truly affect national political dynamics or the vast flows of financial capital that today primarily determine people's life chances within the global economy.

Neither limitation is a black mark on faith-based organizing. No single organization or field of organizations can address every issue, and no one has developed a successful strategy for shaping international capital flows in ways that tie them to broad human development needs. And the mobilizing capacity documented above suggests that in many settings faith-based organizing may have sufficient political power to wield significant influence over city and state initiatives to improve the quality of life for low-income Americans. But the first limitation does suggest the need for other kinds of political organizing work—faith-based organizing is no panacea for all our democratic ills. The second limitation presents a crucial challenge to all farsighted strategists, funders, and analysts of faith-based and other forms of political organizing: how can we move beyond marginally improving the life chances of working families to shaping the central political and economic dynamics that determine those life chances?

Fuller reflection on this question must await the concluding chapter of this book. But one facet of the answer surely includes faith-based organizing federations having the ambition to address higher-level arenas of political life in America, beyond the city and county governments that now provide the focus for much of their activity. We can learn something in this regard from instances where such work is already occurring; the stronger federations in all the faith-based networks are addressing regional and statewide issues, some of them having won significant victories on statewide policy in large, powerful states.

Power Flowing Upward: Projecting State-Level Influence

Faith-based organizing efforts have attained state-level influence only in a few places. The most noteworthy such cases are the Industrial Areas Foundation in Texas and more recently the PICO California Project.[21] The latter effort—in a state with some thirty-four million people with a famously professional and sophisticated political arena—arguably represents the highest-level political influence achieved by faith-based organizing to date.

Projecting power into state-level political venues represents a qualitatively different challenge from the traditional local work of faith-based organizing. It demands coordination among leaders widely separated geographically who can meet only occasionally, facilitated by local organizers who may see state-level work as an additional burden. Furthermore, it involves facing political opportunities that may not correspond to the issue campaigns being developed by local federations, and confronting political obstacles that local leaders may not understand. The complexities of state-level politics, the greater number of political players there, and the difficulties of projecting power rooted in local neighborhoods or cities into distant state capitals all make political dynamics less predictable at the state level, and thus political outcomes less certain. Although full attention to all these factors is beyond my purposes here, I trace the Oakland Community Organization's engagement in the PICO California Project to gain some initial understanding of these dynamics.

Gradually, OCO worked to parlay its local influence into the beginnings of some wider public power. In October 1995, at a PICO-sponsored action with the California superintendent of public instruction and the U.S. secretary of education, Oakland provided several of the key public leaders and some 350 attendees in a crowd of some two thousand people from twelve PICO organizations around the state. The action focused on increased funding for school-to-work transition programs for high school youth, and both officials strongly endorsed the organizations' agenda. A year later, the secretary of education announced twenty-five million dollars in new federal funding for California school-to-work programs.

In a 1998 action similar to that described in the introduction—but this one under a conservative Republican governor—PICO again convened more than two thousand people from around the state, urging a bipartisan group of political leaders to provide after-school programs to schoolchildren. The organization also urged them to place on an upcoming ballot a measure to begin rebuilding California's crumbling infrastructure of public schools—once among the nation's best, now badly deteriorated after two decades of disinvestment (Schrag 1998). This initiative led directly to the 1998 After-School Learning and Safe Neighborhood bill that provided fifty million dollars in new funding for a variety of after-school programs, signed into law by a conservative governor who had initially opposed it. It also led to the placement of Proposition 1A on the November 1998 ballot, through which California voters overwhelmingly approved $9.2 billion for school repair and construction.

Meanwhile, PICO's Sacramento-area affiliate had begun an experimental collaboration with the local school district, an effort to strengthen parental involvement in the schools, focusing on low-income, low-education households where such involvement is often weakest. PICO organizers and leaders used the one-to-one model to train public school teachers in how to do home visits and use them to encourage parental engagement. Though the teachers—already overburdened by the demands of teaching in understaffed schools—were initially quite hesitant to be involved, once they had actually visited students' homes many of them enthusiastically endorsed the experimental program. In 1999, PICO used this effort as the basis for convincing the California legislature to pass fifteen million dollars for a new parent-teacher home visitation program in over four hundred public schools—three-fourths of them low-income schools.

Through these campaigns, PICO organizers and leaders gained confidence in their ability to coordinate state-, city-, and neighborhood-level organizing efforts. This led to the Healthcare for All campaign to address the crisis in health coverage for nonunionized working-class residents. That campaign culminated in the May 2000 action described in the introduction, which shifted political dynamics surrounding health care provision in California in significant ways. Within two weeks of the action, Governor Gray Davis revised his budget proposal, meeting some of the demands made at the action. More significantly, following the action the leaders of the two houses of the California legislature, Bob Hertzberg and John Burton, became PICO's key partners in advancing its health care agenda. When funding for that agenda was in jeopardy during committee hearings, representatives of all sixteen PICO federations in the state traveled to Sacramento and successfully defended the money budgeted.

By July 2000, the state legislature and governor's office had approved the budgeting of fifty million dollars in additional funding for primary care clinics around the state; the governor also simplified the reporting process for Medi-Cal programs, making it much easier for 1.5 million Californians to sign up for and retain Medi-Cal coverage. PICO staff persons report that members of the governor's staff had told them that the May rally had directly led to his shift of position on both issues. Thus were met two of the three core demands presented at the action. The endorsement of other powerful organizations at the action, such as the AARP, the California Medical Association, and the California Labor Federation, no doubt helped move the issue forward. But all these organizations publicly recognized PICO's leadership on this issue; essentially the entire multiracial three-thousand-person turnout at the action was the work of PICO federations, and the heavy lifting in terms of issue work and coordination was done by the PICO California Project. Gains of this magnitude are not won by single organizations; they require powerful grassroots support, alliances among various constituencies, and leadership from political elites. PICO directly provided the first, played the central role in coordinating the second, and was the key public partner to those who provided the third, Hertzberg and Burton.

The new primary care funding strengthened the medical infrastructure through which many poor and working-class Californians, including vast numbers of immigrants, get their health care. Bureaucratic simplification should facilitate medical coverage for hundreds of thousands of uninsured children and their parents, though that outcome remains to be verified. But the governor vetoed additional funds for core operating expenses for clinics, as well as funds providing dental coverage for the working poor in California; the latter was seen as an entirely new entitlement that was not politically viable.

Thus, while important, the gains flowing immediately out of the action were only partial victories. More important was the fate of Senate Bill 673, sponsored by State Senator Martha Escutia. The bill committed a large portion (over $130 million per year) of California's tobacco settlement money to extend health coverage to parents of poor children under the state's Healthy Families program, which covered only the children themselves. PICO advocated that California supplement this money with some $600 million in federal funds, which the state was at risk of losing because it had failed to enroll eligible children in the Healthy Families program. Thus, SB 673 represented the crucial vehicle for implementing the third, and by far most substantial, demand made by PICO at the May action: health coverage for low-income working families.

As the state legislature worked through the summer, SB 673's fortunes rose and fell but gradually progressed through the legislative process due to considerable effort by Burton, Escutia, and a handful of other legislators, and with intervention at strategic moments with local legislators by PICO leaders from around the state. The governor's signature on the bill remained in doubt until the end but appeared likely given strong support from powerful legislators.

But first, of course, the bill had to pass. The legislative leadership had lined up the votes required, and the final vote on SB 673 was scheduled for the closing day of the 2000 legislative session, August 31. In the final hours of that day, a computer breakdown, related procedural errors, and perhaps some incompetence resulted in forty pending bills being lost—including SB 673.[22] Desperate attempts to revive the bill ran up against a midnight deadline, and the bill died.

Thus, PICO leaders and organizers had to swallow defeat after coming within an eyelash of winning major new health care funding for their low-income constituents. Organizational time had to be invested in not letting this defeat demoralize or, worse, demobilize the local leaders who had given themselves tirelessly to this campaign. By the end of September, they took some consolation when Governor Davis signed the key legislation creating the policy revisions to allow more parents to be insured under the Healthy Families program. But since the money for implementation had died with SB 673, they had to wait for the legislature to reconvene before they could seek funding. Meanwhile, their work helped ignite a public uproar over the federal funds scheduled to be lost, and ultimately California was authorized to keep 60 percent of that money—some $400 million.

Prospects looked good in January 2001, when the state legislature reconvened and Davis included $201.5 million in his proposed budget for the expansion of Healthy Families to include parents. But prospects soon turned grim: the California energy crisis quickly drained several billion dollars of the state's budget surplus, creating a fiscal crisis. All bets were off for any programs asking for new funding—particularly social program expansions like Healthy Families. But by this time, buttressed by PICO's proven ability to mobilize supporters statewide, leading Democratic politicians in the state were standing behind the health care proposals, and health policy researchers continued to produce analyses showing the difference state funding for parental health insurance could make.[23] Furthermore, PICO mobilized its constituents at key junctures in the legislative process to keep the health care expansion alive, with behind-the-scenes issue work and turning out several hundred supporters on two occasions.

Ultimately, they gained far more than most believed possible in the midst of California's fiscal crisis: In July 2001, Davis signed a state budget—after wielding his line-item veto powers to cut more than $600 million from other programs—that included $250 million dollars to expand Healthy Families to parents making up to 250 percent of the federal poverty level (currently $42,500/year for a family of four), the highest cap in the nation. This will extend coverage to approximately 518,000 of the 1,247,000 uninsured parents in California in 2001 (Brown, Ponce, and Rice 2001, 80). The governor also signed legislation committing 100 percent of the state's share of funds from the national tobacco litigation settlement to health programs, and providing a nearly 50 percent increase for state-funded health clinics serving very low-income and undocumented immigrant populations.[24]

Together, these measures signaled a significant turnaround in public policy regarding health care in California—a state often seen as a harbinger for public policy nationally. Indicative of the extent of the turnaround: when Gray Davis was elected governor, health care for the uninsured was entirely absent as an issue in his campaign. PICO had to generate sufficient political pressure to get it onto the political agenda at a time when 90 percent of the "frequent voters" (to whom elected officials look to test prevailing political winds) were already insured and when health care for the uninsured was nowhere near the top priorities of frequent voters.[25] PICO was capable of sustaining for two years the democratic mobilization required to push these changes forward—and to defend them despite a state fiscal crisis that hit during the legislative endgame. These achievements provide powerful evidence that faith-based organizing is, in the right hands, capable of projecting democratic power sufficient to protect substantive interests of working families.

Caveat: Power Flows to Money

None of this analysis suggests that these organizations can fully transcend the power of mobile capital or macrogovernmental structures. Neither PICO's experience nor that of faith-based organizing more broadly provides an easy antidote to Manuel Castells's pessimism regarding the political potential of social movements. The flow of money internationally through financial markets and capital investments, and nationally through weak campaign finance regulations and virtually uncontrolled political action committees, continues to place disproportionate power in the hands of economic elites. Faith-based organizing (on its own and as currently fragmented between networks unwilling to coordinate their work) cannot begin to touch the power of these economic elites.

But the experiences of PICO and the other networks do suggest that sophisticated organizing within strong moral communities may offer leverage to restrain the irrationalities of markets and governments. This offers no excuse for easy optimism, no rationale for a simple reversal of Castells's insight into the limits of urban movements. But it does offer reason for some abiding democratic hope that we can turn our cities, our economy, and our government toward more humanly defined ends.

PICO has established a five-year track record of projecting power upward into the top political arena in the most populous, economically most powerful, and politically influential state in the nation. This is partly a story of strategic calculation and organizing acumen, but it is also crucially the story of the slow construction of a political culture within the organization. That story awaits us later—after we have considered a second model for empowering low-income urban residents, CTWO's model for multiracial organizing.

Chapter 3

Race-Based Organizing in Action

The multiracial model for community organizing developed by the Center for Third World Organizing promotes democratic engagement by linking racial identity to grassroots political work. Through this model, CTWO has not only developed its own successful projects but has staked out an influential role in many other organizing projects by training "activists from communities of color" from around the country.[1] By focusing on CTWO's project in Oakland, People United for a Better Oakland (PUEBLO), we will see multiracial organizing on the ground and get a glimpse of the organizing process and internal cultural dynamics that make it work.

PUEBLO organizes in precisely the same broad neighborhoods of Oakland as PICO's local project, OCO, with a clientele that is equally multiracial (albeit with a different racial mix). But it operates within an organizing model founded on a different cultural strategy: appeal to racial identity as "people of color" as the basis for building a

PUEBLO leaders perform street theater in downtown Oakland as part of the Campaign for Community Safety and Police Accountability, August 1994. Photograph by John Anner. Courtesy Center for Third World Organizing.

multiracial political culture of organizing, rather than an appeal to religious culture. This chapter explores CTWO's organizational culture for the lessons it offers about race and political engagement in America, and in order to lay the groundwork for chapter 4's comparative analysis of race-based and faith-based cultural strategies. It begins with a narrative of an "accountability session," CTWO's term for the kind of political event that PICO called an "action." The chapter then examines the work of PUEBLO's professional organizers and local leaders by describing the meetings, organizing process, and relations with public officials associated with this accountability session. Finally, it analyzes the interplay between the organizing techniques used, the beliefs and worldviews held by participants, and the broad ethos surrounding this model—and how these have generated important organizational victories as well as significant organizational limitations.

Putting Faith in Direct Action

On a summer evening in 1994, a few months after the Saint Elizabeth's action described in chapter 1, streets in downtown Oakland were bustling as office workers departed. At the new Federal Building, however, the crowd was incoming: people arrived from West Oakland and East Oakland neighborhoods for an accountability session regarding local funding for the criminal justice system.

In the auditorium, behind the front stage hung a large red and black banner saying "PUEBLO" with its full name in English and Spanish: "People United for a Better Oakland" and "PUEBLO Unido por un Mejor Oakland." On the side walls hung banners declaring "Prevention, Intervention, *Not* Detention" and "Not More Police and Prisons—We want more toys, not guns or cops." In front, a sign on the podium demanded "Put the Money Where It Belongs." At the table to the left were chairs for PUEBLO leaders and organizers; to the right, chairs with labels for the then-mayor Elihu Harris, the deputy chief of police, and the city manager.

At the appointed starting time, among the invited officials only the police representative had arrived. Some one hundred people sat in the audience, grouped in clusters. Most of these clusters were racially homogeneous, but the crowd as a whole was quite diverse: about a third were African American, a third Latino, and a third Asian or Pacific Islander, with a scattering of white folks completing the mosaic. The crowd was relatively young on average, many having come from local ethnic youth centers.

The meeting began without the other city officials having arrived. Wilma Jackson, an older African American woman welcomed everyone and said, "PUEBLO has spent over six years organizing and fighting to improve the quality of life for low-income and racial-minority people." Margarita Sanchez repeated the welcome in Spanish; from here forward, the entire meeting was conducted with summary translation. Maria Leal, a Latina leader, then addressed the deputy police chief and other city officials in absentia: "We want you to open your hearts and listen to us. With only punishment, we'll never stop crime. . . . we want parks, after-school programs, long-term solutions to our problems, not more prisons."

The meeting, being held under the theme of "Building a Safe Community," then continued with a series of speakers from local immigrant groups, racial and ethnic associations, social service agencies, and voluntary organizations. Leaders from PUEBLO and the Vietnamese Fisherman's Association suggested investing in prevention programs, schools, recreation centers, and cultural centers. A representative of the American Friends Service Committee spoke of "the incarceration-industrial complex" having "stolen money from our communities" and suggested that "to really be about prevention, our communities must police themselves." He also first mentioned the goal of the meeting: to force the city police to redistribute to community groups funds they receive as a result of drug busts. State legislator Barbara Lee drew applause when she called law enforcement and prisons "the military budget of the state of California." When she finished her speech, Lee identified herself with the organization by sitting down at the front table with the PUEBLO leaders (or "activists," the organization's preferred term). A city councilor delivered a similar speech, advocating a "partnership between local communities and the police to develop solutions," and also sat with PUEBLO leaders. Representatives of the East Bay Asian Youth Center, the Centro de Juventud, and Empowered Youth Educating Society all endorsed "community-based programs" rather than police as the key to safe communities; the EYES representative said, "Members of communities create safe communities. . . . We need to build *trust* between people. . . . Solutions do *not* come from large organizations, they come from local communities."

Finally, three teenagers from Youth of Oakland United (YOU), the youth component of PUEBLO, denounced police brutality and the lack of attention to youth concerns in Oakland. Nearly all these speakers were people of color; most represented organizations based explicitly on racial or ethnic identity.

At this point, Mayor Harris arrived, dressed in a windbreaker. Next to him, the city manager's chair remained empty, as it would throughout the meeting.

A brief attempt by a PUEBLO leader to explain the organization's strategy for funding prevention programs led to confusion in the audience; the presenter simply did not have the public speaking skills to present the information. Francis Calpotura, the Filipino-American codirector of CTWO at the time of these events, then spoke via speakerphone to Gary Copeland, an official at the U.S. Department of Justice. Copeland explained the "asset forfeiture" mechanism: whereas traditionally money and property seized as part of drug-related arrests were kept to be used in law enforcement efforts only, beginning in 1994 any tangible property and 15 percent of any cash forfeited could be made available to local organizations for prevention and community development. He estimated the potential funds available nationally through this program to be thirty million dollars per year (15 percent of the two hundred million dollars per year forfeited on average in recent years).[2] Finally, Copeland accepted Calpotura's request to make himself available to work with community groups and police departments on this issue, to which the audience responded by chanting "We are here for justice!" This set the stage for the crucial moment of this meeting: presentation of the organization's demands and the response of city officials.

Two middle-aged grandmothers, Joyce Taylor and Rita Cotton, both African American and longtime activists in PUEBLO, presented the organization's demands in the form of a series of "proposals for change" in how the Oakland Police Department handled forfeited assets. Two were central: first, that the OPD agree to distribute 15 percent of forfeited assets to non-OPD community groups, as recently allowed under federal law; and second, that such disbursement give priority to groups working in crime prevention initiatives. In addition, the proposals suggested (but at this meeting did not further pursue) that PUEBLO have a central role on any asset distribution commission.

The invited officials who, in the organization's jargon, were to be "jammed" on this issue had been chosen carefully during strategy sessions among organizers and key leaders. Since any such disbursement would require the endorsement and cooperation of elected city officials, the city bureaucracy, and the OPD, key figures from each of these settings were invited. In response to the first demand, Harris simply said he had not read the proposal, though PUEBLO had sent it to him two weeks earlier. In response to the second proposal, he said that *if* such a disbursement were approved, he would support the money going toward prevention efforts. He concluded by saying, "Let's not get mad at each other. Let's get mad at where the resources are controlled, at the state level. Get mad at Governor Wilson." When he was informed that his time for responding was over, Harris left the auditorium.

The deputy chief of police was simply asked if the police "would follow Department of Justice guidelines that say 15 percent of forfeited funds can go for treatment, jobs, and prevention." He responded, "I'll tell Chief Samuels he ought to do it. . . . If we choose to support PUEBLO or other groups asking for funding, then of course we would follow the guidelines." He then left as well, to loud and sustained applause from the audience. The accountability session concluded with a brief "wrap-up session." Participants assessed the evenings events quite positively: "We got a positive response from the mayor; he will read our proposal and will support money going to prevention. . . . The deputy chief will personally recommend this to Chief Samuels. . . . It's been a very productive evening." The evening ended with activists and staff leading the audience in chanting, "The people united will never be defeated."

To an outside observer, different aspects of this meeting gave contradictory impressions regarding respect for PUEBLO from the official institutions of city life. On one hand, a councilperson and a state representative gave strong endorsements and chose to sit at the same table as PUEBLO activists; the deputy police chief supported their request, at least to some extent. On the other, the no-show from the city manager and the mayor's late arrival, informal dress, and failure to prepare for the meeting communicated something approaching derision toward the organization; even the more positive comments of the police official could be interpreted as noncommitment to PUEBLO's demands.

Less than a year later, however, the Oakland Police Department agreed to distribute asset forfeiture money to community agencies through a process in which PUEBLO would play the dominant role. Over the next four years, over a hundred thousand dollars would be distributed to community-based crime-prevention agencies through this mechanism. Understanding what led to this significant victory—as well as the reasons for its later partial curtailment—requires paying attention to the organizing dynamics that led to and followed this accountability session.

Organizing Process: Primary Community and Power Organization

Four months before this accountability session, fifteen PUEBLO participants had gathered in a typical PUEBLO meeting to plan the organizing leading up to it. Two were professional CTWO staff, one Latina woman and one Asian-American man. The other thirteen were local leaders for PUEBLO; these nine women and four men included eight African Americans, four Latinos, and one Asian American. As they gradually filtered in, the evening began with social time over a potluck dinner.

The meeting was held in the three-floor training center run by CTWO in what was once a large house. In the meeting room, a Puerto Rican feminist-nationalist poster hung on one wall and the face and words of Malcolm X looked down from another:

> I don't think I could incite. How could I incite people who are living in slums and ghettos? It's the city structure that incites. A city that continues to let people live in rat-nest dens and pay higher rent in Harlem than they pay downtown, this is what incites. . . . Don't ever accuse a black man for voicing his resentment and dissatisfaction over the criminal conditions of his people as being responsible for inciting the situation. You have to indict the society that allows these things to exist.

Pasted on the walls, left over from previous training sessions, were sheets of butcher paper defining key words in every community organizer's lexicon:

Action:	A collective activity that brings people with a common problem in direct confrontation with an individual that has the power or influence to solve the problem. . . .
Demand:	Specific claim on a target for what is rightfully ours.
Leader:	A member of an organization who demonstrates initiative in analyzing problems and thinking through solutions, has developed the loyalty and trust of other members in the organization, and commits to being actively involved. . . .
Problem:	Something which members believe lowers the quality of life.
Strategy:	An overall plan to destabilize the position of the target and that gives direction and focus to other elements of the campaign.
Target:	An individual with the power to grant the organization its demands.
Constituency:	A grouping of people whose interests would be served if they supported your organization or campaign.

Originating in the early community organizing work of Saul Alinsky, these are fundamental conceptual building blocks of most community organizing efforts currently practiced in the United States, including the faith-based activities described in previous chapters.[3] Their entire focus is on building a "power organization," i.e., generating within an organization the ability and willingness to exercise political leverage in the interests of the sponsoring community. Like PICO, CTWO both draws upon and reworks this Alinsky model—but CTWO does so in a different direction. Gary Delgado characterizes the older Alinsky model as "hard-nosed, pragmatic, non-ideological, and usually white and male. . . . Locked in the old paradigm of the neighborhood group, traditional community organizing runs the risk of replicating the same power relations as the dominant society in terms of race, gender, and sexual orientation."[4]

PUEBLO is part of CTWO's organizational response to this shortcoming. That response emphasizes building "organizations in communities of color" in which "issues of race, gender, and sexual orientation are addressed" (Delgado [1993a?], 7). This evening's meeting was called to begin formulating the strategy for the next stage of PUEBLO's campaign, which throughout would emphasize these same themes of racial identity, "the dominant society," and an appeal to being "low-income people." The most common shorthand identification for the organization characterized it as focusing on "low-income communities of color." Gender and sexual orientation remained in the more-or-less visible background. With women constituting the strong majority of participants, gender issues were clearly visible, but were rarely made central. Sexual orientation was never explicitly addressed, but organizational life clearly welcomed gay and lesbian participation.

The shared meal at the start of the gathering was chaotic and the food ran out early, but people appeared to enjoy themselves as they chatted informally in small groups scattered around the house. Many sat in groups of the same racial/ethnic identity, but significant crossover occurred among groups, especially by the PUEBLO staff. The informal meal time spilled over into the scheduled meeting time by twenty minutes, but members did not seem to mind much. Only the staff appeared impatient to get the meeting underway; yet one staff person later talked about this as "important community-building time."

Once dinner was over, the meeting began with a welcome to "this multiracial, multi-issue organization fighting for a better Oakland," delivered by Maria Leal and by Zovie, a young African American man. They listed PUEBLO's accomplishments since its founding in 1989: passage of a model lead-poisoning abatement program in the county, improved translation services at the county hospital serving low-income patients, an extensive vaccination program for children, and most recently the establishment of improved "nutrition breaks" for children in several local schools.

Next, Rita Cotton introduced the evening's purpose as identifying potential allies for moving forward with CTWO's Campaign for Community Safety and Police Accountability (CCSPA). CCSPA originated in the CTWO staff's analysis of the shift in city budgetary priorities away from social services and toward law enforcement and punishment, with resulting increases in social disintegration and "police occupation of low income communities of color." The CCSPA used a baseball metaphor to frame the organization's demands for reform of public criminal justice policy. The home run would involve heightening "police accountability" to citizens by establishing a democratically elected community oversight commission. In pursuing this ultimate goal, first base focused on a fifty-fifty split of public money for law enforcement and crime prevention efforts, whereby each dollar of public funds committed to the criminal justice system would be matched with a dollar for educational, recreational, training, and conflict resolution programs. Second base would be the promotion of "community justice," primarily greater reliance on alternatives to incarceration and greater judicial discretion in sentencing. Third base would be the institution of "community-directed policing," which CTWO saw as a substantial step beyond community-oriented policing—the difference lying in giving real control and direction of law enforcement resources and priorities to community groups, rather than such groups serving as tools for police-controlled efforts. Thus, CTWO saw this meeting as an early step in a long-term strategy to redirect state policy from punishment and incarceration to rehabilitation and "community control" of the law enforcement establishment.

Many of those present participated for the preceding six months in PUEBLO-run discussions regarding police-community relations that staff called "political education" sessions. These connected the CCSPA campaign to local residents' experiences of police power and abuse in their neighborhoods.[5] Rosi Reyes, a staff organizer with PUEBLO, reported on these conversations:

> Police brutality is increasing in our community, especially against young black men, and more and more against Latino and Asian men. . . . One example of that is here with us tonight. [Reyes then introduced the widow of a man was killed after his home had been surrounded by thirty Oak-

land police officers.] This kind of brutality occurs in neighborhoods where people of color live all the time. We want to start looking at crime from a very different perspective, looking at prevention.

Gwen Hardy, also African American and a longtime PUEBLO leader, outlined the CCSPA campaign, noted that even first base would be difficult to achieve, and suggested that PUEBLO would need allies in order to pursue it. When someone questioned the need for allies, Dan HoSang, then the PUEBLO land organizer and now director of CTWO, reinforced the idea:

> Why do we need allies? Because in our surveys of people we found a lack of respect by police for Oakland residents, especially low-income people of color. We're going to be implying that there's racism in the Oakland Police Department. . . . Our community is being destroyed, and only we can put it back together. We don't need anybody from uptown to tell us how to do it, but we do need to build our base and look for allies to work with us on this.

By this point, there were twenty-seven people present; all but three were female. The rest of the meeting was given over to small-group discussions focused on planning house meetings, identifying potential allies, and building ties to youth. Of the groups eventually listed as potential collaborators by the allies group, nearly all were racially or ethnically based. Several of the exceptions appeared to be chosen based on shared ideological orientation, since some groups (e.g., a merchants association) were ruled out as "not progressive."[6]

The meeting ended with organizers presenting a goal of having fifteen organizations present for an "allies meeting" a month later. After a two-and-a-half-hour meeting, people filtered out late in the evening, with several people asking for rides home—an indication of the low-income status of some of PUEBLO's participants.

This meeting and many others throughout this organizing campaign reveal two key aspects of CTWO's organizing effort. On one hand, this campaign was clearly about power—like similar PICO campaigns, it was a faithful reflection of the Alinsky organizing tradition in this sense, focused on building a "power organization" to represent the interests of subaltern groups in American society and on projecting that power politically in order to change public policy. At the same time, as indicated by the time taken for a shared meal and the leisurely pace of the meeting, this effort was also about building a sense of primary community. Participants used the organizational forum to knit together face-to-face relationships that were as much informal friendships pursued for their own sake as they were politically oriented relationships focused on the tasks of organizing.[7]

CTWO's emphasis on primary community flows out of its fundamental cultural strategy. In appealing to racial identity as the basis for building a political culture, the organization faces a dilemma: racial identity by itself divides rather than unites participants. CTWO circumvents this by fostering a multiracial identity as "people of color" and by emphasizing "multiracial culture." But such a multiracial culture is a future ideal and a tentatively emerging reality within the organization; it is not a solidly established cultural reality in participants' lives, reinforced by mutual commitment to a shared culture.[8] Indeed, beyond the shared experience of occupying subaltern positions within the racial and wealth status hierarchy of the United States, the strongest cultural links joining the various minority racial and ethnic groups in American society are arguably those embedded in the dominant consumer culture. That is, one of the strongest cultural overlaps between African Americans, African immigrants, Native Americans, southeast Asian immigrants, and various Hispanic-origin groups—at least those that have been in the U.S. for any length of time—is American consumer culture. This is precisely the cultural commitment CTWO most wants to help members shed, and thus hardly a good basis for organizing. So new participants, though they may be committed to multiracial culture as an ideal, carry only a tenuous commitment to any concrete expression of multiracial culture. This provides only a weak solidarity within the organization to carry it through the political tasks of organizing. CTWO bolsters this solidarity by fostering a sense of primary community within the organization.

The combination of power organization and primary community produces an ongoing tension within the organizing process: members are often focused on building their interpersonal ties to one another, and the staff often must push to move meetings toward the political tasks of organizing. Occasionally, this tug-of-war produces exasperation in the PUEBLO staff or irritation in the members, but also provides some of the dynamic tension that keeps the multiracial organizing model moving forward.

Political Action and Cultural Action

The ensuing weeks of organizing proceeded rapidly. A series of membership meetings and smaller organizing meetings served to generate enthusiasm for and focus attention on the current campaign for the fifty-fifty split of public funding for prevention programs and for punishment. Attendance at these meetings varied from seven to eighteen people, always with a majority African American presence and a smaller Hispanic presence, sometimes with a few biracial, Asian immigrant, Asian-American, or white individuals present.

Through extensive staff research, the overall call for a fifty-fifty split of money for prevention and law enforcement was narrowed to the asset forfeiture arrangement that had recently been allowed under federal law. Door-to-door campaigns were carried out on weekends by the two professional organizers, three organizers in training visiting for the summer, and a few leaders. They sought to draw new members into the organizing campaign, activate some of the four hundred or so individuals and families currently listed as members of PUEBLO, and tap into extended family networks by inviting relatives of existing contacts.

In June, representatives of fifteen social service and advocacy groups came together at the meeting of groups identified as potential collaborators. Representatives of the American Civil Liberties Union, the East Bay Asian Youth Center, the American Friends Service Committee, Copwatch (a group opposing police brutality, led by a former Black Panther), and the Narcotics Education League endorsed the effort to divert money from enforcement to prevention.

During the weeks of work leading up to the key August accountability session, several things were noteworthy. First, seven staff members, organizers in training, and leaders joined participants from four other cities in a three-day lobbying and media exposure drive in Washington, D.C., focused on police accountability. Although a press conference in Washington at which CTWO codirector Francis Calpotura was the key speaker generated only limited local publicity, the opportunity to engage politically at such a high level was an important formative experience for some leaders. It also helped CTWO cultivate the contacts that led to the Justice Department's participation via speakerphone in the August action in downtown Oakland.

Second, the organization successfully overcame the minor crises and confrontations (work not done, expectations not fulfilled, and interpersonal conflicts) that inevitably crop up during the course of organizational life—especially in organizations dedicated to transforming an always-intransigent social world. But PUEBLO's primary approach to surviving such difficulties involved paying no attention to them in group settings. For example, deep consternation resulted when the only three PUEBLO members chosen to receive further training during a CTWO-run organizing apprenticeship program were African Americans. One Latina leader, Margarita Sanchez, challenged the decision publicly, saying in Spanish, "Why aren't any Latinos participating? I wanted to be part of this, and would leave my job in the dust in order to participate in this if I could, but I can't because of the language barrier." An awkward silence followed before the staff intervened and identified the problem as a lack of funding for translation throughout the summer program, and noted that this was only a pilot program. Sanchez expressed dissatisfaction once again, but then relented and nothing more was said publicly. As far as I could ascertain, it was never pursued privately either. In any case, the key point here is the public downplaying of internal group conflict. Likewise, though the organization tried to hold leaders accountable for fulfilling tasks to which they committed, it proved difficult to maintain discipline in this regard. In practice, the staff and leaders showed a great deal of tolerance for task commitments that went unfulfilled. This tolerance flowed not from any belief that completing such tasks was unimportant—indeed, participants at a number of points expressed to me privately their frustration in this regard—but rather grew unintentionally from the organization's cultural strategy. Since that strategy led to an emphasis on primary community within the organization, focusing on such interpersonal conflicts risks undermining a core organizational commitment. This in turn leads participants to suppress internal conflict.

Another prominent characteristic of the organizing process was the centrality of shared meals and PUEBLO-sponsored cultural events, which entailed a significant burden upon the organization. Most of the meetings (anywhere from one to several per month) began with a meal either partially or fully provided by PUEBLO. At a discussion forum with immigrants, PUEBLO provided food and had the most multiethnic gathering of the year, with four or five young people of each of the following ethnicities: Chinese, Vietnamese, Laotian, Hmong, and Mexican. One visiting organizer motivated the participants to bring more people to the accountability session by saying, "This will be our first test: we've been able to get people out for food, but can we get them to come out for an action?" More striking still, a significant amount of organizational energy went into festive occasions that were essentially cultural events rather than strategic steps toward the goal of the fifty-fifty split. For example, from May through December, PUEBLO sponsored a Cinco de Mayo and a Juneteenth celebration, focused on Mexican and African American culture, respectively; a three-hundred-person dinner honoring graduates of CTWO's summer activist training program; and a two-hundred-person organizational fund-raiser called the Annual Community Dinner, coinciding with International Human Rights Day. These events reflect the way PUEBLO operates as a primary community for many of its core participants, as well as PUEBLO's understanding of what it means to be a multicultural organization—a quite different understanding from PICO's, with different political implications, as we shall see.

Such cultural events are nonstrategic in the sense that they are not oriented in any immediate way toward achieving the political objectives of the organization's campaign for police accountability. This is not to say that they are politically irrelevant: constructing a political culture that spans the racial and ethnic cleavages in American politics may have important long-term political implications, whether done under the guise of faith-based or race-based organizing. The key point here is that this nonstrategic organizational focus is in fact quite rational, *given the organization's fundamental cultural strategy.* That is, given the combination of an appeal to racial identity and commitment to cross-cultural solidarity that lies at the heart of CTWO's multiracial organizing model, it makes a great deal of sense to dedicate organizational energy to affirming particular racial and ethnic cultures while constructing an organizational "multiculture." Indeed, this appears to have become the key interim goal in PUEBLO's efforts: while the long-term goal remains transforming the wider society through political action, "constructing a multicultural organization" in itself has become an important subgoal, to be pursued immediately. In this way, nonstrategic events become opportunities for what might be termed "cultural action," in which the focus is on transforming the dominant culture and building an alternative political culture. In the multiracial organizing model, this cultural action occurs by splicing together elements from diverse cultures in an effort to create a coherent whole.

PUEBLO's organizing process culminated in the August accountability session described above. Although both attendance at the action and the mayor's lukewarm (at best) response fell short of PUEBLO's expectations, in the staff's judgment two factors made the event a success. First, it contributed to leadership development by giving activists the opportunity to carry significant roles in a fairly large public forum controlled by PUEBLO. Second, the forum demonstrated to the deputy police chief a sufficient level of community support to make PUEBLO a credible community representative. This would lead directly to the organization's first success in the CCSPA campaign several months later.

Relations with Officialdom: Negotiation, Conflict, and Early Victories

The months following the accountability session were spent drawing the police department and city administration into actual negotiations over the use of asset forfeiture funds in Oakland. Through contacts with Deputy Chief Donahue and intervention in the city council's community policing task force, PUEBLO parlayed its influence into a series of meetings between its own representatives, the Oakland Police Department, and the city attorney's office. Through those meetings (at which PUEBLO's typical delegation included the two organizers, four leaders, and myself as translator), the police department ultimately acceded to the idea of disbursing 15 percent of asset forfeiture funds to community groups and accepted PUEBLO as the organization representing "the community" on this issue. Most crucially, the city agreed to set up a five-member committee to allocate any funds to be disbursed, with one representative from the OPD, one from the city manager, one from PUEBLO, and two from "prevention programs working with young people"—with PUEBLO naming which programs would be represented.

But almost immediately a series of conflicts occurred as the two sides negotiated the details of that arrangement, in preparation for presenting a plan to the city council. Typical of these conflicts was the following exchange over who would hold fiscal responsibility for any asset forfeiture funds distributed:

City attorney:	The responsibility for the money *has to be* in some city agency. That's the way these things work.
PUEBLO representative:	So the funds stay with *you*?
City attorney:	It is lots of work to control these funds, be sure the money is spent where it is supposed to be.
PUEBLO representative:	We're willing to do the work. That's why we're here. You're going to audit *yourselves*? I don't know how to say this. . . .
City attorney:	You just have to trust us.
PUEBLO:	Why should we trust *you*?
Police representative:	You have to trust *somebody, sometime!* [cut off by PUEBLO representative] . . . *let me finish!*

Minor conflicts of this kind occurred frequently in PUEBLO's relationships with representatives of official institutions. This pattern appears to result primarily from taken-for-granted aspects of PUEBLO's internal culture, as opposed to being a product of strategic or tactical decisions by leaders; at least the organizing process did not include the kind of conversations regarding the strategic use of conflict that we saw in chapter 1. However, this pattern does appear to serve a strategic function in that confrontation separates the organization from officialdom and thus keeps it from being swallowed up by "dominant institutions." It also appears to serve an expressive function by allowing participants to vent their anger at those institutions, which itself becomes the basis for solidarity within the group. However, as we shall see below, this pattern also makes collaborative relations with official institutions more difficult.

In spite of these tensions—and perhaps in some measure because of them—within a few months the city and the OPD agreed to a formal asset forfeiture arrangement.[9] Under this arrangement, asset disbursement was heavily influenced by PUEBLO through its role in helping define funding criteria and its preponderant influence on the allocations committee.

This victory was announced at an April 1995 press conference. Shortly thereafter, PUEBLO won another victory in helping defeat a youth curfew under consideration by the city council; it was fought on the grounds that it would be enforced primarily against young people of color. Together with earlier victories in fighting lead poisoning in East Oakland, extending the school lunch program to more children, and gaining translation services for low-income patients at the county hospital, these achievements established a track record of successfully confronting mainstream institutions through grassroots organizing and direct action.

But limitations on the democratic power PUEBLO could generate through its cultural strategy and associated direct action tactics would soon become apparent. An overview of the multiracial organizing model as a whole will help reveal the origins of those limitations.

The Political Culture of Multiracial Organizing

Understanding the political culture of CTWO's multiracial organizing model requires recognizing how CTWO has transformed earlier versions of community organizing. That transformation emerged from the social struggles that occurred within the United States from the late 1950s to the mid-1970s, which formed the experiential and analytic prelude to the multiracial organizing model. In an interview Rinku Sen, then codirector of CTWO, described the organization's origins: "CTWO has existed since 1980 and was formed as a model for multiracial organizing and training. We were especially African American based originally. The roots of our work are in the welfare rights movement, labor union struggles, and the civil rights movement." Dan HoSang connected these movements explicitly with the Alinsky model. When asked what traditions of organizing underlie PUEBLO's work, he responded:

> Well, probably some of the nuts and bolts are what people call Alinsky-style organizing, which is very pragmatic. For the most part, I would say that we use that as a base, and then the CTWO spin on it is [to shed Alinsky's nonideological framing]. . . . Tactically, I think we're heavily influenced by the farmworkers and the house meeting model they developed, and some of the direct action stuff they've done. Also, different kinds of union organizing, the kinds that value militant direct action. . . . I would trace some of it back to the welfare rights movement of the 1970s. . . . Gary Delgado's background is in ACORN and in a lot of the welfare rights organizing in the 1970s.

Thus, CTWO and its organizing projects strive to synthesize in their own model the experiences of multiple movements of earlier decades: Alinsky-style community organizing, the black civil rights movement, the United Farm Workers' struggle, and welfare rights movement. While any detailed exploration of CTWO's debt to these struggles is beyond my purposes, a few notes are important here.

First, like PICO, CTWO both embraces and rejects key portions of Alinsky's model. As noted by HoSang and shown in the organizing terminology posted on the training center's walls, CTWO incorporates much of Alinsky's practical organizing model. The focus on organization building, developing leaders who consciously seek to accumulate organizational "power", and the central role of staff in "cutting an issue," identifying a "target," and holding this target "accountable" through some specific "demand" are all standard Alinsky formulations of the community organizing process.

These general orientations and specific techniques (shared by PICO and many other organizations) are adopted by CTWO with significant divergences, all revolving around two axes: race and ideology (Delgado [1993a?]; Anner 1996). While Alinsky worked in various ethnic and racial settings, he never focused on race as the basis of organizing. CTWO was founded explicitly to train organizers from minority communities to work among communities of color. CTWO staff describe Alinsky-style organizing as nonideological and pragmatic, whereas they see their own model as clearly based on a set of ideological commitments, discussed below.

Thus, when CTWO staff identify the organization's roots in the black civil rights movement, they connect it most strongly with the later "Black Power" trends in that movement associated with the Student Nonviolent

Coordinating Committee and the Nation of Islam rather than with the earlier civil rights movement associated with black churches through the Southern Christian Leadership Conference.[10] Thus, Malcolm X rather than Dr. Martin Luther King Jr. adorns the wall of CTWO's training center. Similarly, the connection with the United Farm Workers links the multiracial model to radical, nonbureaucratic versions of labor organizing and to the Chicano power movement.

Likewise, key CTWO staff personnel and advisers had their crucial organizing formation within the welfare rights movement and the Association of Community Organizations for Reform Now (ACORN), one of that movement's current descendants. In both its guiding ideology and its organizational experience, that movement emphasized disruptive tactics as the most effective means of gaining benefits from "the system," and downplayed or actively criticized more institutionalized forms of political participation (Piven and Cloward 1977; Delgado 1986).

Elements of these cultural strands have been woven together to give shape to CTWO's multiracial organizing model, and particularly the *internal political culture* of the organization. One way to understand this organizational culture is to think of it as a "cultural system" (Geertz [1973] 2000) made up of a set of *practices* for how this community does things; a set of central *beliefs* that make sense of those practices, the world, and one's place in it; and a general *ethos* or "feel of life" within this community.[11] The interaction among these elements, and the way relations of authority and power shape all of them, structures the cultural dynamics within race-based organizing. We turn now to analyze CTWO's core practices, beliefs, and ethos and how they shape CTWO's projection of power into the public realm.

The Practices of Multiracial Organizing

While, as noted above, much of CTWO's organizing work is inspired by the power focus of the Alinsky model, CTWO enacts that power focus through its own set of practices. The most important of these are door-knocking campaigns, political education, direct action, meals as ritual social events, accountability sessions, and cultural action.

Door-Knocking Campaigns

Door-to-door visits in poor and moderate-income minority neighborhoods are a key part of CTWO's work, though not a constant focus as in the neighborhood-based organizing work of groups like ACORN (Swarts 2001;

Delgado 1986). Thus, PUEBLO staff and (to a lesser extent) leaders periodically spend a weekend doing "outreach" in this way.

Door-knocking campaigns are CTWO's equivalent of PICO's one-to-ones. During this study, they were done to invite people to attend "issue study groups" in preparation for the CCSPA campaign; to garner support and attendance during the asset forfeiture element of that campaign; to identify people who had suffered police abuse or knew others who had; and to survey residents regarding police practice and attitudes. Though time-consuming and staff intensive, this process is PUEBLO's primary vehicle for bringing in new participants. A typical recruitment story was that of Gwen Hardy, whom we met earlier:

> I've been involved in PUEBLO since 1989. . . . I got involved through an intern that was doing a health survey. She was asking me questions about accessibility of health care. . . . I had a completely bedridden husband and needed transportation to make sure that I was able to get him back and forth to his doctor appointments. So she invited me to a meeting telling me that some members of the community were coming together to talk about issues of concern for them. [She said] that if need be they would pick me up. I did attend the first meeting. For the first two or three meetings that I attended, maybe a little longer, I mostly just sat and listened to see what was going on. And of course I liked what I was hearing and the direction that the people sitting around the table wanted to go. So I've been attending meetings ever since.

Hardy has since become one of the four or five key leaders within PUEBLO. Her account shows the way door-to-door efforts combine with individual needs and self-interests to draw participants in; only subsequently do interpersonal ties, shared cultural elements generated within PUEBLO, and political education cement that participation into place. She notes:

> Our main outreach is going into the community and doing door knocking. That's our primary outreach. Going into the community. So when you go into the community and you are talking to people about the issue as well as listening to what they have to say and listening to their pertinent concerns, sometimes you can get a feel for the potential of the people that you're talking to. If you can recruit them and sign them up in membership and bring them into the fold, what you do is you encourage these individuals, you stand beside them, you give them information that will be helpful to them, you make them feel that they are just as good or

better than anyone else. People who show leadership ability, things of this nature, those are the people that you empower.

Door-knocking thus extends PUEBLO's network into the community and identifies potential leaders. It also serves to legitimize PUEBLO's claim to represent the community, as they can cite large numbers of neighborhood visits to back up their framing of issues and demands.

Political Education

In keeping with their rejection of the "nonideological orientation" and "sheer pragmatism" of Alinsky's model, CTWO organizers actively seek to provide political education to leaders. While clearly ideologically informed (as in the PUEBLO staff's analysis of police accountability issues in the CCSPA campaign), these are not simple indoctrination sessions. Rather, they seek to draw on the experience of CTWO constituents by validating, framing, and interpreting that experience. Dan HoSang describes this process:

> PUEBLO, for example, did very explicit political education pieces, where we looked at community policing, civilian review boards. To do that, the organizers had to understand these different kind of institutions. . . . And then you have to figure out how to put that into a program that involves the members. And mostly, in my experience, folks have the analysis. They're very clear on who wins and who loses on these things. It's just specifics that people need to sharpen, to actually give them a point of entry into fighting back. So for example, if your daily experience is that the cops are crooked, that they take people's stuff and that there's nothing going into programs, as an organizer you just have to understand the idea of asset forfeiture and make it accessible to people. Normally it won't be accessible to people, because no one has any interest in making it accessible.

But of course organizers make choices about what aspects of participants' experience to validate, what lens to use to make it accessible, and how to interpret its political implications. HoSang continues:

> We value political education in the context of organizing, and we also value a particular race, class, and gender analysis. That's important. So organizers are organizers, but they're also leaders. And they're, in some ways, trainers as well. And we value that kind of relationship, the reciproc-

ity between an organizer and a constituency, in terms of its ability to create informed and well-rounded members of the organization.

Thus, CTWO staff understand themselves as both peers and mentors to the leaders with whom they work. They are peers in distinguishing only partially between their own role and that of leaders, but mentors or "trainers" in fostering within leaders a political analysis oriented by categories of race, class, and gender.

This "particular race, class, and gender analysis" explains social inequality in America primarily as the product of three dynamics: (1) institutional racism, i.e., the way the historical legacy of racism has generated institutions that privilege white status even where individual racist attitudes have been eliminated or suppressed; (2) the class privilege of wealthy and middle-class Americans vis-à-vis poor, working-class, and low-status immigrant sectors of American society; and (3) male patriarchy and dominance over women, as well as the normative privilege granted to heterosexual orientation. In this analysis, it is the "interlocking oppressions" created when these three factors reinforce one another that primarily shapes contemporary inequality.[12]

In practice, political education occurs both in the daily context of organizing and in special meetings called issue study groups. Rinku Sen described how these functioned in launching the Campaign for Community Safety and Police Accountability:

> From October [1993] to April [1994] we had a series of issue study groups to consolidate our research and make policy recommendations. We had something like twelve sessions, each on different aspects of policing: philosophies of policing, civilian police review, immigration and the INS, use of force, public records on force, police discipline, 'cops on bikes', the economics of various policing programs, community policing, alternatives to incarceration. . . . This is our way of deepening the discussion on issues, developing a culture of this kind of discussion.

Much of the research that went into these issue study groups was done by CTWO staff; that same staff research gave rise to the sophisticated analysis behind the home run strategy of the CCSPA campaign. Together, staff research and the issue study groups represent quite a substantial organizational investment in generating knowledge of police practices. In these sessions, that knowledge was linked with participants' anger by portraying the role of police in the community in quite unambiguous fashion; for example, one issue study session provoked discussion of police use of force by showing video clips of police beating demonstrators.

Direct Action

Because the formal democratic institutions of American political life are seen as excluding low-income people of color, CTWO's efforts give direct action a central tactical role. Direct action in CTWO is conceived of as disruptive politics, an alternative to participation in institutionalized politics. As Dan HoSang described it, "Action in this context means removing all barriers between institutions that influence or impact a community and the community members themselves. And bringing pressure to bear through direct confrontation on those institutions." Thus, PUEBLO's repertoire of tactics prominently included unannounced takeovers of city offices, disruptions of public meetings, and the like.

Certainly, PUEBLO engaged in a significant amount of more institutionalized politics, what staff called "mainstream politics" or "civic engagement." But in the staff's self-understanding, direct action is to remain "the linchpin" of organizing. Note that the tactical repertoires of race-based and faith-based organizing are essentially identical: just as PUEBLO could engage in institutionalized politics up to and including negotiation with official representatives of dominant institutions, so OCO has in the past engaged in disruptive political action. It is not simply that one is inclined toward mainstream politics and the other toward alternative politics. The key question, rather, is why in times of organizational difficulty or crisis each organization tends to gravitate toward one mode of political engagement or the other. I argue in the following chapter for specific reasons for this, grounded in their internal political and cultural dynamics.

Meals as Ritual Social Events

Meals play a politically significant role in PUEBLO, although that role is easy to overlook as simply a prosaic part of the week-to-week organizational life. Significantly, the largest events sponsored by PUEBLO or CTWO during the course of this study were three large fund-raising dinners held on such celebratory occasions as the anniversary of PUEBLO's founding and the graduation of activist apprentices from CTWO's training program. The largest of these drew some three hundred participants; the largest political action drew a little over one hundred.

Both as preludes to business meetings and as separate events, meals were far more prominent within PUEBLO's organizing than they were in faith-based organizing. Although under both models large meals occasionally

serve to celebrate special events, raise funds, or build networks with potential new allies, only in PUEBLO did they become central aspects of
organizing meetings themselves. Since PUEBLO serves as a primary affective community for many key participants, these meals provide a critical
opportunity for ritualizing interpersonal, affective bonds, drawing on the
symbolism of family to stabilize organizational solidarity.[13]

Accountability Sessions

Though this analysis highlights the divergent internal cultural dynamics
of multiracial organizing and faith-based organizing, the similarity of their
primary political events is striking. Superficially, accountability sessions in
multiracial organizing are nearly identical to actions in faith-based organizing (which indeed sometimes calls them accountability sessions). The session described earlier in this chapter, which sought to garner city support
for the asset forfeiture campaign, was typical. Participants were recruited
through a combination of family networks and social agencies, primarily
service agencies based in specific ethnic or racial communities, or advocacy
groups whose ideology focused on issues of race, class, and gender. In re-
cruiting members, appeals to race and low-income status are especially
prominent. In contrast to PICO, staff often participate along with leaders
in taking important "up-front" roles during the accountability session and
are often interviewed along with them by media reporters. These sessions
typically include significant translation, particularly into Spanish. Like
OCO, but perhaps even more extensively, PUEBLO often draws on youth
to articulate their own perspectives on issues.[14] But in both organizations,
older, more experienced leaders play the key public roles.

In setting up accountability sessions, PUEBLO drew explicit or implicit
endorsement from sympathetic public officials, as signified in the August
event by the participation of a state representative, a city council representative, and a federal official, as well as the assistance of a U.S. congress-
person's aide in gaining use of the Federal Building auditorium. They only
succeeded in "turning out" attendance of just under 100, however, rather
than their target of some 250.[15] While sufficient to gain somewhat grudging
and limited attention from some of the targeted officials, this level of turnout delivered mixed results in getting the organization into the negotiating
realm it sought; as we have seen, PUEBLO at least temporarily convinced
the upper echelons of the Oakland Police Department to negotiate regarding asset forfeiture, but gained little access to the mayor's office or city manager.

The accountability session described here was typical in other ways. It

combined a sense of expected accountability and responsiveness from public officials with a tenor of skepticism regarding the legitimacy of those same
officials, implicated (as they are within CTWO's race-class-gender analysis)
as representatives of dominant institutions guilty of complicity in the marginalization of CTWO's constituency. This perception was essentially independent of the race of officeholders—at different times in the broader organizing process, an African American police chief or mayor and a Latino
city councilor were all regarded as skeptically as were most white officials.
Also, in the absence of being able to turn out massive numbers of participants, the dynamics of the session relied on the staff's sophisticated issue
analysis and development of elite allies in order to place the organization
in a position of strategic strength on the asset forfeiture issue.

Cultural Action

A set of organizing practices that I term "cultural action" coexist with direct
action and accountability sessions as PUEBLO's fundamental strategies for
asserting itself in the public realm. Cultural actions are public events whose
primary focus lies in generating a multicultural experience for participants
in such a way as to build a shared political culture. In the cultural actions
sponsored by PUEBLO or CTWO during this study, the focus was on both
affirming particular racial and ethnic identities and at the same time striving to *transcend* those identities in the name of a broader experience of being "people of color." So Latino members were encouraged to attend Juneteenth and Kwanza celebrations hosted by African American members or
outside organizations, and black members were encouraged to attend Cinco
de Mayo festivities. The political culture under construction during these
events might best be described as a culture of resistance: that is, it encourages resistance as the primary mode of participation in current social institutions.

The Beliefs of Multiracial Organizing

Beyond these organizing techniques and practices, a broad set of beliefs
underlie CTWO's cultural dynamics. These are not so structured as to be a
fully developed ideology, but are certainly more than simply coincidentally
shared beliefs. They can be best understood as a relatively coherent and
interlocking set of perceptions shared by participants, their viewpoints having converged through the influence of factors such as the experience of
being racial and ethnic minorities in America; the lack of understanding or
outright racism they experience in interacting with social institutions and

various sectors of mainstream culture; the political education process within the organization; the informal socialization at dinners and cultural events; and (in the case of most staff organizers) socialization in the university campus environment.

The "Statement of Purpose" from PUEBLO's sixth-anniversary dinner in 1995 summarizes the beliefs informing CTWO's organizing model.

> People United for a Better Oakland is a membership organization of individuals and groups working together to take back power over our lives and our communities.
>
> We are Black, Latino, Native American, Asian, and White people of all ages and economic backgrounds who demand accountability from those in positions of power over the issues that affect our lives. We firmly believe that:
>
> - everyone, if given the opportunity, recognition, and support, can become an active intelligent contributor to the well being of our communities.
> - children and young people are vital resources for building vision for change.
> - quality, affordable and accessible health care is a human right.
> - safe and affordable housing is a human right.
> - quality employment is a human right.
> - services should be relevant and culturally sensitive to the populations reflected in the community.
>
> Ultimately, we believe that Oakland should celebrate all of its diverse population by promoting justice for everyone that lives here, regardless of age, race, sex, sexual preference, immigration status or income.
>
> Only by uniting ourselves and our communities can we create the power to force change in the conditions which affect our lives.

This statement combines two different thrusts, which coexist uneasily within the organization's overall belief system. On one hand, a strong flavor of ethnic particularism pervades the statement, as reflected in the call to celebrate diversity and in the second paragraph ("We are . . ."). This corresponds to CTWO's emphasis on racial identity as the basis of organizing. On the other hand, the statement also incorporates a powerful universalism that transcends any such particular identities: it emphasizes universal and very extensive "human rights," calls for "justice for everyone," and premises successful egalitarian change on unity across diverse communities. In the tension within this combination lies much of CTWO's dynamism.[16] But

I will argue in the following chapter that this tension also leads CTWO to a difficult organizational dilemma.

While tensions exist within CTWO regarding how central particular beliefs might be and how they ought to be prioritized, several perspectives are broadly shared among key participants. As one participates in the organization, the first core belief becomes clear immediately: that race and ethnicity comprise a fundamental fault line along which people can and should be mobilized. Thus the prominence in CTWO literature and in interviews of phrases such as "communities of color," "people of color," and "We are Black, Latino, Native American, Asian, and White." This core belief is obvious enough that I do not belabor it here; the key point is that race is taken explicitly as a strategic divide along which organizing should occur. But note that this assumption is not inevitable; other bases of organizing are possible, even within the same constituency.

Second, the cultural expressions of blackness, Latino-ness, Asian-ness, and so on must be knit together into a multiculture that borrows from them all and can animate the political coalitions necessary for transcending racial divisions. Thus, "building a multiracial culture" and "multiracial organizing" are the two most frequent ways that participants refer to this model of organizing.

Third, while racial and ethnic identity as people of color represents in practice the most frequent and most fundamental grounds of cultural appeal in the multiracial organizing model, in theory it holds equal status with economic class and gender as the fundamental categories in CTWO's social analysis. Thus, all the CTWO staff people interviewed explicitly identified race, class, and gender as the keys to their analysis of society.[17]

For example Rinku Sen noted, "We use race, class, and gender as factors to recruit people." When asked if one element was more fundamental than another, Dan HoSang answered: "I think they're all equal. They might be emphasized more or less at different points." He went on to describe how these affect PUEBLO's organizing work:

Take any particular issue, like toxic dumping. At the time CTWO took up that issue [late 1980s], the environmental movement was very white. And it wasn't really looking at the impact that corporate dumping was having on low-income communities. That's a simple example of bringing that [racial] analysis, [and asking] "How does it effect people of color?" And also, How can people of color be organized to fight back, as opposed to how can a set of white liberal advocates be mobilized to get involved?" So I think that's key. And the same thing with the crime and safety debate: we

know that the folks that are pushing this initiative are very much interested in blurring its effects on people of color, blurring its inherent racist
bent. And I think the same thing with gender. CTWO's now developing a
women's organizing campaign. Women's organizing is a particular and
necessary facet to an organizing project.

This analysis sees race, class, and gender as interlocking systems of oppression and holds as a primary goal the unveiling of that oppression in dominant institutions. Still, racial and ethnic identity remains the primary practical grounds of appeal, a kind of first among equals within CTWO's belief
system. Thus, nonstaff participants in PUEBLO, more immersed in the practical work of the organization than in theoretical analysis, articulate the
race dimension more prominently than the others. For example, when
asked what PUEBLO's goal is, Gwen Hardy responded, "The goal is to bring
persons of color together to work on the issues of concern for them and
their families." [18]

We might summarize these core beliefs by saying that CTWO's primary
cultural strategy involves an appeal to racial identity, done in order to build
a multiracial organization and a political strategy in which race, class, and
gender provide the central analytic categories. As Dan HoSang writes:

I would add that part of our intention in fashioning a type of multiracial
consciousness is to respond to a shifting racial landscape within the city.
As people of color have assumed higher-profile leadership positions locally, the emphasis on securing racial justice within public policy initiatives, especially for low-income people, has receded. Issues like police brutality against low-income people of color, health care access, education
reform, and housing rights are not framed [in city politics] as racialized
concerns per se. PUEBLO has a specific concern in raising the racial dimension of these issues, and that's one reason we attempt to consciously
frame the racial politics of the organization. [19]

In addition to these core beliefs, a few other beliefs merit mention due
to their centrality in CTWO's model and the way they distinguish that
model from other community organizing efforts, including faith-based organizing.

CTWO staff believe that people of color should form separate, minority-
controlled organizations that keep the dominant culture at arm's length in
order to foster the development of minority activists whose leadership

might be suppressed if greater white involvement were present. Thus, although a few whites do participate to some degree in PUEBLO, the core leadership is essentially African American and Latino. Likewise, since PUEBLO's founding all but one of the staff organizers have been people of color.

Fifth, CTWO staff also share the commitment to equality and democratic participation that animates most community organizing efforts, but in CTWO this belief finds expression in a prominent emphasis on "rights." Though rights language is of course common in many forms of political engagement, it is used far more prominently here than in most other efforts at community organizing derived from Alinsky. Here, human rights are a primary basis of appeal for organizational demands. This contrasts significantly with the pattern in faith-based organizing, in which a similar commitment to equality and democracy grounds organizational demands, but typically through the language of human dignity and shared quality of life in the city. Thus, apparently similar emphases lead in two rather different tactical directions: to the polarizing language of rights violated on one hand, and the common-ground language of shared interests (sometimes backed up by tactical polarization and conflict) on the other. The experience of CTWO and PICO show that both tactical directions can be effective, but they lead in different directions—directions characteristic of the two organizations—and with different strategic outcomes, as we shall see.

Finally, CTWO-affiliated organizations affirm in relatively unambiguous terms a conflict model of society, in which dominant social institutions inherently exclude whole social groups, whose marginalization results unidirectionally from that exclusion. Although CTWO's work challenges poor people's acquiescence in their own marginalization, the organization's belief system places little focus on that challenge. If it did, it might treat marginalization as a temporary product of both exclusion and apathy, to be overcome via participation. Instead, in the absence of such a focus, marginalization is treated as a fait accompli to be unveiled and confronted—but not, in any immediate sense, to be overcome.

I do not suggest that a full consensus exists regarding these beliefs, but rather—as in any community or organization—that a shared set of partially coherent and partially contradictory orientations underlie CTWO's internal life. These orientations allow participants to collaborate and at times provide the common ground that allows them to argue with one another productively.

The Ethos of Multiracial Organizing: Democratic Multiculturalism

PUEBLO's statement of purpose articulates nicely the spirit and "feel of life" within the multiracial model of organizing. The appeal to racial identity as the basis of organizing accurately reflects the primary cultural strategy at work in PUEBLO, but note that this appeal coexists with an effort to transcend narrow "nationalist" identities in favor of cross-cultural collaboration. The appeal to human rights as the moral grounds of political claims too reflects the primary ethical language invoked during PUEBLO's organizing work. Both mirror the ethos of the more sophisticated strands of the multicultural movement.[20]

Among the first impressions of a visitor to PUEBLO meetings (an impression that endures over months of participating as well) are the demonstratively expressed positive affective bonds among individuals within the organization and the conflictive tenor of their relations with mainstream social institutions. Participants are friends bound together partly by their negative experiences and negative evaluations of wider social institutions. Thus, many elements of the shared cultural life of the organization evince a certain pessimism about American institutions, a sense that they inevitably collude to marginalize people and communities of color. Finally, the professional staff who run the organization appear to integrate successfully their ideological commitment to the race-class-gender analysis described above and a warm human commitment to the people with whom they work. There is little public trace of the condescending attitude toward their constituents common in ideologically driven organizations.

The overall ethos that takes shape under the race-based strategy of organizing can best be described as *disruptive democratic multiculturalism*. The term is meant to convey two crucial elements of the organization's internal life and external relations.

First, CTWO's democratic multiculturalism involves a fundamental commitment to a multicultural process and outcome. Multicultural process in CTWO means drawing on the cultural practices of diverse minority groups in constructing its internal political culture. The multicultural outcome sought by CTWO means building toward a future American society that is not only multiracial in its demographic composition, but that values and celebrates the diverse cultural expressions of minority communities and somehow fuses them into a shared political culture. Both aspects of this commitment are rooted in an affirmation of particular cultural forms as authentic expressions of communities of color, a presumption of equal value to these various cultural expressions, and a determination to preserve them from being overwhelmed by the dominant culture.[21]

But such cultural expressions are always under threat of being undermined or "washed out" by the power of dominant cultural forms from white society. The commitment to sustaining them thus leads CTWO to keep dominant cultural forms at arm's length, in favor of celebrating subaltern cultural forms. So key celebrations during the course of a calendar year included the Cinco de Mayo, Juneteenth, and Kwanza celebrations noted above.

Furthermore, this power of the dominant culture exists not only in mainstream cultural forms and institutions, but also imprints itself in the self-conceptions of dominated individuals and groups. The "in-your-face" tenor of PUEBLO's relations with official institutions and its tactical reliance on direct action against them can be understood as an alternative to more violent responses to this "internalized oppression" advocated by some (Fanon 1965); both involve the rejection of negative self-images by acting directly against oppressors. Clearly, this can be effective in leading marginalized groups to experience some sense of their own power. CTWO's experience shows that in the hands of expert organizers, it can also generate significant pressure for democratic reform. Less clear is whether it can provide a cultural basis for routine participation in democratic institutions and thus actually overcome marginalization.

The second crucial element of CTWO's ethos conveyed by the term "democratic multiculturalism" is the organization's insistence that attaining this outcome must be achieved through a radically democratic process. Within the organization, this insistence produces a strong version of democracy combining participative and representative elements.[22] For example, a great deal of decision making is carried out or at least ratified by all the participants at a meeting, but a smaller core group of leaders and staff are entrusted with key strategic decisions. Membership in this core group shifts regularly. The primary qualifications appear to be willingness to invest time in this work and having garnered respect and trust from other participants. The organization's commitment to political education flows partly from this commitment to internal democracy; for internal democracy to thrive, organizers must teach leaders the analytical skills necessary for formulating organizational strategy.

Outside the organization, this insistence takes the form of demands for something akin to direct democracy in official institutions. As seen from within this organizational culture, all mainstream institutions are tainted by virtue of being part of the dominant system or the hegemony of white culture. Thus most ways of participating in those institutions are suspect. When asked to identify the key values and principles lying behind the CTWO organizing model, Dan HoSang first notes "that people do have the power to confront the institutions and individuals that control their lives . . . that our society basically teaches and socializes people not to exercise that power." This wariness of social institutions leads CTWO activists to their commitment to direct democracy; when asked to elaborate further on CTWO's values, HoSang continues, "We value action. We really value action. We don't value talking. [What do you mean by action?] Action in this context means . . . bringing pressure to bear through direct confrontation on those institutions."

Participative democracy internally and a highly confrontational version of direct democracy externally thus characterize the democratic strand of CTWO's ethos. Both are rooted in CTWO's stance of cultural egalitarianism; participants come together representing diverse minority cultures each seen as equally valid. They thus accept one another relatively smoothly as equals in a participatory democracy. But they share relatively few cultural traits beyond their subaltern status in American society and their suspicion toward some elements of the broader American culture. They therefore have few shared cultural supports for mutual trust, and their intervention in mainstream institutions thus takes the form of direct confrontation rather than representative participation.[23]

Relations among staff, leaders, and agency personnel have a distinctive character in keeping with CTWO's organizational ethos. First, staff bring significant *expert authority* to the organizing process. This results both from their knowledge of organizing techniques and from their greater cultural capital as university-educated people working mostly among less-educated residents. *Moral authority* in CTWO's organizing work, or the authority of legitimacy, derives essentially from one's status in the hierarchy of race, class, and gender; being from a community of color and of low income, and to a lesser extent being female, brings a certain ethical weight to one's opinions. Staff, leaders, and outside agency personnel all partake of this authority to varying degrees. Some potential *practical authority* adheres to those leaders who have sufficient networks of contacts to mobilize large numbers of people to accountability sessions, but the organization's strong reliance on door-to-door campaigns led by staff limits this authority.

Overall, CTWO's model shows relatively little specialization of authority functions, and thus relatively few checks and balances among staff, leaders, and agency personnel. In particular, outside agency personnel wield little authority comparable to that of pastors within faith-based organizing: although PUEBLO has attempted to use social agency staff to mobilize their constituents for accountability sessions, agency personnel have proven to be relatively ineffective in doing so and thus hold little power in the organization. Also, in reaction to the strong staff/leader distinction in traditional Alinsky-style community organizing—a distinction preserved in most faith-based organizing—the organization has intentionally blurred the dividing line between staff and leaders. For example, in the accountability session described above and others I observed, staff played a far more prominent role onstage during the event than would typically be true in faith-based organizing. Indeed, CTWO in part distinguishes its model of organizing precisely by separating the two roles to only a minimal extent, and participants frequently refer to both as activists. Thus, rather than a role-defined, pluralistic system of checks and balances to distribute power within the organization, PUEBLO relies on the relational dynamics of primary community to do so. Within those dynamics, staff carries a great deal of authority.

Thus, three factors—the cultural diversity resulting from the multiculturalist strand of CTWO's internal culture, the egalitarianism resulting from the democratic strand, and emotional dynamics resulting from the emphasis on primary community—together produce a culturally rich and sometimes chaotic internal organizational life within PUEBLO. But it is a chaos with a direction: CTWO's disruptive democratic multiculturalism emphasizes creatively confronting the dominant institutions of society regarding the ways that they reinforce racial, economic, and sexual inequality. It is in this sense that the organization ultimately places its faith in action—in the direct, disruptive action of interrupting the routine workings of institutions seen as excluding subaltern voices. This central thrust to CTWO's culture is rooted in its members' experience of marginalization, but in that experience as interpreted and given meaning by the staff's analysis of social domination.

Power Flows Relationally: The Strengths and Limitations of Disruptive Power

The combination of direct action as a tactic and multiracial organizing as a strategic model, both pursued within a spirit of disruptive democratic multiculturalism, has led to significant organizational success on a variety of issues. In addition to those noted above, in the mid-1990s PUEBLO (working in an unusual collaboration with OCO) launched a Kids First! campaign that sought to protect social service funding directed toward children in the face of demands for constantly greater tax revenue to go to the criminal justice system—with partial success.[24]

Yet subsequent events also showed the limits of disruptive power pursued in this way. By 1996, CTWO and its Oakland organizing project faced setbacks in each of their key previously won victories. First, the superior court in the state capital had declared unconstitutional the Lead Act, which had been enacted by the state legislature in 1991 and subsequently provided the legal basis for PUEBLO's antilead campaign. The 1996 ruling found the Lead Act's assessment of fees on industry for funding anti-lead-poisoning efforts to be a tax that violated California's antitax Proposition 13. The staff noted that, if upheld, this would "defund PUEBLO's entire antilead program." Based on the political opportunity provided by previously enacted laws, PUEBLO's disruptive tactics had enabled the organization to force local officials to enact and fund a substantial lead abatement program. But those tactics had not allowed the organization to generate sufficient political clout or to develop adequate alliances among state-level institutional elites to generate funding within the normal political process.

Likewise, in 1996 the county hospital serving low-income patients faced massive budget cuts as the county strove to balance its budget; an eroding tax base and declining state and federal support for social programs for the poor had undermined the county's financial position. As a result, the translation services PUEBLO had won in a previous campaign were not being implemented.

Finally, as the Campaign for Community Safety and Police Accountability moved forward after 1996, it led to some new victories but also some weakening of previous victories regarding asset forfeiture. The next stage of the campaign involved an extensive effort to document "police brutality at the hands of the Oakland Police Department." PUEBLO staff and leaders sought out people who had in the past filed complaints of excessive force and spent hours knocking door to door to find other victims of police abuse. They hoped to organize people who had suffered abuse and flood the system with documented complaints. But they met stiff resistance from the police department when they attempted to file new excessive-force charges.

This new stage in the CCSPA campaign was intentionally confrontational, designed to publicly embarrass a police department believed to be unwilling to police its own officers' interactions with communities of color. In a sense, confrontation worked all too well: publicity surrounding the campaign so heightened tensions between PUEBLO and the Oakland Police Department that even the previously established collaboration on asset forfeiture became problematic. Indeed, public confrontation served to embarrass precisely those police leaders who had encouraged the police department to work collaboratively with PUEBLO—key potential allies for the long-term CCSPA effort. In an interview during this period, one such high-ranking police official characterized the organization as follows:

> They're a tough bunch. . . . They're always wanting to operate in an antagonistic way. They always need to be confrontational. It's ridiculous when right now we're sharing asset forfeiture money with them. And they refuse to be partners with us, to do anything with us. They say, "We don't want to be identified with you." Well, fine, they don't have to be—but then don't take our money.

When the OPD resisted PUEBLO's accusations of widespread abuse of force, the organization escalated its tactics, staging small direct action demonstrations at public hearings and sit-ins at police and city offices. PUEBLO's turn to police abuse as a central organizing issue, the tensions between the group and the police, PUEBLO's confrontational tactics, and the resulting retrenchment on the part of the OPD eventually led to a breakdown in the asset forfeiture disbursement procedure. By 1997, the city had restructured the way the disbursement committee was appointed, giving PUEBLO a less preponderant role—although the city manager's office continued to consult with the organization in making appointments.

In each of these cases—the rollback of lead abatement fees, the cutbacks of translation services, and the scaling back of its central role in asset forfeiture disbursements—CTWO found itself at the mercy of structural forces beyond its control. On each issue, CTWO's disruptive democratic multiculturalism has been unable to project sufficient power to defeat countervailing forces (the antitax sentiments from economic elites and the political power of police departments to resist encroachment on what they see as their terrain). The following chapter will trace the roots of this political impasse to both PUEBLO's cultural strategy and structural breakdowns in the American political system. For now, I note only the evidence for real limitations to disruptive power.

Note how the faith the organization places in direct action and confrontation with dominant institutions was both the cause of its success in gaining a voice in government policy and one source of its ultimate limitation in this regard. In one sense, the asset forfeiture campaign served its purpose in becoming a point of leverage for the organization's home run goal: greater civilian control over the police department, at which it has had some success. But that PUEBLO was unable to sustain its dominant place at the table controlling asset forfeiture moneys must be counted a partial defeat, at least until it wins on the other bases of the home run strategy.

Conclusion

Properly understanding CTWO's multiracial organizing requires taking a step back from this partial setback on the asset forfeiture front and placing it in the context of CTWO's organizing vision and continuing experience. If the organization were focused narrowly on this issue, if leaders and organizers had built its internal culture around this issue as an ultimate end, such a defeat might well have destroyed the organization. Frustration and disbandment are the fate of many organizations that fail to implement an alternative public policy.

But CTWO's organizing vision does not center around such particular issues. Rather, issues serve as tools for reinforcing CTWO's envisioned role: as a catalyst in the effort to pursue what former CTWO codirector Francis Calpotura calls the "two intertwined dreams" cradled by all progressive organizers:[25]

- The equitable redistribution of wealth and power to assure each person the necessities of healthful physical survival and the maximal realization of human potential, in viable communities, on a planet safeguarded from degradation.
- A multicultural, communal space where our various identities can shine and interact in an environment of equally shared power and mutual respect.

Since these twin goals take priority over any specific issue campaign, defeat on an issue does not count as real defeat as long as pursuing it contributes to these ends. Indeed, CTWO's organizing vision follows a logic that places the internal construction of culture as its immediate goal: "Perhaps, if [we] forge a diverse and respectful community culture, then creative and cohesive work to build organizations to redistribute power will follow."[26]

CTWO's experience since 1997 further illuminates how the organization keeps particular defeats from undermining its vitality. Following the stagnation of the asset forfeiture campaign, rather than stepping back in the face of institutional resistance, organizers and leaders pushed further into their Campaign for Community Safety and Police Accountability. They sidestepped their faltering partnership with police and some city officials by forging stronger links with the federal Department of Justice and used those ties to try to institutionalize stronger civilian review of police operations. The Oakland city council had established a civilian review board in 1980, but it had remained very weak, with no subpoena power, limited jurisdiction, and only a half-time investigator on its staff. As part of the CCSPA campaign, PUEBLO and the local American Civil Liberties Union pressured the council to strengthen this civilian review board, which gradually occurred in the late 1990s. As of 2000, it had four investigators, subpoena power, jurisdiction expanded to include policy recommendation, and greater access to internal police information. PUEBLO continues to push it to more fully investigate accusations of excessive use of force by police.[27] Multiracial organizing thus continues to wield real political influence, albeit somewhat tenuously and only up to the level of city politics.

The cultural strategy adopted by CTWO, emphasizing racial and other subaltern identities as the basis for building a political culture, thus represents a stark contrast to the cultural strategy of faith-based organizing. Out of this cultural strategy flow important elements of CTWO's organizing dynamics, institutional ethos, and political capacity as well as the tenor of its relations with official institutions. In tracing how this cultural strategy plays out in CTWO's internal life and external relations, we have begun to see the strengths and limitations implicit in appealing to racial and other subaltern cultural identities as the basis of political work. In the next chapter, we turn to contemplate the more external, public implications of the alternative cultural strategies at the heart of faith-based and race-based community organizing. What might they mean for the future of democratic life in this country?

Chapter 4

Reweaving the Social Fabric: Social Capital and Political Power

The faith-based and race-based community organizing models adopt divergent cultural strategies that generate the significantly different organizing dynamics that we see within PICO and CTWO. This chapter compares the external effects of these two cultural strategies—that is, their political outcomes. I first draw on recent studies of democracy for the light they shed on these organizations' divergent political development. Mindful of their many similarities (political opportunities, material resources, issues, organizing practices, and participant demographics), I then trace their differing political outcomes to their divergent cultural strategies. The key argument here concerns how those strategies shape their access to social capital; although both have had significant success, PICO has had greater mobilizing capacity, attained greater success

Top: CTWO leaders unveil their community safety strategy at a National Press Club briefing in Washington, D.C. Photograph by John Anner. Courtesy Center for Third World Organizing. *Bottom:* Longtime OCO leader Fran Matarrese addresses city officials and community residents at a celebration launching the demolition of the Montgomery Ward building in Oakland, California. Photograph by Michelle Longosz. Courtesy Oakland Community Organization.

in higher-level political arenas, and achieved a stronger "structural position in public life."

Understanding Democratic Life

In order to account for the successes and dilemmas experienced by faith-based and race-based community organizing efforts, I draw on theoretical and empirical writing on democratic life.[1] In particular, the concepts of the *public sphere, democratic skills,* and *social capital* help illuminate both democracy as an ideal and the distortions that undermine that ideal.

The Ideal Public Sphere: Multilevel Arena of Dialogue and Conflict

Leaders in both faith-based and race-based organizing frequently speak of holding government and corporate leaders and institutions "accountable" to describe their work. Along with PICO's more recent addition of the concept of "partnership" with government, this represents these organizations' primary ways of talking about their role in what democratic theorists call the public realm.[2]

For present purposes, we may think of the public realm as made up of all those arenas of social life in which members of a community reflect upon, argue about, and make decisions regarding the problems they face and the rules under which they live. The public realm clearly includes all levels of government from local to national, particularly those settings in which elected representatives make the rules by which the wider society lives. These settings include the legislative process in city councils, schools boards, state legislatures, and Congress; judicial review at all levels; and executive policy formulation by mayors, governors, and presidents and their aides. Especially to the extent that these government settings make decisions in ways not purely technocratic but involving deliberation through dialogue with constituencies, they are key components of the public realm.

But the public realm also includes far more than government. Indeed, the most crucial dynamics for long-term political change arguably do not lie within government at all, but in the formation of political will and aggregation of interests among both the general citizenry and leaders of nongovernmental institutions in society. Two kinds of social locations are crucial for these processes.

The first is "political society," all those arenas lying outside government but at least loosely linked to it.[3] Most notably, political society includes political parties, lobbyists and political action committees, labor unions and business associations, think tank institutions associated with interest groups, and similar organizations with political goals. Within political society, citizen demands are channeled and possible responses are formulated. As the reach of government into society has lengthened, political society has gained a central role in policy formulation. But the relative weight of different actors within political society has also shifted; political parties, once fairly robust channels of popular participation, are now largely organizational shells for raising the vast sums of money needed for electoral campaigns. Labor unions still play significant political roles but are much weaker than they were two decades ago, despite recent reinvigoration. In contrast, the roles of business associations, policy institutions, and political action committees have grown considerably.[4]

The second nongovernmental segment of the public realm is located in "civil society": all those organizational settings that are not part of political society or government and in which members of a society reflect upon and form values and attitudes regarding their life together, social problems, and the future of their society.[5] These politically relevant conversations occur in myriad settings throughout society—civic groups, political discussion groups, issue study groups, ethnic associations, and churches, to name only a few. The concept of civil society provides a way of understanding how the associational life of voluntary groups helps form political identities, shape political attitudes, and generate the solidarities that underlie political mobilization.

The public realm that lies across the levels of state, political society, and civil society exhibits two facets that must be kept in creative tension to do justice to the complex reality we call modern democracy. Analysts who see societal consensus as central emphasize the responsibilities of all of society's members, fearing that centripetal forces of alienation and self-interest will lead to social fragmentation. Analysts who see conflict as the central dynamic of society emphasize the rights of the weak, who must be protected from the strong. Though these are often presented as mutually exclusive understandings of the core of political life, they are best seen as complementary features of politics, both necessary if real insight into democracy is to emerge.[6] The first perspective depicts the public realm as a space in which occurs a societywide dialogue about the means and ends of the good life and the common good of society. Ideally understood as a conversation or mutual discourse about shared aspirations and problems, this *discursive* or *dialogical* model of the public realm highlights the (potential) freedom of all to participate in constituting society's future.

But this discursive model hides the constraints that limit the ability of some groups to participate in that conversation or deny that ability altogether. That is, while modern democracies in theory guarantee the right of all to participate in the public realm, the actual workings of economic and political power prevent some sectors from doing so. These marginalized, oppressed, or subaltern groups face an uphill struggle if they wish to redeem their theoretically guaranteed right to participate. Thus, leaders and organizers in both of the organizations studied here spoke of having to "fight to get any kind of place at the table where those decisions are made, to get our voices heard in that conversation."

Thus, alongside the dialogical model of the public realm we must place a *conflictive* model that draws attention to the way groups must mobilize—and often mobilize contentiously—to have their voices heard in the public realm. They enter into conflict over the appropriate goals of society, their relative priority, the role of government and other institutions in pursuing them, and (explicitly or implicitly) the understanding of the good life that informs those goals. Conflict is a constitutive element of the public realm, and thus ever present.

If the dialogical model highlights the way communication structures relationships in the public realm, the conflictive model highlights the way power does so. A healthy democracy entails strong institutions to promote dialogue and fair conflict; an adequate analysis of democratic community organizing must pay attention to both. Through work in both dimensions, participants seek to "reweave the fabric of society," to use a phrase often heard in faith-based organizing circles.[7]

Social Capital and Democratic Life

Social scientists have recently rediscovered the importance of the bonds of everyday life in civil society for sustaining political democracy. In their 1993 book on Italy, *Making Democracy Work,* Robert Putnam and his colleagues report on an elegant study of democratic institutions.[8] New regional government institutions were established in the early 1970s in Italy, and Putnam studied their development over the next two decades, as some thrived and others stagnated. His key finding: the most powerful predictor of successful performance of democratic government is a region's prior stock of "social capital": social ties between relative equals (as opposed to hierarchical ties between superiors and subordinates) and the extent to which citizens trust one another and thus are willing to collaborate.[9] More recently, in *Bowling Alone: The Collapse and Revival of American Community*, Putnam applied this insight regarding trust and social ties to the United States, marshaling systematic evidence that social capital in America declined dramatically over the last three decades of the twentieth century. He argues that this drop in social capital across all social sectors has deeply eroded the foundations on which democratic political processes are built. Exactly what Putnam's evidence means is hotly debated, but it does provide strong evidence that the kinds of democratic efforts studied here may face increasing difficulty in tapping into trust-carrying social ties as the basis of their work. One thing is clear: movements to deepen American democracy in the years ahead will have to find ways to overcome the erosion of social capital that emerges clearly in Putnam's account.[10] Race-based and faith-based organizing struggle to represent the interests of poor and working families in America in the context of this challenge; to the extent they overcome it, they represent important models for reinvigorating democracy.

A weakness in *Bowling Alone* suggests another way in which the democratic organizing efforts studied here are important. Putnam's focus on documenting America's declining social capital and our resulting social ills leads him to pay little attention to some of the key institutional, political, and economic forces that have caused or exacerbated that decline. Especially important here are the dislocation of blue-collar "good jobs," weakened political institutions, erosion of public education, attenuated labor unions, and beleaguered urban neighborhoods of the last thirty years. These and similar forces have presumably contributed mightily to eroding American social capital; strengthening American society in all these areas is also the focus of much of the community organizing studied here. Thus, social capital erosion *both* threatens to undermine this kind of organizing *and* offers all the greater reason why such organizing is important.

The approach I adopt here in order to draw on the strength of Putnam's analysis while avoiding the explanatory conundrums to which it gives rise is to treat social capital *not* as a broad-scale measure of national "civic culture"—an approach that shapes much of Putnam's work, through his reliance on the classic book by that title (Almond and Verba 1963)—but rather as a key resource on which marginalized groups draw as they work to make political and economic institutions respond to democratic pressure.

Seen from this perspective, social capital becomes one important influence on whether grassroots organizations can effectively deepen democracy: if organizations rooted in marginalized communities can generate or tap into social capital resources and parlay them into significant influence within the public arena, our political life will develop in more fully democratic directions.[11] If, on the contrary, they are unable to do so, marginalization will be reinforced and extended.

Democratic Skills as Political Resource

In *Voice and Equality* (1995), Verba, Schlozman, and Brady examined how Americans participate in political life, and how equally we do so. Two forms of participation are crucial: donating money and getting personally involved. The effectiveness of the former depends upon how much money one donates; the effectiveness of the latter depends upon the democratic skills one brings to political work.[12]

Verba and colleagues studied how these factors affect the equality of participation ("voice") and of outcomes ("equality") in American politics. Unsurprisingly, the donation of money works in favor of the wealthy; they have more money to give and use it to increase their influence on the political process and to encourage political decisions that protect their interests.

The acquisition of democratic skills is a more complex story, but also by and large favors those better off. American adults learn democratic skills in three kinds of prepolitical settings: the workplace, voluntary organizations, and religious congregations.[13] Of these settings, both the workplace and voluntary organizations strongly favor those of high socioeconomic status. That is, democratic skills acquisition on the job and in voluntary organizations goes predominantly to those better off; the wealthy and upper middle class over all others, men over women, and whites over most minorities. This systemic bias in American life means that those of high socioeconomic status are more able to protect their interests through the political process—with negative implications for both democratic voice and equality. Only in religious institutions, the third setting for learning democratic skills, does this systemic bias break down. Religious congregations teach democratic skills relatively equally to those of lower and higher incomes, to women and men, to minorities and to whites.[14]

Voice and Equality thus documents how our political process is structured by money and skill building in ways that disadvantage the poor, working class, and even core middle class—and thus distorts American politics by perpetuating a "democratic deficit" in American life. The large gap between haves and have-nots is partly the result of this long-term democratic deficit, this lack of effective political voice for the lower half of American society. Faith-based and race-based organizing strive to overcome this democratic deficit by working with the communities and families that make up that lower half. They strive to deepen democracy by generating more political voice and greater economic equality in American society.

Summary: Distortions of Democratic Life

The public realm is thus ideally a dialogical and conflictive space within civil society, political society, and the state, within which people discuss and make decisions about the future of society. More accurately, this public space *potentially* exists at these three levels, but must constantly be reconstituted by groups actually entering into this potential space and engaging in public deliberation. That is, public life must be regularly reenacted by groups drawing on social capital and democratic skills to project democratic power; otherwise, public life withers. Democratic theorists argue that only when this occurs vigorously across many levels of society does democracy flourish and does democratic decision making really guide societal direction.

This broad sketch of democratic life obscures a crucial fact—the three levels of the public realm exist in rather different organizational spaces: in government; in political associations like parties, unions, and political action and lobbying groups; and in civic associations. Linking them analytically does not suffice to make the public realm an effective arena for societal deliberation; rather, there must exist *institutional linkages* to facilitate communication across these three levels. Political parties have historically provided the institutional means for linking political society downward to civil society (via their roots in ethnic associations, business groups, workplaces, families, etc.) and upward into the state (through electoral influence and the exercise of political power). But political parties' downward linkages have weakened considerably in recent decades, replaced by the new technologies of opinion surveys, mass marketing, and fund-raising through direct mail.[15] These anemic downward linkages erode democracy in America by reducing the exposure of political parties—and through them, elected officials—to democratic pressure from below. Since so few institutions today substitute for these linkages, we lack the degree of political accountability needed to foster strong democracy; this is a fundamental institutional dilemma of American democracy today.

Thus, alongside our picture of an ideal, democratic public realm that fosters societal self-reflection and constructive conflict, we must juxtapose a reality falling well short of this ideal. Organizations that foster democratic skills, build social capital, and use both to empower the less privileged may invigorate democracy by making possible the effective political participation of less privileged members of society. *If* CTWO and PICO succeed in marshaling democratic skills and social capital at the grass roots of American society—either by tapping into existing stocks in poor communities or by cultivating them anew—and use them to project power into the public realm in ways that effectively protect the interests of low- and middle-income families, they will strengthen democratic life. In so doing, they may provide models for other groups striving to bridge the yawning gap between haves and have-nots.

In striving to check the unfettered exercise of economic and political power, both groups turn to government as a potential ally. When they do so, they face state institutions already structured by political power and deeply penetrated by economic power. How successfully each organization can turn that alliance to its own ends depends greatly on the strength of its structural position in society.

Society Faces the State: Comparing the Structural Positions of CTWO and PUEBLO

Putnam's account of the civic roots of political democracy, refocused in more politically centered terms as above, provides a framework for explaining the divergent external impacts of faith-based and race-based organizing. How successfully PICO and CTWO tap into stocks of social capital in the community may be crucial to explaining how successfully each organization overcomes the contemporary institutional dilemma of democracy. While Putnam's large-scale account of Italian political institutions offers strong empirical evidence that social capital factors matter and a powerful theoretical argument for why they matter, it offers little empirical account of *how* they matter. That is, the quantitative data available to Putnam and the macrosocietal focus of his study do not lend themselves to understanding just how, at the micro level, social capital shapes the course of democratic institutions.

The rest of this chapter offers just such an analytic account of social capital and political democracy. On this broad level, the strong examples of contemporary religiously based and race-based community organizing examined here have much in common. Yet, as shown in the case studies of previous chapters, the political cultures and political capacities of CTWO and PICO, the style and substance of their political organizing, and what they contribute to making democracy in America work diverge quite dramatically. We can best account for this difference by considering how their divergent cultural strategies lead them to quite different structural positions in public life. As used here, *structural position in public life* refers to each organization's position in relationship to other institutions within the state–political society–civil society dimensions of the public realm.[16]

My core argument holds that differing cultural strategies give CTWO and PICO differential access to social capital; based on these differential resources of social capital, the two organizations develop differing political capacities and thus attain divergent structural positions in public life—and different political outcomes.

CTWO's Cultural Strategy, Social Capital, and Structural Position in Public Life

PUEBLO in Oakland and local organizing projects in other cities based on CTWO's model organize low-income urban residents primarily through a cultural strategy based on appeal to racial identity. While social class and gender also play significant roles in the organization's conception of its mission, participants explicitly target communities of color and highlight racial and ethnic identity in their organizing campaigns.

Clearly, racial identity has provided a powerful basis for social movements in the history of the United States: examples include the Black Power, Chicano, and American Indian movements, the Nation of Islam, and the Ku Klux Klan and other white-power movements. But CTWO's commitment to democratic multiculturalism excludes the kind of cultural strategy of ethnic or racial nationalism used by these movements to mobilize exclusively along racial lines. Such a strategy might give the organization access to the intraracial trust and social networks that still exist in minority communities. But CTWO staff learned from the experience of divided ethnic power groups of the 1960s and 1970s that minority communities working in isolation from one another are easily balkanized and defeated. Successfully reforming society demands a broader movement.

As a result, CTWO seeks to build an explicitly multiracial organization. In doing so, however, it faces a dilemma: the trust and social networks to which it gains access through appeal to racial identity are largely intraracial resources. Trust within ethnic identity–based social networks primarily exists as trust of others in one's own ethnic group. This is not to say that open racism is common. During this study, PUEBLO occasionally faced outright racism among ethnic minorities it strove to recruit, such as stereotypes held by immigrant Mexicans and other Hispanics toward African Americans and vice versa. But such problems were not terribly common; rather, interethnic trust and social networks are simply anemic.

Certainly, many members of CTWO were remarkable for the extent of their cross-cultural friendships. The rich racial diversity present in their gatherings remains rare in contemporary America. But PUEBLO must either find individuals *already* embedded in extensive cross-cultural networks or *develop* leaders capable of and interested in multicultural organizing. But the former individuals are rare. So the latter approach predominates, with the result that bonds are initially thin within the organization and staff must expend a considerable part of its effort on building and maintaining a multiracial identity within the membership.

The difficulty of doing so becomes clearer when one considers the paucity of shared history or culture among urban African Americans with their historical experience of slavery, Native Americans, recent immigrants from all over the world, and Asian Americans or Mexican Americans long resident here. Certainly, the subaltern status of many of these groups and their experience of racism in various forms and to various degrees of virulence give them shared experiences within American society and thus shared interests. But constructing a self-conscious reform movement out of those shared interests demands constructing what Fantasia calls a "culture of solidarity" (1988)—a difficult task given the distinct cultures carried by these groups. The task is more difficult still, since the elements of culture that *are* widely shared among these diverse groups come, unsurprisingly, from the one cultural world in which all are immersed: American popular culture, with its indelible marks of the dominant consumer culture. Since CTWO's cultural system rejects that culture, it is of little use in constructing a culture of solidarity.

Note that none of this suggests an *absence* of social capital within CTWO's organizing efforts. Using its race-based cultural strategy, CTWO does gain important access to interpersonal networks, but those networks tend initially to be intraracial networks, with little cross-racial trust; when such trust exists, there are few expectations of reciprocity. In other words, these networks provide little of the "bridging social capital" that might help build an organizational culture to link diverse ethnic groups (see below).

So CTWO puts considerable effort into building its own multiracial culture within the organization, drawing on social capital and cultural symbols rooted in the various ethnic cultures represented among its constituents. The extensive presence of what I called cultural action within the CTWO organizing process partly stems from the need to build such a culture; these actions serve to build a reservoir of shared symbols and ritualized experiences to mark group identity. The organization must do a great deal of work to generate this shared culture and sustain the cross-cultural trust and social networks needed for democratic mobilization; thus, it invests significant time and effort in cultural action and informal social contact among members.

To achieve its ultimate goal of being politically effective in the public realm, CTWO thus must focus on both the political tasks of mobilizing its membership *and* the cultural tasks of generating trust and sustaining social networks through a shared multiracial culture.

CTWO's Organizational Dilemma

The constant need to face both sets of tasks produces an organizational dilemma: at any given time, should CTWO concentrate its energies primarily on political action or cultural tasks? Of course, these are not inherently in conflict. Indeed, PUEBLO successfully combines them in an "action/reflection" model, but with two results. First, it mobilizes fewer people than OCO does, both internally during the organizing process and publicly during accountability sessions. As shown in chapter 3, PUEBLO succeeds as much through sophisticated staff work in background research and developing issues as by mobilizing large numbers; indeed, its turnout is comparable to a single medium-sized OCO local organizing committee. So it projects less power into the public realm and has less influence there. Second, PUEBLO's less stable internal culture forces the organization to find other ways of producing internal cohesion. External conflict and a fairly stereotyped view of mainstream institutions may represent strategies for doing so; such solidarity-generating strategies are common in sectarian communities (Kanter 1972).

The organization appears to recognize the dilemmas arising from its relatively weaker access to social capital for mobilizing; it has periodically attempted to draw on staff allies in social service agencies to involve their clientele in PUEBLO-sponsored accountability sessions. These patron-client networks are functionally similar to the vertical networks Putnam observed in Italy: like there, in Oakland they fail badly at fostering effective democratic participation. PUEBLO must organize nearly all its own turnout at accountability sessions, through door-to-door campaigns and extended family networks. The organization can turn out over a hundred people at a time through these efforts, which is no small feat. So far they have gained sufficient leverage from such efforts to extract concessions from local government regarding public services and funding, but not to win the larger-scale issues to which they aspire.

CTWO's Structural Position in Public Life

PUEBLO's structural position in the public realm resulting from these factors looks essentially like a classic institution of civil society, similar to a myriad of cultural associations that have been present throughout American history. But it is a civic institution with a highly systematized political ideology and that attempts to project itself rather directly into the workings of government. Several characteristics are noteworthy in this regard.

First, the salience within PUEBLO's work of "cultural action" events, the fact that these produced the organization's largest attendance during the course of this study, and the role of the organization in offering participants a sense of primary community all point to its status as essentially a civil institution (in contrast to PICO, as discussed below).

Second, to the extent that CTWO focuses on political education and cultural action, the organization's efforts are directed at changing a limited corner of American culture on the level of members' lives in civil society. That is, political education attempts to refashion individual perceptions and attitudes, rather than to impact political institutions.

Third, to the extent the organization does strive to influence public policy, it does so primarily through direct action aimed at unmasking the at least implicitly racist inner workings of government and other societal institutions. Little effort is made to address the intermediate level of political society, to reform institutional politics by calling it to live up to its ideals or by showing officeholders a compelling political imperative for doing so. Though CTWO's accountability sessions are superficially similar to PICO's political actions, recall that no appeal was made to the ideals or self-interest of individual decision makers in political institutions. As players within the institutions of the dominant culture, these individuals are distrusted, and most such political institutions are bypassed in favor of disruptive direct engagement with governing institutions, aimed at disclosing the power relations at work there. In a sense, this disclosure becomes an end in itself with the result that political influence is sacrificed.

In terms of structural position in public life, PUEBLO might best be characterized as a *politicized civic association:* essentially located and focused in civil society, with a highly politicized internal culture and limited (though by no means negligible) political leverage on the wider society.

This interpretation of how CTWO's cultural strategy has shaped the po-

Figure 4.1 Schematic of CTWO's Development

litical experience of its Oakland project is summarized in figure 4.1. With this structural position comes a significant strength; CTWO can focus on cultural tasks that it sees as contributing to a desirable societal future. In contrast, PICO's different cultural strategy and its resulting greater access to social capital allow it a different and, in an important sense, more powerful structural position. This is not to imply that one structural position is better than another; shaping political perceptions in civil society has real political implications, and different organizational actors will prefer different modes of public engagement. Indeed, gradually transforming the political culture of America and reshaping the race relations underlying American politics are critical civic goals.[17] But it does constrain the organization's immediate prospects for influencing social reform, leading it to look more like the social movements analyzed by Castells, who regarded their immediate political prospects with sympathetic pessimism.

PICO's Cultural Strategy, Social Capital, and Structural Position in Public Life

Recall that PICO's turn to religious congregations as the basis for organizing represented a new strategy for the organization. This new cultural strategy was associated with a dramatic increase in PICO's effectiveness, as indicated by the number of participants involved, the total number of federations organized, and the political capacity of those federations (see appendix 2). But was it the cause of that increased effectiveness, or would PICO have blossomed even if it had not adopted the new cultural strategy? The timing of its expansion provides prima facie evidence that its religious turn was important in this regard, but an analytic account of precisely *why* religion mattered can make that evidence a great deal more compelling. I argue that PICO's recent success has resulted in large measure from its religious cultural strategy and the opportunities it made available: new access to the social capital within the churches, a new kind of structural symbiosis with them, and the resulting opening up of a new structural position for PICO within the public realm.

PICO's Cultural Strategy

Though initially the turn to a more explicitly faith-based model of organizing was made for fairly narrow strategic reasons, over time PICO organizers came to draw increasingly on symbols, rituals, practices, stories, and concepts that were explicitly religious as a key basis for their organizing. As this occurred, they gradually came to make increasing use of a more ethically reflective process within the organizing work, which led them toward their first tentative forays into working out a model that would be relationally based, ethically reflective, and institutionally collaborative. Over time, PICO's understanding of the role of its organizers coalesced around this model and the new faith-based cultural strategy that was central to it.[18] How are we to understand this strategic turn and its long-term implications? The answer turns on two factors: new cultural dynamics (examined in later chapters) and newly strengthened access to social capital (examined here), both of which resulted from the new cultural strategy.

In the terms discussed above, instead of working in the context of generalized mistrust and attenuated social ties that had come to characterize many urban neighborhoods, working through the churches brought heightened access to social capital resources. Drawing on those resources, PICO was able to mobilize sufficient numbers of participants to influence deeply the political process in Oakland. This, in turn, led some PICO staff to take more seriously the organization's partnership with churches, enter into deeper conversation with some of their early collaborators among Catholic, historic black Protestant, and mainline Protestant clergy, and seek out leaders and staff who were more scripturally and theologically articulate. Thus, it was the social capital embedded in the constituent churches, combined with the presence of some theologically articulate individuals and the organizing expertise of professional staff, that enabled PICO's breakthrough into Oakland political society. One might debate whether this initial breakthrough represents a cultural effect or an institutional effect of the PICO-church collaboration—did it arise from PICO's link to religious culture or to churches as institutions? But the two factors presuppose one another in two ways.

First, mobilization of the church's social capital depended upon its prior buildup within congregations, itself the product of the workings of religious culture among the church's adherents. On one hand, whatever social capital the churches held had been developed precisely through the cultural dynamics of worship, prayer, Bible study, etc. discussed in later chapters. On the other hand, PICO could mobilize the trust and relationships embedded in these religious communities only because it shared significant cultural elements with them; it articulated its organizing model in terms of religiously grounded values, understood its need for the churches' ethical teachings regarding relational integrity, and understood its work as "religiously inspired" even when not explicitly an expression of faith. Although at this early stage PICO used religious cultural elements only to a limited extent in day-to-day organizing work, it could thus work with churches "in good faith" rather than manipulatively.

Second, whatever the degree of institutional logic and self-interest behind the initial partnership with churches, PICO's experience within that partnership soon drove organizers toward a full-blown effort to incorporate religious language, symbols, and meanings into the organizing work itself. The dynamic behind this move into an explicitly religious cultural basis for organizing, as it can best be reconstructed ten or fifteen years after the fact, was as follows. Once staff began to work through church relational networks to identify issues and organize members, they frequently encountered people who articulated their commitment to civic engagement through the language of religious faith; religion as well as self-interest based on common residence in neighborhoods provided the shared language through which people talked about what moved them to action. As we will see later in exploring the worship lives of congregations, religion also provided the shared cultural elements around which these social networks took shape.

Together, these factors and the desire among many staff organizers to make ethical sense of their roles led PICO over time to draw more extensively on religious culture in the day-to-day practice of organizing. Presumably, PICO's reliance on church institutions as the basis of organizing and the pastors' effective veto power over what occurs in their churches further encouraged this turn to a more explicitly faith-based cultural strategy to complement the traditional focus on self-interest and a vague language of values.

As this cultural strategy gradually deepened, it came to restructure PICO's work in at least three ways. Most importantly, many individuals among the key sectors in the organizing process—staff, leaders, and pastors—came to think of their political engagement as an expression of both their faith and their civic responsibility. In the terms used by one current study (Coleman forthcoming), they developed parallel languages of "discipleship" and "citizenship" to make sense of their political experience, rather than relying solely on the latter.

In addition, the public face of organizing began to change. As the participants came to draw more extensively on religious self-understandings in the internal life of the organizations, they found it quite natural to incorporate religious elements more vigorously into its most public settings as well. Prayer, reflections that framed a given issue in light of religious teachings and values, and Scripture-based appeals to social justice became far more prominent at actions. All these changes opened up space for greater participation in public by pastors, further cementing the PICO-church collaboration.

Finally, this deeper "embeddedness" (Granovetter 1985) of PICO's work in religious networks enriched the organization's reach into society for its recruitment of participants, strategic contacts, and—crucially—professional staff. PICO, like most activist organizations, had previously drawn its staff largely from the ranks of aspiring social movement professionals who were disproportionately university trained, white, and secularly motivated. In recent years, its reach and profile in religious sectors of urban communities have substantially diversified the kind of people interested in working as PICO staff. Thus, while some new PICO staff continue to come from the traditional pool, the majority deviate from the traditional profile in at least one of several ways:[19] those whose primary cultural capital comes from formation in local churches rather than universities, those from minority communities, and those who became involved as leaders from their "indigenous" religious institutions and now wish to become professional staff out of a combined sense of democratic commitment, religious calling, and the need to make a living. Noteworthy is the fact that even those staff members who are not personally committed to a faith tradition are explicitly expected to respect and support the faith commitments of others.

Together, these mutually reinforcing tendencies resulting from PICO's cultural strategy allowed the organization to draw on the heightened trust existing among members of some congregations by virtue of their shared membership in a moral community. They have afforded PICO greater access to the social networks embedded in congregations—including (in the most supportive congregations) full access to phone lists, computer data-bases, church social and ministerial groups, announcement times at ser-vices, bulletin space, etc. This heightened access to the moral resources and social capital of church life gradually strengthened existing PICO federa-tions during the late 1980s. This success led to its expansion into new cities in the early 1990s—from four to twenty-five federations between 1988 and 1995, and nearly forty in existence or under formation today—as word-of-mouth led to invitations to establish federations in new cities, as success led to the recruitment of new professional staff, and as PICO developed networks of clergy supportive of its work.

These changes soon shaped PICO's work in all its projects. By the early 1990s religious faith, church institutions, and community organizing had become more fully articulated in some PICO projects. While earlier the im-plications of this dynamic interaction were vaguely understood by PICO's national staff, by this period the possibilities became quite clear to them. The dramatic success of those federations that led the way in adopting the faith-based cultural strategy began a process of diffusion to other federa-tions. This diffusion originated in Oakland and New Orleans and eventually spread throughout the network, except where local conditions (usually weak pastoral support) have made it difficult. This organizational learning was possible because of the coordinating role of PICO's central structure; this self-conscious move is what shapes it into a "cultural strategy" as op-posed to random experimentation.

It led to a political capacity PICO never had before adopting the faith-based cultural strategy. The success of those federations that pioneered the new cultural strategy taught even the most reluctant and secular partici-pants that some forms of religious belief could provide a solid basis for dem-ocratic organizing: by the early 1990s, the New Orleans federation turned out over five thousand people to an action, several California federations turned out fifteen hundred to two thousand, and a federation in Camden, New Jersey—with a total population of some seventy thousand—turned out over one thousand people.

PICO's Structural Position in Public Life
PICO's symbiotic relationship with religious institutions, in turn, has al-lowed it to assume a new structural position in public life. Clarifying this structural position will help make clear what makes this kind of organizing successful and why it holds promise for democratic renewal.

In one sense, the structural position of local PICO federations is clearly within civil society: they are rigorously nonpartisan, withhold endorsement of specific political candidates, and actively strive to avoid close identification with political officeholders.

Yet these federations exist precisely to pursue power to address public issues, albeit not as contenders for political office. The most successful of them—in places like New Orleans, Oakland, San Diego, Denver, San Jose, San Francisco, and Orange County—by the late 1990s had attained sufficient influence within city politics to have become players at the level of political society. Mayors and their key staff people attended working retreats with organizational leaders to formulate policy; some federations formed tactical alliances with labor unions to promote overlapping agendas; and in some places political officials regularly consulted with federation leaders regarding upcoming political decisions. This new structural position is even clearer in the PICO California Project's high-profile role in educational, medical, and housing policy in California.[20]

PICO's heightened structural position is evident in the federations' ability to influence public policy on complex and substantive issues like educational reform and economic development. An example of this occurred in New Orleans, long depicted as having one of the most corrupt and reform-resistant police departments of any major American city. Though attempts at police reform had been made, until the mid-1990s mayors in New Orleans were too politically beholden to the police department and police officers' union to be effective in initiating such reform. In 1995 the first significant steps toward real reform were undertaken by a new mayor, Marc Morial. A crucial factor in this development was investigative work by federal law enforcement officials, but for the first time a New Orleans mayor backed up such investigation with effective political action, including appointing and supporting a reformist police chief. So a second crucial factor appears to have been equally decisive: Morial's relative autonomy from the political dictates of corrupt law enforcement institutions. That autonomy has several roots, but prominent among them was Morial's relationship to the local PICO federation as a civic channel offering an alternative to patronage politics.[21] Suggestive in this regard was an interview with a New Orleans political insider and long-time confidante to Morial; when asked how much difference Morial's ties to the PICO federation made, the respondent answered:

> How much difference politically, you mean? All kinds of difference, that's how much. He can work with them, and it gives him some freedom of movement with other groups that'd try to box him in. [Interviewer: And

on the police corruption issue?] Especially there. He could never have
done what he did with that by himself.

PICO federations thus also function partially as institutions of political
society, oriented toward power and focused on shaping the decisions of
elite decision makers.

Together, these two facets of PICO's work constitute the organization's
structural position in the public sphere; it can best be understood by seeing
PICO federations as *bridging institutions* that straddle the divide between
civil society, political society, and the state. Analogous to the classic role
of political parties, bridging institutions aggregate the interests and value
commitments of individuals and collectivities in civil society and channel
them into the decision making processes of governing elites, "holding them
accountable to the community." Faith-based federations play this role, yet
in subjecting the dynamics of political power to the ethical traditions and
moral-political vision of moral communities, the more sophisticated of
them hold political society and the state at arm's length and remain rooted
in civil society. With a foot in both worlds, PICO provides precisely the
kind of democratically controlled links from society to the state that are so
scarce in contemporary American society.

This structural position has become possible because PICO's close structural ties to the religious institutions of civil society have substantially
unburdened the organization of the need to generate meaning and create
primary community in members' lives, in contrast to CTWO. Member
churches carry the primary burden—and, for believers, provide the primary
grace—in these areas. In this division of labor, members turn at least partially to their churches for the work of psychological integration, symbolic
meaning construction, and face-to-face community that are in many ways
the specific strengths of religious and other moral communities. PICO is
thus partially freed from these tasks to focus on its specific specialty: linking
these moral communities with the political process that determines the social conditions of their lives. This division of labor allows the organization
to remain grounded in the life-world contexts of civil society while projecting itself into political society. In return, PICO delivers to the churches
concrete improvements in their local settings, a deeper grounding of their
religious mission in members' daily struggles, members with new leadership
capacities, and greater effectiveness in shaping political priorities in line
with their social and ethical teaching.

Figure 4.2 depicts the developments in PICO, from its adoption of the
new cultural strategy beginning in the mid-1980s to the organization's cur-

Figure 4.2 Schematic of PICO's Development

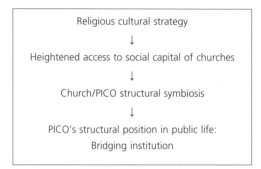

rent position as an influential player in city and in some cases statewide politics. Churches thus provide an anchor in civil society that allows faith-based organizing federations to venture far out into political society without losing their mooring in the moral worlds of individuals' everyday lives. At the same time, faith-based organizing offers the churches a way to channel their ethico-political positions more effectively into the public realm.

Faith-based organizing federations also perform a different bridging function in American life: they provide links among communities that frequently coexist in relative isolation from one another. Often termed "bridging social capital" (Warren, Thompson, and Saegert 2001; Gittell and Vidal 1998), such links—especially across different racial/ethnic groups, but also other social dividing lines—are a rare commodity, and may be especially crucial for minorities (Putnam 2000, 322 and passim). As shown in the case studies of previous chapters, the Oakland chapters of both CTWO and PICO promote this kind of social capital quite extensively.

The Interfaith Funders study (Warren and Wood 2001) provides data with which to assess whether faith-based organizing nationally generates bridging social capital. Two kinds of ties are of interest here: cross-racial ties and interreligious ties. No individual-level data are available in this regard, but congregation-level data are for the 82 faith-based organizing federations that responded to a question concerning the predominant racial/ethnic makeup of their member congregations. As shown in table 4.1, 56 percent of the federations were biracial or multiracial; that is, at least two racial/ethnic groups predominated in at least 15 percent of member institutions (and no group predominated in more than 65 percent of member institutions). In only 13 of the 82 federations (18 percent) did one racial/ethnic group predominate in more than 80 percent of member institutions. Fur-

Table 4.1 Racial Diversity across Local Organizations in Faith-Based Organizing

	Number	Patterns within This Category*
Monoracial	9	3 white
(100% one group)		3 black
		3 Hispanic
Racially dominant	4	2 white dominant[a]
(one group >80%)		2 black dominant
Racial majority	21	14 white dominant[b]
(65%–80% one group)		6 black dominant[c]
		1 Hispanic dominant[d]
Biracial	35	22 white/black[e]
(only 2 groups >15%)		8 white/Hispanic
		3 black/Hispanic
		2 white/Asian
Multiracial	9 with 3 groups >15%	9 white/black/Hispanic[f]
(3 or 4 groups > 15%)	2 with 4 groups >15%	1 white/black/Hispanic/Asian[g]

Source: Data from Interfaith Funders study of faith-based organizing groups nationally (Warren and Wood 2001); table also appears in Wood and Warren forthcoming. Of the one hundred respondent organizations, eighty-two provided data on this question.

* Secondary group listed when ≥ 10%. Two cases were indeterminate—one in which 11 of the 12 partici- pating groups were interracial, and one in which 50 percent of the participating groups were white and 43 percent were interracial.

a. Listed as dominant/secondary group, the patterns are 1 white/Hispanic, 1 white/black & interracial, and 2 black/white.
b. Listed as dominant/secondary group, the patterns are 6 white/black, 3 white/Hispanic, 2 white/black & Hispanic, 2 white/black & interracial, and 1 white/interracial.
c. Listed as dominant/secondary group, the patterns are 3 black/white, 1 black/Hispanic, and 2 black/ white & interracial.
d. Listed as dominant/secondary group, the pattern is 1 Hispanic/white.
e. Listed in order of concentration: 12 black/white, 10 white/black, 4 white/Hispanic, 4 Hispanic/white, 3 black/Hispanic, 1 white/Asian, and 1 Asian/white.
f. Listed in order of concentration: 3 black/white/Hispanic, 2 white/black/Hispanic, 2 black/Hispanic/white, 1 white/Hispanic/black, and 1 Hispanic/black/white. Groups include Asian, black, Hispanic, Native American, and white. Interracial group excluded from analysis. If groups had equal proportions, then listed in alpha- betical order.
g. Listed in order of concentration: 1 Asian/black/Hispanic/white and 1 white/Hispanic/Asian/black. If groups had equal proportions, then listed in alphabetical order.

thermore, as the right-hand column shows, even where one racial group was dominant, that group was as likely to be African Americans as to be whites, and only somewhat less likely to be Hispanics.

We have similar data on interreligious social capital. The three core reli- gious groups within faith-based organizing are Roman Catholics, mainline (theologically liberal and moderate) Protestants, and congregations of the historic African American church traditions. Table 4.2 shows that federa- tions are quite interreligious, at least across these three Christian traditions:

Table 4.2 Religious Diversity within Local Faith-Based Organizations

	Number	Main Patterns within This Category
Monoreligious 100% one group	3	All Roman Catholic
Dominant > 60% one group	13	7 Roman Catholic dominant 4 mainline Protestant dominant 2 historic black Protestant dominant
Majority 50–60% one group	11	4 Roman Catholic majority 5 mainline Protestant majority 2 historic black Protestant majority
Bireligious 2 groups > 20%	35	20 Catholic/mainline 9 historic black/mainline 4 Catholic/historic black 1 traditionalist/historic black 1 mainline/non-Christian
Diverse 3 groups > 20% or 4 groups > 15%	31	9 with largest group mainline 9 with largest group Catholic 4 with largest group historic black 9 with two essentially equal primary groups (mostly historic black, mainline, or Catholic)

Source: Data from Interfaith Funders study of faith-based organizing groups nationally (Warren and Wood 2001); table also appears in Wood and Warren forthcoming. Of the one hundred respondent organizations, ninety-three provided data on this question.

66 of the 93 federations for which we have data (71 percent) are bireligious or more diverse—that is, have 20 percent or more of member congregations affiliated with at least two religious traditions. In only 27 of the 93 federations (29 percent) do a majority of member congregations represent the same religious tradition; and those 27 federations are fairly evenly divided among Catholics, mainline Protestants, and historic black Protestants as the majority tradition.

Beyond these three core traditions, institutional membership in faith-based organizing includes significant presence from the following religious traditions: Jewish (2 percent of member institutions), Unitarian Universalist (2 percent), and black evangelical (mostly Church of God in Christ; 2 percent). Largely *absent* from faith-based organizing are traditionalist Protestants (including white evangelicals) and the Hindu, Muslim, Buddhist, and other non-Christian congregations that make up only a small percentage of American congregations but have a significant presence in urban America.[22]

Nationally, faith-based organizing thus fosters significant cross-racial and interreligious ties, bringing racial/ethnic groups and religious traditions into greater contact and collaborative work than they would be likely to otherwise have. The resulting bridging social capital helps to fill an important void in American civic life.[23]

Faith-based organizing thus plays two important bridging roles, one of which is also played by CTWO.[24] In fostering bridging social capital—especially among different racial groups—both faith-based and race-based organizing make significant indirect contributions to long-term democratic possibilities. In serving as a bridging institution, faith-based organizing makes a direct contribution to the long-term deepening of democracy, a contribution that few other institutions are poised to make as effectively.

Contrasting Strengths, Contrasting Challenges

The robust national economy of the late 1990s allowed the well-off to live in the illusion that everyone was doing well, but the less well-off were often balancing two or more jobs just to stay afloat. On the more tenuous economic terrain of the new millennium, low-income Americans are yet more vulnerable. In both contexts, the work of CTWO and PICO and similar efforts around the country provide an important counterpressure: they generate democratic pressure from relatively marginalized groups so that economic resources and public goods flow toward poorer communities and the threatened middle class, not just toward established interests and new elites. Furthermore, both organizations do so rather effectively and in ways that address, explicitly or implicitly, one of the deepest scars on the American body politic: the stark divide between racial and ethnic groups. In place of privileging white culture and status, these organizations create spaces in which multiple cultures can interact and collaborate in advancing their democratic interests. This is no small feat; that they do so in quite different ways only enhances the struggle for a richer and multihued democratic culture.

By building democratic skills within low- and middle-income families, establishing relationships across the racial, cultural, and geographic barriers among subaltern groups, and forging links between these groups and elite decision makers, both faith-based and race-based organizing make it more likely that democratic alliances and constructive political action will take shape in the face of the next economic downturn or political crisis.

These shared aspirations and democratic impacts of the two forms of community organizing examined here should not, however, keep us from recognizing their different dynamics and different implications for democracy. Each brings its own distinctive contribution to the democratic challenges of our time, and each faces its own distinctive obstacles to contributing effectively.

CTWO's distinctive ethos of radical democratic multiculturalism, built on the practice of direct action to interrupt the routine workings of dominant institutions, suggests that its organizing projects are likely to remain political outsiders permanently. This brings real strength to the organization's adopted role as social critic and representative of highly marginalized groups, as its uncompromising stance can sting the consciences of elites and disrupt dominant routines. Such tactics can have powerful effects, at least in the short term; witness how direct action tactics shut down the World Trade Organization meetings in Seattle in early 2000.[25] In addition, CTWO's organizing does focus more keenly on the most marginalized communities of urban America; proportionately, those engaged in CTWO's race-based model were more likely to come from extreme poverty and be least connected to social institutions such as schools, churches, or full-time employment.[26] Finally, and partly as a result of its disconnection from these institutions, CTWO is more likely to engage in political organizing around such controversial issues as sexual orientation, transgendered identities, the right to life versus the right to choose, police abuse, and racial profiling— all issues on which faith-based organizing is unlikely to focus (though in some locales it has addressed the latter two issues).[27]

The organizational dilemma arising from CTWO's appeal to racial identity probably does mean that CTWO will play the more constricted role I describe as a "politicized civic association." That is, the organization with its current cultural strategy is unlikely to break out of its present position as a significant but isolated voice from marginalized sectors of civil society. Playing this role creatively and with integrity represents an important organizational and political vocation, albeit one unlikely to shift the fundamental power dynamics of public life.

Faith-based organizing faces a different set of opportunities and challenges. The organization implicitly accepts the fundamental institutions of political democracy and the market economy, but works to project sufficient political power to hold those institutions accountable to their own ethical claims and democratic ideals. Faith-based organizing has succeeded sufficiently in this regard to gain a role as a bridging institution linking grassroots civil society and the higher arenas of the public realm located in political society and government. This was clearly illustrated in the work of the PICO California Project, depicted in the introduction and chapter 2.

In this linking role, faith-based organizing holds great democratic promise not only by addressing the distributional challenges of modern society, but also by addressing a fundamental institutional dilemma of contemporary democracy.

The links to the mainstream institutions on which faith-based organizing relies do bring real constraints and dilemmas, however. The most obvious constraints concern the issues that faith-based organizing will address; these are unlikely to include such highly divisive issues as discrimination on the basis of sexual orientation, the politics (pro or con) of abortion, or even school vouchers. For some, these organizations' inability to address such issues makes them unattractive avenues of political engagement; for others, it means these organizations are likely to focus on issues of greater concern. This highlights the importance of sustaining diverse avenues for grassroots political engagement; having a hundred ways to hold our economic and political systems accountable to democratic pressures is surely a good thing.

The dilemmas confronting faith-based organizing include how best to reinsert religious language into the public realm. Faith-based organizing clearly does so, and needs to do so to bring its full political potential to bear in the political arena. But at a time when some fundamentalists are pursuing a similar course in ways that smack of Christian hegemony, this is a political minefield. If American democracy is to institutionalize an appropriate relationship between religion and politics, it will be crucial for organized voices of faith communities to establish an appropriate tone and content in their political interventions (even when their policy prescriptions disagree sharply). Similarly, faith-based organizing must decide how best to incorporate diverse religious voices into its organizing work, in a way that encourages the vigorous incorporation of religious language into public life and yet is acceptable in contrasting traditions.

But faith-based organizing's most crucial dilemma flows directly from its success: its growing political power. PICO's commitment to the ethical ideals affirmed by the wider society, links to mainstream institutions, ability to institutionally bridge the gaps between civil and political society *and* between racial and religious groups, and capacity to project significant power into the political arena together allow the organization to play a complex insider/outsider role vis-à-vis the political system. In multiple cities around the country and at the state level in California and Texas (and increasingly in a variety of other states) faith-based organizing represents a powerful potential political partner for political, corporate, civic, or union leaders willing to embrace an agenda built around "working families"—or to negotiate toward such an agenda.[28] This brings the risk of faith-based organizing's becoming or being perceived as "captive" to the interests of corporate or union leaders, political officeholders, or political parties. The stronger faith-based organizing becomes, the more appealing it will be as a target for such efforts at co-optation. In becoming a partner to established political interests in order to pursue shared goals, these organizations must also retain their commitment to being vocal critics of those same interests. Getting this right will be a key factor in whether faith-based organizing can sustain a credible role as a bridging institution in pursuit of ethical democracy.

A last dilemma should not go unmentioned: because they rely on resources from similar sources, seek finite media attention, and face a limited supply of talented organizers, the four major networks and the smaller regional networks that together sponsor the lion's share of faith-based organizing compete with one another. Furthermore, interpersonal conflicts rooted in past feuds and organizational conflicts arising from broken agreements and turf battles make that competition truly fierce at times. This poses a very real strategic challenge; if they wish to fully exert the political capacity they enjoy, the networks will have to coordinate their action to some degree. None alone has sufficient national presence to exert federal pressure, but together they have a significant presence in all the biggest electoral battlegrounds and many of the key congressional districts around the country. Overcoming their conflicts in order to coordinate their action will not be easy, for little trust exists on which to build collaborative relations. But if they fail to do so, any political goals they achieve will be dwarfed by the democratic potential they forgo.

Conclusion

This chapter has argued that the divergent cultural strategies of faith-based and race-based organizing provided each model with differential access to social capital, which in turn explained much about their development, the dilemmas they face, and the potential they hold for contributing to democratic renewal in America. We might think of these as the indirect effects of their divergent cultural strategies of organizing.

But all of this leaves out of the analysis the direct effects of cultural strategies: i.e., how differing cultural strategies lead organizations to construct their internal political cultures differently, and how this leads to divergent cultural dynamics within the two models. The following chapters pursue this *cultural analysis* of community organizing. They address a series of questions concerning the cultural dynamics of community organizing, and in particular whether distinct cultural dynamics help determine distinct political outcomes. PICO's close links to religious congregations means that its organizing process occurs within a context informed by the worship experience of those communities. Likewise, CTWO's strong appeal to participants' identities as people of color bathes its organizing process in cultural themes attached to those identities. Does religious culture contribute anything in particular to PICO's democratic success? Does CTWO's appeal to racially and ethnically rooted culture contribute to its democratic success? Analytically, do their internal cultural dynamics differ, and are these connected to PICO's greater political capacity?

To ask these questions draws attention to a different aspect of these organizations' work: to considering their organizational life as a cultural process destined not just to get people to show up at events, but to get them to think politically, find meaning in being politically engaged, and invite others into an understanding of human life that makes politics interesting and compelling. Ultimately, I will argue that beyond the specific policy victories these organizations win, their most important contribution to the democratic struggle may well lie in their revalorization of the political dimension of human life, and the gradual transformation of American political culture that this makes possible.[29]

Part II   Thinking Culturally about Politics

We do not usually think of politics as a cultural enterprise, but rather in terms of voting, raising campaign contributions, convincing others of a certain point of view, accumulating power, and using that power to win future power struggles. But even as it focuses on these tasks, politics is profoundly also a cultural enterprise because it is about creating meanings. When we engage in political action, talk about politics, or simply vote, we do so on the basis of the meanings we attach to the world around us—meanings about our economic self-interest, political commitments, and moral beliefs. Social scientists, in an older terminology, speak of this in terms of "values" that guide our politics, but this lends itself to the illusion that such values are stable preferences, internalized by individuals in the course of being socialized, with little real initiative on their own part. In contrast, the focus here on *meanings* emphasizes the contingent, often temporary quality of political commitments, commitments that are constantly being restructured.

In individuals, this contingent quality of meanings is hard to study, often obscured in their interior lives. But for political organizations, we can watch the process of meaning creation occur in vivo precisely because they must *create shared meanings* among their participants. Meaning creation in PICO and CTWO is thus an explicit and visible process—if we pay attention to it.

To see this process at work, it helps to think ecologically. Imagine these organizations as living creatures surrounded by their environments (Hannan and Freeman 1989). Rather than using food and water, however, these community organizations draw different kinds of resources from their environments: *money* from supporters, participants, and foundation donors; *personnel* from the neighborhoods or churches they serve, or from universities and other community organizations; and *knowledge* about organizing practices and specific policy issues from the national organizing networks, policy experts, books, and a variety of other sources. Beyond these kinds of resources, voluntary organizations must keep people involved by helping them find a sense of *meaning* to the work they do.[1]

In community organizing, that meaning comes partly embedded in the personal ties among participants. But just as important is direct work to create cultural meaning; organizers and leaders engage in extensive effort to construct shared meaning within the organization—that is, to construct an organizational culture that binds participants together (Pedersen and Sørensen 1989; Schneider 1990; Cole 1989; Ott 1989). Because CTWO and PICO strive to hold together large numbers of people and to get them to act politically in coordinated fashion, I term each organizational culture an "internal political culture." That is, each organization must construct a *political culture* at least partially shared by its constituents—a set of shared assumptions, perceptions of the world, symbols, and concepts that help them interpret and act in the political world.[2] I use the term "political culture" in a profoundly different sense than the dominant tradition in social sciences, represented in the classic cross-national study by Almond and Verba (1963) and more recently by the work of Ronald Inglehart (1988). Whereas their approach emphasized widespread value orientations that putatively characterize the broad mass of the population in a given society, and thus the overall culture of a nation, I use the term in a much more bounded sense: to denote the organizational culture of a group of people pursuing broadly political purposes, especially as that culture relates to their associational life and political commitments.

Political organizations rarely build their political culture from scratch; typically, they draw on the prior cultural experience of those involved. But potential leaders come already embedded in multiple networks based on racial and ethnic identity, political affiliation and experience, educational and employment status, religious commitment, age and generational status, family ties, sexual identity, etc. No community organization appeals simultaneously to all these aspects of their potential leaders' social terrain. Rather, each relies on a *cultural strategy:* a more or less conscious decision to construct an organizational political culture by drawing cultural elements from some particular segment of their potential participants' social terrain (Gould 1995). Of course, political organizers can insert cultural elements of their own or create new ones in collaboration with local leaders. But this is an arduous process and is greatly facilitated if it is built on a foundation of cultural elements already institutionalized in participants' lives.

In adopting a cultural strategy, an organization focuses attention on some segments of participants' cultural terrain rather than on others. This area of primary attention becomes an organization's *cultural base* for its work in developing leaders and building a political culture. That is, while organizers may well still draw on various dimensions of participants' cultural identities, their cultural work will revolve much more closely around that dimension of participant identities associated with the organization's primary cultural base and strategy.

The choice of cultural strategy and cultural base is crucial for at least two reasons. First, it represents one of the few areas in which challenger groups can choose their own terrain of struggle: political organizers have little choice (at least in the short term) regarding the structure of political opportunities they face or the material resources on which they can draw. But since real human communities have complex and multifaceted cultural traditions, organizers have a great deal of leeway in adopting a cultural strategy. Second, the choice matters enormously: as argued below, the foundation on which a group constructs its internal political culture and the cultural patterns it institutionalizes shapes its ability to project power into the political arena and gain a voice in public life. The initial choice of cultural base and cultural strategy, along with standard practices and the ongoing cultural work within the organizing process, together give rise to the internal political culture of the organization; this, in turn, partially determines the organization's ability to project social power from civil society into the political arena, and thus the degree of political effectiveness of the organization.[3] This process can be schematized as shown in figure II.1.

At first glance, the task of building an internal political culture looks simple; in working together, human groups tend naturally to generate some shared culture. As participants in a political organization begin to work together, some kind of internal political culture will develop. Though many voluntary organizations rely on whatever spontaneously generated culture

Figure II.1 Cultural Influences on Political Effectiveness of Challenger Groups

Cultural base + Cultural strategy	→	Internal political culture	→	Projection of social power	→	Degree of political effectiveness

emerges out of this process, gaining long-term political influence requires more. The best community organizers recognize that to rely on a naturally emerging political culture allows the organization to fall into traps created by the blind spots of unexamined cultural assumptions: that conflict should be avoided, that certain groups cannot be trusted, that one engages in political work only as a prophetic witness or to express one's values rather than to actually succeed, that all institutions and all authority are inherently suspect, that God cares about individual moral worth, not about social problems, or any of a myriad of other assumptions of American culture.

To circumvent these accepted cultural meanings, organizers engage in *cultural work* (Hart 2001).[4] As I will use the concept here, cultural work includes both intentionally importing cultural meanings from the organization's wider environment and reworking these cultural meanings within the organization.

Cultural work happens partly just by bringing participants into the organizing work. They bring with them multiple sources of meaning, from their family ties, ethnic or racial backgrounds, work experience, religious tradition, formal education, American popular culture, etc. When participants invoke cultural elements from the wider society (symbols, ideas, words, and practices), cultural meanings come embedded in those elements and are drawn implicitly into the work of organizing.

A more explicit kind of cultural work occurs when participants analyze their political experience by drawing on the cultural resources available to them—that is, when they apply cultural elements to interpret their political action. This happens to some extent spontaneously, but is a practice and skill that better organizers develop and encourage systematically. However, if the meanings of the cultural elements thus brought to bear politically are themselves taken for granted and fixed in participants' minds, then only a relatively narrow range of cultural work is possible. The best organizers develop a rich set of cultural tools within their leaders by doing explicit cultural work on the cultural elements themselves. They draw on the cultural orientations participants bring into organizing, and the symbols, stories, images, and ideas that are relevant to them, and rework them. They reflect with participants on their received cultural elements, emphasizing some elements, critiquing others, and reinterpreting still others by fostering critical appropriation of them. Organizers will also occasionally incorporate new cultural elements from sources unfamiliar to participants: from books and articles, from religious traditions, from writings on radical democracy or organizational management, from more experienced organizers, etc. But they do so judiciously, balancing incorporation of new elements with reflective and critical appropriation of elements from participants' own traditions.

Thus, moving from a cultural base and cultural strategy to an effective internal political culture involves extensive cultural work. Part 2 analyzes how this occurs and how it shapes the political outcomes of these organizations.

This presents an analytic problem: I argued in the previous chapter that the differing political outcomes of CTWO and PICO are explained by divergent access to social capital. With only the two cases under study here, perhaps the social capital factors already discussed fully account for the differences between CTWO and PICO and we need not refer to their distinct cultural dynamics. How can we disentangle whether there really is any autonomous cultural influence on their outcomes?

These chapters do so by taking advantage of the fact that three congregations within PICO all had strong social capital yet had very distinct political capacities and outcomes. A social capital–based argument cannot explain these divergent outcomes, but an analysis of their cultural dynamics can: the three congregations embodied divergent religious cultures, so PICO's work built on somewhat different cultural bases in each congregation. As a result, their efforts built differing political cultures, or at least substantial variations on PICO's broad political culture. If we can develop a convincing cultural analysis that links the differing outcomes of these three congregations to their internal cultural dynamics, we will have evidence that culture matters in ways not reducible to social capital alone.

The following chapters pursue this cultural analysis. Along the way, we shall see that distinct internal political cultures also contribute to the different political outcomes of CTWO and PICO, reinforcing the differences in social capital emphasized in chapter 4. Chapter 5 explores the organizational culture of faith-based organizing by analyzing the practices, beliefs, and ethos that shape it. Chapter 6 provides a framework for a more rigorous analysis of how culture matters for politics and applies that framework to CTWO and one local congregation within PICO, the Saint Elizabeth organizing committee whose highly successful work we have already seen.

Chapter 7 disentangles the cultural and social capital explanations of organizing success by characterizing the limitations of particular forms of religious culture for this kind of democratic work, showing how cultural dynamics can undermine organizing success even when congregations carry plenty of social capital.

By linking recent advances in cultural and political sociology with classical and contemporary work in the sociology of religion, these chapters provide new insight into one way culture shapes politics: by contributing to the political capacity of challenger groups.[5] By paying close attention to the microdynamics and institutional context of the organizing process, precisely *how* culture matters is brought into sharper focus.

Chapter 5

The Political Culture of Faith-Based Organizing:
Practices, Beliefs, Ethos

Without an informed public capable of responding morally to its
own needs, there can be no democracy.

—José Carrasco, PICO

The strong political position of faith-based federations
as bridging institutions, discussed in chapter 4, is a
product not only of religiously rooted social capital, but
also of the internal political culture of these organizations.
PICO participants work to shape organizational cultures
that help develop the informed, assertive, morally reflective democratic participants for which José Carrasco calls.[1]
They do so by generating an internal public sphere, or
what feminist theorist Nancy Fraser (1992) calls a "subaltern counter-public," within the organization—settings
in which participants talk to one another about public
policy, political alternatives, and how to shape their
shared future.[2] Each federation then projects power out of
that internal public sphere into the wider public arena of

Gloria Cooper, president of the San Diego Organizing Project, and Fr.
Eduardo Samaniego address participants at a PICO action. Courtesy
San Diego Organizing Project.

city government and public schools, and occasionally of neighborhoods and state government. This chapter describes in detail the internal cultural system that allows faith-based organizing to project power in this way.

The organizing process described in the first two chapters is multiplied across more than 30 American metropolitan areas in which the Pacific Institute for Community Organization works, and—with some variation—across over 130 other cities in which other faith-based organizations work. In order to overcome the opposition or inertia of entrenched economic and political interests and to promote public decisions in the interest of less privileged sectors, the more effective organizers I observed helped their organizations simultaneously develop in three ways.

First, these organizations rely on leaders with the skills to effectively organize people, run public meetings, and negotiate with political representatives and economic elites. This is the task that the vast majority of organizers I interviewed cited when I asked them about their work; most said, with some variation, that their primary role is to develop leaders—i.e., to help leaders cultivate the civic skills necessary in public life. But in fact, their task is broader than that, involving at least two other dimensions.[3]

Second, these organizations powerfully articulate a *moral vision* of society, how society ought to be. Because these organizations can rarely force their will on public officials, their influence comes from the combination of concrete political power based on the demonstrated capacity to convene hundreds or thousands of people, sharp analysis of issues affecting urban residents and the possible solutions to them, and—crucially—the ability to present their proposals in an ethical framework. That is, though in the final analysis these organizations may gain political allies or change the minds of elected officials by exerting raw political power, in the *process* of organizing, the ability to gain adherents and present a convincing rationale for a given proposal requires not simply arguing that the proposal should be adopted because the organization demands it, but also arguing that it is *right,* reflects things as they should be.[4] Such a moral vision does not replace the political power needed to change society but rather provides an ethical critique that can open up the status quo to alternatives promoted politically. As in mechanics, where a lever can vastly increase the ability of a given amount of force to move an object, such ethical leverage in public discourse can vastly increase the impact of democratic power.[5]

Third, effective community organizing requires sustaining the emotional engagement of participants with the issues addressed and channeling that engagement toward long-run objectives. Because organizing moves forward only slowly—for organizations must gradually accumulate sufficient power and expertise before they can take action at a level that can make much impact on their community—this key task involves attention to the flow of emotion during the organizing process.[6] Though until recently social science scholars have neglected the role of emotions in social movements, here we must pay attention to that terrain. Keeping participants engaged in the slow work of organizing requires careful cultivation of both *anger* at present inequalities and *hope* that society can actually be transformed.

All three—building skills, generating a vision, and engaging participants' emotional lives—entail cultural work. PICO carries out this work partly by drawing on the moral-political traditions of democratic organizing inherited from Saul Alinsky and other left and populist organizers of the last fifty years, and more distantly from the radical democratic and Jacksonian traditions of American life.[7] But those traditions had largely waned by the 1970s, at least as vibrant aspects of Alinsky's work and writing.[8] In his later years, Alinsky's organizing had become a rather blunt instrument for forcing elites to respect the power of nonelites—no small achievement, to be sure, but devoid of much of the humanist worldview that originally had inspired it. More broadly, much of the morally rooted fervor of the civil rights movement, the anti–Vietnam war and early feminist movements, and United Farm Workers organizing drives had, by the 1970s, given way to cynicism and demobilization resulting from official opposition, internal sectarian factionalism, and the rejection of their own cultural and institutional roots—part of the 1960s reaction against all things traditional (Tipton 1982). This chapter argues that religion is central to how PICO and other organizations overcome this recent anemia of the democratic strands of American culture. It is the first step in arguing that religion matters *as religion,* not just as a source of legitimacy, money, or social capital.

More broadly, this chapter analyzes how PICO avoids falling into antidemocratic, bureaucratic patterns common in political organizations—that is, succumbing to the "iron law of oligarchy" (Michels 1915), the sociological truism that oligarchic pressures from inside political movements ultimately undermine their democratic thrust. Through the patterns of organizational culture examined here, participants cultivate the skills, vision, anger, and hope that sustain their commitment. I argue that the key to those patterns of organizational culture lies in understanding how participants infuse meaning into the work of organizing by drawing on ethical traditions rooted in democratic strands of religious belief—and how this, in turn, places the work of faith-based organizing in a moral-political context that is its greatest strength. Thus, though the most visible and politically effective aspect of this work lies in the kinds of political actions we have seen in previous chapters, the real source of faith-based organizing's success lies in the backstage processes that generate its moral-political culture.

As one moves from church to church in Oakland or from federation to federation around the United States, the organizational cultures of faith-based organizing shift somewhat to reflect regional cultural differences, differing mixes of ethnic groups and religious traditions, and different leadership styles within a local organization. Nonetheless, a shared culture clearly joins these PICO federations, reinforced by shared practices, beliefs, and organizational ethos.[9] Chapter 1 described the key practices; I here look at them more interpretively, with an eye to how they contribute to the cultural work and ethical leverage of faith-based organizing. Next, I consider the primary beliefs that inform those practices, as expressed in official mission statements and in interviews; these include beliefs rooted in grassroots democratic traditions and in religious ethical traditions. Finally, I analyze the ethos or feel of organizational life that shapes these practices and beliefs—including the role of anger, conflict, and joy in the organizing process—describing it as an ethos of "ethical democracy." This ethos is carried by relational and authoritative organizing techniques *as those techniques are infused with* moral-political meaning drawn from the incorporation of religious symbols, commitments, stories, and assumptions. Throughout, I argue that most of the real "action" in faith-based organizing is built upon this combination.[10]

Interpreting the Practices of Faith-Based Organizing

Several practices of faith-based organizing not only serve to build the organization by creating what social movement scholars call "mobilizing networks," but also provide settings in which significant cultural work occurs. We thus turn to a more interpretive look at some of the organizing practices first described in chapter 1, in order to better highlight the cultural work embedded in these practices, including their strengths and weaknesses.

One-to-Ones

Recall how central the practice of relationship building through one-to-one meetings is within the faith-based organizing model. A core part of this one-to-one organizing process is building trust. Ultimately, it is interest in a specific issue plus the trust built up through the one-to-one process that gets people to the large political actions sponsored by faith-based organizing.

In doing one-to-ones, initial access to a person's own preexisting friends comes easily, due to the trust already embedded in the friendship. With others, once a relationship has been established, trust can be built up through ongoing contact. But gaining initial access to launch this process beyond one's circle of friends, with strangers and even neighbors, can be enormously difficult. Trust is simply too scarce in many settings (Putnam 2000; Nohria and Eccles 1992). Here, the church context becomes critical; in an initial phone call or encounter at church, leaders gain acquiescence for in-person contact by citing common membership in a church (or, to a lesser extent, even different churches), noting the pastor's endorsement of the organizing process and using shared linguistic markers to show their church association. Such markers include citing the pastor's name or discussing this work as part of the church's ministry. They thus avoid having to make cold contact and talk their way into the front door and are instead usually welcomed into the home.

Religion and the symbolic authority derived from it are central in one-to-ones in another way. During one-to-ones, participants often spoke in religious terms: "I just know God wants something better for my kids"; "Jesus does not want us livin' holed up here, afraid to go out on the streets"; "God bless you for comin' all the way over here to talk with me; I'll come to your action, 'cause you ministered to me here today"; "If you're working in the Spirit, I'll be right there alongside you." When I conducted one-to-ones as part of my own role as a marginal participant during ethnographic fieldwork, such language was a regular feature of these meetings.[11] Occasionally, I sat in shared prayer at an interviewee's request at the start or end of a one-to-one. One such occasion led to the following prayer: "Lord Jesus, help us work together to change things here. Thank you for this new friend. Give us your Spirit and your power, and we will turn this city around for [his son] and for everybody."[12] Far from being otherworldly escapes from real engagement in concrete social conditions, such language often appeared to be leaders' most heartfelt and "grounded" expression of passionate commitment to social engagement.

Credentials

The strategic function of the organizational "credentials" that start most public meetings in this model is to assert a powerful public profile of the organization by claiming to represent the interests of thousands or tens of thousands of constituents. Beyond this, though, the credential serves several crucial cultural functions within the organization that shape and strengthen the self-identity of the group as a whole and of the individuals that compose it.

First, given that most local organizing committees meet in church facilities and are made up primarily of church members, faith-based organizing must work to construct a sense of organizational mission that transcends the interior world of the church. The credential is one tool for doing so. Through it, each meeting begins by affirming that this organization transcends purely internal church matters and exists in order to address the situation of the wider society. The strongest such credentials articulate this role both in terms lying close to the heart of the religious tradition present (as part of "Jesus' ministry," "God's call in our lives," "the work of the Spirit," as rooted in "human dignity," etc.) *and* in civic terms familiar within the secular political milieu ("improving the quality of life," "bettering conditions in our neighborhoods," or again reflecting "human dignity"). In combining the two elements, these credentials help participants understand the organizing work as in keeping with their own sense of religious calling as understood in their tradition, while at the same time linking the psychological dynamism of religious experience to the effort to transform the social world.

Second, by requiring leaders to articulate the power basis of the organization, over time the credential may socialize them into greater comfort with the instrumental and broadly political nature of community organizing. This may appear to be a minor concern, but multiple encounters with new participants expressing discomfort with the instrumental character of organizing convince me that it represents a significant challenge. The credential, in asking members to articulate—in a church context—an understanding of their organization as a "power organization," helps leaders to contextualize organizing within their religious tradition's understanding of the moral dimensions of social reform.

Prayer

Though public prayer within the organizing process provides a forum for significant cultural work, I wish to avoid reducing it to a narrowly instrumental dimension. People pray for a great variety of reasons, and some draw profound spiritual sustenance from their prayer practices, both public and private.[13] Still, the practice of public prayer colors the organizing process so extensively that ignoring it would distort our picture of the political culture of faith-based organizing.

Most crucially, prayer located the organizing process within the context of a reality transcending instrumentalist power politics. Prayer was the most visible marker communicating to new participants that this was not just another effort to exert power around narrow self-interests, but rather something linked to a broader vision of the common good and their own religiously grounded view of social justice.[15] Of course, prayer alone does not make this claim a reality. But public prayer signals to participants and outsiders that this is a different kind of political organization; this in turn creates pressure to back this claim up in the day-to-day work of the organization internally and in negotiations with power holders. One resulting message is that political work—both that of elected leaders and that of the organization—will be judged not just by how successful it is, but also according to ethical values embedded in religious traditions, such as social justice, the rights of the poor, the responsibility of authority, the call to service, etc.

Like the credential, public prayer also provides a forum for identity work for both the organization and the individual, one that roots political work in shared faith commitments of participants. Including prayer in public meetings prevents participants from easily compartmentalizing themselves into a "secular self" separate from their "religious self" enacted in other settings; instead, this creates a setting in which these often fragmented identities can be integrated and enacted publicly as "whole selves." Given the vibrancy of religious commitment and experience in many Americans' lives—for some, one of the few settings in which they feel "authentic"— this serves to buttress the passion and confidence with which they approach political engagement. They *feel* God's presence with them as they move onto a public stage.

Actions

Even the most instrumental of organizing practices, the political action or accountability session, is also used as an opportunity for cultural work by organizers. This is obviously true in the sense that all of the above practices occur as part of or in connection with political actions, but it is also true in a larger, less obvious sense: public conflict itself is used by organizers as a tool to do cultural work on the organization itself.

Understanding this requires some attention to the relationship between faith-based organizations and elected officials. Though those relations are sometimes quite conflictive, the interest of organizers in using government to make real improvements in participants' quality of life appears to orient them strongly to establishing "partnership" relationships with elected officials, in order to gain a voice in shaping policy. But this runs a risk of being co-opted by established political interests. In order to avoid being drawn into too-cozy relationships with political officials, organizers typically believe it critical that local organizing committees demonstrate their willingness to enter into public conflict with elected leaders. In interviews, many said such conflict establishes a public profile that commands respect in the rough-and-tumble political arena and deepens the confidence of leaders. Crucially, it also serves as a kind of ritual affirmation of the community organization as an autonomous authority structure, not simply beholden to and thus not a tool of elected political authority.

Organizers and experienced leaders will therefore periodically argue for initiatives they know elected officials may not support, denounce a lack of responsiveness from a given official, or otherwise "raise the tension level" in political relationships—all in order to keep the internal culture of their own organization capable of dealing constructively with official conflict. This tends to be played out as front-stage political strategy, but often is at least in part a form of backstage cultural work on the organization. Because organizers see a periodic need for this kind of cultural work, the tension within faith-based organizing between partnership and political conflict is not likely to disappear. It sometimes bewilders public officials, who would prefer a cozier relationship with these organizations and instead find them occasionally "needlessly confrontational," as one said in an interview. But conflict helps keep organizations from becoming complacent, and thus potentially able to keep pushing institutional politics in a democratic direction.[15] A key cultural task of organizing thus involves engaging in conflict when appropriate, yet sustaining an ethical and political tone that positions the organization to enter into partnerships—even with those with whom it has been in conflict.

Evaluation Sessions

Cultural work in evaluation sessions occurs in several ways. Along with trainings, evaluation sessions give PICO staff their primary forum for leadership formation. Given the very backstage role taken by staff during actions, evaluations are their opportunity to coach leaders—which they do very strategically, encouraging specific lessons from whatever occurred in actions or meetings. By giving their own feedback and by eliciting feedback from other leaders, staff use evaluations to invite leaders to think critically about their own roles during public events.

Evaluation sessions also provide an opportunity for the staff to assess whether their own work has been effective. Given the perception of staff organizers as experts, less experienced leaders are often reluctant to assess staff roles critically; thus, the best organizers I observed structured evaluations so that leaders were asked specifically what the staff had done well and what they had done less effectively. But this occurred only sporadically, as it requires staff confident enough to risk public criticism of their role.

Finally, staff use evaluations to shape the long-term dynamics and assumptions underlying the organizing process. For example, on one occasion an organizer applauded the way one moderator had drawn on religious symbols and language to "give spirit" to the action—later explaining to me that he wanted to undermine leaders' assumption that religious believers need to censor all religious language in the public realm. Likewise, organizers used evaluations to draw attention to the productive aspect of some of the conflict that leaders had experienced vis-à-vis the targets of the action, and thus to encourage leaders to accept conflict as a potentially constructive force.

Trainings

A variety of training sessions serve to develop leaders' relational, analytic, political, and public speaking skills. Trainings occur briefly during regular organizational meetings, more substantially during periodic half-day or daylong workshops, and very intensively during national leadership retreats. Many trainings are quite participative, employing pedagogical techniques pioneered by Paulo Freire (1970, 1973) in Brazil but now commonly used in adult education worldwide.

A local organizing committee meeting at one Oakland church, Saint Columba's, provides an example of a typical training. Art Rose, trained as a minister in the African Methodist Episcopal denomination but now a full-time organizer with PICO, sought to explain the faith-based organizing model to new leaders. He began by drawing a large, irregular shape on a blackboard, saying this "rock" represented the "issue" or "problem" around which the group would be organizing at a given time. He continued:

> Most issues we're concerned about in our community are big enough
> that even all of us here together can't move them. So what do we do?
> Well, how do you move a rock that's too big to move? You use a lever,

don't you? [draws a long lever at an angle, wedged under the rock]. The length of that stick, that lever, is the amount of knowledge we have together about this issue. The more we know about it, about possible solutions to it, the more leverage we have. . . . But a stick by itself isn't enough to move a rock, is it? What else do you need? Something to pry against [draws a fulcrum for the lever]. That firm place, that thing we'll pry against to move the issue, that's our decision to do something about this issue. We have to have decided that we're going to change things, and be firm about that.

What else do we need? We need some force at the other end of the lever, don't we? We have to push at the other end, in order to move the issue [draws an arrow, pushing down at end of the lever]. That force is the number of people we turn out for an action; that's what provides some force to move an issue. Together, it's our knowledge about an issue, plus our numbers, that move an issue. . . . Research gives us knowledge . . . it has to be good knowledge, deep knowledge, because if the stick is too thin, it will break.

In this example, Rose stuck with secular themes, striving to help leaders understand organizing practices. But he immediately connected it to religious themes, motivations, and meanings by noting that practicing these techniques would allow the group to "do the work God calls us to do in this world." Later in the meeting, he invited the group to close with a prayer, during which they asked in fervent tones for the confidence to "really build relationships with people," for God's guidance in "cultivating power to change the situation for our youth," and for the ability to gain the knowledge they would need to do so.

This training sought to provide techniques to achieve instrumental goals, but these goals are linked explicitly to spiritual practices and self-understandings rooted in faith. Other trainings I witnessed "worked" more directly on religious culture by reflecting on the Gospel of Mark in order to understand the ways that Jesus engaged in conflict with the authorities of his time—thus suggesting religious sanction for the conflict inherent in community organizing.[16] Still others extended the Alinsky democratic tradition by asking how it related to "biblical values" or Catholic social teaching, and by reflecting critically on whether political leaders were necessarily corrupt or might be important partners for constructive political change. The success of faith-based organizing is often rooted in this kind of cultural work; its weaknesses are often tied to failure to dynamically combine diverse cultural strands.[17]

Challenging and Holding Accountable

Challenging and holding accountable (discussed in chapter 1) are the key tools of internal organizational discipline in faith-based organizing and thus are crucial to understanding its political culture. Challenging occurs mostly in one-to-one settings; holding accountable occurs mostly in group settings. Through them, the interpersonal, organizational, and political skills of leaders, pastors, and organizers are developed and channeled into the work of the organization. Much of what leaders in interviews cited as their personal development through organizing appears to occur through being challenged and held accountable by others—not always comfortably.

Together, these practices represent the core techniques of the faith-based organizing model. They also serve as a template for transferring that model to new cities; it is largely on these practices that PICO focuses when expanding its network to new cities. But practices do not exist in isolation; they come infused with a set of beliefs and an organizational ethos that are as much a part of PICO's internal culture as are these practices—though often less noticed.

The Belief System of Faith-Based Organizing: Civic and Religious Meanings

Participants use a variety of cultural elements to express their understandings of what faith-based organizing is all about. In this sense, the beliefs underlying PICO's organizational culture represent less a unified whole than a rope of many fibers. But two main cultural traditions intertwine to form the main cords of the culture of faith-based organizing: the civic and political traditions of grassroots democracy and the ethical traditions of religion. Each cord, in turn, is made up of several related cultural strands.

Official mission statements provide some initial clues to these organizations' fundamental beliefs—or rather, those beliefs they wish to highlight publicly. The most extensive mission statement that appears in official PICO documents in recent years reads:[18]

> PICO's mission is to assist in the building of community organizations with the power to improve the quality of life of families and neighborhoods. PICO carries out its mission through leadership training seminars; the recruitment and development of professional community organizers; and ongoing consultation and technical assistance.

Through the PICO Network, people learn to participate in and influence our political system and democratic institutions. Those who were previously ignored, excluded or apathetic become involved. People's stake in
our society is made real. Family life is strengthened. The once-torn fabric
of neighborhoods and communities is rewoven. At the very heart of this
mission is the process of helping people help themselves.

Local organizing activities within the PICO Network are guided by the
principles and concepts found in the Congregation-Community Model of
Community Organization. Congregations of all denominations are the
building blocks of the community organization. The members of a local
congregation and those living in the neighborhood join together in a powerful expression of unity that transcends racial, ethnic, and income differences. PICO seeks to involve all elements of a community based on the
following principles:

- Respect for human dignity
- Creation of a just society
- Development of the whole person

Such official statements of purpose reveal several key beliefs within faith-
based organizing, the self-understanding of its participants, and some of
the assumptions that underlie their efforts.

First, organizing staff quite self-consciously understand their role as the
"building of community organizations"—which they pointedly distinguish
from "activism," "mobilization," or being part of a "social movement." But
of course they do mobilize people, and analytically the field of faith-based
organizing clearly constitutes a social movement. Categorizing themselves
as engaging in "organizing" in contrast to a "movement" represents organizers' way of setting off faith-based organizing from the activist movements that they perceive as having failed in the late 1960s and 1970s because they failed to build an organized base. They see these movements as
closely tied to ideological assumptions about what lower-class people ought
to believe and as rooted in university life-worlds largely divorced from the
experience of lower-class neighborhoods and families.

Second, the mission statement's treatment of "power" captures both the
belief that Alinsky's work represents a key touchstone for faith-based organizing and the belief that the field has successfully transcended the limits
of his work. The opening reference to "building community organizations
with power" as PICO's central mission directly echoes Alinsky's constant
emphasis on building "power organizations." Yet the statement taken as a
whole considerably mutes this emphasis by embedding it within references

to society, family, reweaving the social fabric, congregations, racial and class unity, and ethical principles drawn from (though not here explicitly connected to) faith traditions.

This muted emphasis on power, rather than being a product of organizational weakness, appears to reflect real organizational strength: the strongest faith-based federations are confident enough of their access to political power that they need not hit this note particularly loudly. However, these organizations remain true descendants of the Alinsky tradition: all aspects of organizing are focused on building sufficient power vis-à-vis the political environment to address the problems of involved communities. As a result, remarkably little explicit attention is paid to formalizing power within the organization: on one hand, as noted in chapter 2, this can allow fluid power relations among staff, pastors, and leaders; on the other hand, power dynamics within faith-based organizing are left so unscrutinized that it is sometimes unclear where real power lies.

The mission statement's reference to "improving the quality of life" as the ultimate goal serves as a kind of unobjectionable final goal used to galvanize involvement while avoiding ideological arguments that might bog down the organizing process. But of course every organization must ultimately choose some goals over others. "Improving the quality of life" as the central goal brings with it the danger that the organization will address only those issues most immediately and obviously affecting local residents (e.g., crime and street improvements) rather than more distant or complex issues that affect local residents at least as deeply (e.g., job loss, economic restructuring, and the decay of the political process). Organizers' commitment to keeping overarching goals vague appears to flow from their belief that any articulated ideology risks organizational stagnation and only opens the organization up to political critique. In the hands of more sophisticated organizers, "quality of life" serves as a kind of contentless cipher that focuses participants' attention while organizers gradually build an experienced leadership base and reflect *with local leaders* on what changes might actually make the most difference to their communities. In less skilled hands, it serves to evade deep political analysis of goals and trade-offs.

A fourth foundational belief common in the culture of community organizing is carried in the phrase "participate in and influence our political system and democratic institutions." The implicit assumption behind community organizing is that American political institutions can be forced to open up to participation and influence by previously marginalized groups. Faith-based organizing thus tends to accept the legitimacy of liberal political institutions even while pushing them in more democratic directions and to reject the antiestablishment stance more typical in some versions of radical democracy. However, important strands of radical democracy are preserved in faith-based organizing, primarily in its commitment to organizing in poor and less-affluent areas, as reflected in the phrase "those who were previously ignored, excluded, or apathetic." This phrase echoes a common pair of beliefs expressed in interviews with organizers: that American political institutions are so dominated by money that they effectively exclude those without access to money, but that marginalization is not inevitable and that those excluded must be challenged to organize themselves to redemocratize our political institutions.

The salience in PICO's mission statement to the principles of "respect for human dignity," "creation of a just society," and "development of the whole person" gets replicated in trainings, literature, and interviews throughout the network (sometimes with additional "values" such as "community" or "unity"). While clearly rooted in Scripture and other Jewish or Christian sources, as phrased here in nonreligious language they provide an ethically grounded cultural basis for participants regardless of their religious affiliation.[19]

Though a useful place to begin to discern the key beliefs informing modern faith-based organizing, official mission statements fail to express the full legacy of the various cultural currents that have shaped the internal culture of the field. A fuller understanding requires looking at the way participants actually talk about their work.[20]

Grassroots Democracy

We have heard the grassroots democratic cultural strands of civic republicanism, populism, radical democracy, and the New Left at play in political actions whenever participants have invoked such themes as community, citizenship, democracy, accountability, and power.

One belief lying at the core of nearly all community organizing efforts in the United States, with roots in political thought at least back to Machiavelli, is the notion that effective political action must be built around participants' "self-interest." Alinsky dedicates whole sections of his books to convincing his reader of the importance of self-interest in politics; he thus writes:

> From the great teachers of Judaeo-Christian morality and the philoso-
> phers, to the economists, and to the wise observers of the politics of man,

there has always been universal agreement on the part that self-interest plays as a prime moving force in man's behavior. The importance of self-interest has never been challenged; it has been accepted as an inevitable fact of life. (1971, 53)

This assertion seems rather baldly one-dimensional, but the notion of self-interest at its core serves as the nexus for much of the early training of organizers and leaders. The key question, of course, is what is really meant by "self-interest." We examine this meaning below; here, I note only that its centrality for politics constitutes a core belief of faith-based organizing.

A second key belief flowing from the grassroots democratic strand of faith-based organizing culture is that organizers see their main job as "developing leaders." Denise Collazo, now the director of PICO's project in San Francisco, thus described her mission as an organizer:

> The way I think of community organizing is getting people the tools to change their communities. So it's not doing things for people, because if I do everything and then I leave, what happens? I think of it as teaching people how to look at things [so that] once I'm gone they can continue to make change in the neighborhood. It's more than just winning an issue. . . . Taking people who when you first met them would never dare go talk to someone else in a one-on-one, and then taking them to the point where they will play a role in a citywide action. Most of our work is leadership development. It's not just winning issues.

Though Collazo focuses on contrasting leadership development with "winning issues," implicit here as well is a contrast with what organizers see as ideologically driven political organizing, in which organizers are believed to impose their issue commitments on others. But of course organizers bring passionate commitment to some issues and not to others, and have significant power to shape which issues are taken up by an organization, as we saw in chapter 2. The focus on developing leaders serves to partially subject this passion to the power of leaders to set their organization's agenda. Promotion of this belief among organizers appears to serve two functions: to keep organizers focused on long-term development of organizational capacity, rather than becoming overly invested in the up-and-down rhythm of particular issue campaigns, and to keep organizers grounded in relationships with participants rather than primarily motivated by prior ideological positions to which other participants are not committed. The commitment to developing leaders as a primary goal thus becomes a unifying belief intended to substitute for any shared ideology.

A third core democratic belief is best described as an affirmation of the sheer joy and political importance of collective action. Participants previously marginalized out of public life take pleasure in experiencing themselves as effective agents, whether in winning issues or simply being taken seriously by those who hold local power.[21] Thus, Willie Mae Randerson's joy in recounting how her organization in a very low-income neighborhood in Pensacola forced a meeting with the local police chief:

> We had called for an appointment and they kept giving us the run-around. So finally fifteen of us loaded into our cars and went down. We asked to see the chief of police, saying, "We are taxpayers and we have a right to see him." So he sends another person out to tell us, "The chief is busy, he doesn't have time to see you." [But] these people in the neighborhood pay the same taxes as the people in the upper-class neighborhood, and I told them we were going to sit and we were not going to move until we saw the chief of police. After forty-five minutes he came out and he opened the door and told us to come in. . . . Now that felt good!

The political importance of collective action was expressed in the populist vision of participatory democracy expressed by Florida community organizer Peter Phillips:

> [Community organizing] is the next natural progression of democracy because our institutions don't work at the polls. There is a need to give people in communities a mechanism to participate and to reweave the fabric of communities which have been so destroyed over the last forty years. The other thing that makes this an extension of democracy is that everyone can participate in this, because it's not set up for activists. It's set up for everybody, so our strongest leaders are not activists. They're not previously activists, they're mostly people who have never done anything in the community before.

The key influence of grassroots democratic traditions on the culture of faith-based organizing are found in the principles that organizers are taught as part of their training. No canonical list of faith-based organizing's core principles exists, but PICO organizer Jim Keddy suggested the following as central (drawn from Alinsky's writings, PICO trainings and verbal traditions, and common political wisdom):

- Power rests in relationship
- No permanent allies or enemies, only interests
- Action *in* reflection
- Never do for others what they can do for themselves
- People can't be held accountable for what they don't understand
- Self-interest moves us
- Further away from a problem, easier to philosophize
- Go in stupid, come out smart
- Power only respects power
- Push a negative far enough, it becomes a positive (and vice versa)
- Power defines the rules
- Take people where they are/Stay within experience
- Real power is hidden
- Relationships are reciprocal
- Challenge in relationship
- Change involves tension
- Organization is not about issues, it's about people (who care about issues)
- Small is beautiful
- Define the situation and you'll control the outcome
- Empowerment is developmental
- Power is taken, not given
- Rewards go to the people who do the work
- First revolution is internal
- When in doubt, do one-to-one's.

One striking aspect of this list is its combination of a predominant focus on power as a core organizing principle and the way power is understood in highly relational terms, so that power accumulation remains embedded in processes of interpersonal communication between relative equals. The former is what makes faith-based organizing effective in bringing politicians and other elite decision makers to public meetings and to the negotiating table. The latter at least partially counteracts the risk of being "colonized" by the logic of power—that is, allowing the relational and communicative processes intended to humanize and democratize political decision making to become distorted by precisely the narrow power dynamics the organization is striving to change.[22]

A final politically oriented belief that drives the faith-based organizing process—at least where it has most fully entered the policy making arena—represents a step beyond the Alinsky legacy. In some places, faith-based organizing today appears to have embraced a stance more indebted to the heritage of representative democracy. This cultural shift both reflects and allows the organizations' practice of partnership and negotiation vis-à-vis institutional leaders in the political and economic arenas. For example, New Orleans city councilperson Jim Singleton contrasted PICO's stance in dealing with him to that of another community organization rooted more exclusively in a radical-participatory democratic heritage:

> [Other organization] tries to intimidate you. They try to take control of things. They try to take credit for things that they had no part in. But the big offensive part to me was that they didn't always tell the truth. They'd lie if necessary in order to get their point over. Everything they did was for the public relations value. . . . PICO is a community-based organization and their basic value is to organize and get people involved . . . and these were all basically law-abiding, religious-type people who attended a church and who had a great deal of respect for their pastor or their priest. Anybody would be a fool to say no to PICO. . . . I haven't found them to be the kind of people who disrespect my position.

Though this passage reflects multiple dimensions of PICO's work, one facet of it is the way this politician sees PICO in New Orleans as respecting authority, apparently including his own role as a political representative. Radical democratic distrust of elites would make partnership and negotiation with political elites morally and politically suspect. PICO's partial embrace of a more representative understanding of democracy makes such partnership imaginable and desirable.

Religious Social Ethics

Faith-based organizing rests on extensive cultural beliefs drawn from religious social ethics, including strands rooted in traditions of Catholic social teaching, African American social ministry, white Protestant social gospel, and Hispanic popular religiosity (including extended family and *compadrazgo*). More recently, elements have been incorporated out of the traditions of Jewish social ethics, social evangelicalism, liberation theology, Pentecostalism, etc.[23]

We have seen some of these religious cultural elements in action in the descriptions of organizing events. The organizing process regularly draws on such religious cultural elements as the concepts of social justice, following Jesus, community, the Kingdom of God, liberation, the Jewish concepts of mitzvah and tzedakah, etc. All these concepts are invoked in the course of faith-based organizing in order to present a common set of insights: God does not embrace worldly injustice, but rather calls prophetic figures to denounce it; God wants people to engage in this-worldly work for societal transformation; God accompanies and sustains them when they dedicate themselves to this work; and, in the words of an African American pastor quoted in chapter 1, holding a Bible, "This is a book of *liberation!*"

All these are powerful beliefs, strongly present for many participants, typically carried within believers as orientations and assumptions rooted in worship life, biblical teaching, and individual prayer—as well as articulated in official documents.[24] To emphasize the latter, however, risks misrepresenting these beliefs as primarily intellectual traditions. They are often more affectively held than that, in ways linked to worship and prayer; later chapters analyze this further, in examining the role of specific religious cultures in faith-based organizing.

Whether or not the religious cultural strands are important for the work of faith-based organizing is a matter of some difference of opinion among organizers. The "first language" in which many organizers express their views on this is the abstract language of "values"; a typical expression in interviews was "religious faith provides the values that guide our work." This provides a convenient way of bridging different faith traditions, but does not do justice to the way the religiously committed actually *carry* those values: attached to specific symbols, stories, songs, and intuitions of the divine. When asked how faith shapes the organizing process, organizer Denise Collazo began with the abstract values language, but immediately connected it to more concrete cultural elements:

> I think one most important thing is that [our work] is value based. The ability to talk about why we are doing this [comes from] looking at the Bible and the specific stories we all know. We have all been brought up hearing and using these examples or symbols as the reason why we do this.

More clearly still, when asked what role religious values play, organizer Art Rose drew on the fluent social Christianity of his African American church tradition:

> Values [pause]. Well, yes, but it's just much more real than that. It's people's *faith* that God's with them. When we read Exodus, we *know* a God of freedom. When we sing the songs, we *feel* that. When I preach, I'm not talking about values, I'm talking about *Jesus!* [emphasis noted by italics]

That is, biblical stories, songs of the faith, the preached word, and religious symbols help participants articulate why they do the work of organizing, thus helping generate meaning, motivation, and solidarity in the organizing process. As we shall see, these gain their resonance through the ritual dynamics of worship: shared commitment through assent in hearing the Word, partaking in communion, and the other rituals of faith traditions.

Participants also commonly affirm that, by drawing on religious motivations and teachings, faith-based organizing can and does transcend ideological divisions between left and right. Given the primary geographic location of these organizations in urban areas, and their orientation toward working-class economic issues, those who identify as strong political conservatives are less common among faith-based organizing participants. But they are certainly present—and organizations often go out of their way to try to make them feel welcome. Reverend Paul Bryant, a Southern Baptist minister in Pensacola, Florida, articulated the notion of religiously anchored transcendence of political divides:

> See, the ironic thing is I'm a conservative, biblically and politically. You usually don't see that kind of bird involved in this type of work, but I believe we have to avail ourselves of this model. This is not something for the left or right, it's something for God's people to be engaged in.

Whether this transcendence of political differences can be sustained over the long term is an open question, beyond my purposes here. But many participants believe that it can be and appear committed to ideological diversity.

Another belief expressed regularly by organizers and less often by pastors holds that churches often foster good intentions and networks of social ties but are markedly ineffective in making those intentions or social networks relevant in the political realm. Thus, Reverend Willie Gore, a pastor in Mobile, Alabama, notes, "PICO has given us some courage to do things we should have been doing all along. They have helped to show you how to do these things. We [the church] know a lot of things but we just don't know how to go about it." This was echoed by Mike Kromrey, a PICO organizer in Colorado: "A lot of stuff in the churches is all about prayer and relationship, but they never move the relationships to do anything."

A final key organizing belief rooted in religion appears to be drawn from Catholic distinctions between the role of laypersons and clergy. Father Joseph Justice of Orange County, California, expressed the belief that the primary work of organizing is properly the province of laypersons, but that clergy have primary responsibility for seeing that it continues to reflect and draw on religious inspiration and ethical guidance:

> My whole goal is to get the laypeople involved in this. My role in it is to keep the faith orientation going. We have a reason why we are doing [faith-based organizing]. It is not disconnected from everything else we do. All this time we spend at Mass and at prayer, at catechism classes and all of those things, somewhere it has to be expressed. And this is one of the important ways of expressing it. . . . I think we would be deficient without community organizing because it seems to me this is very much what so many of our church documents talk about. And it does it in a respectful, healthy, good way. I think for some pastors the temptation would be to take it over and impose their agendas as well. And I think that is a dangerous thing, because that basically is taking away people's authority and power.[25]

Linking Civic and Religious Meanings: The Legitimacy of Authority

The belief that political elites can be legitimate representatives of community interests rests on a broader organizational assumption nowhere articulated explicitly: the belief that authority *itself* can be exercised legitimately. This may be the most subtle but crucial cultural element that faith-based organizing draws from its institutional base in churches; it not only allows organizers, pastors, and leaders to adopt authoritative roles with one another and with potential participants, but also lets the organization collaborate with political and economic elites believed to operate responsibly and accountably.

Even in the midst of such collaborative partnerships, however, note how organizer Judy Reyes conditions partnership on respect for the organization's autonomy. In reflecting on PICO's relationship with the then-mayor of Oakland, she said:

> I don't know if there can really be collaboration, if he doesn't perceive us as powerful enough to be his equal. So to me, this is a principle: If you are on equal terms, or each of you sees the other with equal respect, you can be pretty collaborative. But if that doesn't exist, there isn't a good reason to do it, because someone is going to exploit you.

Thus, sufficient organizational autonomy and power allow the stronger federations to enter into mutually beneficial partnerships with elected officials. Yet such partnerships themselves can only develop if the organization sees elite leaders of political institutions as legitimate—or at least potentially legitimate. One source for such an orientation comes from participants' encounter with elites in other institutions, including their religious congregations: if they have experienced authority being legitimately exercised in those institutions, they may be more open to the possibility that authority can also be exercised legitimately—and accountably—by political elites. At an abstract level, then, authority becomes a key cultural resource transported from one institutional setting into another.

Summary: Beliefs in Faith-Based Organizing

These main cultural strands of grassroots democracy and religious ethics coexist with other cultural currents flowing into faith-based organizing from contemporary American society: spiritualist escapism, therapeutic culture, expressive individualism, utilitarian individualism, antigovernment resentment, consumptive narcissism, cutthroat competitive culture, and others. But those discussed above are key in setting the internal political culture of faith-based organizing apart from the wider culture. Organizers affirm them throughout the organizing process and use them to undermine the latter, less politically constructive cultural currents. This is a crucial aspect of their role as architects of a counterhegemonic political culture.

Religious ethics and realistic political beliefs sometimes coexist uneasily within the church-PICO nexus. Yet eloquent testimonies from numerous leaders suggest that combining them well can radically transform people's political identities. Mary Ellen Burton-Christie, a leader in the PICO federation with a background in the radical Catholic Worker tradition, reflects on this:

> I think there was a time when singing "God Bless America" would have made me ill. But [today] if we had an action and we sang it together, it would make me cry because of who was singing it and because of how much they meant it and because it wouldn't be "God Bless America instead of everybody else," it would be "God be with us in our lives, we need you here." I am not usually very sympathetic to patriotic kinds of things like that, although I think organizing is a very patriotic thing to do. I think that being active in a democracy is very patriotic. We are being active participants in a democracy. That means a lot more to me now than it did ten years ago.

The Ethos of Faith-Based Organizing: Ethical Democracy

The faith-based organizing process integrates the practices and cultural beliefs discussed above within an ethos or "feel of life" within these organizations best described as a commitment to "ethical democracy." Underlying this process is the anger at the status quo—the lack of health care, poor schools for their children, dearth of good jobs, violence in their streets—held by those who suffer the most under current social arrangements. The channeling of this anger into public life occurs within an organizing context shaped by ethical passion and constraint rooted in religious culture and radical democracy. Characterizing the overall tenor of faith-based organizing as ethical democracy offers a way to summarize both its democratic and ethical facets and how anger becomes a constructive source for democratic action.[26]

Imagine the complex political culture of faith-based organizing, with all its variations and subtleties, as a musical composition as complex as jazz; one can pick out notes and subthemes from many of the political currents at play in American culture today, including strong strands from various religious cultures plus periodic fragments of shallow pragmatism, therapeutic culture, and antigovernment populism. But as the main theme in a jazz masterpiece is constantly reinvoked, the dominant themes in faith-based organizing are participatory democracy and representative democracy.

Participatory democracy is the core of the *internal* organizing process within PICO culture. This generates constant consultation with neighbors, friends, and coreligionists through the one-to-one process—to elicit their involvement, but also to check out their support and/or distance from the direction being contemplated in the organization. It explains, too, the emphasis placed by staff on developing leaders as the most satisfying dimension of their work. For many of them, democratic renewal is primarily a matter of forming enough leaders capable of sustaining reformist civic participation.

Since professional organizers carry highly influential roles as bandleaders within the organizing process, this dominant chord of participatory democracy is crucial. In its absence or diminishment, the organizational structure might easily become a tool manipulated by a few, rather than a forum for engagement by the many. This generates extensive grassroots participation—albeit in a fairly controlled form, what participants term "discipline." The plural sources of authority within faith-based organizing help check this tendency, but the constant emphasis on participatory democracy within the organizing process remains the most crucial countervailing force.

However, the *external* face presented by faith-based organizing in its relations with officials, political actions, and other public settings is far less participatory; rather, the tenor is one of representative democracy on two levels. First, those who have played key roles in the organizing process represent the entire constituency to external institutions and actions never include an open forum for discussion. Second, political officials are largely treated as legitimate representatives of the body politic—or at least assumed to be so unless participants come to believe they have forfeited that legitimacy. While officials are kept on remarkably tight reins at political actions, sometimes with as little as two minutes to respond to the organizations' proposals, and shown little tolerance if they strive to expound much or "take over our agenda," they are not typically treated disrespectfully nor asked to subject themselves to endless participatory politics. The *external* tenor of organizing is that of representative democracy, held to accountability by a participatory process that occurs in *internal* settings.

I term PICO's ethos *"ethical democracy"* because the participatory and representative components of its ethos function within the context of a set of orientations regarding the good life and how human communities can thrive; organizers explicitly draw upon these ethical orientations to question the social status quo. In this way, alternatives that in an ethically neutral setting might be considered simple "social choice" material are highlighted as connected to fundamental values of the organization and thus as morally charged.

For example, in Oakland in the middle and late 1980s, local PICO leaders confronted the rise of crack cocaine and accompanying neighborhood deterioration. In an ethically neutral setting, this might have led the organization to sign onto the war-on-drugs strategy of increased prison construction, greater funding for law enforcement, and prisonlike conditions in some inner city neighborhoods. Instead, participants (leaders, pastors, and organizers) reflected together on the ethical implications of embracing the war on drugs and its impact on poor neighborhoods.[27] Out of these conversations, they chose to pursue better funding for treatment and prevention programs *along with* strong law enforcement to drive drug markets out of poor neighborhoods. It was also the ethical implications of this issue that helped organizers move the organization toward addressing the need for educational reform and economic development in Oakland.

The ethical spirit of democratic practice within PICO is, for many participants, central to their reasons for staying involved. Judy Reyes articulated this theme well:

> I really believe it's about the relationship and community building and that the grounding in the faith keeps us from getting too wild or too way out there as far as I am concerned. In other words, it keeps us from trashing people, our opponents, which is real important to me that we don't. We have to respect their dignity, and I think that comes from the faith base.

That this has significant political repercussions was made evident in the way some of those opponents—or, more accurately, "targets" who have been sometime opponents and sometime allies—talk about these organizations. Echoing Councilman Singleton from New Orleans (quoted above), Mayor Tom Daley of Anaheim, California, noted that, despite political differences and tensions with the local PICO organization, "I hung in there with them because they are good people—concerned, active citizens."

It is thus the modus operandi of constantly connecting practical organizing steps with the moral commitments and righteous anger of participants, long-term vision, and sophisticated political strategy that produces the ethos of ethical democracy in faith-based organizing. Sustaining that ethos requires a constant organizational balancing act.

Balancing Instrumental Politics and Ethical Reflection

Finding such a balance is not easy, as attested by the fact that participants periodically expressed displeasure with the uneasy fit between the organizing process and their own ethical comfort zone. Thus, one pastor noted, "I just don't like treating our elected officials that way. It just doesn't sit right with me." Likewise, a leader said after an action, "I can see how he [action target] got mad about us only giving him two minutes to respond. I wouldn't like that either. It doesn't seem quite fair or Christian or something." Whether or not these ethical concerns are well-founded is a judgment that belongs to organizational participants. The point here is that they represent real ethical dilemmas that, if left unaddressed, are likely to eviscerate the commitment of those who hold them. Equally importantly, when such concerns *are* well-founded they are not simply moralizing tendencies that obstruct the organizing process. Rather, they can be used to help the organization think more clearly about what kind of a public sphere it is constituting through its work. So it is in the organization's interest to get issues on the table and address them communally, as opposed to the typical practice of having individual meetings with those raising ethical concerns.

Effective community organizations thus experience an ongoing tension (at least, if they are at all responsive to the ethical issues): as active participants in the political world, they are exposed to all the instrumentalizing pressures of politics, in which relative power colors all relationships—indeed is the medium of exchange in all relationships.[28] To be effective in that arena, faith-based organizations must constantly monitor their status in the balance of power within the city's political arena. Because their low-income constituents hold few of the resources that provide political influence, these organizations cannot simply slide into the public conversation that informs policy debate. Rather, they must consciously act to accumulate sufficient power to be heard and taken seriously by more powerful actors in that realm. All these factors pressure the participants in community organizing toward an instrumental orientation in order to make democracy work for them.

At the same time, faith-based community organizations are not simply political actors. They depend enormously on the sponsoring religious institutions for access to members, in-kind contributions, financial support, and the like. Those institutions are moral communities: whatever the levels of actual moral practice within them—which of course vary widely—they share a discourse and raison d'être involving attention to the way people treat one another, the moral tenor of relationships. Equally importantly, most participants come to this work through these religious institutions and some bring deeply held moral commitments against using people. This creates an ambience within the organizing process that countervails pure instrumental calculation: treating others as manipulable means to political ends, always a possibility and often a reality in any form of political organizing, runs up against religiously grounded presumptions of human beings as ends in themselves.

This ambience does not eliminate the pressure toward instrumentalization, nor prevent it from being enacted at times. But the voices of articulate advocates of ethical constraints within political organizing are strengthened when they have recourse to a shared moral discourse that transcends calculations of political efficacy. Faith-based community organizations thus have some leverage against the instrumentalizing tendencies of power politics—and long-term effectiveness demands that they engage in ethical reflection to counterbalance those pressures.

Evaluation sessions would seem to be a natural venue for such ethical reflection, but in fact little occurs in that context. Evaluation sessions typically occur right after actions, which themselves follow weeks of intense preparation. Participants are tired, and evaluations are thus kept brief, focused narrowly on assessing the effectiveness of the action in terms of achieving organizational goals. Little effort is made to reflect on how well the event "fit" with the ethical traditions of the religious institutions, unions, or schools sponsoring the organizing process. I did not observe such reflection being actively suppressed. Rather, it is simply out of bounds; the whole organizing process assumes that organizing exists to reshape the social world and already embodies these ethical traditions.

The most viable venue within the organizing process for discerning how best to balance its ethical and instrumental dimensions are "reflections," meeting times specifically set aside to learn about or discuss the moral, political, and cultural bases of organizing. Some federations incorporate reflections regularly in their work; others rarely. A typical reflection occurred at a citywide leaders' meeting in Oakland. Some sixty PICO leaders gathered on a Saturday at a church-affiliated liberal arts college; Father Ignatius de Groot, whom we encountered in chapter 1, was first on the agenda:

> I want to reflect with you on the values we draw from the road map
> that we worked on together at our August meeting. Keep them in mind
> all day, as the values that come from our faith. . . . First, we value the *dig-
> nity* of every person. We believe that God is our Creator and Source, and
> human beings are the image of God. We must have dignity and freedom
> to be creative. . . . Often, we just fight for security, for economic benefit.
> But we are called to live as we were made, as we were meant to live. . . .
> So, for example, we believe it is better to work for home ownership, not
> just low rents; it better reflects human dignity.
>
> Second, we value *family and children*. There is no stronger quote of
> Jesus in all of Scripture than his anger at those who cause a child to fall.
> We should have this anger inside us as well, when we see what is happen-
> ing to children and to immigrants, to all those without a voice. . . .
>
> Third, we value *community and unity*. We live in a society based on
> competition; we're rarely in unity. But Scripture says that the real good,
> the right good, for women is also the good for men; the just good for His-
> panics is also the good for blacks [some leaders in the audience here say
> "yes, yes!"]. When one group receives a real good, it is good for all. . . .
> We must reject the way society sets us in competition. . . . We must work
> together. . . . Cooperation and unity are real gospel values.

Fourth, we value *justice.* All of you are church-related people. . . .
There's a danger in church groups: we want to be kind and good to people, but we do not want to set them free [again, "yes, yes!"]. . . . But we
must call for justice, out there in the world and inside our churches. . . .
We face the temptation to buy peace at the cost of justice, to trade justice
for social tranquility. But God calls us to work for justice, not just give
people things.

Here and in many reflections, PICO participants use religious language
and symbols to construct a counterhegemonic vision of citizenship.[29] That
is, they draw on religious ethical traditions, worldviews, and self-identities
to construct their understanding of the organization's work, and with it an
alternative understanding of what it means to be a human person and a
citizen of America. During my fieldwork, I witnessed reflections drawing
on Christian scripture, Catholic social teaching, the Jewish ethical tradition, the "social gospel" and Protestant denominational statements, liberation theology from Latin America, and the writings of Dr. Martin Luther
King Jr. and W. E. B. DuBois. One common purpose of these reflections
appeared to be to encourage leaders to rethink therapeutic, privatized elements of American culture and thus invigorate their public engagement.

Though reflections often draw on the key authoritative texts and symbols of particular religious traditions, they typically do so in an instrumental sense, to legitimize the issue being addressed and to mobilize the
affective commitments and interpersonal solidarities of participants. Reflections at public actions—in the heat of the battle, so to speak—typically
fit this instrumental mode.

Reflections in a less instrumental mode typically occurred during pe-
riods of less intense organizing. At such times, they often emphasized
grounding the overall organizing process within the particular religious traditions present. This occurred under themes such as scriptural endorsement
of this-worldly involvement in working for justice; organizing as an expression of personal faith, a particular religious identity, or a way to "follow
Jesus"; the need to cultivate a spirituality to sustain one through the joys
and disappointments of political organizing; and how a specific denominational tradition understands and articulates the social role of Christians.

These slower-paced reflection settings are the venues that make possible
the kind of deliberation and conversation through which faith-based federations can balance the ethical and instrumental demands of organizing.
This occurs very occasionally, as when participants engage in reflective discussion of policy issues, the role of conflict in organizing, or the ethical

trade-offs between different possible policy initiatives. Much more frequently, the pressures of the instrumental tasks of organizing win out. So such conversations occur in private, very sporadically in communal settings, and often not at all. Ethical reflection could much more profoundly guide the long-term workings of faith-based organizing if it were incorporated more systematically into communal settings of these organizations' internal public sphere.[30] We can witness the resources for and obstacles to such ethical reflection within the political culture of faith-based organizing by looking at the most consistent training received by participants: the leadership retreats sponsored by the national networks.

National Leadership Trainings

Intensive multiday leadership training workshops are offered by PICO twice a year at various locations in the United States and on similar schedules by the other networks.[31] Most of the key leaders in each federation have attended a national training, which serves as a primary means to reproduce the networks' internal political cultures. Understanding how the seeds of those cultures are planted during national trainings requires looking at the interplay there between instrumental and ethical values.[32] The central concepts in the culture of faith-based organizing that represent instrumental values are power and self-interest. Echoing Alinsky, participants constantly define local federations as power organizations and whenever asked to define their mission say something very close to "we work to build power to improve the quality of life in our communities." Staff work hard to promote a positive understanding of power within organizational culture, initially by undermining the negative connotations of the term. Thus, on the second day of a national training,[33] PICO associate director Scott Reed quickly moved a discussion of the forces causing fear and frustration in urban neighborhoods toward a focus on power, correcting a common misquotation: "We need to challenge [ourselves and others] to participate in efforts to *change* these forces. This is where power comes in. . . . Lord Acton did *not* say 'power corrupts, absolute power corrupts absolutely,' but that 'power *tends* to corrupt, and absolute power tends to corrupt absolutely.' " He went on to note that the Latin root of the word *power* means "to be able to," meaning a "capacity to act," and that "power is to responsibility like powerlessness is to irresponsibility. . . . People cannot be responsible if they do not have the power to change things—and without any power, they tend to act irresponsibly. . . . Together, power and responsibility make ownership."

Other sessions also focused on power, including one drawing on political philosophy and recent feminist writings to draw distinctions among the "three faces of power": exploitative power, manipulative power, and interactive power. Building the last of these was presented as the goal of organizing, which might have offered entree to talk about balancing instrumental and ethical demands. But given limited time and a full agenda, the ethical implications of thinking of power as interactive were not explored.[34]

Self-interest represents the second key locus of instrumental values in faith-based organizing. The term *self-interest* can be interpreted in a narrowly individualistic way and on that basis is often found objectionable by participants steeped in religious teachings against selfishness. Indeed, leaders often reacted hostilely to the idea that self-interest should be the driving force behind their involvement in community organizing. In this emphasis, faith-based organizing remains very much a descendent of Alinsky's legacy and at times mired in it. But the fundamental meaning of self-interest in faith-based organizing today has a different emphasis, well captured at the same training event by Scott Reed. The discussion of self-interest had begun in a narrowly individualistic mode, with leaders questioning the whole idea of self-interest driving their political action. In response, Reed drew on the chalkboard a diagram linking "selfishness," "self-interest," and "altruism." Reed suggested that, when he spoke of self-interest, the leaders were thinking of selfishness, and rightly rejecting this. But in rejecting selfishness, he suggested, they immediately jumped to the notion of altruism, which he characterized as acting on behalf of others with whom one has no concrete relationship. He suggested that such altruism is "often very selfish," motivated by one's own needs rather than by any real understanding of the other's needs.

Reed then argued that, properly understood, self-interest bridges individual interests and the common good—paralleling the classic understanding in Tocqueville's work ([1835–40] 1956). Reed ended by entirely jettisoning an individualistic connotation of self-interest, noting, "It's the self-interest of *our communities*. . . . We need to tap into something in real depth, important in our community."

Usage of the concept of self-interest in faith-based organizing thus can fall anywhere along a spectrum: at the simplistic end, participants sometimes insist on an individualistic interpretation, reflecting a Machiavellian, amoral understanding of self-interest. At the opposite end of the spectrum, the term can reflect a richer, morally grounded understanding. Why then use the phrase "self-interest" at all? In a sense, it remains central simply as a remnant of faith-based organizing's roots in Alinsky's work several decades ago. Yet beyond this status as received tradition, the phrase appears to serve an important political purpose as well: it prevents participants from pursuing issues with little constituency by forcing them constantly to tie their engagement back to concrete interests.

Note that beneath contrasting understandings of self-interest lie different notions of the self that holds interests: what I have called the amoral position assumes isolated selves protecting only individual interests or, at best, what is sometimes called "amoral familism," a denial of any legitimate interests beyond one's own family connections (Banfield [1958] 1967). The altruistic position assumes politically disembodied selves, doing good in the abstract and often without input from supposed beneficiaries. The "self-interested" position—perhaps poorly described by this term—assumes "selves" who are connected to other members of the community, clear about their shared interests as neighbors, residents in a city, or citizens.[35]

In its better moments, the culture of faith-based organizing thus extends self-interest in two directions; "selves" are understood as connected irrevocably to all others in the community, and "interests" are understood to encompass not just narrow economic or political stakes but also the human need for self-development and a share in the decision making that defines the community's future. Thus, the self encompasses concentric circles extending outward toward the whole community, and potentially to all humanity. Likewise, interests are linked to an understanding of the human person as an economic, political, developmental, and ultimately even moral-spiritual being.[36]

Thus, faith-based organizing's central instrumental concepts—power and self-interest—both provide at least some resources for ethical reflection, via the idea of interactive power and an expanded understanding of self-interest. But both are also sufficiently ambiguous to put up barriers to ethical reflection, especially given the pressing political tasks of organizing. A strong anchor for ethical reflection in faith-based organizing must come from other sources.

Institutionalizing Ethical Democracy: Reflection and Anger in Faith-Based Organizing

In fostering ethical reflection within PICO, the concepts of "unity," "community," and "human dignity" are invoked and matter, but are too abstract to provide a great deal of direction in the day-to-day life of the organization. The language of "building relationships" is invoked regularly by organizers and, because American culture values relationships as ethically laden, provides a means for mediating moral values into the organizing process. Yet on its own, the language of relationships offers too thin a reed to provide much moral guidance within the rough-and-tumble world of politics. Much more substantial is the ethical anchor provided by the fact that the whole organizing process is bathed in the social context of religious congregations as moral communities.

Balancing the instrumental demands of political organizing with the moral resources of congregations demands institutionalizing ethical reflection within the organizing process. This entails setting up regular opportunities for participants to talk about the ethical tensions within organizing, learn about the religious and democratic ethical traditions of American life, and reflect upon how the latter can best guide the organization.

Where talented and ethically grounded organizers combine with effective leaders and pastors dedicated to the public mission of their congregations, such reflection already occurs. The resulting combination of instrumental and ethical values can lead to real partnership between these organizations and political officials. Thus, at the end of the presentation cited above, Scott Reed noted, "In San Diego, we strove to capture the imaginations of bureaucrats, not just force their consent." But he was quick to note that none of this implies that political relations will always be smooth; sometimes, political leaders are recalcitrant and unaccountable, and "the exercise of power may become fairly uncomfortable." He gave as an example PICO's relationship with the then-mayor of New Orleans, reported to have responded angrily to the local federation's exertion of political influence, saying, "If you take me on, I'll take on the weakest one among you and take him down, embarrass him." Reed noted that, though the organization prefers interactive power, it does not eschew the rawer forms of power in such circumstances: "We do sometimes have recourse to [negative] power, if the mayor refuses to come to terms with power as interactive. . . . We use all three faces of power, but we'd better understand when and why we are doing it."

Answering this "why" question about the exercise of raw political power ultimately requires a moral-political answer anchored to an ethical worldview.

Yet this, in turn, creates a dilemma: ethical constraints on instrumental power may produce a "nicer" politics that fails to vigorously project power into the political arena. This may undermine any democratic impact, for marginalized social groups may have to generate substantial political heat simply to be heard within the political process—recent calls from political elites for a more "civil" politics notwithstanding.

Here, the flow of anger within the community organizing process becomes central. Anger about inequality; anger about kids not given an adequate education or being denied health care or being victimized by violence at school; anger at being disrespected by political leaders; anger at jobs lost—all these and more are channeled into the organizing process and used to intervene passionately in the political process. In this sense, anger indeed underlies the whole ethos of faith-based organizing.[37]

Yet these are not angry activists getting together to grind an ax or gore an ox. Participants in faith-based organizing, where it is most successful, focus this anger on particular situations, use it to build political power, channel it into conflict with those standing in the way of needed changes, and mobilize it to create passion and drama in the public realm. The term "cold anger," often applied to faith-based organizing, accurately captures this process, with one caveat: at the end of the day, when an issue has been won, even cold anger gives way among these participants to a cathartic joy expressed in celebratory postaction events.[38] This dynamic interplay of contrasting emotions helps sustain faith-based organizing and places ethical reflection at the service of long-term political effectiveness.

Conclusion

Thus, the political culture of faith-based organizing walks an interpretive tightrope, balancing between instrumental and moral values, between the pursuit of political power and relational ethics, between self-interest and common concern. The overall ethos within PICO dances precisely along this tightrope, between the demands of projecting power into the political and economic systems and the ethical constraints on directly exercising political power. At their best, faith-based federations embody in their own organizations and, through their work in congregations and other institutions, extend to the wider political culture a particular model of public engagement that integrates the political exigencies of effective organizing and an ethical vision rooted in religious practice and relational ties. One of the critical tasks of an organizer is to maintain this dynamic balance. At its best, this balancing act generates a complex understanding of self-interest (akin to Tocqueville's notion self-interest rightly understood) and a sophisticated understanding of power and authority. In the hands of less careful organizers, it can degenerate into a simplistic emphasis on self-interest narrowly conceived, on power as a bludgeon, on government as an enemy, and on the manipulative use of relationships for purely instrumental purposes.

The active incorporation of religious traditions into the organizing process introduces religious ethical leverage into the organizing process—and when done systematically, bathes that entire process in an environment of ethical reflection. In effective federations, these factors tended to produce a delicate balancing of instrumental and ethical orientations. Though purely instrumental orientations can build organizational strength in the short term, long-term thriving—in community organizing as in personal life—demands that such strength be tempered with ethical insight. If political action and negotiation are the heart of faith-based organizing, its soul lies elsewhere: in this artful balancing of the drive for political efficacy with the moral demands of religious and democratic traditions. This interweaving leads participants to affirm what I have called the symbiosis of churches and the faith-based organizing efforts examined here. In the words of Reverend Bernard Yates, pastor of an African American church in Pensacola, Florida, "PICO is saturated with the church."

This symbiosis and the ethico-political organizational culture it fosters helps sustain participants in long-term political engagement. When asked whether she could sustain her commitment to organizing without its church ties, long-time PICO leader Mary Ellen Burton-Christie replied:

> No, I don't think I could. I think that when we organize, people really do feel like they are opening up and letting God work through them. I think there are a lot of people who are really serious about that. It sounds simple to say that your faith makes a difference, but I think that's one way you hang onto hope. . . . Somehow I do, and it's not because I think that things are going to get better fast. It's because I think there's God. I think there's God.

Chapter 6

Cultural Dynamics and Political Action

Many frontline leaders of faith-based organizing testify eloquently—as did Mary Ellen Burton-Christie at the close of chapter 5—that their spiritual commitments sustain their political engagement. Indeed, some spoke movingly of a "spirituality of organizing." That leaders find such strong religious meaning in this work must be taken seriously as evidence that religion somehow may matter here, but by itself it does not prove the case. To make a stronger case, we must answer a more analytic question: In constructing an internal political culture of organizing, does appealing to religion as the cultural base for that work make a significant difference? That is, does religion *as religion* (as opposed to religion as a source of social capital or legitimacy or funds) matter politically? Chapter 5 offered evidence suggesting that it might—that specifically religious cultural dynamics may explain the ability of strong PICO federations to project political power and gain a strong institutional position in public life.

Fr. Marco Antonio Figueroa leads OCO leaders in "Prayer of Hope for a New School" at a vigil in front of the Montgomery Ward building in Oakland, California, February 1998. Photograph by Michelle Longosz. Courtesy Oakland Community Organization.

But suggestive evidence and the subjective impressions of participants leave one wondering both whether religion really does make much difference in faith-based organizing *and* how generalizable such a difference might be—that is, even if religion matters in this case, would we expect it to make a difference in other cases of community organizing, and in other settings entirely. To answer these questions, we need a more analytic and theoretical account of the cultural dynamics of political organizing that applies both to religion and to other kinds of cultural systems. This chapter pursues such an analysis.

But why turn to cultural dynamics to explain how religion matters? Given the argument in chapter 4 that differential access to social capital explained the divergent political outcomes of PICO and CTWO, why introduce cultural dynamics to explain the same thing?

Attention to cultural dynamics is necessary here for three reasons. First, if we are interested in whether religion matters qua religion, the social capital argument is not very satisfying; there may be nothing specifically religious about religiously based social capital. Attention to cultural dynamics offers greater insight into religion as a specifically cultural phenomenon.[1] Second, the social capital argument offers little real insight into how non–religiously based organizations can meet the challenges of political organizing; if their fundamental cultural strategy is not religiously oriented, suggesting that they tap into greater social capital reserves is a nonstarter unless they can find other deep reservoirs of social capital in poor communities. Third—and most crucially—the social capital argument cannot explain the fact that, *within* PICO's organizing effort in Oakland, congregations with uniformly strong social capital perform very differently; some succeed impressively, some muddle along, some fail. As we shall see, close analysis of the cultural dynamics within these congregations can explain these outcomes.

This chapter offers a new theoretical framework for a cultural analysis of democratic organizing. It also argues for an original cross-institutional approach to analyzing political culture and applies this framework to the comparison between faith-based and race-based community organizing. The next chapter then provides a comparative analysis of how cultural dynamics in contrasting congregations shape their experience of faith-based organizing.

Political Culture within Challenger Groups: Theoretical Insights

Organizations striving to develop effective political leadership from marginalized constituencies face a series of challenges. I will focus on those related to sustaining effective long-term participation in public life, rather than on the early challenges related to framing issues and mobilizing initial participants in a social movement (Snow and Benford 1988, 1992; Tarrow 1994). This analysis applies only to organizing efforts within formally democratic political regimes. As I argue below, democratic institutions create specific pressures on these organizations, which affect what cultural dynamics contribute to organizational success. In seeking to have a democratic impact, organizers face three key challenges. These challenges, in turn, demand four specific qualities in the political culture of challenger groups. In the following section, references to the challenges are underscored to distinguish them from the *qualities*, which are in italic type.

Three Challenges, Four Key Qualities of Internal Political Culture

The first challenge facing such groups is that they must maintain stability along two dimensions: organizational continuity and continuity of individual involvement. The importance of organizational stability can best be seen through the insight of the social movements literature. In a classic study, Gamson concluded that one key to social movement success was simple organizational longevity (Gamson 1975; see also the subsequent debate in Gamson 1980, Goldstone 1980). As long as a "challenger" organization could remain in existence and continue making demands, eventually it was likely to gain material concessions and political recognition. The importance of stability of individual involvement flows from the nature of community organizing itself. Few of the skills of leading meetings, analyzing political opportunities, and developing political relationships can be taught quickly or in a classroom; gaining these skills requires repeated exposure within the context of real political engagement. If leadership changes frequently, little opportunity exists to draw on the previously gained expertise of past leaders or to develop such skills in inexperienced leaders. Stability in the sense of continuity of leadership allows such cumulative learning.[2]

Culturally, what leads to stable organizations and enduring commitment? We know that relational networks provide the key routes along which organizations establish themselves (Granovetter 1983, 1985; Krackhardt 1992; Zucker 1977). But not all relational networks matter; the net-

Figure 6.1 Institutionalization of Cultural Elements Leading to Political Success

works most capable of lending stability to an incipient organization are networks with high levels of "institutionalized elements," i.e., things agreed upon by most individuals and collective actors within the organization (Zucker 1988). Institutionalization occurs through a process of common agreement leading actors to perceive the shared cultural elements as transcending themselves, and thus as worthy of commitment. Combined with the insights regarding stability and success drawn from Gamson, this process is shown schematically in figure 6.1.

Study of this process suggests that "shared cultural elements" (symbols, paradigmatic figures, rituals, narratives, even language itself) increase the likelihood of group members generating shared meanings regarding their action and therefore the likelihood of the group enduring and perhaps succeeding.[3] Organizational culture—not just resource flows, selective incentives, or psychological identity—plays a key role in confronting the challenge of maintaining stability.

But not just any shared cultural elements will do. Some symbols, rituals, and narratives are more valuable than others. The organization must elicit from participants sufficiently vibrant commitment to its shared cultural elements to hold the group together during challenges to organizational stability. Vague acceptance of shared symbols or meanings can help a group cohere during calm times. But in the more raucous waters of political engagement, with the constant threat of fragmentation through conflict or dissipation through loss of commitment, more deeply held cultural elements become important for holding a group together. So the group must have or develop intensely shared cultural elements sufficient for stabilizing the group. Thus, the first key quality of the internal political culture that challenger groups must seek is *high intensity of shared cultural elements.*

The second organizational challenge constantly confronting political organizers is to develop leaders' ability to <u>adequately interpret their complex political environments</u>. Political environment here includes all those institutions, politically connected individuals, and issues that an organization might hope to influence. Interpreting that environment includes deciding what alliances to forge, what issues to pursue, what political or business leaders to target, and what information to gather. In short, community organizations must constantly seek to understand and make judgments about an ever changing and ambiguous political world.

The literature on the sociology of organizations provides a sharper perspective for analyzing this aspect of organizational culture. In his seminal work, Karl Weick ([1969] 1979, elaborated further in Weick 1995) suggests that the fundamental challenge that every organization confronts involves interpreting ambiguity; every organization must develop an interpretive framework sufficiently complex and subtle to encompass the ambiguity in its environment. It must *match* this external ambiguity with sufficient internal ambiguity to encompass and not prejudge it, then *process* this ambiguity in coherent fashion in order to take appropriate organizational action.

In the case of community organizations representing marginalized populations, examples of ambiguity in the external environment abound: Are alliances with more powerful elites desirable in order to promote our agenda, or do they inevitably co-opt that agenda? If talented residents of marginalized communities become leaders in mainstream institutions, have they sold out the community or are they exemplars for it? Of course, in any given instance, either thing may be true—that is the nature of the ambiguity that these organizations must process. If they prejudge the case, they may respond inappropriately or ineffectively, or miss an opportunity for accumulating greater power. So they must approach each instance with an attitude of ambiguity and then make a judgment. More precisely, each organization must start with internal cultural resources sufficiently flexible to contemplate a range of outcomes ("match ambiguity in the environment") and then choose among them and take action ("process ambiguity"). We will see examples of the success and failure of these processes in the community organizing case studies shortly. For now, the key insight is that an organization's political culture must provide symbols and interpretive frameworks sufficiently flexible to encompass an ambiguous political environment. Thus, the second key quality of a challenger group's internal political culture: it must *provide sufficient capacity for ambiguity to interpret a complex political world.*

The third challenge facing political organizations is that they must <u>act effectively in the public realm</u>. Participants typically give their time to these organizations because they want to improve life in their neighborhoods or wider communities. The organization must help them experience a sense of efficacy or they are unlikely to continue giving their time. Shaping public policy is no easy task, but on it depend not only participants' long-term involvement but also continued funding from foundation sources and sponsoring congregations, who expect public results from their investment. More critically still, the democratic promise of these organizations rests on this capacity for public action.

Here, the second half of Weick's formulation, regarding the processing of ambiguity, comes to bear. By "processing," Weick means that an organization must not only match its external ambiguity, it must also sustain sufficient internal coherence to understand its options and take effective action within its environment. In the case of challenger political groups, this means the ambiguity inherent in confronting the political realm cannot overwhelm the organization's capacity to act; it must sustain sufficient clarity and coherence to make choices and act vigorously in pursuit of its agenda.

Strongly shared symbols and a high capacity for ambiguity by themselves may help a group endure—but these organizations do not seek simply to endure, they seek to exert political power in favor of the interests of relatively marginalized social groups. Political elites rarely welcome new contenders for political power, so conflicts arise as challenger groups push to overcome entrenched opposition from powerful interests. Thus, the third key quality of the internal political culture of challenger groups: organizational culture must provide *resources for contestation* in the social world; that is, reasons for struggling against opposition and for contesting power. Only through such struggle can these marginalized constituencies get to the table of power, where decisions affecting them are made.

The fourth key quality also arises out of this challenge to act effectively in the public realm. Contestation and conflict can get challengers to the table of political power, but once seated there, rather different skills are required if an organization wishes to exert influence—and avoid being shut out again in the future. In particular, an organization must be capable of negotiating and trading off some goals over others, that is, capable of engaging in the dialogical dimension of democratic political life (see chapter 4).[4] So the organizational culture of challenger groups must also *permit negotia-*

Figure 6.2 Political Tasks Leading to Crucial Qualities of Internal Political Culture

To be successful, challenger groups must necessarily:	generating need for:	Shared culture with specific qualities:
—maintain stability	→	intensity of shared cultural elements
—interpret environment	→	capacity for ambiguity
—act effectively to shape public realm	→	resources for contestation; resources for compromise

tion and compromise. Figure 6.2 summarizes this theoretical argument regarding the cultural basis for projecting social power in a democratic polity.

Cultural Analysis across Institutional Boundaries

The approach to analyzing political culture suggested so far—like much cultural analysis in recent years—focuses on how cultural elements are invoked, used, and reworked within a single institutional setting, in this case the organizing process. Though this talk-centered and intraorganizational focus provides real insight into how political cultures are shaped,[5] it leaves out a central fact: every cultural element invoked as part of building a political culture, unless it is generated de novo within the organizing process, is itself the product of cultural dynamics going on elsewhere, often in institutional settings entirely beyond the lenses that scholars typically bring to bear on social movements.[6] To extend examples already cited: when an organizer draws on the legacy of Malcolm X, it is not the actual historical person Malcolm X brought into the organizing process, but rather a specific cultural object (Griswold 1992) laden with interpretations by other 1960s black nationalists, his contemporary critics, revisionist scholars of African American history, the Nation of Islam, political commentators, and the media. These multiple layers of cultural meaning are part of what makes Malcolm X a potent cultural element within the process of constructing a political culture. Likewise, when a pastor invokes the power of the Holy Spirit over a political action, the potency of the symbol comes not only from whatever charisma the pastor carries, but also from a reservoir of meanings and experiences built up in church worship settings, prayer groups, and devotional-spiritual materials. To try to interpret the meaning of these symbols only on the basis of what is said in the organizing process itself—even with sophisticated and fine-grained attention to "talk" there—is to miss the central settings in which these symbols are constructed as cultural objects.

Thus, although up until now this analysis has paid attention primarily to how cultural elements are invoked within the organizing process itself, it now begins to look at cultural dynamics from a dual perspective. That is, it brings cultural dynamics into sharper focus by paying attention to how cultural dynamics *beyond* the boundaries of community organizing instill cultural elements with meaning, shape participants' sense of commitment, and give rise to assumptions and orientations that influence the organizing process.

Given the salience of congregations as the institutional base of faith-based organizing, and religious culture as the key cultural base for its organizing base, the crucial institutional context providing this binocular view of how culture shapes democratic organizing will be religious congregations. Of course, one thing religious congregations do is generate social capital, whose impact on organizing was the focus of chapter 4. Here I pay attention to a different aspect of congregations: how they invoke and constantly reinterpret symbols, images, stories, and worldviews and reinforce commitment to them. Moreover, though this occurs in multiple settings within congregations (prayer groups, soup kitchens, worship, healing services, individual prayer, penance, private counseling, shared meals, Scripture study groups, classes, etc.), my analytic attention will focus on the central worship services of participating congregations. This focus is in keeping with the classic sociological insight (Durkheim 1965) that the "collective effervescence" generated in group religious ritual provides the crucial mechanism through which religious experience shapes individuals and generates commitment to religious symbols.

Analyzing worship services leads to hard choices regarding research design; adequately interpreting how worship shapes religious cultural elements, and through them the cultural dynamics of faith-based organizing efforts, requires careful and detailed attention to only a few settings, as opposed to more superficial study of multiple settings. In the course of my fieldwork, I attended worship at all of the congregations then active in PICO's Oakland project—many of them several times. Gradually, I chose to focus on three congregations, analyzed here and in the following chapter. These were selected because all were successful congregations (in the sense of thriving worshiping communities) that appeared to embody strong internal social capital but had very different religious cultures. Ultimately, they showed significant variation in their organizing outcomes, but I could not know that at the time of deciding on which congregations to focus. I then attended worship at least a half-dozen times at each of these three congregations, as well as dozens of monthly community organizing meetings associated with them.[7] The service recounted here from each congregation represents, in my judgment, a "modal" service—that is, a service reasonably representative of worship within this faith community, neither particularly strong or weak along any of the key axes of analysis used here.

We first consider how the cultural elements used in a highly successful community organizing effort are first infused with meaning and commitment, by returning to where we started: Saint Elizabeth Catholic Church in Oakland, California.

Experiencing a Moral Universe: Worship at Saint Elizabeth Catholic Church

Saint Elizabeth Church shows how religious traditions can evoke commitment to symbols, worldviews, and other cultural elements in ways that foster political engagement—even when those traditions are not presented in an overtly politicizing manner. Chapter 1 introduced the efforts by Saint Elizabeth's members to fight the ravages of economic restructuring in their neighborhood of East Oakland; Saint Elizabeth is also a crucial element of the PICO California Project, which has exerted influence on educational, health, and housing policy throughout the state. Participants in the organizing effort at Saint Elizabeth see both their local and statewide work as avenues for creating more social justice in America, of building a more moral society. But their intuition of what a more moral society might be differs markedly from that promoted by the Christian right or by utilitarian or expressive cultural strands of American life. Their vision of a moral society is deeply linked to their experience of a moral universe through the worship life of their parish. It is there that their understanding of the "Lord's will" as entailing social responsibility, of a God "who does not abandon us," of who Jesus was, of a Holy Spirit who brings power to their lives— all images invoked during the organizing process—are shaped, infused with meaning, and become the object of their commitment. So we now see the grassroots leaders introduced in chapter 1 in a different institutional setting: Sunday worship.[8]

When I arrive on Sunday morning, mass is just beginning in the large sanctuary, built in the shape of a cross and now about half full. The stained glass side windows throw green, yellow, blue, and purple onto the interior walls. The congregation sings in Spanish, led by a youth chorus and accompanied by guitar, mandolin, and piano:[9]

> Today, Lord, we give you thanks
> for life, the land, the sun;
> Today, Lord, we yearn to sing
> of the greatness of your love.
>
> Your hands work the clay
> of which I am made,
> My soul is your divine breath,
> Your smile lights up my eyes . . .

Ten minutes into the service, the church is overflowing; some twelve hundred people are present, a hundred of them standing in back. Nearly all are Latino, including many families with young children. The front of the sanctuary is rich in imagery: a crucifix on a green and white background behind the altar, and below the crucifix the tabernacle;[10] flowers and candles and the Bible around the altar; on the left of the altar, next to the youth chorus, a statue of Saint Francis of Assisi; an image of the Virgin of Guadalupe and statues of Mary and Joseph in the European style on the right. No one image stands out, but all focus attention on the front, where scripture will be read, the sermon preached, and communion celebrated. Father Ignatius de Groot and the choir lead the congregation in singing:

> Glory to our God in highest heaven
> and on earth peace to all whom he loves.
>
> Lord, we praise you; Lord, we bless you;
> together we adore you,
> giving you thanks for your immense glory.
>
> You alone are the Lamb who takes away sin,
> have mercy on us and hear our prayer.
>
> You alone are holy, you alone are most high,
> with the Holy Spirit, in the glory of the Father.

Next comes a reading from the prophet Malachi:

And now, O priests, this command is for you. If you will not listen, if you will not lay it to the heart to give glory to my name, says the Lord of hosts, then I will send the curse on you and I will curse your blessings; indeed I have already cursed them, because you do not lay it to heart. . . . But you have turned aside from the way; you have caused many to stumble by your instructions; you have corrupted the covenant . . . and so I make you despised and abased before all the people, inasmuch as you have not kept my ways but have shown partiality in your instruction. (Malachi 2:1–2, 8–10)

The prophetic reading is followed by a song:

The right hand of the Lord has done wondrous works
The right hand of the Lord has saved me.
Jesus rose from among the dead,
over him death will have no dominion.
Christ rules the universe,
the Lord Christ reigns on his throne.

After the song comes a reading from the Gospel of Matthew:

Then Jesus said to the crowds and to his disciples, "The scribes and the Pharisees sit on Moses' seat; therefore, do whatever they teach you and follow it; but do not do as they do, for they do not practice what they teach. They tie up heavy burdens, hard to bear, and lay them on the shoulders of others; but they themselves are unwilling to lift a finger to move them. They do all their deeds to be seen by others. . . . Call no one your father on earth, for you have one Father—the one in heaven. Nor are you to be called instructors, for you have one instructor, the Messiah. The greatest among you will be your servant. All who exalt themselves will be humbled, and all who humble themselves will be exalted." (Matthew 23:1–12)

These are the sorts of texts that have at times been used to justify anti-Semitism. But here, Father de Groot puts them to quite different use in his sermon:

Jesus' words to the religious leaders criticize their way of acting: they do not fulfill the spirit of the law. . . . We priests, and all with leadership authority, must hear this. . . .

But there's also a message here for *all* of us. We have a temptation: reject authority itself, not just the misbehavior of those in authority. Jesus does not give us permission to reject authority—we should relate to those in authority who fail to fulfill their duty. Do not follow their example, but they are your brothers, not fathers. At times we look to human authority for what human beings cannot give us, what only God can give us. If we put our soul and heart in human hands, we will be disappointed. Only God has the goodness and faithfulness in which we can trust completely.

The pastor gives two examples of how this occurs. First, he notes that young people's anger often reflects a transition from childhood idolization of parents to a teenager's discovery that their parents have faults:

We feel cheated or tricked. We do not want to accept this. But we eventually reach a point of being able to respect their authority, receive their good advice, but not idolize them. They become our brother and sister, with faults, and we need no longer feel tricked.

Second, religious leaders may fail to live up to our expectations:

Priests often offend us, fail to be all they ought to be. But priests must not be seen as Jesus, who *does* deserve all our love and respect. Priests do not deserve this—we must see them as brothers, not as someone perfect and then reject them and all authority because they do not live up to our expectations.

The pastor summarizes his sermon by applying this teaching to all sorts of social authority: in the family, in politics, and elsewhere.

Following the traditional creed affirming orthodox Catholic beliefs, public prayers are offered by lay leaders in the parish. In addition to standard prayers for the sick and deceased, for vocations to the priesthood, and for good leadership in the church and in society, the congregation prays "for the poor and weak, those without prestige or respect in the world, that they might be the most respected in the church," and "that the Kingdom of God might come in power to transform our world and our society." The priest closes the prayers by asking that God "help us put all our faith and confidence in you. . . ."

The rest of the service follows the standard Roman Catholic liturgy of the Eucharist, involving the taking forward of the bread and wine; prayers and songs associated with the consecration of the bread and wine; the Lord's Prayer; and reception of communion. All this is done in quite solemn fashion, even as young children play in the pews and parents strive futilely to keep them quiet. Key texts during this second half of the Mass included the song when bread, wine, and financial contributions were brought to the front of the church:

> Today, Lord, I bring my heart,
> aflame with a love and truth I cannot explain.
> The offering today of bread, our lives, and the wine
> will become that love and truth.

There are also brief prayers from the official prayer book; a prayer expressing trust that "you accompany your church, giving us courage and faith"; prayers for "the future world to come" as well as prayers for quite church-centered and otherworldly concerns; the traditional whispered "my Lord and my God" at the moment of consecration, common in popular Catholicism; and the "amen" chanted beautifully by the priest. The words sung during Communion express this congregation's understanding of who Jesus is for them:

> He is among us, yet we do not recognize him;
> he is among us, his name is the Lord.

> His name is the Lord and he is hungry,
> and he cries out through the mouths of those hungering
> and many who see him pass him by at a distance
> may be hurrying on their way to church.

> His name is the Lord and he suffers thirst,
> and he lives in those who thirst for justice
> and many who see him pass him by at a distance
> may be busy in their prayers.

> He is among us, yet we do not recognize him;
> he is among us, his name is the Lord.

The service closes with a prayer and a song affirming a personal relationship with Jesus as divine savior, in quite traditional language:

Christ is with us. He hears our prayers, for our families, our problems, and for our church. Lord, feed us with your bread and your Word. May we be worthy of participating in your divine life.

I give you thanks, Jesus
for having found me
for having saved me
Lord, I give you thanks.

Worship services similar to this one, in both Spanish and English, constitute the core religious culture within Saint Elizabeth. Of course, participants in the organizing committee there are also shaped by American popular culture and various Latino subcultures. But this core religious culture is shared by all participants in the organizing committee and provides many of the cultural elements used to frame the organizing process.

Note that this worship service at Saint Elizabeth Church included no revolutionary innovations in liturgical content or form. The service at several points referred to the broader social world and the political life of the community but was not explicitly politicized in ways that made political issues the center of attention.[11] The liturgy does not imply support of a specific social agenda as a precondition to membership. Even less is liturgical innovation pursued for its own sake. Outwardly, this was a rather traditional Hispanic Catholic service, with moderate but important innovations introduced through song, prayer, and preaching. Saint Elizabeth represents "institutional religion" that takes tradition seriously, innovating only enough to adapt tradition to local conditions and social realities.

These innovations happen subtly rather than provocatively; little here makes traditionalists uncomfortable enough to leave the community, and the church is filled to overflowing for most of the six masses every Sunday, mostly with traditional Hispanic Catholics. By remaining connected with meaningful traditions, the service remains linked to members' past religious experience; at the same time, it innovates with and interprets those traditions in order to construct a more intimate experience of God's presence in people's lives and draw out its implications for their social lives. Note, for example, the words sung when bread, wine, and financial contributions were carried forward: "I bring my heart, / aflame with a love and truth I cannot explain. / The offering today of bread, *our lives,* and the wine / will become that love and truth." This song ritualizes the process of gradual transformation of identity by explicitly engaging believers' emotional lives and incorporating their whole selves into the offering; linked to prayers for "good leaders in society," "for the poor and weak," and especially "that the Kingdom of God might come in power to transform our world and our society," it places their Christian identity on the side of societal reform.

Likewise, the sermon represents an innovation with deep political implications beyond politics narrowly conceived. Its message regarding authority makes no dramatic call to disobeying authority; indeed, it explicitly calls the congregation to respect the working of legitimate authority. But it does call members to a complex and critical stance vis-à-vis authority, both in the church and in the wider society. In doing so, it rejects both unquestioning subservience to authority *and* unthinking rebellion against all authority as illegitimate and coercive. It legitimates social authority as a positive good, but also emphasizes that such authority is fallible; therefore, it must be exercised responsibly by those holding it and approached critically by those subject to it.

This message addresses in a complex manner a central polarization in contemporary American culture and acutely in American Catholicism. How is authority to be exercised? Can authoritative roles in church and society coexist with a culture deeply suspicious of hierarchy? The sermon implies that it can and calls both sides of authoritative relationships to take responsibility for doing so. Pastors, political leaders, parents, and other elites are urged to use their authority responsibly, for the good of all; those under authority are urged to respect its legitimate use and to call it to account when it is exercised irresponsibly. This is reflected in the organizing committee's ambiguous relationship to political authority shown in chapter 1: members were willing to respect and collaborate with their political representatives, but also willing to challenge and confront them.

Symbolic elements of the worship service were largely traditional: crucifix, tabernacle, the Virgin of Guadalupe, Saint Francis, Mary and Joseph. However, in many traditional Catholic churches these images are spread throughout the worship sanctuary, providing multiple opportunities for prayer but also diffusing attention. At Saint Elizabeth, they are concentrated at the altar, in the front of the worship space; they thus focus the congregation's attention forward to where the sermon is preached, the Eucharist blessed, and communion served. This innovation helps constitute communal identity around these shared ritual experiences rather than around diverse and privatized spiritual practices that happen to occur within the same building. Personal prayer is certainly encouraged, but encouraged in a way that promotes a shared focus on a communal identity.

The communion ritual, or Eucharist, represents the other central symbolic experience at Saint Elizabeth, as in all congregations of this tradition.

Two aspects were noteworthy. A far higher proportion of people in the congregation participated in communion than is typically true in traditional Hispanic communities. Approximately two-thirds of those in attendance (not counting small children, who are usually not eligible) took communion; typically, well less than half would do so.[12] Also, the lyrics sung during this key ritual moment vividly connect Jesus with those "hungry" and "thirsty for justice" in this world. In the Catholic understanding, this Jesus—present in the poor and in those who work for justice—is literally being internalized in the act of taking communion. In this most intimate of religious acts in the Catholic tradition, the central object of faith is understood as an embodied, this-worldly, and politically relevant person; at least the songs ask communicants to understand Jesus this way.

The central beliefs informing the faith life at Saint Elizabeth are of course many; three seem especially relevant. First, the community is presented with a symbolic understanding of God as *powerful,* as acting in the world. Given this understanding, when participants in the PICO committee pray for God's aid in their efforts, they are invoking a presence that can act on their behalf and, perhaps more importantly, support them as they act on their own behalf.

Second, the "Kingdom of God" as interpreted here is a this-worldly social reality. This is not simply the "kingdom within" of much contemporary popular spirituality, with its underpinnings in therapeutic psychology.[13] Nor is it a purely transcendent reality, something for life after death. Rather, the Kingdom of God as spoken of here links a transcendent God to active societal reform in the here and now: When this community invokes the Kingdom, members pray that it "might come in power to transform our world and our society."

Finally, even in the midst of these this-worldly emphases, the service preserves a strong sense of otherworldliness, of an intimacy with a God who transcends this-worldly relations. The worship is flavored throughout with the orthodox Christian understanding of Jesus as both truly divine and truly human. And even as this community grounds religious experience in the realities of peoples lives and social world, it simultaneously emphasizes transcending this-worldly struggles through an encounter with the Spirit.

Considering the broad context of worship led by de Groot (with his past experience in ministry with farmworkers in general and Cesar Chavez's United Farm Workers in particular), the overall ethos at Saint Elizabeth can be characterized by a phrase from Catholic social teaching: "the faith that does justice." This phrase represents a moderating strand within worldwide Catholicism today, in that it is often embraced by both liberationist Catholics focused primarily on societal reform and by more traditional Catholic leaders focused on sustaining traditional institutions but also committed to placing those institutions on the side of social reform (the theologically and morally conservative but socially progressive profile common among bishops and cardinals promoted by the Vatican in recent years). At Saint Elizabeth, the emphasis falls on "faith," in keeping with the fact this is a religious community committed to a particular understanding and experience of God among them. The *fact* of faith sustains members' commitment to transcending the current limitations of their lives, but the *content* of that faith rejects an escapist interpretation of "transcendence." Instead of encouraging believers to repress or escape from limitations imposed on them by social inequality, this understanding of transcendence demands attention to this-worldly struggles against those limitations.

We can summarize this interpretation of the cultural dynamics at Saint Elizabeth Church in terms of the crucial qualities of political culture elaborated above. Not too surprisingly, the home congregation of the highly successful faith-based organizing effort depicted in chapter 1 measures up well against these key cultural qualities: the overall worship experience of this community appears to generate (1) moderately intense commitment to shared cultural elements; (2) an exceptionally strong capacity for dealing with ambiguity; (3) moderately strong cultural resources for contestation; and (4) strong cultural resources for compromise.[14]

Cultural Analysis of CTWO's Organizing Effort

The Oakland organizing effort of the Center for Third World Organizing was analyzed on its own terms in chapter 3; the implications of the limited social capital to which it has access were explored in chapter 4. Here, I return to consider CTWO's internal cultural dynamics in light of this chapter's theoretical framework and as an important comparative case. As before, the strength of this comparison lies in the fact that CTWO in Oakland organizes in the same neighborhoods and political environment as PICO—indeed, partly in the Fruitvale neighborhood of East Oakland in which Saint Elizabeth Church is located—but separately and under a race-based cultural strategy.

The organizational culture in CTWO's multiracial organizing model displayed great complexity regarding the four key facets examined here. A core group comprised of staff and a few key leaders shared an intense commitment to a set of paradigmatic figures political ideals and a vision of a multiracial American society. Furthermore, they and most CTWO constituents shared experiences of racism and marginalization in American society, which served the organization as a key touchstone for its efforts to constitute a common identity.

But CTWO faced a dilemma. Recall that many potential participants appeared to be far more rooted in and committed to their own ethnic cultures than to the multiracial culture of CTWO. The organizational multiracial culture appears to them not as a shared culture, but rather as an amalgam of diverse cultural elements, some of which they embraced and others of which they rejected or kept at arm's length. The intensity of shared elements across the overall organization was thus fairly low, while within the core group it was fairly high.

Similarly, CTWO displayed an uneven capacity for facing the ambiguity of its political environment. On one hand, its organizers and leaders sometimes dealt with that ambiguity in very sophisticated ways. That is, CTWO sustained constructive relations with official representatives within the police department, city government, and so on even while at times engaging in highly confrontational relations with the same institutions. On the other hand, its cultural resources for making sense of this ambiguity were more limited. Its organizational culture emphasized a salient division between "dominant institutions" and "subaltern institutions" (the latter term used by some of the more formally educated CTWO staff). "Dominant institutions" included all institutions affiliated with government and, in the organization's highly racialized worldview, all those led by white elites. "Subaltern institutions" appeared to include organizations led by people of color whose social analysis emphasized the dimensions of race, class, and gender. This sharp distinction undermined the organizations' capacity for ambiguity in facing their political environments by eliminating or making more difficult collaboration with potential allies not "saved" by sharing the right political analysis and racial identity.

CTWO dealt with this difficulty with reasonable success. But the fact that this tension was embedded in the core categories of CTWO's political culture meant that it required ongoing staff attention and could never be fully resolved. The understandings of racial identity available to CTWO staff as cultural elements "out there" in the American social world simply did not incorporate sufficient complexity and ambiguity to build an organizational culture more effective in this regard. That CTWO managed to operate relatively effectively in spite of this limitation testifies to its organizers' deft use of what cultural categories are available ("people of color," "communities of color," "dominant institutions," etc.). But the underlying cultural realities—rigid racial/ethnic categories arising from America's racialized history, combined with the language of "dominant institutions" coding for institutions believed to serve the interests of the dominant racial majority, regardless of the racial identity of those leading them—exerted a logic of their own.

This logic was shown most clearly in CTWO's asset forfeiture campaign (see chapter 3)—CTWO's campaign to force the Oakland Police Department (OPD) to accept CTWO as its primary partner in determining which social service agencies would receive a share of forfeited drug assets. While successful in the short term—CTWO indeed became the key community representative in the forfeited asset distribution process—CTWO was unable to convert this success into constructive relations with the OPD for its other campaigns; from the point of view of key OPD community relations representatives, CTWO was simply too confrontational to treat constructively. One high-ranking OPD officer who had contact with the organization during this period said in an interview, "They're just not worth dealing with. It's too conflictive, too much trouble. I don't mind working with people who don't particularly like the police, but there's gotta be some give-and-take. They just think we're the bad guy."

CTWO's organizational culture has been constructed quite directly to address the political tasks the organization faces. As a result, on one level it was quite coherent with those tasks; its sharp distinctions between the white elite and people of color and between dominant and subaltern institutions, its history and ethos of conflict-driven political organizing, and the priority it places on direct action as a political strategy all gave CTWO powerful resources for contesting power in the public realm.

But on another level, CTWO's suspicion of official institutions and contempt for the compromises made by officeholders within those institutions (including the African American chief of police in Oakland) presented obstacles to constructive negotiation and compromise. Thus, even their erstwhile allies resented their tactics. As one Oakland political aide noted:

[CTWO] seems to do confrontation above everything else. They pushed through the police reform work, and [a specific city council member] sponsored some amendments that would really reform the police department. But then CTWO pushed so hard, kept saying it wasn't enough, that he just said "forget it" and walked out of the room.

In spite of such tensions, CTWO's organizing efforts did give its members access to political elites, and the organization did negotiate successfully with those elites on some significant issues. Yet their ties to these elites remained quite politically or ethically dubious in the minds of participants; in "backstage" conversations, members often belittled the very leaders with whom they were striving to form alliances and expressed reservations about those alliances. While similar self-questioning also went on among PICO leaders, the latter discussions more clearly articulated reasons why such alliances were a good idea—they succeeded in making moral sense of a political necessity. In contrast, CTWO members found it harder to make sense of the same experience: they saw the political necessity of forging such alliances, but seemed to feel morally dubious in doing so—for reasons rooted in the sharp distinctions cited above. The only place in PICO that similar cultural dynamics occurred was at Gospel Church, with an organizational culture paradoxically similar to CTWO's in this regard, as we will see in chapter 7.

All these dynamics sapped significant organizational focus and energy over the course of CTWO's organizing efforts. In interviews, decision makers in city government recognized these struggles. For example, one spoke of dealing with CTWO as "a pain in the ass," since "you never know how they're going to approach you, as friend or foe." Although this tension with city officials no doubt kept CTWO from being co-opted, this could advance the organization's political goals only if those same officials could be obliged to continue negotiating with its leadership. At no point during this study was CTWO able to bring more than a hundred people into a room for a political action; hostile political leaders could therefore shun the organization when they chose. As a result, CTWO's significant political victories never coalesced sufficiently to enable the organization to project power at the level of Saint Elizabeth's organizing effort. Sophisticated staff research and marshaling of political support from outside groups allowed the organization to continue as a player in Oakland politics, but always a marginal player.

We can summarize this discussion of CTWO's internal cultural dynamics in terms of the four crucial qualities of political culture. Through its appeal to the racial identities of residents of color in low-income communities, CTWO appears to generate (1) only tepid commitment to shared cultural elements; (2) a fairly weak capacity for dealing with ambiguity; (3) exceptionally strong cultural resources for contestation; and (4) moderately weak cultural resources for compromise. Overall, CTWO generates what we might term a culture of "oppositional multiculturalism."

This analysis of the cultural dynamics of multiracial organizing thus clarifies the challenges facing CTWO in striving to build an effective political culture on the basis of an appeal to racial identity. Though racial identities in America are often strongly held and thus capable of motivating vigorous political engagement, this cultural strategy risks undermining democratic organizing in two ways: by diminishing the organization's interpretive resources for facing the ambiguity in its environment and by undermining participants' willingness to compromise and find the powerful allies needed for a successful fight.

This confirms the earlier finding regarding the weaker political outcomes and structural position of race-based organizing relative to faith-based organizing. American history and culture make race a key site of social conflict yet provide only very thin nonreligious, cross-racial cultural resources for engaging in that conflict. The distortions of America's racialized past and present continue to burden all players in the political arena—not least those struggling to overcome it.[15]

Conclusion

This chapter provided the conceptual tools for a more rigorous analysis of how culture contributes to the political outcomes of democratic organizing efforts and applied those tools to illuminate the cultural dynamics within some of the strongest local organizing efforts of PICO and CTWO. We now have a partial answer to one of the questions with which this chapter began: religion does make a difference in democratic organizing, in ways traceable to specifically cultural dynamics. Religion qua religion matters, at least in some circumstances.

But what are those circumstances? How generalizable might this be? Does religion always contribute positively? In order to more adequately answer these questions, we need to consider other forms of religious culture. The next chapter examines the organizing process in a particular institutional setting with a distinct religious cultural base: a strongly evangelical and Pentecostal church (part of the Church of God in Christ denomination) with a heavily African American membership; and a second Catholic church that worships in a vibrant Afrocentric style, with a split black-white membership. Combined with the brief case studies in this chapter, we will then have strong comparative leverage for an institutional analysis of cultural dynamics.

Chapter 7

The Limitations of Religious Culture:
Moralistic and Therapeutic Faith

From downtown Oakland, the drive to either East or West Oakland is vaguely depressing.[1] The drive southeast leads past Saint Elizabeth's neighborhood, through another disemboweled factory district, and through miles of empty or struggling industrial yards. Surrounding East 14th Street's fast-food restaurants, used car dealers, and boarded-up storefronts lies an enormous residential area once home to the workers and foremen of the now-abandoned factories along the freeway, the laborers in the economic expansion of the 1940s, 1950s, and 1960s. As of the late 1990s, these houses and apartments are home to various groups: retirees from good factory jobs, now living on fixed incomes; two-wage middle-class families; working single parents; low-wage service workers; those unemployed and surviving at the margins of urban society. Here in the heart of East Oakland stands Gospel Church,[2] a large, predominantly African American church of the Pentecostal Christian tradition.

If, from downtown Oakland, one instead drives north-

PICO leader Alvin Spencer prays at the statewide action in San Francisco sponsored by the PICO California Project, February 2001. Photograph by Sean Masterson.

west, the first mile of San Pablo Avenue is lined by low-end retail stores and fast-food restaurants, used furniture stores, and old apartment buildings. Then the avenue suddenly—and briefly—turns neon, fueled by a construction miniboom associated with a new shopping mall built to capture the disposable incomes of those commuting on the nearby freeway. Just as quickly, San Pablo Avenue fades again into makeshift storefronts, empty lots, and barbed wire. Islands of relative prosperity occasionally interrupt this dismal progression: here, a concentration of successful Black Muslim businesses; there, an intersection anchored visually by a Buddhist prayer center and a Missionary Baptist church and buoyed economically by traffic into the nearby mall. But urban decay again claims primacy on these hard streets. Just at Oakland's northwestern city limit, in the midst of one of the less prosperous sections of the avenue, stands Saint Columba Catholic Church, a majority black but quite interracial congregation whose worship service incorporates African American and Afrocentric cultural traditions.

Both East and West Oakland were ravaged by the economic restructuring of the 1980s, as unionized working-class factory jobs disappeared. Some neighborhoods in these sectors of Oakland remain predominantly African American, but others are heavily Latino or Asian or white; still others extensively integrate people from all these ethnic groups. The areas immediately around Gospel and Saint Columba churches do not have the boarded-up, bombed-out look of some urban areas, but they are bleak: well-kept homes are interspersed with houses in disrepair and an occasional drug dealer's abode, nearly all with window shades drawn closed. Dilapidated cars stand idle in front of many houses, but in front of others are practical late-model cars, occasionally a luxury sedan. The streets are dirtier than those in the suburbs; at night in the mid-1990s, they were also darker, because the city had turned down the streetlights to save money.[3]

This chapter traces the faith-based organizing efforts associated with these two contrasting religious congregations. Both brought strong resources of social capital to their participation in PICO's Oakland efforts. But they also brought to that effort profoundly different religious cultures. Their contrasting cultural bases for faith-based organizing led both to less than ideal outcomes, via quite different paths and for quite different reasons. For each congregation, we trace first its cultural base as elaborated in worship, then connect this to particular outcomes in the faith-based organizing process.

Worship at Gospel Church

It's eight o'clock on a Sunday morning in the heart of East Oakland, and Gospel Church is already rocking. People are streaming in as a gospel choir accompanied by organ, guitar, and drums joyfully sing gospel classics: "That's why I praise you, I lift you up, I glorify your name . . . that's why my heart is filled with praise," and "create in me a clean heart; renew in me a right spirit." The congregation of some one thousand African Americans, a few Hispanics, and a few whites reportedly includes many former drug dealers and prostitutes and certainly includes many veterans of East Oakland's hard street life.

The front stage contains the musicians, a prominent podium, and lots of open space in which the pastor and lead singer move about. Behind the altar, lettered large on the front wall, are the words: "We are taking the City of Oakland for our Lord Jesus Christ." Otherwise, the church is essentially devoid of visual symbols. Bodies begin to sway rhythmically with the music:

> Jesus, you're the center of my joy,
> all that's good and perfect comes from you;
> you're the cause of my contentment the hope of all I do.
> Jesus, you're the center of my joy.

Prayers are offered by a lay leader, chanting powerfully: "We invoke his name: Be with us, Jesus. We thank you, Jesus, for your precious blood, for saving us, Jesus." As he continues, his voice growing in urgency, many in the congregation begin to "pray in tongues," a low murmur rising all around. Others pray in English, ecstatically, deeply focused within themselves. Some are "slain in the spirit," dropping into the arms of those around them. The chant continues for perhaps ten minutes, reemphasizing Jesus as "the center of my joy." The music rises and falls in a complex interplay among musicians, the congregation, and the Spirit as they construct and encounter it here. As the music crescendos and hits a climax, some bodies shake in paroxysms of joy or relief. It is stunning to witness, and even many who looked around awkwardly at first now have their eyes closed, swaying with the chant.

After more music, Pastor Ron Owens enters and launches his opening salvo: "We hope you don't leave the way you came in. Anybody saved this morning?" Voices from several parts of the church cry "yes!," and calls of "praise the Lord" go up from all around. He calls forward one young woman, saying "she's having trouble this morning." She kneels shyly as a sense of expectation builds. Owens speaks of her troubles, his voice rising in urgency, and tells of her familial and addiction troubles, relating them to the struggles that "we all face in life." He continues, "But by His stripes we are healed. . . . Demon, come out of this woman. I take authority over thee in the name of Jesus." As the pastor prays over her, the woman groans and her body shakes visibly; she goes weak, and attendants help her back to her chair, where she slumps, eyes closed, apparently praying.

Next, visitors are asked to stand and are warmly welcomed. Owens now asks each person in the congregation to turn to those nearby and repeat each phrase after him, as he says, "As long as I'm in the church / I'm in the safety zone. / I don't know about you / but I am going to stay in the safety zone." The congregation stands, apparently spontaneously, as the musicians launch into another hymn ("Rejoice in His holy name. This is the day that the Lord has made, be glad about it"). Soon, almost all are dancing. Some cry out "hallelujah," while others are clapping or jumping up and down. The music slows, and the congregation quiets for about thirty seconds—and then rocks again, loudly, piano and drums in a driving rhythm. The place is jumping. It's a rock concert for Jesus, and folks are screaming.

As the music moves to a slower rhythm, Owens brings everyone back into the present, saying "Thank you, Lord, thank you . . . for getting us up early this morning, for giving us a mind for the Lord . . . a right mind, thank you, Jesus, thank you . . . for giving us a right spirit . . . for power over the devil . . . thank you, Lord, thank you."

Announcements come next; of the ten announcements, eight have to do with religious events or meetings in the coming week, with special emphasis on next Saturday's "door-to-door witnessing" effort. The remaining two messages are from the Civic Committee (this church's name for its local organizing committee associated with PICO), which announces its weekly meeting, and for a church-sponsored "business directory" comprised of congregation members. Soon, the pastor moves into his sermon by saying, "let's all say 'praise the Lord' . . . isn't it beautiful not waking up with a hangover . . . let's all say 'I do need the Bible.' "

In this church tradition, the sermon is based on a text selected by the preacher. In this case it is Matthew 5:27–28, in which Jesus addresses his followers: "You have heard that it was said, 'You shall not commit adultery.' But I say to you that everyone who looks at a woman with lust has already committed adultery with her in his heart."

Adultery quickly emerges as the central theme of the sermon. Owens repeatedly calls people to turn away from adultery, and says, "If you don't say 'amen,' then say 'ouch!' " (I interpret this to mean: "If this teaching is difficult for you to embrace, it is probably because it's about you.") He goes on to identify "temptation" with alcohol, drugs, "partying," sexual attraction to men or women not your spouse, male homosexuality, and lesbianism. "Every time you're tempted, take it to the Lord. The devil will leave you. . . . Take authority over your *own* mind."

Soon after the sermon, the service ends with an altar call: all congregation members who feel a particular need for prayers are asked to come and kneel in front of the congregation. Eventually perhaps eighty people come forward as the pastor invokes specific sins and "calls them out":

> Spirit of fornication, come on out of there today. In the name of Jesus, I
> call you out of there. . . . We've got backsliders here, I know, come on out
> of there today. Religious spirits [spirits inhabiting those whose faith is
> lukewarm, as opposed to the truly faithful], you're so lukewarm, come on
> out of there today. . . . I see the devil coming off you, brother. Yeah,
> yeah, I see the devil coming off you, sister. . . .

The service ends with a song of celebration; all present are encouraged to go next door for various classes.

Other worship services at Gospel Church elaborated on similar themes, consistently invoking a dualistic view of reality, rigidly dividing the world between good and evil, with the latter associated with the flesh. For example, in response to a reading from Paul's Letter to the Ephesians that referred to "the spirit that is now at work among those who are disobedient," the pastor preached that there is no middle ground: "You're either under satanic or Holy Ghost influence, either in the Kingdom of God or the Kingdom of Satan."

Readings that could have been interpreted in politically relevant ways were instead given quite individualistic meanings. A reading of the Beatitudes ("Blessed are the peacemakers. . . . Blessed are those who are persecuted for righteousness' sake. . . .") led the pastor to identify peacemakers with those who intervene to prevent gossip and persecution with criticism from the unsaved. Likewise, a degree of quiescence marked the way religious meaning was constructed at Gospel Church. A reading that depicted Jesus sleeping tranquilly on a small boat as a storm raged and his disciples panicked (Mark 4:35), drew this commentary from the pastor:

If you're tired of the storm, just wake him up, give him the praise . . . just wake up Captain Jesus [here, there was dancing and hollering in the congregation] wake him up if it's too much for you. . . . But if you really know the Word, that storm isn't taking you nowhere—you don't need to wake him up. Just get you a little pillow and lay down next to Jesus, and sleep on, sleep on. . . .

Interpreting Gospel Church Worship: Intense, Moralistic Religious Culture

To truly understand religion in urban America today, we need insight into the powerful worship life of the Pentecostal tradition, represented here by this African American congregation, an affiliate of the Church of God in Christ—one of the fastest-growing denominations in America today.[4] Understanding Pentecostal religious experience and its influence on this congregation's efforts at community organizing requires seeing them within the context of members' social setting and personal biographies.

According to dozens of interviews within this congregation, many younger Gospel Church members were products of the breakdown of urban families over the last generation. Some—males more than females, but a significant portion of both—had spent some time involved in a gang life founded on violent competition, sex as conquest, and confrontation with authority, either as full gang members, marginal participants, or girlfriends of members. They thus possessed at least elements of the character traits Sanchez Jankowski (1991) calls "defiant individualism," with a worldview marked by social Darwinism, in which other people are seen as predatory by nature. During this period of their lives, they thus would have denied the importance of moral bonds or claims upon their lives.[5] Though most Gospel Church members were not directly involved in these activities, many were surrounded by them during their adolescent years. The resulting insecurity and moral chaos touched the lives of nearly all members of Gospel Church. In addition, like all Americans they were deeply exposed to a consumer ethos based on the constant pursuit of pleasure and the eroticization of all aspects of life through television, music, and billboard advertising.

In settings like East Oakland, this exposure is especially difficult to overcome, since most residents' low socioeconomic status denies them access to some of the more edifying products of American culture. In the public world of urban street life, prostitution, sexual promiscuity, and drug use are not abstract "lifestyles"; they are not hidden from view by the fences of suburban America or the privacy codes of a university setting. Rather, they are concrete life experiences whose resulting human degradation is displayed in the surrounding world, as well as recalled in many members' past histories or recent lives.

In providing this social context for the Gospel Church worship community, I do not mean to suggest that the neighborhood is simply chaotic, for this is not the only characteristic of life in East Oakland. Life there has significant structure and meaning for its members, and there are vital countervailing influences at work, particularly those rooted in African American traditions of family, church (and, more recently, mosque), and to some extent labor unions. But residents—under the pressure of the destruction of entry-level and skilled manufacturing jobs, labor force competition from new immigrant groups, the proliferation of drugs, and a violent culture of survival around them—find it ever more difficult to sustain stability and structure. These countervailing institutions have lost enough influence that their ability to shelter youth from the effects of the forces outlined above has eroded badly.

Thus, many Gospel Church members in services and in interviews bear witness to a disturbingly chaotic personal past in which sex, friendship, and family ties became tools for pure personal gratification. These chaotic currents in the individual biographies of congregation members are crucial for understanding worship at Gospel Church.

For those embedded in this milieu, the experience of salvation at Gospel Church should be seen in part as having pulled them beyond a life centered on a Hobbesian worldview, deep exposure to or engagement in predatory individualism, and denial of moral solidarity. The contrast between that life and the moral community of the congregation gives Gospel Church its powerful pull on members' lives.

The tenor of worship at Gospel Church responds to and brings order into this chaotic experience. It is from a deep moral chaos (as well as from the hell they believe awaited them) that Gospel Church members believe themselves to have been saved. More accurately, it is from this deep moral chaos that many *experience* themselves as having been saved, redeemed, set free. Church members testify to having found new meaning and purpose here. Of course, worship at Gospel Church (like religious services anywhere) is part ritualized performance: the dramaturgical presentation through prayers, songs, sermons, and actions of a cultural system intended to produce specific kinds of religious experience in participants' lives. But it is precisely *through* such ritualized performance that members experience what they call "the power of the Spirit," the transcendence of everyday life that they feel working change in their everyday lives. In interviews, when I asked about the church's influence in their lives, I frequently heard testimony like that of one member:

> This church and Pastor [Owens] have saved my life, they've saved my life. This church pulled me up when I was down, I mean really down, down in the gutter in the worst way. They gave me Jesus, showed me his love for me, showed me I don't need all that other stuff I was mixed up in. . . . I was living in Satan's world, and now I'm living in God's world and I just can't believe how happy I am.

Of course, we must assume that for some in any congregation, worship may be simply an opportunity for socializing, for entertainment, for good music, for an escape from hard realities. But we do justice to Gospel Church only if we appreciate the way worship there appears to have helped some members transform their lives in meaningful and productive ways. Appreciating this, we can better understand the key cultural elements at work in this religious culture.

Symbolism at Gospel Church

At Gospel Church, Jesus and the Holy Spirit he sends into worshipers' lives are front and center, to the exclusion of other symbolic appeals. No other contemporary, historical, or literary figure is presented prominently as a model for just *how* to follow Jesus. Thus, belief that "Jesus is Lord" is highly normative here, but precisely how this belief applies in one's own life is left in the first instance entirely to the individual believer, as inspired by the pastor's preaching and biblical citations (and whatever social control the believing community exerts).

This Jesus is above all else the Great Comforter, who heals the faithful of the wounds sustained in life—wounds that may be physical but are especially moral and psychological. The Comforter brings a profound interior tranquility to replace the chaos of life past, a tranquility resting on the assurance that one is loved personally and profoundly by Jesus. "Captain Jesus" allows the faithful to rest, to "sleep on, sleep on." In a chaotic social setting, this comfort is deeply welcome: members of Gospel Church attest in private conversation and public testimony to having experienced this kind of solace, and they ask for it through songs and prayers.

The symbolic world of Gospel Church also rests on the power of demonic symbolism, the invocation of the presence of Satan in the world and in members' lives. For people educated without reference to the concept of the devil (or where "evil" has been reduced to "dysfunctional behavior" or the political categories of oppression), such a worldview seems deluded. But the real question is what worldview best provides resources to help people confront and transcend their experience of moral chaos and personal degradation. With the help of such concepts as evil and the devil, Gospel Church appears to have successfully supported its members' efforts to, in their words, "take authority over their own mind." Partly as a result, despite its social quiescence, faith at Gospel Church is not at all a complacent Christianity. Rather, there is an urgency to its message: the devil is out there in the world, so we must act to limit him, change the world, "Take the City for Jesus."

But this urgency comes at a price; at another service, the pastor criticized those "who spend more time with sinners in the world than with the saints in church," saying "they were on rock, now they're standing on sand." We shall see below how this suspicion of those beyond the community's boundaries constrained Gospel Church members from engaging in the world effectively. I argue that it ties them so inflexibly to "the saints" that the church actually *loses* power to transform society beyond the lives of its members—at least within the democratic organizing model studied here.

Beliefs

The core beliefs underlying the Gospel Church worship experience and acted out by and for the congregation include beliefs about the relationship between God and the individual, the biblical concept of "the reign of God," the nature of religious action, and the relationship between the church and the world.

This community sees Jesus as relating to each member as an isolated individual, in a kind of radical spiritual individualism. It is the essence of what has been called the "American religion" (Bloom 1992): the Lord, though here mediated by the pastor's interpretation of scripture, *in principle* directly confronts each person as an individual, radically and without mediation. This encounter occurs in the experiential here and now, in which Jesus stands at first in divine judgment over an individual's life, demanding repentance, the rejection of its evil; and then, once this occurs, in divine mercy, accepting the now reborn person. This brings a vivid personal quality to that encounter, but also a nearly complete disconnection from one's social and historical context; this is both the strength and the weakness of this particular religious culture.

For Gospel Church members, the reign of God (and the parallel concepts of the "kingdom of heaven" and "eternal life") is very real and very present—perhaps more vividly than at any of the other churches discussed here. At times, there is a hint of its relevance in the wider social world, as when members speak of "converting the city to be more like God wants it to be" or of running for public office because there they may be able to "be an instrument of God's will in Oakland." Through these phrases, Gospel Church members communicate their desire to make Oakland a better place socially, not simply to convert or coerce residents into becoming Christians. But these social connotations remain always vestigial, an appendix in an ecclesial body whose whole being is oriented to a reign of God understood individually. In this conception, God's reign "comes into my heart." It is an interior, psychological reality experienced as "a kind of peace that surpasses all understanding" and calls one to engage others only so that they may have the same experience.

Religious action, then, is seen above all else as those practices that lead oneself and others to the experience of interior tranquility, via Jesus' saving grace. This includes charismatic worship, praying in tongues, singing and dancing in worship, and biblical study, as well as everything the church does under its understanding of evangelization: personal witnessing, sending hundreds of people to do door-to-door evangelizing, and sending "SWAT teams" to other cities to Spread the Word Around Town.

Worship at Gospel Church presents a specific understanding of the relationship of the church to the world—or, in this case, the relationship of the saved to the unsaved. The barrier between this church and the wider world (Douglas [1973] 1996) is very high, since the world represents a tainted realm experienced as morally chaotic. The world must be kept at bay, for it always threatens degradation. Within the confines of the sanctuary provided by the church, members are referred to as "saints." Though they are not presumed to be without sin, they are believed to exist in a realm in which they are constantly called to shed sin and thus become saints, or at least more saintly. Those outside are referred to as "sinners" and are always morally suspect.

Together, the worship practices, symbols, and beliefs at Gospel Church structure an overall ethos that might be best described as *enthusiastic evangelical moralism.* The underlying belief that if you are "right with the Lord" things will go right in your life and the environment of constant "praise" together encourage Gospel Church members to present an optimistic public face. To be sure, behind this front-stage evangelical enthusiasm one catches glimpses of a less optimistic backstage in moments of prayer when members lament their difficulties and struggles, and in leaders' invocations to Gospel Church members to rein in their complaining and gossiping. But the front-stage enthusiastic optimism of life within the confines of Gospel Church represents a core aspect of organizational culture there, and the congregation invests considerable cultural work in sustaining it.

Finally, the powerful emphasis on salvation from moral temptation and maintaining one's status among the saints through moral individual behavior—and its juxtaposition to the hard life on the streets of East Oakland—makes Christian moralism the central axis around which revolves the whole congregational world of Gospel Church.

Underlying this core ethos of enthusiastic evangelical moralism lies the religious encounter constructed in worship at Gospel Church—this congregation's enactment of what Robert Bellah has called the "felt Whole" of worship (1970). But it is a whole only in the sense of two dichotomized parts held up alongside each other: the unredeemed social world and personal sin always threaten to overwhelm the saved. As a result, that social world, one's own sinfulness, and anyone who seems to represent these must be kept at arm's length.

All this leads to the sense of the Gospel Church as the "safety zone," as expressed in the worship service. Redemption here occurs within an almost entirely individualist salvation economy: you enter the safety zone as an individual, and Jesus holds you there until you enter that final safety zone promised in the next life. All this makes enormous sense in a social context in which "safety" cannot be taken for granted at all. But it also leads to the Gospel being presented as a resource for personal tranquility and peace of mind, with virtually no social or political content at all.

In spite of this, Gospel Church's leaders and members could not avoid the reality of a threatening social world around them; indeed, at night Gospel Church and other stable churches felt like islands of stability and safety within neighborhood seas of uncertainty and fear. Owens and key lay leaders at Gospel Church were keenly aware of these wider social realities buffeting their congregation's members, and felt real responsibility to try to do something about that. So Gospel Church did strive to organize its members for civic engagement to transform the wider society, in part by joining Oakland Community Organizations. In doing so, the church started from within a cultural base that embodied shared cultural elements of exceptionally high intensity, and whose central categories of saved/unsaved and Jesus/Satan gave them potentially powerful cultural resources for political contestation. But could those same cultural elements meaningfully interpret ambiguity in the congregation's political environment and enable them to successfully collaborate and compromise with political officials who might or might not be saints? That is, did a cultural foundation of dualistic moralism give leaders from Gospel Church the cultural tools they needed to succeed in a democratic political realm? We now turn to consider their experience in that realm, and how that experience was shaped by Gospel Church's religious cultural dynamics.

Gospel Church's Organizing Effort: The Civic Committee

Over the course of the two years I observed the organizing effort at Gospel Church, the church invested significant time and talent in the faith-based organizing effort, via its Civic Committee. The pastor offered the group regular meeting space, access to announcement time at services, and asked Karl Morrison, introduced to me as one of the congregation's most promising and able leaders, to head the effort. The committee leaders had full access to Gospel Church's extensive organizational network, which included ministries for everything from men's, women's, and youth groups to evangelization, hospitality, nurseries, and prisons to Sunday school and Spanish classes. Furthermore, participants in the Civic Committee were assured that they "personally represent the church and Pastor Ron in all you do."

Yet the committee experienced significant difficulties and what might be termed "dissipative crisis"—that is, not sudden crises bursting forth to destroy the group, but rather a gradual dissipation born of low morale and slackening participation. Understanding these developments requires a look at how Gospel Church's internal culture was incorporated into the organizing process.

Like most other PICO-affiliated organizing committees, the Civic Committee always began its meetings with a prayer, here reflecting the charismatic Pentecostal tradition. The following two prayers, taken from different meetings, are typical examples:

> Oh Jesus, be here with us, Jesus . . . we are taking the city back in your
> name, Jesus, and not only the city but the whole country. Help us make

this a righteous city, help us take this city and give it back to you in
righteousness, Jesus . . .

Help us bring down the principalities and powers, Jesus, for you brought
this ministry into existence. May we turn to you when we face disappoint-
ment and dejection. Renew in us our commitment, Jesus, to your name.

Through such prayers and in myriad interpersonal exchanges, organizing in this setting was indeed "saturated with the church," as a pastor
quoted in chapter 5 described it. But at Gospel Church, this meant that the
surrounding world was portrayed rather unambiguously as hostile to the
lives and commitments of the saints who have been saved from it. That
stance affected the Civic Committee's work in several ways.

First, this translated into an aggressive, uncompromising posture vis-à-
vis city government: elected officials not explicitly among the saved were
seen at best as useless, and at worst as "principalities" or tools of the devil.[6]
Thus, at one meeting, Morrison described the Civic Committee's role in
fiery "culture wars" language (Hunter 1991):

> Politics is war without bloodshed . . . we're at war here, actually and spiri-
> tually. Use government as a tool to get your ideas, values, and culture into
> place. This is what we want to do. You don't build a cabinet without
> tools; we have to use the tool of government to impose our vision on soci-
> ety. In this way, we'll influence everybody around us. We want to be up-
> front about this, not manipulative. Politicians do this with manipulation,
> like with the Willie Horton ads, manipulating people to scare them. The
> only way to implement our values and culture is by using the tool. We
> *will* take the nation, improve everybody's lives. . . . We fight the principal-
> ities. We are soldiers in a war, both actual and spiritual.

I will consider below how PICO worked to moderate this aggressive stance
or, perhaps more accurately, to rechannel it in more democratic directions.

Second, in keeping with the "sect" type of religious organization
(Troeltsch 1981), Gospel Church's understanding of "the saints" does not
extend much beyond its own membership and perhaps members of similar
congregations.[7] This led to difficulties with the ecumenical relations necessary for collaborating in PICO's Oakland federation of two dozen churches.

Third, this stance led to distrust of potential allies beyond the bounds
of the church congregation. For example, among the Civic Committee's
ground rules was a stipulation that "no outsiders are allowed; members of

this committee must be [Gospel Church] members for at least six months."
Exceptions to this rule were made, so that ultimately the organizer could
attend consistently and I was allowed to attend all Civic Committee meetings over the course of a year and a half. But these were exceptions that
had to be made against the overall thrust of Gospel Church's internal culture, with its distrust of those not saved by inclusion in the community's
orbit.

Even the "praise the Lord" greeting invariably used by church members
to mark the bond of trust they shared may have carried political disadvan-
tages. If its use marked a person as trustworthy, it also presumably brought
an assumption against trusting anyone else, such as nonbelieving or differently believing potential allies in the political world.

The rigid division of people into the saved and unsaved thus became
an obstacle to effective organizing, even when the church leadership saw
such civic engagement as a significant priority. The rigid categories of saved
and unsaved translated poorly into the political realm; the pluralism there
demanded more nuanced categories of judgment.

Gospel Church's particular religious culture shaped the organizing process in other ways. For example, the church is part of a tradition that understands all legitimate authority to flow from the Bible. This made it difficult
for teachings not entirely based on Scripture to be taught authoritatively.
When the head of the Civic Committee was to introduce to members some
uncontroversial civic principles, he began his presentation by playing down
his own role: "God knows everything already, so don't let this teaching
distract you. I'm going to go over some stuff, but God already knows everything, so I'm not trying to puff myself up here." Similarly, when one leader
sought to present some ideas regarding civic life she had learned at the PICO
national training, another immediately challenged the validity of doing so,
saying "I want to know, before we do anything more, is our direction scriptural or PICO's?"

The model of authority that functions within Gospel Church encourages individuals in leadership positions to use their role to dominate others
in the group. Thus, at some meetings Morrison would hold the floor for
the first two-thirds of the meeting. When he stepped aside as head of the
Civic Committee for a few months, he was replaced by a woman who had
sat through many such meetings and expressed resentment of his style to
me in private—and proceeded to carry her authority in much the same way.
Similarly, tasks were frequently delegated authoritatively to the group by
the head of the committee, rather than being taken on voluntarily by members themselves. For example, when encouraging leaders to attend a large

citywide action sponsored by OCO, the head of the committee essentially ordered everyone to participate: "Everyone is absolutely required to be there." Perhaps as a result, though four of the five people present in the room attended the action, they brought few others with them.

These elements of Gospel Church's religious culture so constrained its efforts at civic engagement that this highly organized and otherwise successful church struggled mightily to sustain any community organizing during the course of this study. For a year and a half, a small handful of people came to Civic Committee meetings, and while they were occasionally joined by one or two others, there were never more than six people involved at one time. Attendance averaged about four people, and several meetings were canceled because no one attended. This powerhouse congregation never successfully "moved an action" on its own, and with two or three thousand people attending worship services every weekend, the Civic Committee turned out a maximum of twenty-five people to any citywide PICO event, to which similar-sized congregations often turned out several hundred. By early 1996, the Civic Committee had ceased meeting.

Thus, in spite of the availability of extensive motivation and organizational resources, Gospel Church never succeeded at sustained civic engagement. Though the church constructed intensely shared cultural symbols, the content of those symbolic resources undermined core cultural tasks associated with sustained political action in a democratic political regime. The Civic Committee had a difficult time dealing with an inherently complex and ambiguous political world. Perhaps more critically, the cultural resources of the congregation appeared not to motivate very many people to dedicate themselves to changing society; salvation and spiritual experience simply lay in other priorities. Likewise—and rather paradoxically—those who did enter into this work had few cultural resources for either contesting the authority of public officials (who partook of the general legitimacy of authority at Gospel Church) or for seeking to negotiate with them (since they were tainted by association with unsaved institutions).

Before turning to examine a very different religious culture, several caveats are in order.

First, Gospel Church's difficulties of course do not suggest that Pentecostal or evangelical Christians cannot mobilize politically. Indeed, evangelical churches make up a large part of the Christian right's power in America today. But the Christian right has succeeded especially at (1) mobilization of political pressure through mass mailing and other media strategies that are the antithesis of the kinds of grassroots organizing studied here and (2) grassroots organizing around such "moral issues" as abortion and school prayer, which can be more easily framed in rigid religious categories than the complex issues of economic development and broad educational reform that PICO increasingly pursues.

Second, Gospel Church's problems should not be interpreted as implying that the Pentecostal religious culture is incapable of generating this latter type of civic engagement. In a sense, during my fieldwork Gospel Church never truly *tried* the faith-based organizing model; potential participants were too focused on otherworldly salvation or individual moral reform to engage fully in community organizing. But this need not have been the case: not far from Gospel Church stands another nondenominational but broadly Pentecostal church called Love Center Ministries. Its worship life is externally similar but its religious categories are far more flexible and nuanced than Gospel Church's, and it has been far more successful in community organizing.[8]

Third, since 1996 PICO has continued to organize at Gospel Church; as the largest African American church in a city with a largely African American political establishment (though the latter has changed very recently), it is a potentially powerful voice in the city's civic life. This has met with some limited success through extensive cultural work to develop leaders and foster their understanding of faith-based organizing from a Pentecostal perspective. Thus, religious culture is not destiny in any deterministic sense; rather, some religious cultures face more significant limitations than others in generating a political culture capable of sustaining democratic action. If the foregoing analysis is correct, otherworldly and dualistically moralistic religious traditions like that at Gospel Church will have to overcome significant cultural obstacles if they wish to act effectively in the public realm and will have to moderate their antagonistic stance toward a pluralistic public world.

Worship at Saint Columba Catholic Church

It's a Sunday morning in January 1993, and strains of gospel music flow from Saint Columba Catholic Church as a mixed-race choir warms up. Today happens to be the holiday honoring Dr. Martin Luther King Jr., but Dr. King's photograph *always* stands prominently on the left of the congregation, gilded in the green, black, and red colors representing Africa.[9] A photograph of Malcolm X stands less prominently but also quite visibly at the rear of the church. The congregation of some six hundred people includes young couples, young and middle-aged families, older couples, and single adults of all ages. Between two-thirds and three-quarters are African American; the rest are mostly of European descent.

As the opening procession carries forward an African-made crucifix portraying Jesus as a black man, the congregation accompanies the choir in a driving rendition of "The Battle Hymn of the Republic." It is sung with a conviction I never heard growing up in white America:

Mine eyes have seen the glory of the coming of the Lord;
He is trampling out the vintage where the grapes of wrath are stored;
He hath loosed the fateful lightning of his terrible swift sword;
His truth is marching on.

In the beauty of the lilies Christ was born across the sea,
With a glory in his bosom that transfigures you and me;
As he died to make us holy, let us die that all be free!
Our God is marching on.

The opening prayer is led by the pastor, Father Paul Vassar, who sits inconspicuously in the congregation. Visual attention is focused on the choir leader, who introduces the next song as "a spiritual, a song of struggle of our ancestors." The spiritual draws on biblical images of liberation from slavery in Egypt, Jesus' healings, and Mary's mourning at the spilling of her son's blood. The lead singer invites believers to "wade in the water" and cries out "the vision has power, believe!" Many in the congregation sway with the music, eyes closed.

The congregation sits and hears a series of quotes from Dr. King, read as short communal meditations:

All you need to serve is a heart full of grace, a willingness to serve. . . .
Everyone is somebody because they are made in the image of God.
. . . Hatred and bitterness cannot heal the disease of fear, only love
can. . . . Hatred darkens life, but love illuminates it. . . . When individuals no longer participate, the content of democracy is meaningless.

The pastor, still seated in the midst of the congregation, then prays:

Our society has more guns than people, and we live in a world where violence reigns . . . but today we celebrate a vision of nonviolence: Dr. King's belief in the power of goodness. . . . We can only ask forgiveness, on our-

selves and on a church that has too often been silent. . . . Lord, we pray
for your forgiveness, knowing that you love us beyond all our brokenness.

Two biblical passages are read in a slow, storytelling style: a passage from
Samuel (3:3–10, 19) in which God calls Samuel, and a passage from the
Gospel of John (1:35–39) in which Jesus calls two of his disciples.

An African American religious sister, Marie de Porres Taylor, is the invited homilist. Draped in an African liturgical robe, she begins by "calling
down our ancestors of the civil rights movement," as she slowly and rhythmically voices the names of Harriet Tubman, Ella Baker, Fanny Lou Hamer,
Martin Luther King Jr., Frederick Douglass, and others. She speaks of King
as "a modern-day saint, and a man of peace" and asks:

> Are we really living the dream? We need to get back on track. . . . We are
> worse off today than when Dr. King went to Birmingham: more young
> black men in jail than in college; more black women dying of AIDS than
> any other group; higher infant mortality in Oakland than in any African
> country; young rap artists consistently disrespecting black women. Have
> we taken up the call of Dr. King? Or are we waiting for another King, an-
> other Ella Baker? They led a nation; we are called to effect change here
> where we are. Are we bringing a better world into this world? . . . I am
> not asking you to do anything but to be active where you are, to serve Af-
> rican Americans, people of color, and people in general. . . .
>
> We *must* begin again to truly mentor our children. Having survived
> the Middle Passage, *will* we survive what is going on in our community to-
> day? As an African American people, we are in some terrible days . . . we
> are *far* from the mountain. . . . Dr. King's challenge today is this: to
> change *within our own lives*. Without this, we have nothing. . . . Being a
> Christian means worrying not just about the supernatural, sweet bye-and-
> bye, but also to begin to deal with the nasty here and now. . . . We can-
> not rest until our world, our country, our city, our neighborhoods are
> at peace . . . we cannot rest until there is justice, equality, and peace
> for all.

As the sermon concludes, fervent amens rise from many in the congregation. After a few moments of silence for meditation, the priest for the first
time becomes visually prominent. Until now, the focus of attention
throughout the service has been the choir, the Word and the woman
preaching it, and the crucifix behind. The priest now stands center stage
and offers prayers:

that we might all work for the Kingdom of God . . . that we might be re-awakened to the cause of justice in society and in our families and community . . . for those who use violence so frequently . . . for all of us when we are enslaved to money or to profits . . . for the Church throughout the world, that we might remain faithful. . . .

He then connects the sermon's call to mobilization back to the liturgical setting:

These realities, of violence and vile language, are not just out on the streets. They infect our homes, our lives, and often our attitudes toward one another. I invite you to stand now and pray for wholeness, that we might not give in to the brokenness of the moment, but receive the healing and wholeness God offers us and our world.

After the collection is taken, and as the offerings of bread, wine, and donations are being brought forward, the altar is draped in a colorful African kente cloth matching the one draped behind the crucifix. Another of different, equally bright colors hangs overhead, evoking the Spirit hovering over and among the community.

The rites of consecration of the bread and wine are done in the standard Catholic manner, but punctuated by African drums and led by a priest draped in vestments of African cloth. The traditional prayers are offered, including invocations for the sake of the church, religious and civic leaders, and the historic saints of the church. A sentimental version of the Lord's Prayer is sung as many members hold hands.

Before communion, a hauntingly beautiful, blues version of the "Lamb of God" is sung by the choir:

Lamb of God who takes away the sins of the world,
have mercy on us. . . .
Lamb of God who takes away the sins of the world,
grant us your peace.

Laymen and laywomen, black and white, distribute communion with kente cloth sashes over their shoulders. The congregation files forward as the choir sings a classic of the gospel tradition:

Precious Lord, take my hand, lead me on, let me stand,
I am tired, I am weak, I am worn;

Through the storm, through the night,
Lead me on to the light,
Take my hand, precious Lord, lead me home.

When they return to their pews, most kneel and pray in silence while music
continues in the background. The priest then offers a closing prayer: "May
we always work for the sake of your kingdom of love and justice, Martin
Luther King's beloved kingdom." The congregation leaves the church singing the "black national anthem":

Lift every voice and sing, till earth and heaven ring,
Ring with the harmonies of liberty,
Let our rejoicing rise high as the listening skies.
Let it resound loud as the rolling sea.
Sing a song full of the faith that the dark past has taught us.
Sing a song full of the hope that the present has brought us.
Facing the rising sun of our new day begun,
Let us march on till victory is won.

Interpreting Saint Columba's Worship: Evocative Therapeutic Religion

The main Sunday Mass at Saint Columba was a vibrant "Catholic Mass in
the African American tradition," as the weekly church bulletin noted.[10] The
rich texture of worship there also incorporated Catholic social teaching and
therapeutic strands of American popular culture—particularly the inclination to see religion and other sources of meaning as valuable to the extent
they serve one's individual psychological well-being. Thus, the prayers and
sermon during this service carried a clear social message, yet also returned
regularly to focus on "our brokenness," "healing," and change "within ourselves." This undertow of therapeutic religion is understandable enough,
given the pain in members' lives as they wrestled with falling standards
of living and family crises. The combination of a therapeutic emphasis on
psychological healing and a call for social justice drew members from
nearby cities as well as from the surrounding neighborhoods. Saint Columba's strong social message and the aesthetic appeal of its music and visual
imagery would seem to make the church a natural candidate to succeed at
faith-based organizing. Yet its organizing effort generated only limited
gains, and ultimately faltered badly. Both the make-up of the congregation

and the core cultural commitments shaped through worship at this dynamic church contributed to this outcome.

Four groups made up the bulk of the membership at Saint Columba in the early and mid-1990s. First, a group of older black couples who migrated to the Oakland area from the Deep South some forty years earlier, during and after the wartime construction boom, made up a core of established leadership in the congregation. Second, a larger group of younger and middle-aged black couples, families, and single adults from Oakland and surrounding communities were attracted by Saint Columba's vibrant worship life and African American emphasis and were often seen as "new leadership" for the congregation. Third, a smaller group of white members, many from a local ecumenical seminary, were also attracted by the church's reputation for engaging worship and a multiracial congregation. Finally, there was a small but growing group of southeast Asian immigrants who had moved into the surrounding neighborhood in recent years.

The personal biographies, social backgrounds, and current situations of Saint Columba members were thus quite diverse. Yet this diverse membership did not lead to a watered-down or culturally thin worship experience; the church specialized in Afrocentric worship and successfully offered a worship experience vibrant enough to attract a large congregation. It did so by constructing worship as an emotionally and aesthetically engaging experience that coherently integrated Roman Catholic theology with African and African American cultural traditions.

But these traditions were often presented in ways that left unchallenged the therapeutic expectations brought to worship by members as a result of their formation in contemporary American therapeutic culture.[11] Thus, there was an emphasis on the emotional healing and psychological wholeness of the individual, within a worship service that otherwise confronted worshipers with a more historical, societal, and communal understanding of Christianity and of liberation. On the whole, this church wove these strands together in a way that many members said they found richly meaningful and socially relevant. However, the therapeutic strand in the congregation's religious culture came to undermine the organizing effort.

Symbolism at Saint Columba

As at Gospel Church, the central symbol at the heart of the Saint Columba community was Jesus. But in contrast to the other congregation, the official parish mission statement carefully avoided Christian triumphalism by identifying parish members "as sinners ourselves" whom God embraces and calls to transform the world. Likewise, this community understood Jesus differently than the Gospel community; less as Comforter than as a kind of transformative Healer. In an interview, the pastor spoke of the importance of presenting a Jesus who meets people "where they live their lives," heals them of the brokenness they experience, and transforms them to re-engage constructively in the world around them.

Many symbolic elements made this Jesus present to the congregation and relevant to members' lives, while still remaining rooted in traditional Christian beliefs. African artifacts, from the crucifix to kente cloth to drums, represented otherwise-traditional understandings of Jesus' death and resurrection, the sending of the Spirit, and the Spirit's presence among the believing congregation. Key figures in African American struggles for justice served to communicate what it might mean to follow God's call. The red, green, and black colors present in many parts of the liturgical space affirmed many members' ancestral origins in Africa and perhaps commitment to black liberation. And both testaments of the Christian Scriptures were interpreted consistently and explicitly in relationship to both Jesus and societal transformation.

Together, these symbolic forms served to build religious identity and commitment within the congregation by drawing upon accepted cultural icons and offering new ones within a context of traditional Christian meaning. Many members found these symbolic forms highly meaningful and evocative. However, this embrace of Saint Columba's cultural emphasis was uneven; while many of the younger and middle-aged members expressed strong support for the church's African and African American emphasis, many of the older members expressed views ranging from vague discontent to active resistance. This division existed within both the black and white segments of the worshiping community. The small Filipino segment of the community largely shared the sentiments of the older members, but mostly stayed out of this debate. Saint Columba was thus a community with intense commitment to cultural elements shared across a large portion of the membership but with an influential minority of members less committed to those symbols.

Beliefs

As at Gospel Church, the core beliefs underlying the Saint Columba worship experience included beliefs about who Jesus was, the biblical concept of "the Kingdom of God," the nature of religious action, and the relationship between the church and the world. But the content of these beliefs diverged quite starkly from those at the Pentecostal congregation.

Most importantly, Jesus was understood to have come into the world to herald the breaking of the Kingdom of God into human history; thus, he was not the center of attention, but rather pointed beyond himself. As at Gospel Church, there was a deeply personal dimension to the experience of God's reign, in that God was understood to call individuals personally and intimately into communion. But at Saint Columba, this reign of God referred less one-dimensionally to the interior life of the individual; it was understood as an explicit invitation to engage in relationships of equality among people and justice in the world. The concept of the reign of God as used at Saint Columba clearly included all these dimensions—personal, interpersonal, and social—but referred most explicitly to the social world, and especially to the just relationships to be built there. In this sense, it is important not to overemphasize the therapeutic aspects of worship there. Rather, it embodied the Catholic emphasis on social justice we saw at Saint Elizabeth, combined with a particular strand of therapeutic culture.

In keeping with this emphasis, religious action at Saint Columba took on a more social dimension than at Gospel Church. It included an evangelical strand that emphasized inviting others into the community and into the "light of God's love." But this was done more through the implicit testimony of the quality of one's life and relationships than through explicit evangelism.[12] The social dimension of religious action at Saint Columba took the form of food programs for the hungry, visitation programs for those suffering from AIDS, congregation-sponsored low-income housing for the elderly, subsidizing an elementary school attended primarily by low-income non-Catholic African American children, and involvement in PICO's work in Oakland.

Worship and preaching at Saint Columba encouraged members to understand God as active in their lives and in the world in ways consistent with how God had acted previously in history, to "know God" more fully by looking within the historic life of the community. Thus, the community sang of God's liberation of the ancient Hebrew people from slavery in Egypt, with its echoes in the liberation of African Americans from slavery; cited heroes of the struggle for black dignity and civil rights as exemplars of the life of faith; drew parallels between the current plight of poor African Americans and the horrors of the Middle Passage from Africa into slavery; and sang songs of the Civil War and the civil rights struggle. All this represents a traditional Catholic notion of "salvation history" as seen through an African American and black liberationist lens. It avoids dichotomizing the world into the saved and unsaved by positing God's action as at work in all of human existence, both within the church and within the world. It likewise avoids identifying the Kingdom of God with the church by locating the former clearly in the wider world, in the concrete historical dimension of social life—while also identifying the church as a partial, though always imperfect, embodiment of that Kingdom.

The predominant belief at Saint Columba regarding the relationship between the church and the world can best be understood by contrasting it with historic Christian dualism (Casanova 1994, chap. 1). Historic Christianity in Western Christendom understood the universe as divided into two worlds, the present world and an "other world" to be encountered after death. In addition, the present world was divided into two realms, one "sacred" and one "secular" or "profane"—with the sacred identified with the Church and the secular identified with "the world" and subordinated to the sacred. In place of this classic understanding (which has lost plausibility in the modern world, after the rise of Protestantism, the Enlightenment, and scientific worldviews), much of Catholic theology since Vatican II understands reality as reflecting a kind of limited dualism in which two realms interpenetrate even as they are experienced as distinct. The first and spiritual realm is one in which people experience the holy, find their true relationship to a loving God, and are transformed by it. The second realm, that of everyday living, is where they are called to express this spiritual experience through the way they work, love, and relate to others. In this understanding, the sacred and the secular, the spiritual and the material, each carry religious significance. Spiritual transcendence does not occur by escaping from the material realm. Rather, the material realm is the context within which spiritual transcendence occurs—in part, through this-worldly struggles to make society reflect or embody the Kingdom of God.

Worship at Saint Columba constructed religious experience in ways that closely reflected this limited dualism, but with little clarity regarding how power and conflict shape this-worldly struggles for justice. Similarly, though its clear call to working for justice helped the church transcend therapeutic expectations in significant ways, it left unchallenged the aversion to interpersonal conflict that is central to American therapeutic popular culture (though in a sense inimical to psychotherapy). Thus, Saint Columba's religious culture carried an apolitical tenor—quite paradoxically, given its foundations in Roman Catholic and African American religious traditions, with their powerful resources for social critique.[13]

Ethos: Evocative Social Christianity

Through these symbols, beliefs, and worship practices, the dynamics of worship at Saint Columba presented a particular understanding of God to the congregation. It first constructed a realm of redeemed experience, and then tied this realm back into the congregation's this-worldly setting. The worship embodied a moderate emotionalism with a deeply reflective dimension, all focused around symbols interpreted in ways relevant to the social world and contextualized in this community's historical experience. Although the resulting ethos was not dramatically different in tone from the ethos of Gospel, it carried a quite different content; it strove to be both personally transforming *and* socially directed. Saint Columba integrated these elements with relative success by affirming members' experience of the deep brokenness and sinfulness of human life *and* the deep beauty and promise of human life. Both were illuminated by the power of God's promises to humanity: promises of liberation, of equality, of healing.

The overall ethos at Saint Columba might be described as having a main current of *evocative social Christianity,* with a strong therapeutic undertone. The church combined a main cultural current of social Christianity built upon an understanding of believers as persons deeply embedded in a wider community and in history, with great attention devoted to creating a communal worship life that members found engaging and evocative. In these broad outlines, religious culture at Saint Columba embodied many of the crucial characteristics for successful democratic engagement: strongly shared cultural elements carrying a high capacity for interpreting ambiguity in a complex world, including a positive regard for institutionalized authority to allow constructive negotiation and compromise with political officials. But to get to that point, Saint Columba's community organizing effort would first have to get to the negotiating table. This involved conflict with political authority, and proved to be a difficult hurdle.

The Saint Columba Organizing Committee

Saint Columba initially became involved in community organizing through PICO's Oakland Community Organizations in 1991. As at the other churches, organizers were given access to church membership lists and the use of announcement time and bulletin space, and the pastor identified key potential leaders and encouraged them to participate. By mid-

1992, the fledgling committee was engaged in the standard cycle of community organizing practices: one-to-ones, issue analysis, and research. The next year saw a gradual increase in attendance at meetings, from an average of six in 1992 to twelve by late 1993. Typically, two-thirds of participants were black and one-third white. Twice during this period, Saint Columba sponsored public actions focused on public safety issues. In planning for these actions, the committee estimated that, at this very local level, a public meeting with one hundred people present would be "a significant political event." The police chief attended a December 1992 meeting with just over one hundred people present; he committed to and subsequently assigned additional foot patrol officers in the area, which became the initial step toward community policing in the city. He also agreed to research the possibility of an antiloitering ordinance but refused to commit to establishing a police substation in the area, saying he did not consider this a wise use of funds.[14]

In late June 1993, the Saint Columba leaders succeeded in getting the mayor to a public action, again attended by slightly more than one hundred people. The meeting itself was fairly typical of such actions in faith-based organizing. More interesting were the dynamics between the mayor and the pastor. On the telephone the day of the action, and again upon arrival, the mayor complained bitterly that she had not received the agenda (the leaders said they had faxed it to her office several days previously) and insisted to the pastor that she be allowed to make opening remarks and then run most of the meeting under a question-and-answer format. Such a format would favor her political interests by allowing this skilled politician to exert control of the meeting. Professional organizers see such efforts to take over a meeting's agenda as standard practice for many politicians: use intimidation and the opponent's fear of conflict to force a meeting to happen on the politician's terms. Without consulting the organizing committee leaders, the Saint Columba pastor initially agreed to the mayor's demands. But one leader objected to this arrangement, and the mayor acquiesced to the planned agenda, under which the Saint Columba organizing leaders would run the meeting.

But the mayor gained a partial victory in the process. As the choir finished its last opening song, with lyrics about the "power in doing Lord's work" and lyrics proclaiming "God has given unto us a spirit of power" rather than of fear, the pastor began the meeting by cautioning against hostility toward the mayor, expressing his concern that the meeting would be confrontational, and asking for "cooperation, not politics" from those in attendance. He then prayed for "a spirit of responsibility, unity, and cooperation." None of this was unusual in an opening prayer, but given that up until this moment the only confrontation had been initiated by the mayor, it set a tone of appeasement. He then invited the mayor to make opening remarks—which was not on the agenda, as she had already backed down from this demand. Furthermore, over the next several minutes, the visual geography of the meeting shifted noticeably. Originally, the mayor and the Saint Columba leaders had been seated on opposite sides of a central podium; just in front of the podium was a microphone for use by the audience. Together, these symbolically constituted the public realm. But after making the opening introductions, rather than sitting among the audience (as he did during worship services), with his leaders, or even directly behind the podium, the pastor walked behind the mayor and sat next to her.

One further deviation from the agenda occurred. The agenda was set up so that, following the welcome, prayer, and credential, the first major item on the agenda would be the "research report." Organizers see this as a way to frame the discussion so that the community's problems as presented by the organization are prominent and thus taken seriously. Following this, city officials in attendance were to be introduced. Instead, after allowing the mayor to make opening remarks, the pastor introduced six city officials.

None of these relatively minor changes drastically altered the substance of the meeting. The mayor agreed to pursue community policing if a study then under way supported such a move and noted that five hundred thousand dollars had been set aside for that purpose (perhaps partly the result of Saint Columba's previous action). This eventually became the seed money for the city's move into community policing. She resisted committing her support for an antiloitering ordinance, saying it would be impossible to enforce without infringing on civil liberties. The meeting ended with the pastor calling the audience to "a vision beyond politics, to the Kingdom of God."

But in terms of the dramatic flow and dynamic process of the meeting, these factors combined to weaken the political leverage of the organization by demobilizing the emotional engagement of the congregation. In the action described in chapter 1, such emotional engagement was used to counter the effort at intimidation and control exerted by an invited political leader. In this action at Saint Columba, leaders were unable to summon the resources for contestation needed to do so. Within the general cultural climate of the congregation, with its aversion to conflict, leaders did not manage to defend their agenda in the face of hostility emanating from their invited political leader. Within that culture, the pastor's insistence on "respect" (appropriate in other contexts) served to delegitimate any conflictive response from leaders and thus undermined the effort to empower leaders to operate on an equal footing with their political representatives. As a result, the meeting in effect failed to generate a public realm in which constructive conversation could occur between political officials and organized citizens. Instead of frank dialogue that would give leaders a sense of initiative and efficacy—and perhaps give the elected leader a sense of rootedness in the community—the meeting ended in frustration and ambiguity. *Dramaturgically,* the meeting was a flop; no strong gains were made, little excitement was generated, and no significant conflict added spice to the proceedings. In spite of having carried off a mildly successful action, leaders at the evaluation session spoke of the experience as frustrating, and turned this frustration to dissension within the organization. They spoke of weak leadership and of the action having failed to extract a clear mayoral commitment to a concrete outcome.

Dissension and Decline

This dissension festered for several weeks, then was voiced extensively at a leadership retreat at which fourteen key participants were to chart future directions for the Saint Columba organizing effort. Dissatisfaction and acrimony emerged immediately, with discontent directed at one leader's "egotistical style," "struggle for power," and "disrespect for the group." Other participants expressed concern that the pastor was not working in unison with the group, saying, "He should not have kowtowed to the mayor" and "He has his own agenda . . . if he's going to chair [an action], he should be at the meetings, understand the strategy, be unified." Another leader expressed uncertainty regarding the direction of the organizing: "I'm frustrated . . . we worked so hard, and nothing . . . where are we going? What is OCO all about?" Finally, one participant expressed doubts about "the integrity of this group"; he elaborated on this by expressing discomfort with even the mild conflict with the mayor that did occur at the action. Clearly, significant unease existed within the committee—despite concrete improvements in police presence some members saw flowing from the action.

Saint Columba had sponsored a relatively successful political action, yet was facing significant internal tension produced by the stresses of instrumental organizing within a moral community. In response, the organizer did some further training on "public life" and the role of conflict there. The group also spent some time studying Catholic social teaching and Scripture, particularly how Jesus entered into conflict with the religious and political leaders of his time (Borg 1984; Cassidy 1978). Following the retreat, several representatives met with the pastor to ask him to be more engaged in the organizing process. The pastor responded by agreeing to support their work more fully but challenged the leaders to root themselves more fully in the ethical tradition of their church: "We need to reflect on things as faith issues, not just as political issues. The mayor was at times voicing Catholic social teaching, and we were opposing her. So we need to learn and reflect more of our own social teaching."

While I am unconvinced that the mayor had in any substantial way "voiced Catholic social teaching," what is interesting here is the pastor's partial acceptance of the leaders' challenge and, at the same time, his counterchallenge to them. He did begin to attend meetings more regularly and was quite supportive of their work. At one meeting attended by fourteen people, leaders expressed discouragement with not having more people involved. Vassar responded by emphasizing the group's success: "Don't underestimate what it means in this parish to have fourteen people around a table in one room. How many other groups here get this many people to a meeting? None."

The role of the pastor during this period was complex: he supported the organizing effort by encouraging people to be involved and making parish facilities available, but always with some apparent hesitancy. His ambiguous position appeared to flow from ethical concerns about the conflictive orientation of political work. He insisted that the organizing effort avoid demonizing political leaders, wanting to counter the trend common in American popular culture by the 1990s. For example, during preparations for one of the actions, he cautioned: "One thing I won't go along with is that we assume the worst about politicians, be cynical about everything they do. . . . Be very careful not to be judgmental or cynical during the research report." Also, he chastised the group at one point when it seemed to be mischaracterizing the mayor's position: "We can't pretend the mayor has not responded when she has. . . . We're manipulating the mayor cynically, propagating an untruth. We can't call others to task and not call ourselves to task."

The pastor thus repeatedly pushed participants to abide by ethical teachings to which they were in principle committed. Such a role seems perfectly appropriate in that it corresponds to the moral authority inherent in leading a religious congregation. But this legitimate concern for ethical integrity can easily be manipulated politically when integrity is understood as a way of avoiding conflict. As the organizing process moved forward, these leaders' discomfort with conflict and their pastor's frequent expressions of concern that they might enter into conflict with political leaders gradually eviscerated their work.

During the subsequent months, the Saint Columba organizing committee continued to promote community policing and began a project to develop apprenticeships and long-term jobs for youth from the area. The police department ultimately launched an extensive community policing initiative in late 1994, partly though by no means solely the result of the committee's work. Thus, during the period from mid-1992 to early 1994, the Saint Columba group had achieved at least moderate success: it sponsored two fairly large local public actions, gradually increased in size, gained credibility in the public realm, became an official ministry within the parish (including some financial support), and contributed to "moving" a significant initiative that eventually became public policy. That success, however, would soon run aground on the rocky shoals of wider parish dynamics.

In mid-1994, Vassar's tenure at Saint Columba ended when he was promoted to a position of higher authority by the local bishop. His departure and the subsequent conflict over who would replace him generated a great deal of turbulence throughout the parish community for a year and a half, distracting members from other matters.[15] Initially, conflict arose at a community meeting called at the diocese's request to decide what qualifications in a new pastor were important to the community.[16] A faction of older parish members discontented with the church's Afrocentric focus used this meeting to attempt to seize authority during the transition. Although this attempt was rebuffed, it paralyzed any authoritative representation of the community's interests during the ensuing effort to find a new pastor.

A five-month period without a resident priest at the parish followed. This rudderless period, following the earlier conflict and recriminations, contributed to eroding trust and fraying social networks within the parish. When a traditionalist priest was eventually assigned, he came to be perceived by various factions as incompetent, a "good priest" but a bad match for this parish, or as a "long-suffering servant." The diocese eventually transferred him elsewhere, partly due to strong objections from Saint Columba members. By this time, the worship life of the community had also changed dramatically, becoming more like a traditional black Catholic parish; the gospel choir still sang but participation declined and neither kente cloth nor the images of Dr. Martin Luther King Jr. and Malcolm X adorned the worship space. Great dissension split the community during this period, and community organizing, like other forms of participation, deteriorated badly.

A few numbers may convey the erosion. From October 1994 (by which point attendance had already declined, according to anecdotal evidence) to October 1995, average attendance at the three weekend services at the parish had declined from 554 to 428. Average weekly collections over the first ten months of the year had declined from $10,139 (1994) to $8,913 (1995) (from parish budget statement, November 1995). More importantly, but more difficult to measure, participation in ministries reportedly had declined, and distrust and alienation had spread.

Community organizing at the parish also withered. Attendance at organizing meetings gradually fell off, to only four or five people by late 1994 and even fewer in early 1995. By late 1995, when my intensive fieldwork ended, no organizing meetings had occurred for several months. Several factors must be cited in explaining this erosion. The decline of networks and trust in the parish were surely a factor. But the aversion to conflict within Saint Columba's religious culture, and members' resulting inability to deal constructively with political conflict either within the congregation or in relation to political officials, also critically undermined their efforts at community organizing. Finally, the difficult workings of authority in the American Catholic Church clearly contributed to this decline as well. Given the fact that when the pastor was present all decision-making authority resided ultimately in him, it is unsurprising that the community found it difficult to suddenly exercise democratic authority in his absence. This is a structural deficiency, rooted in the Catholic culture of authority. The pastor wanted lay leaders to take greater authority in the organizing process, but they were hesitant in doing this and he was unable to facilitate it effectively. Once a crisis hit, the community could not overcome its inexperience in exercising egalitarian authority.

Ultimately, the organizing effort would be rebuilt, but this would require several years. As of 2001, a new pastor has been named who seems committed to reemphasizing African American and African cultural expressions within the congregation's Catholic liturgy. Social networks and trust at Saint Columba have reportedly been repaired to a significant degree. Over time, the church's leadership may choose to cultivate a less conflict-averse religious culture, and the church clearly has the cultural resources for doing so. But religious leaders face market pressures to tailor religious culture to whatever congregation members seek, and many of those members are deeply immersed in popular culture with its therapeutic emphasis. Likewise, American Catholics may in the long term gain sufficient experience in democratic participation and authority to help overcome these kinds of crises—perhaps partly through exposure to faith-based organizing. But at Saint Columba during the mid-1990s, all these things were still too new or too shallow. As a result, leaders there were unable to sustain a truly vigorous political culture of organizing.

Culture in Action: A Cross-Institutional Cultural Analysis

In this and the previous chapter, we have looked at how the internal cultural dynamics of four local organizing efforts—those of Saint Elizabeth, PUEBLO, Gospel Church, and Saint Columba—were shaped by cultural factors from outside PICO or CTWO and in turn shaped their organizing success. What can a cross-institutional cultural analysis of these four cases tell us about the cultural dynamics of political work, especially in light of the conceptual framework developed in chapter 6? Can we trace their divergent success to specific aspects of their internal political cultures?

Given that all four organizations work in the same low-income and racially diverse neighborhoods of Oakland with similar organizing techniques, expertise, political opportunities, and—in the case of the three churches—social capital resources, the primary variation among these organizing efforts lay in their divergent cultural dynamics rooted in contrasting religious and secular cultures. We are now in a position to more systematically compare the cultural dynamics within democratic organizing. Table 7.1 summarizes the principal findings from the case studies, using the theoretical framework from chapter 6 and a simple scheme to indicate facets highly conducive (++), moderately conducive (+), or not conducive (−) to political engagement in the public realm. Where these factors are especially mixed, the table indicates this (+/−). The table also suggests

Table 7.1 Cultural Traits and Expected/Observed Political Capacity of Four Organizing Projects

	Saint Elizabeth	Gospel	Saint Columba	PUEBLO
Intensity of shared elements	+	++	+/−	+/−
Capacity for ambiguity	+	−	++	+/−
Cultural resources for contestation	+	+/−	−	++
Cultural resources for compromise	++	+/−	++	+/−
Expected political capacity	high	low	moderate	low-moderate
Observed political capacity	high	low	low-moderate	moderate

what political capacity one might expect on the basis of this analysis, and the actual political capacity observed.

A closer comparative look at the similarities and differences among the case studies summarized in the table will illuminate broad patterns consistent with theoretical expectations, as well as a mild divergence from them.

Intensity of Shared Elements

The three religious congregations all appear to elicit significant commitment to shared cultural elements among their members.[17] Though Mass at Saint Elizabeth was not particularly impressive in eliciting obvious external signs of enthusiastic commitment, this is probably not a reliable marker of felt commitment. In the more subtle signs of congregational members' devotion during prayer and participation in the ritual of communion, the church did appear to elicit at least a moderate intensity of shared commitment. Gospel Church—in the fervor and raw power of its worship service—may have been the most effective in this regard, as suggested by this church's astounding growth over ten years from a small storefront congregation to one with weekly attendance among the largest in the city. Similarly, Saint Columba appeared to generate strong commitment among the majority of its members, those open to its Afrocentric cultural elements. This was attenuated, however, by the presence of a significant minority at Saint Columba that resisted the incorporation of those cultural elements. In contrast, PUEBLO confronted a complex dilemma; it had to appeal to potential members on the basis of cultural elements rooted in their own racial and ethnic histories—held fervently by some participants, much less so by others—while *simultaneously* eliciting commitment to a multiracial political culture that combined and transcended those ethnically rooted cultural elements. As a result, organizational culture appeared to many of PUEBLO's members not as a shared culture but as an amalgamation of diverse cultural elements with little to hold them together; this led to a lower intensity of shared commitment.

Note that PICO faced a similar dilemma in Oakland: various Christian traditions held quite diverse symbolic emphases, cultural styles, and religious self-understandings. But religious culture—though sometimes enormously divisive—can also provide rich universalistic resources for drawing people together across religious and ethnic lines. PICO could draw on overarching symbolic elements and religious practices shared across even the most diverse Christian denominations and congregations: God, Jesus, Spirit, shared prayer and songs, and so on. Such overarching symbols and practices appear to be less common across the racial and ethnic divides of American life. Where they do exist, if they are not religious they are likely to be rooted in American consumer culture—precisely the cultural commitments from which PUEBLO wishes to help members to extract themselves. Of course, this approach becomes more difficult where faith-based efforts incorporate high levels of religious diversity, including Jewish, Unitarian, Islamic, Baha'i, or other congregations for whom the Jesus-centered language of some Christian traditions is unacceptable; nonetheless, some federations appear to have done so successfully.[18]

In addition, PICO relied on another factor that helped keep the universalism/particularism dilemma from undermining its internal cultural dynamics. Although some of its member churches were quite interracial, others were quite homogeneous; the organization's structure thus allowed those more comfortable within their own ethnic culture to focus on organizing there, while still drawing them into interracial collaboration on the citywide level. Members could choose to worship in a style strongly rooted in Hispanic or African American or middle-class white cultural traditions—and still be pulled into much more multicultural settings for political action and shared prayer across cultural boundaries. Though not immune from the cultural dilemma of race-based organizing, faith-based organizing brought broader cultural resources to the task of overcoming it.

One further note regarding the institutional settings of shared culture: just as interviewees from these churches often spoke of the interpersonal bonds within their congregation being central to their lives, PUEBLO members often did so regarding their friendships within the organization. As moral communities, all four organizations helped their members establish social connections, meaningful direction, and a sense of relatedness to a reality transcending their immediate confines. All also served as bulwarks of stability and communal focus in neighborhoods in which residents often felt unsafe, vulnerable, and isolated. But in the churches, this sense of moral community was generated primarily in worship, i.e., a setting *separate from* the immediate organizing context. In PUEBLO, it was generated *within* the organizing context. Though this often meant that the political work of organizing was deeply meaningful for PUEBLO participants (since it was infused with the emotional power of moral community), it also meant PUEBLO had to be both a political action organization and a moral community. This burdened the organization with the need to devote staff time and organizational focus to building primary bonds with and among members.

Though this enhanced rather than lessened emotional intensity within PUEBLO, it did distract from other organizational goals.

Capacity for Ambiguity

Regarding the second key cultural characteristic for democratic challenger organizations—their capacities for confronting, interpreting, and processing ambiguity in their external political environments—the four organizations diverged quite dramatically. The religious culture at Gospel Church was weakest in this regard, offering remarkably thin resources for matching the complexities and ambiguities "out there" in the social world. In this religious culture, two lines starkly divided good and evil in the world. One line ran between individuals: people were either good by virtue of being saved or were presumed to be immersed in evil. The other line (perhaps encompassing like-minded congregations) ran between the congregation and the rest of the social world; institutions controlled by this church or staffed by its members were embraced, while all other institutions (including government) were suspect.

In spite of a superficially similar worship style, Saint Columba's religious culture contrasted sharply with that of Gospel Church. This contrast partly reflects differing Pentecostal and Catholic theological commitments; organizational culture at Saint Columba (as well as at Saint Elizabeth) promoted a vivid sense of good and evil in the world, but here the line between good and evil ran through every individual. People were seen as fundamentally good and "created in God's image," yet as capable of engaging in *both* good and evil. Institutions were seen in a similar ambiguous light; whereas Gospel Church divided the world into godly institutions associated with the church and satanic (or at least suspect) institutions beyond and PUEBLO divided the world into legitimate and suspect institutions on the basis of their relationship to multiculturalism and "dominant society," in the organizational culture at Saint Columba, government and other extraecclesial institutions were *neither* assumed to be illegitimate nor embraced unquestioningly. Institutions were assessed gradually during the course of learning more about them rather than judged according to predetermined categories not reflective of the ambiguity surrounding the organization. In this and other ways, Saint Columba had perhaps the strongest cultural resources for confronting ambiguity, drawn from the historical experience and rich traditions of social criticism and political engagement of its Roman Catholic and African American religious currents.

This is not to suggest that "theology" (in the sense of disembodied ideas) drives these organizations' experience. Rather, it is ideas *enacted through organizational practices* that do so, by shaping individual identities and collective worldviews. Ritual enactment, when entered into fervently by believers (political or religious), shapes the assumptions and affective ties at work among believers by inscribing differing symbolic commitments into the selves engaging in political organizing. The symbolic commitments ritualized at Saint Columba and Saint Elizabeth led members to approach potential allies and opponents pragmatically, recognizing in them the possibility of both good and evil. Individuals were therefore assessed on the basis of what they could contribute to the organization's efforts in a given area and their integrity in doing so—rather than prejudged according to their status in a moral hierarchy of salvation (whether secularly or religiously derived). Organizers could then draw on this reservoir of symbolic commitments to construct a political culture capable of confronting ambiguity in the organization's political environment.

The organizational cultures at Saint Elizabeth and PUEBLO showed intermediate capacities for ambiguity, but for quite different reasons. Saint Elizabeth drew much of its complex cultural resources from the intellectual tradition of Catholic social teaching, supplemented by the pastor's prior experience with the United Farm Workers as well as by some strands of liberationist Catholicism from Latin America. But its resources for interpreting ambiguity were not so deep as at Saint Columba, because Saint Elizabeth's religious culture was not enriched by the civic traditions of black Christianity in America.

PUEBLO's intermediate capacity for processing ambiguity arose from a different source. On one hand, the organization had invested considerable effort in a process of "political education" that encouraged participants to reflect upon and talk about the complexities of the political world. This process did in fact appear to foster among participants, including those with little formal education, an inclination toward substantive and not simplistic analysis. On the other hand, PUEBLO's internal political culture, with its strong distinction between dominant and subaltern institutions, was paradoxically reminiscent of Gospel Church's categorization of institutions as under the influence of Satan or under that of Jesus. Though these distinctions functioned *politically* in ways very different from the application of the Christian message at Gospel Church, they functioned *culturally* in ways closely parallel to the church's dualistic theology. In both cases, dualistic distinctions made the formation of alliances and the interpretation of political ambiguity more difficult.

Cultural Resources for Contestation and Compromise

In order to attain politically feasible outcomes that at least partially reflected their organizing commitments, the religious cultures at Saint Elizabeth and Saint Columba were strongly oriented toward compromise with political elites. In contrast, Gospel Church's dualistic religious culture and PUEBLO's oppositional multiculturalism showed only occasional willingness to compromise with elites. In both cases, this was connected to their evaluation of elites as religiously or politically illegitimate. In PUEBLO, this stance was moderated—but only partially—by the organization's desire to make a political impact.

The four organizations diverged much more fully in the cultural resources for contestation on which they could draw. PUEBLO was clearly strongest in this regard; its consistent oppositional stance, ritualized and reinforced in direct action to interrupt the routine functioning of dominant institutions, structured an organizational culture premised on contestation. Gospel Church, whose view of political elites as linked to ungodly institutions might have provided powerful resources for contestation, in fact found itself unable to engage in conflict with those elites; its particular religious culture promoted an unquestioning stance toward authority within the congregation, which did not translate easily into a critical stance vis-à-vis political authorities outside the church. In the rare instances when the organizing committee at Gospel Church had personal contact with an elected or appointed city leader, they so deferred to the latter's authority that they were unable to "hold them accountable."

Two points of this analysis seem contradictory: how can Gospel Church's oppositional posture toward government as an institution coexist with its uncritical stance toward political authorities, and how do both arise within the same organizational culture? This apparent contradiction must be understood as part of the disjuncture between what we might call the institutional analysis promoted at Gospel Church and the day-to-day experience of members there. The institutional analysis embedded in the church's preaching, prayers, and theological assumptions indeed delegitimated current political authority—that is why the church yearns to "take the city." But the Pentecostal tradition of strong pastoral authority meant that the day-to-day encounters of members within the church provided them with little actual experience of questioning authority when facing it personally. So institutional delegitimation of government actually combined rather seamlessly with uncritical personal acceptance of political authority.[19]

For their part, leaders at Saint Elizabeth had over time cultivated enough experience in the public arena to value and see the need for public contestation and conflict, though in a form moderated by the organization's embeddedness in religious traditions of respect for authority. Finally, the organizing effort at Saint Columba demonstrated the politically debilitating effects of the latter traditions if they are combined with a strong dose of the orientation toward niceness above all else that emanates from American therapeutic culture.

Expected and Observed Political Capacities: Summary of Comparative Cultural Analysis

On the basis of each organization's match with the crucial traits of organizational culture needed for effective political organizing in a democratic polity, table 7.1 leads us to expect the organizing effort at Saint Elizabeth to display the highest political capacity, due to the at least mild intensity of its shared culture, fairly strong capacity for ambiguity, and balanced cultural resources for contestation and compromise. We would expect the lowest political capacity to emerge at Gospel Church, due especially to its weak capacity for ambiguity and only thin resources for contestation and compromise. All other things being equal, this cultural analysis leads us to expect the organizing efforts at Saint Columba and PUEBLO to develop moderate political capacities, since both had mixed or weak scores on three of the four cultural traits. At risk of stretching the analysis too far—but, as we shall see, doing so in a direction that places a heavy explanatory burden on my argument—we might expect PUEBLO to have a slightly lower political capacity than Saint Columba, due to its strong scores on only one key trait, cultural resources for contestation.

The actual political capacities observed in the case studies—the fruits born of their efforts—largely reflected these theoretical expectations. As expected, Saint Elizabeth Church demonstrated the strongest political capacity in having won the most substantial and politically complex issues, having sustained community organizing over the longest period, and having turned out the most members for actions (up to four hundred for its own local actions, up to four hundred for citywide actions with two thousand people present, and three hundred for statewide actions in Sacramento, San Jose, and San Francisco). Also as expected, Gospel Church showed the lowest political capacity, having been unsuccessful in winning specific issues, having seen its organizing effort wither after only two years, and having turned out only two dozen members at the height of its collaboration with PICO. Saint Columba and PUEBLO both demonstrated moderate political capacity in turning out members (each with slightly over one hundred people for their own actions).

This overall pattern strongly supports the theoretical framework developed here for analyzing the cultural dynamics of democratic organizing. But within the "moderate" political capacity, the actual outcomes at Saint Columba and PUEBLO partially contradicted the outcomes predicted purely on the basis of their political cultures; PUEBLO won on more (and more complex) political issues and more successfully sustained its organizing effort than did the local organizing committee at Saint Columba, which essentially disbanded for an extended period. Explaining these outcomes requires going beyond the analysis of cultural dynamics.

I account for this anomaly as follows: PUEBLO managed to sustain its organizing effort more successfully than Saint Columba, and more successfully than its internal political culture would predict, for two key reasons. First, it concentrated a high level of resources on a relatively small organizing effort; indeed, the financial resources PUEBLO dedicated to organizing in Oakland were comparable to those of PICO's entire Oakland effort, dwarfing those that PICO dedicated to Saint Columba alone. Second, due to PICO's structural symbiosis with churches, PUEBLO was more organizationally autonomous than Saint Columba's organizing effort could be. Thus, PUEBLO was not pulled down by crises within its sponsoring institution, as when Saint Columba's organizing effort fell prey to turmoil at the church. Although organizational crises occurred within PUEBLO, staff could devote themselves nearly full-time to troubleshooting these internal crises, preventing them from stopping the organizing altogether.

Conclusion

To suggest that religious culture in some generic sense is a fruitful cultural base for democratic organizing is thus far too simplistic. As in the case of secular cultural forms, some versions of religious culture bring the kind of interpretive resources necessary for vigorous engagement in the democratic public arena, and other versions of religious culture have a paucity of such resources. But this is only to say that some religious cultural traditions must invest more work than others in bringing out and elaborating the resources for democratic engagement that lie latent within any human community. The devil—and the grace—is in the details, and all cultural forms, whether secular or sacred, traditional or postmodern, face challenges in bringing insight and passion to bear on our contemporary democratic dilemmas.

Chapter 8

Making Democracy Work in America

This book has explored how democracy can be made to work more fully for all Americans, through efforts to empower people who previously lacked much voice in our national political and economic life. In particular, it has sought to discover what sources exist for reinvigorating democratic political engagement among poor, working-class, and middle-class Americans. In focusing on race-based and faith-based organizing as practiced by CTWO and PICO, I have sought to understand how each organization's cultural strategy has shaped its political development, and in particular to explain the rapid spread and stronger political influence of faith-based organizing. That success is all the more intriguing given the fact that the classic study of urban social movements—published just before PICO's striking growth—found little reason to expect much success:

Thus urban social movements are aimed at reaction, not an alternative: they are calling for a depth of existence with-

Community leaders hear California state treasurer Phil Angelides at a PICO-sponsored press conference, June 2001. Photograph by Claudine Niski. Courtesy California Primary Care Association.

out being able to create that new breadth. They project the profile of the
world they want, without knowing why, or how, or if. When institutions
remain insulated or unresponsive. . . . police take over the streets again
. . . meaningful space continues to disintegrate, and urban social movements no longer call for an alternative city. (Castells 1983, 327)

Castells followed this diagnosis with a warning of the risks run by society
should we fail to address constructively the call for participation and fairness that urban residents make through these kinds of organizations. The
paragraph continues:

Instead, their fragmented elements undertake the destruction of the city
they reject. We observed and analysed their hope for society as projected
by their desired space and cherished city. If such appeals are not heard, if
the political avenues remain closed, if the new central social movements
do not develop fully, then the urban movements—reactive Utopias that
tried to illuminate the path they could not walk—will return, but this
time as urban shadows eager to destroy the closed walls of their captive
city. (327)

We have witnessed this kind of destruction in recent years in the riots
surrounding the Rodney King verdict and similar incidents, the urban gang
wars of the 1980s and 1990s, the bombing of the federal building in Okla-
homa City, and the more recent string of suburban schoolyard shootings.
All these can be seen as symptoms of "urban shadows eager to destroy"
their captive society—or, in some cases, symptoms of rural and suburban
shadows. On the world stage and at an entirely different level, something
akin to this reflexive destruction can be seen in recent terrorist attacks on
the United States. We must condemn their violence and undermine their
ability to inflict future terror. But that condemnation should not blind us to
the costs of political, economic, and cultural institutions that fail to foster a
worldwide political culture of inclusion, fail to give a hearing to all reasonable claims to fairness and social justice. An intelligent response to the mute
violence of the marginalized and alienated must focus upon deepening democracy—in the United States and around the world—by building a political culture offering greater voice and greater equality to all.

The Cultural, Social, and Institutional Underpinnings
of Democratic Life

The first half of the book documented the crucial role of social capital in allowing organizations of low-income residents to successfully project political power to protect their interests. On the basis of the race-based social capital embedded in communities of color and strong staff work to build alliances with other organizations, multiracial organizing is able to achieve a significant role as a politicized civic association. On the basis of the more extensive social capital embedded in religious institutions, faith-based organizing is able to achieve a more influential role in city and state politics, as what I termed a bridging institution in the public realm, linking civil society upward to political society and the state.

The second half of the book analyzed the cultural dynamics *within* these organizing efforts, drawing on cultural elements infused with meaning *outside* these organizations (particularly in religious worship). On the basis of this new cross-institutional analysis, I argue that the content of an organization's culture matters greatly for political action, but in subtle and complex ways. For example, religious culture in general does not necessarily enable *or* inhibit democratic political organizing. Rather, certain forms of religious culture—like certain forms of any culture—enable such participation, and other forms of religious culture constrain it. To understand the complex dynamics of political culture, cultural analysts must stay grounded within the concrete social settings in which political action occurs.

Thus, the framework for cultural analysis proposed here is not deterministic; political culture does not unilaterally determine organizational outcomes, but it does provide powerful structuring tendencies shaping those outcomes. Alongside this cultural structure, other factors including resource flows, organizational structure, and strategic leadership continue to exert autonomous influences of their own. But analyzing political organizing without paying attention to the construction of political culture runs a risk of missing a great deal of the action. In Margaret Somers's words (1995a, 132–34):

> The causal autonomy [of cultural dynamics] in turn allows, even mandates, a central role for culture in structuring political outcomes. . . . By existing as something apart from either the economy or the state, a political culture, when *acted upon,* will shape the outcome, the meaning, and the very course of political action and social processes.

In keeping with Somers's emphasis on the causal autonomy of culture, the second half of the book showed that culture (religious and secular) shapes politics in ways not reducible to social capital or other factors.[1] By controlling through research design the factors of material resources, social capital, and political opportunity, it isolated for analytic purposes the cultural dynamics within democratic movements. In extending recent work on culture in social movements, on the political culture of democratic engagement, and on the cultural underpinnings of the public sphere, it strove both to illuminate the challenges that face democratic movements in contemporary America and to provide a stronger theoretical account of just how political cultures shape political outcomes.

Thinking Institutionally: A More Complex View of Religion and Politics

Institutions matter enormously to both the social capital and cultural underpinnings of democratic life. Whether political organizers can construct a cultural foundation to sustain democratic work lies not just in their own hands, but depends crucially upon cultural work done in sites outside the political arena. Given Americans' high levels of engagement in religion, among the most important such sites are churches, synagogues, mosques, and other houses of worship. In those institutions, vivid affirmation of the reality of good and evil appears to help make worship meaningful and engaging in ways not available to those not willing to make such judgments. "Vivid affirmation" sometimes becomes simplistic interpretation, but not necessarily: a culture that understands good and evil complexly, as potentials in every person, lends itself to sophisticated interpretation of the political world, whereas conceptualizing good and evil in absolute terms of "us" and "them" tends strongly toward simplistic political interpretation.[2] In this way, religious commitment to a transcendent dimension of human life may lead either to escapism or to strong ethical leverage against the status quo; it may lead to political quietism or to motivation for political transformation. Some religious congregations construct the worship experience with otherworldly dimensions that eviscerate political engagement; but others tie that transcendent dimension back to this world in powerful ways, with different political repercussions.

Linking transcendent dimensions of religion to this-worldly political work makes especially critical the kind of cultural work analyzed by Stephen Hart (2001). My use of this concept draws on Hart's insight regarding the importance of integrating culture and politics, but in place of his focus on "expansive discourse"—the way people within democratic movements *talk about* their moral and political commitments—my analysis focused on the way those commitments are constructed *ritually* in institutions *outside* the immediate context of organizing. Language and symbolic action both matter, and we must pay attention to them within democratic organizations *and* in the nonpolitical institutions where much cultural commitment is generated.

Each of the Christian traditions examined here (and the major strands of religion generally) offers deep cultural resources for political engagement. But as Americans have come to behave more like consumers in a religious marketplace (Butler 1990; Finke and Starr 1992; Iannacone 1994; Warner 1993), religious leaders have come under pressure to make worship more entertaining and engaging. This market pressure has led many religious leaders to be better at generating vigorous worship than at subtle social interpretation, political conflict, or compromise and negotiation. As a result, these religious traditions require significant cultural work to highlight elements within them that can enable political engagement. For example, song, rhetoric, symbolism, and ritual that combine strong aesthetic appeal and rootedness in the worshiping community's own traditions appear to contribute to full engagement in worship life and thus the intensity of shared culture. But these cultural elements must be presented and interpreted in ways that highlight their social implications, not just their potential to offer psychological healing. Their resources for helping members think politically must also be sufficiently complex to interpret a complex political world and to encompass the full array of human political life.

In all these ways, religion in the modern world continues to penetrate deeply the key dynamic that Somers places at the core of democratic public life: the mutually constitutive quality of community associational life, local political cultures, and the construction of public spaces. In social contexts steeped in religious faith and practice—and the global trend in this regard is up, not down—social theory can illuminate democratic life only if it understands the complex interplay of religion and political culture in society. It thus bodes well that political sociology has recently found religious culture near the heart of some of its core concerns: the challenges of democratic mobilization, the impact of culture on politics, and the constitution of a democratic public realm.[3] This study adds theoretical grounding and new empirical insight into the micro-level dynamics through which culture shapes politics. Religious culture matters because it is taken seriously by large numbers of people—and thus orients their lives either toward or away from political engagement and the habits of the heart that can sustain it.

Religion, Race, and the Political Culture of America

Recent writing on grassroots political culture in America clarifies the nature of the tasks confronting those who would deepen contemporary democracy. In *Habits of the Heart* (1985) and *The Good Society* (1991), Robert Bellah and his colleagues argued that unchecked individualism and the power of the market have distorted our core institutions: corporations, government, schools, marriage, and religious institutions. They argued that only deep reform of some of these institutions can reorient us toward the good society and that such reform requires critical reengagement with cultural traditions that can provide ethical, democratic guidance during the long struggle to reform our institutions. They call this critical reengagement "paying attention." Paying attention may sound like too easy a prescription for strengthening democracy. Bellah's argument, however, is not that paying attention is enough, but that it is a necessary foundation for sustaining long-term, widespread reform; paying attention represents a critical first step toward generating a political culture capable of deepening democracy.

Just how difficult even paying attention has become in American culture is made clear in Nina Eliasoph's important book *Avoiding Politics* (1998). Eliasoph shows that political apathy and the avoidance of politics are not natural states, but rather culturally constructed—that is, built up through face-to-face interactions between people as they create meaning and mutual expectations. By closely observing and astutely dissecting the interpersonal interactions in country-and-western bars, voluntary organizations, and other semipublic settings, Eliasoph shows how some strands of American culture lead people away from critical engagement with substantive political issues. Guided by cultural norms around them, Eliasoph's subjects create vacuous public spaces in which any move to engage in political conversation seems absurd and naive. Thus, certain strands of American culture create apathy and disengagement. The democratic cultural challenge thus involves not only "paying attention," but also drawing people out of actively constructed cultural patterns to which they are committed, in which *not* paying attention is seen as a positive virtue.

Eliasoph vividly shows how political (and antipolitical) cultures are constructed and used by participants in them. Though her work shows how this has politically debilitating and antidemocratic effects within the cultural mainstream, it also shows how important it is to learn from those who have found ways of constructing more engaged and democratic political cultures. Likewise, her work suggests that though the voluntary sector and civil society more broadly may indeed have important democratic potential, redeeming that democratic promise is not easy. Certainly, simply getting more people involved in voluntary organizations will not of itself generate a more democratic society. Rather, deepening democracy requires *certain kinds* of voluntary organizations that shape participants in democratic directions.

While Eliasoph emphasizes the politically debilitating strands of popular culture, Paul Lichterman shows that politically empowering strands also exist. In *The Search for Political Community* (1996), Lichterman focuses on a form of individualism he calls "personalism." Personalism incorporates elements of individualism, but in a variation that derives satisfaction and meaning from engagement with politics. Lichterman's study shows that in certain settings personalism can and does provide the basis for long-term political engagement. This highly individualized but politicized identity is portable across different kinds of issues and organizations, even without grounding in the cultural traditions and institutions emphasized by Bellah and his colleagues. Thus, in the right circumstances, some individuals can transcend individualism from within, so to speak, rather than needing strong cultural traditions and institutions to sustain commitment. Lichterman argues that personalism can provide a politically empowering cultural mooring for those uninterested in engaging with cultural traditions and institutions.

But can such personalism provide the basis for the kind of *broad long-term* movement that will be necessary to achieve real democratic reform of American economic and political life? Is it capable of attracting the vast numbers of citizens needed to push democratic reform in a recalcitrant polity, capable of being passed on to new generations of leaders as the basis for sustaining democratic engagement? I am skeptical of this because personalism is essentially a kind of internalized but not institutionalized identity; Lichterman's activists have internalized a political habitus and sense of identity but by and large do not appear to have established the kinds of institutions that might extend the self-understanding and practices that underlie political personalism to large numbers of people.

None of this is to suggest that personalism is void of democratic merit. Lichterman's study breaks new ground in documenting the sustainability of long-term political and civic engagement based on the individualism that sociologists have argued undermines exactly that kind of engagement. If deep democratic reform under conditions of capitalism triumphant is to be successful, a multistrand rope of new citizenship activism will be required. Personalist politics will almost certainly be one strand in that rope, but it alone cannot carry the bulk of the democratic reform agenda. Based on the evidence for organizational symbiosis between religious institutions and faith-based community organizing efforts documented here, I contend that institutionally rooted political organizations enjoy competitive advantages that give them great promise as central strands in the future rope of democratic reform. I do not suggest that faith-based organizing will or should be the dominant element in the coalitions that will lead American society into a new cycle of reform. Rather, faith-based community organizing has proven itself capable of simultaneously generating democratic power and remaining ethically rooted in a democratic ethos and is thus capable of being among the key leaders in such a coalition. Likewise, given the salience of race as a political fault line in American society, race-based organizing will be a significant player in such a coalition. All those committed to democratic reform have a great deal to learn from these organizations' twenty years of experience in building effective multiracial organizations.

Finally, in *Cultural Dilemmas of Progressive Politics* (2001), Stephen Hart shows the kind of "cultural work" needed to build vigorous political organizations. He argues that only by linking their political agendas to strong cultural traditions that provide meaning and guidance to people's lives can progressive organizations hope to reshape American societal priorities. He also suggests that few organizations striving to promote social justice in America today do this kind of cultural work very well.

Recent studies of the grassroots political culture of American life thus point to a series of fundamental dilemmas confronting democratic forces, which I follow Hart in calling the *cultural dilemmas* of American democracy; powerful currents in American culture are politically vacuous or ethically rootless and thus incapable of offering the ongoing moral-political critique on which a healthy democracy depends. Many democratic movements connect their politics only anemically to those strands of American culture that *are* morally and politically robust; these movements are thus less able to overcome the onslaught of antidemocratic economic, political, and cultural forces. And the cultural forces of apathy and antipolitics have colonized even that formidable reservoir of potential democratic change, the voluntary organizations of civil society.

At the same time, democratic organizing faces important challenges arising from the twin *institutional dilemmas* of American democracy. On one hand, weakened political, cultural, and labor institutions have led to the recent erosion of American social capital; on the other hand, institutional linkages between civil society, political society, and the state have broken down. Rebuilding these linkages and strengthening institutions that foster community-based social capital are both crucial for constituting a vital public realm that channels democratic pressure upward into the political and economic systems.

So to make good the promise underlying American democracy, more is required than increasing the store of social capital in poor communities or reinvigorating the voluntary sector, as pursued recently in high-profile efforts by foundations and the president's Office of Faith-Based Initiatives. The social capital thus formed and the voluntary sector thus invigorated both must be linked up systematically to the public realm. This is not to say they must be politically inspired or directly driven by political goals. But if the new citizen activism underlying these efforts is truly to promote a more democratic society, it must at a minimum overcome the avoidance of politics, cultural anemia, and politically eviscerated individualism that Eliasoph, Hart, and Bellah et al. have documented in American political culture and the voluntary sector of civil society. This book shows that the best such efforts do much more; they build political cultures and organizing structures capable of projecting democratic power well beyond the confines of civil society. Some organizations do this by building social capital within their own "politicized civic associations" rooted in civil society. Other organizations draw symbiotically on the social capital embedded in religious institutions or other voluntary organizations, multiplying and extending this social capital outward while reorienting it toward the democratic tasks of societal reform. The advantages inherent in the latter strategy allow the strongest such organizations to become bridging institutions that link popular democratic power from civil society up to political society and the state.

Just how important such bridging institutions can be for the future of democratic reform in America comes into view when we recognize that they draw on some of the richest of American cultural traditions—voluntarism, citizen activism, and often religiously inspired work for democratic reform—to directly attack the fundamental cultural and institutional dilemmas of democracy.

Implications for American Society and Democratic Organizing

The case studies of faith-based organizing suggest the potential promise of drawing on the religious wellsprings of meaning to which many Americans are committed, reinvigorating the social dimension of those religious traditions, and linking them to democratic civic engagement. It suggests that some versions of religious culture are already contributing to reconstituting a democratic public realm in American life and are capable of providing the kind of nuanced yet vigorous cultural elements that will be required to make democracy work in twenty-first-century America.

Faith-based community organizing thus holds significant potential as one aspect of efforts to reconstitute American public life so that it engages the voices and addresses the concerns of people currently left out of institutionalized political debate, namely those of low-income and moderate-income residents of American cities. Its influence may multiply considerably as church-based organizing spreads to wider geographic areas (both nationally and potentially internationally); as local federations learn to link up with federations in other cities in regional and statewide efforts to address higher-level political and economic issues; and as leaders, staff, and political representatives become more adept at negotiating with each other and working in partnership. All this suggests it may be time to revise Castells's pessimistic conclusion regarding the potential impact of grassroots urban reform efforts in the early 1980s; some such efforts appear to have developed sufficiently to justify cautious hopefulness at their prospects, as well as continued sober assessment of the obstacles they face.

The CTWO case study makes clear that turning to religious culture is not the only cultural strategy available for democratic organizing. The race-based model of multiracial organizing also contributes to democratic renewal by revealing to political leaders and the wider society that inequalities rooted in historic and current racism, economic inequality, and gender discrimination continue to exist and to disenfranchise significant sectors of the population from full participation in American life. But this case study also illuminates the difficulties for this cultural strategy presented by contemporary American culture for these groups; at least in poorer communities, contemporary American culture appears to so harden the categories of racial and ethnic identity that they face great challenges in sustaining effective engagement in the public realm. This is true even when that cultural strategy includes a sophisticated understanding of race, class, and gender and an explicit commitment to organizing a multiracial constituency.

As a result, the race-based political organizing model studied here faces significant constraints arising from three sources: (1) the lack of ambiguity and flexibility within polemical understandings of racial identity currently widespread in American culture; (2) the relative dearth of cross-racial cultural resources (particularly social networks and trust) to support multiracial organizing efforts; and (3) the tension embedded in organizational ideology between the universalizing thrust of its democratic ethos and commitment to human rights and the radically particularizing thrust of rooting its appeal in racial identity. These constrain the organization to a role as a politicized civic association rather than an influential player in political society. This outcome appears far more in keeping with Castells's sympathetic but ultimately pessimistic conclusion regarding the social movements of the late 1970s and early 1980s. The burdens of America's racialized history and contemporary political culture continue to burden us all, including those who appeal to it as the basis of democratic organizing.

The political experience of PICO and CTWO also confirms the crucial importance of political culture in fostering the democratic life of communities. But note that this approach to political culture is quite different from the older "civic culture" accounts (Almond and Verba 1963; Inglehart 1988), or even Putnam's adaptation of them (1993, 2000). Rather than focusing on the way a civic culture makes the work of governance easier by leading citizens to trust governing elites, I have emphasized the way a civic culture fosters the work of citizens in holding governing elites accountable to democratic pressures. In this account, rather than political culture being a relatively static national trait explaining effective or ineffective governance, it is a dynamic quality of local communities and their voluntary and political organizations, constantly being put to use in the work of democracy or, alternatively, sliding into disuse.

In partially accepting Putnam's account of the association between political culture and the success of democratic institutions, I also strive to go beneath his macro-level account to consider the micro-level mechanisms through which political culture matters. By exploring the day-to-day experience of the participants in democratic movements, this book provides a clearer picture of just how cultural resources shape the democratic outcomes of such movements. It also shows how, in contrast to religion in Italy as analyzed by Putnam, certain forms of contemporary religious culture can be a powerful resource for making democracy work.

Three further implications of this study deserve mention here. First, this analysis suggests strongly that, though attenuated, sufficient social capital still exists among the working poor and those whom former U.S. secretary of labor Robert Reich called the "anxious middle class" to provide the basis for beginning to reorient America's political future. In shaping a more vigorous public role for these segments of the American populace, a crucial challenge lies in establishing appropriate mechanisms for linking their self-interests, passions, and everyday ethical and political insight to wider public life. That is, what may be lacking are precisely the kind of bridging institutions examined here.

Second, the foregoing analyses of the political experience of faith-based and race-based organizing suggest that democratic theorists' aversion to the politics of inclusion and of reform (Cohen and Arato 1992, 486–563), while valuable as cautionary wisdom regarding the risks of co-optation, may be exaggerated; PICO's experience shows that groups engaging in these kinds of politics do indeed face the risk of being colonized by the logic of power, but need not succumb to it. Vibrant roots in autonomous moral communities can provide some effective check on those risks, and symbiosis between religious and civic institutions can provide an effective institutional counterweight to co-optation.

Third, this study suggests that the cultural strategies employed by these bridging institutions will greatly influence how successful they can be in making democracy work. Since most Americans continue to use religious language as a primary way to voice their ethical commitments, religious culture will remain a crucial contributor to American political culture. To the extent religion provides autonomous organizational space and grounds of ethical appeal in civil society, democracy is more likely to flourish. PICO's experience thus directly addresses current debates regarding the public role of religion in modern democracies. In his outstanding comparative study of public religion in modern democracies, José Casanova (1994) suggests that modern religions can legitimately aspire to a public role if they renounce a privileged status that would deny others an equal voice in public dialogue. But his prescription for how this ought to occur involves limiting religion to a public role at the level of civil society, i.e., excluding religion from the public dimension of political society and the state.

Yet the case study here suggests that—in addition to direct attempts by churches to dictate to political society or the state (which Casanova rightly rejects) and participation at all levels by individual religious believers and the work of religious associations within civil society (both of which he accepts)—there is another form of public religion. This is exemplified in the work of faith-based organizing in channeling democratic power rooted in communal religious commitment directly into political society and the state. This is neither civic participation by individuals who happen to be religious believers, nor public intervention by religious institutions addressing civil society, nor religion dictating to the political structures of wider society. Rather, it is an effort by organized religious believers, affiliated with religious institutions but not directed by religious authorities, to insert themselves into the more directly political levels of the public realm. To make the public square truly accessible to those for whom religious commitment grounds even their most secular political stances, we must preserve the legitimacy of this kind of intervention.

If this is so, how can we distinguish between faith-based organizing and the role of religious extremists at either end of the political spectrum? Are they functionally equivalent, diverging only on the content of their politics? To accept one, must we accept both as appropriate versions of religious engagement in civic life?

I believe not; they diverge in another way that matters critically to their legitimacy in public life. Faith-based organizing insists on a place for religious language there, yet also accepts nonreligious discourse as legitimate "reason" in public dialogue. More importantly, faith-based organizing accepts its responsibility for learning to understand civic participants from secular or divergent religious backgrounds. It engages them as equal participants in public life, even as it asks them to accept the reciprocal responsibility. Embracing this ambiguous position is recognized at least implicitly as the price of admission to the public realm. Religious believers, if they choose to participate in public debate, must unambiguously accept this price of admission; if they do so, extremism will be attenuated.

Finally, this study raises questions regarding the "faith-based initiative" of the current U.S. administration. Seen in this light, the crucial question is no longer whether religious congregations can provide social services more effectively than government agencies; in any case, little good research yet exists to answer this question. The more critical question is whether, if such faith-based social services are indeed effective, they can be funded by government without undermining the organizational, political, and ethical autonomy of congregations.

But if the foregoing analysis is correct, faith-based organizing also presents a significant challenge to those secular intellectuals who strive to pursue a "progressive" politics while rejecting all forms of religious participation in political life. They would do well to hear Casanova's invitation, in the closing words of his book, to enter into dialogue with religious traditions that accept the humanist insight of the Enlightenment while challenging its antireligious assumptions:[4]

Western modernity is at a crossroads. If it does not enter into a creative dialogue with the other, with those traditions which are challenging its identity, modernity will most likely triumph. But it may end up being devoured by the inflexible, inhuman logic of its own creations. It would be profoundly ironic if, after all the beatings it has received from modernity, religion could somehow unintentionally help modernity save itself.[5]

Implications for Race-Based Organizing

Even in CTWO's organizational context of a sophisticated social analysis and a strongly democratic and multiracial vision, its race-based cultural strategy appears to lead into a blind alley, at least if the ultimate goal remains significant political reform and impact on policy formulation. Two responses to this concern seem plausible. One response holds that this tension exists only as long as current understandings of racial identity hold sway and that CTWO's project lies precisely in transforming this understanding of racial identity. So the appeal to racial identity is a temporary tactic, gradually used to build a culture of solidarity around "multiracial identity." This multiracial culture can then serve to organize cross-racially in more powerful ways and thus have greater political impact.

But nothing I observed suggests this response has been successful. That is, the evidence does not suggest that CTWO's organizing process has been sufficiently cumulative to ultimately project a more powerful public presence. It has empowered some outstanding individuals from communities of color to become politically active, and has produced significant improvement in certain social services and in police accountability. But it has not kept enough of these individuals sufficiently involved, nor recruited new participants extensively enough, to accumulate the political power needed to make itself a salient feature of local political society or push through the higher-order political reforms it seeks.

The other response holds that direct political impact simply is not the organization's goal; that its ultimate political influence will come from reshaping American political culture by disclosing and transforming power relations among races, classes, genders, and individuals of diverse sexual preferences and reconstituting those relations within a "multiculture" of solidarity. This response is difficult to assess; long-term cultural change and its political consequences cannot be predicted. But the early fruits of this strategy in the wider society appear to have been fragmentation rather than gradual construction of a political culture to sustain broad social solidarity (Gitlin 1995). Whether multiracial identity can be sufficiently powerful to generate the intensely shared cultural elements needed for sustaining broad social solidarity is a strategic calculation to be made by those involved. If it is to do so, I believe that it will require cultural elements that transcend categories of race, class, and gender. However, with stronger cultural work to generate such elements and to strengthen its resources for ambiguity and compromise, this kind of organizing may help plant the seeds of a more multiracial political culture.

CTWO already is contributing to deepening the resources of political vision and interracial trust held within low-income communities of color. In this way it may be laying cultural groundwork for political initiatives in the future. As importantly, by displaying for public attention the ways its constituents are marginalized from political institutions, left out of economic prosperity, and disproportionately targeted by current law enforcement strategies, the organization holds a mirror up to the wider society that may facilitate effective democratic reform.

Implications for Faith-Based Organizing

The greatest risk posed by the structural position of the stronger federations within faith-based organizing lies in the possibility that they will lose their ethical and democratic vision, coming to look much like purely instrumental political organizations. Accountability and negotiation do indeed draw faith-based organizing partially onto the terrain of power that is the home turf of political society and alien to the (idealized) moral logic of civil society. The struggle for democratic accountability thus poses a risk of being colonized by the logic of power.

However, the alternative may be worse: if those excluded by the practices of institutional politics or overwhelmed by their own life circumstances do not struggle for political accountability, their interests will continue to be poorly represented. Without struggle, the excluded remain excluded. Do leaders of religious and other moral communities face an insoluble dilemma, either to submit their ethical traditions to colonization by the logic of power or to allow the excluded to remain excluded?

PICO's experience suggests not. Where faith-based organizing has successfully pursued accountability and the politics of inclusion and has stayed grounded in the ethical logic of churches and synagogues, it has transcended its own traditional model of accountability vis-à-vis political leaders. Once accountability is achieved, the accountability model can give way to a language of partnership that lends itself to the kind of dialogical relationship with political elites that lies at the heart of the politics of influence. Indeed, PICO staff and other participants speak frequently the language of partnership and actively pursue such partnership with political officials.

Key leaders in faith-based organizing are aware of the risks of such partnership, and see internal and external solutions. John Baumann, director of PICO, emphasizes the internal solution: "The challenge now is to work in partnership without losing the integrity of your organization. The key thing is to keep our ties to the people, keep relationships strong." Jim

Keddy, PICO California Project director, emphasizes the public component. When asked about the dangers of being too closely identified with an official, he responded,

> There's always a danger of that. We could stay out entirely and pretend to be pure; that's the radical activist's solution. But we want to actually change things in the city, to have real power regarding what happens here, make it a better place. To do that, you have to be willing to work with them, and being in partnership gives us leverage. The key thing is always being able and willing to raise the tension level with elected leaders when you need to, and to do that publicly.

Both components are necessary for this kind of partnership to thrive in the long term. Thus, two transitions must occur, one on the community organization side of such partnerships, the other on the political leaders' side.

Within community organizations, the move must be to give up partially the traditional model of accountability and, in particular, that model's virtually *exclusive* focus on building the organization. This involves using far more cautiously one of the key tools such organizations have historically employed to motivate and mobilize constituents, namely constantly organizing *against* established political leaders. Where such leaders reject any substantial accountability, they will still be targeted for such treatment. This is simply the cost of political power exercised irresponsibly.

But partnership requires another modus operandi as well, namely constructive collaboration with some officeholders. While in practice some faith-based organizers and leaders are pursuing this kind of collaboration, others are entrapped in the purely conflictive understanding of "the public" inherited from the Alinsky tradition. This undermines one of the most powerful resources of faith-based organizing: political vision rooted in ethical values and commitments that transcend politics narrowly conceived. It also creates a schizophrenic stance regarding relationships with political leaders. Faith-based organizing actively pursues constructive relationships with such leaders, yet in some locations an older, narrow understanding of public life still encourages conflictive relations even when they may be unnecessary. As one such political leader noted, "This model sometimes jerks around elected officials, sets us up as adversaries. It's brutal stuff, and might have been effective back in the 1960s. But it's not long-term useful now. . . . I don't think the adversarial approach is necessary to motivate the troops." Of course, this critique must be taken with a grain of salt; elected officials would prefer never to have community organizations confront them. The key point here is that by cultivating a more three-dimensional view of the public realm, faith-based organizing may also develop more nuanced judgment regarding when conflict is necessary and when it stands in the way of public partnership.

Are these just civic platitudes irrelevant for the hard realities of political life? I believe not; contemporary faith-based community organizations cannot assume an a priori antagonistic stance for at least two reasons. The first is pragmatic: their acceptability as political partners and the integrity of their partnership with religious congregations depend upon accepting political leaders as potentially legitimate. The second reason is strategic: the overwhelming locus of political power in America lies in the business sector, and community organizations cannot exert influence on these economic actors alone. They need the leverage provided by partnership with strong political leaders. Constantly attacking political leaders—while easy and effective in an age of virulent antigovernment and antipolitician sentiment in America—only weakens the political system through which community organizations must eventually exert leverage on the economic system.

Implications for Elected Political Leaders

The transition needed on the political leaders' side of these partnerships is simpler: political leaders must accept as legitimate the need for community organizations regularly to establish their autonomy from elected officials. Establishing that autonomy means entering into public conflict when interests legitimately diverge. Failure to do so taints an organization as ineffective and demobilizes its constituency—in the long term, bad for the interests of politicians in broad partnership with that organization.

This essentially entails accepting the autonomous character and organizational limitations of this kind of organizing. Given their connections to churches and the diversity of political views typically embedded there, these organizations must remain nonpartisan, and thus will not be particularly useful mobilizing vehicles for electoral campaigns. Also, the participative democratic process underlying their decision making requires long-term investment and planning for an agenda to take shape; asking these organizations to back specific policies without many months of lead time for consultation will not work. In particular, although staff organizers hold significant influence, they do not control these organizations, and attempts to cut deals with them are likely to lead to frustration. In all these ways, these organizations defy the usual modus operandi of the political system's dealings with the "political base." If political leaders need incentives to risk such a transition, they might consider this: these organizations are particularly linked to swing vote sectors of the population (Hispanics, Catholics, working-class whites, immigrants, etc.), which are crucial to electoral success in contemporary America's remarkably split political landscape.

Promise and Limitations of Church-PICO Structural Symbiosis

As this discussion has sought to show, the structural symbiosis between faith-based organizing federations and religious institutions provides the key to understanding both the promise and limits of this kind of organizing. That symbiosis allows faith-based organizing to draw on the trust, reciprocity, and relational networks that are constituted through the worship experience, shared symbolic worlds, and social relations promoted by religious congregations. In this way, it allows these federations to project power into the public realm more effectively.

At the same time, this symbiosis allows churches to promote political engagement among congregation members without crudely politicizing their worship environment and thus alienating currently "less political" members. In this way, it allows churches to make their ethical and democratic values active in the public realm, without undermining the moral community that sustains those values.

Evidence for the success of this symbiosis comes not only from the testimony of both pastors and organizers, but from the increasing political capacity those faith-based federations that have come to operate more and more as institutions of political society, mediating between civil society and the state. The very strongest federations across the country and in several faith-based organizing networks now carry sufficient muscle and voice in the public realm that they aspire to help reshape institutional politics and redefine policy on local and statewide levels.

Thus, faith-based organizing straddles the divide between civil society and political society. Being anchored in religious institutions of civil society and their ethical traditions, as well as in the power logic of political society, directs the attention of leaders, pastors, and organizers to both ethical and political pressures. This produces the creative tension between moral and instrumental values discussed in chapter 5.

If handled poorly, this now-creative tension could erode, leading faith-based organizing to come unmoored from its roots in those religious traditions, perhaps becoming a more centrist parallel to the highly instrumental organizations of contemporary conservatism, such as the Christian Coalition. That would be a long journey from where PICO now stands; its ethos as well as organizational structure militates against that kind of instrumentalization. But it will clearly remain an option.

If handled well, this same tension may allow faith-based organizing to augment its projection of democratic voice and political muscle into the public realm, while at the same time staying firmly anchored in, guided by, and in critical conversation with religious ethical traditions. If this occurs— and such an outcome is by no means guaranteed, but appears a very live historical possibility—religion may once again contribute in dramatic ways to reinvigorating democracy in America. Secular political theorists might then savor the historical irony of religiously rooted organizations providing models for the "self-limiting, self-regulating" social movements rooted in civil society that they believe necessary for reconstituting truly democratic public life in the modern world. That promise remains on the horizon, but it is being nurtured today by growing numbers of community leaders throughout this nation.

Along with this potential promise, PICO's symbiosis with religious institutions does import certain limitations into the organization. These include the issues it addresses, the character of the socioeconomic constituency it mobilizes, and the political style in which it works. Limitations here are in the eye of the beholder; some will find these difficult to reconcile with their own political preferences or opinions, while others will see them as common sense or politically desirable.

The first limitation regards issues; PICO is unlikely to become an organizing vehicle for issues that are highly controversial within most religious communities, such as gay and lesbian rights or either side of the abortion debate. This is not to say that PICO's institutional basis necessarily makes it reactionary on these kinds of issues. Opinion is genuinely split within the organization, and so it is unlikely to become a rallying point on either side of these issues—particularly where divergent opinions are common within each congregation (such as with the abortion debate).

The second limitation regards faith-based organizing's socioeconomic constituency; one great strength of these organizations is their ability to bring people together across class divides. Many federations include strong participation from both the low-income working class and the middle class, as well as the very poor. But along with this strength comes a great risk: that the concerns and interests of less privileged participants from lower economic classes may come to be excluded, or that these individuals come to feel culturally alienated as middle-class values gain ascendancy in the organization. Status markers such as appearance, educational credentials, and cultural skills often connected with higher education all play important roles in this dynamic. Organizers must work to minimize these distortions. Also, most issues to which these organizations dedicate their time (improving public schools, youth programs, local economic development, public parks, and arguably even community policing and heightened police presence in high-crime neighborhoods) represent public goods, which once instituted are available to all. Organizers can work to assure that lower-status participants share fully in such public goods.

In any case, sustaining participation from lower socioeconomic strata and assuring they have equal voice within the organization will be a permanent challenge in any organization that crosses class boundaries as dramatically as many faith-based organizing federations do. Institutionalizing equal voice for poorer and less educated participants is one of the more reliable ways for the organization to keep a critical social perspective in a time of increasing economic polarization in America. Only this kind of diversity will help faith-based organizing keep a critical perspective on issues, such as police conduct, that affect the poor and the middle class differently.

The third limitation presented by faith-based organizing's alliance with religious institutions concerns the style with which it interacts with political leaders. All of the religious traditions present within this kind of democratic organizing include "prophetic" dimensions, and in most of them this prophetic tradition remains salient enough to undergird and make sense of the conflict inherent in civic engagement. But in the United States, at least, most also have sufficiently internalized standards of "polite" Christianity and/or religious teachings of obeisance to authority that public conflict often sits uncomfortably and feels vaguely un-Christian. As shown in the case studies in previous chapters, this does not rule out engagement in conflictual public life. It does mean, however, that organizers must work to draw the attention of leaders' and pastors to conflict-legitimating elements of their tradition (or, better, ask pastors to do so). It also means that faith-based organizing must emphasize the discursive or dialogical dimension of public life (which will include civil confrontation when positions diverge), turning toward conflict only when public events have shown this to be necessary, e.g., when political officials have been intransigent. While in some sense a limitation, this emphasis on dialogue may foster political partnership, institutional influence, and concrete reform. By leading away from polarization and attack as the dominant modus operandi of contemporary politics, and by organizing marginalized groups to exercise political power, it may also contribute to building an American polity that is both more civil and more democratic.

Conclusion

As recent research has shown, and insightful political observers have no doubt known all along, simplistic causal models suggesting that political opportunities, cultural factors, or access to resources alone determine the outcome of social movements fail to do justice to the complexity and contingency of social change. By learning from such efforts—and by thinking institutionally and culturally about them—this analysis has sought to explain more fully than previous accounts just what role cultural factors play in this multidimensional process. An organization's cultural choices do not alone determine its political success, of course, but neither are they superfluous to successful organizing. Rather, they are one crucial feature in a dynamic process through which we mutually constitute the political vision needed to affirm, critique, and transform our society.[6]

I close with the words of a Latina woman raised in poverty in Oakland, who dropped out of college to marry. Years later, after getting involved in faith-based organizing, she returned to college and gained a diploma. At the time of my interview with her in 1994, Judy Reyes was a leader in PICO's Oakland federation; today she is a PICO organizer. When asked how her experience in community organizing had affected her life, Reyes responded:

It's made me feel more idealistic. It's changed me from a cynic who got burned out and never knew how to be effective. . . . I never thought anything made a difference. Organizing taught me that forms of democracy are real important. That we are part of it and it's not just about voting this or that, it's about people feeling empowered. That's what we do, we get people engaged in things they never used to think made a difference. Before, I never did and I had no sense of power, of being able to affect anything in the political realm. . . .

It's really hard, especially for women. We don't get a lot of opportunities to be leaders in society. Just to call myself a leader is a huge thing. I take a great deal of pride in it because I've always had these abilities and I've tried to use them. But before I'd never found the place where they were valued. I was always shut out or shut down. . . . Here, the more I put

into this the more I got. I saw results. Before, the more I did, the more ex-
hausted I got. It limited me, whereas this just keeps making me think of
potential things to do.

I dedicate this book to all those organizing for democratic change and to
all the "potential things" they will do. Through their work, perhaps Manuel
Castells's closing words may begin to be realized: "Our hope and bet is that,
notwithstanding the threatening storms of the current historical conflicts,
humankind is on the edge of mastering its own future, and therefore of
designing its good city. At last, citizens will make cities."[7]

Organizations Sponsoring Multiracial Organizing and Faith-Based Organizing

The following list is compiled from data provided in 2001 by Interfaith Funders and the Center for Third World Organizing, with thanks to Dan HoSang, Jeannie Appleman, and Mary Ann Flaherty. An asterisk (*) denotes organizations within which interviews were conducted for this study (in addition to the organizations indicated, interviews were conducted in organizing projects in Mobile, Alabama, and Pensacola, Florida, that are no longer in existence or have changed names). A dagger (†) denotes organizations affiliated with CTWO's multiracial organizing model.

Organization, by State	Lead Staff Organizer	City
Arizona:		
Arizona Interfaith	Frank Pierson	Tucson
East Valley Interfaith Sponsoring	Molly McGovern-Huerta	Tempe
Pima County Interfaith Council	Petra Falcon	Tucson
Valley Interfaith Project-Phoenix	Tim McCluskey	Phoenix
California:		
Action for Grassroots Empowerment and Neighborhood Development Alternatives (AGENDA)	Sabrina Smith	Los Angeles
Bay Area Organizing Project	Larry Gordon	San Francisco
Californians for Justice†	Norma Martinez	Long Beach
Center for Third World Organizing (CTWO)†	Dan HoSang	Oakland
Contra Costa Interfaith Sponsoring Committee	Don Stahlhut	Richmond
Fresno Area Congregations Together	Manuel Toledo	Fresno
Inland Congregations United for Change	Patrick Kennedy	San Bernardino
Los Angeles Metropolitan Churches	Rev. Eugene Williams	Los Angeles
Metropolitan Los Angeles Organization	Ernie Cortes	Los Angeles
Monterey Bay Organizing Project	Ken Smith	Watsonville
Oakland Coalition of Congregations	Cliff Gilmore	Oakland
Oakland Community Organizations*	Ron Snyder	Oakland
Orange County Congregation Community*	Corey Timpson	Anaheim
Peninsula Interfaith Action	David Mann	San Carlos
People Acting in Community Together	Matt Hammer	San Jose
People and Congregations Together (PACT)	Tom Amato	Stockton

Organization, by State	Lead Staff Organizer	City
California:		
People Organized to Win Employment Rights (POWER)†	Steve Williams	San Francisco
People United for a Better Oakland (PUEBLO)*†	Dawn Phillips	Oakland
PICO California Project*	Jim Keddy	Sacramento
Sacramento Area Congregations Together	Sandy Smith	Sacramento
Sacramento Communities Taking Action for Neighborhood Dignity†	James Johnson	Sacramento
Sacramento Valley Organizing Community	Larry Ferlazzo	Sacramento
San Diego Organizing Project	Stephanie Gut	San Diego
San Francisco Organizing Project	Denise Collazo	San Francisco
South Central Organizing Committee	Sr. Eleanor Ortega	Los Angeles
United African American Ministerial Action Council	Dr. Timothy Winters	San Diego
Valley Organized in Community Efforts	Mike Clements	Pacoima
Colorado:		
Action for a Better Community*†		Denver
Christians Supporting Community Organizing	Marilyn Stranske	Denver
Congregations Building Community	Sandy Brown Windsor	Fort Collins
Metropolitan Organizations for People*	Mike Kromrey	Denver
Connecticut:		
Elm City Congregations Organized	Pat Speer	New Haven
Greater Bridgeport Interfaith Action	Tim Chiavernin	Bridgeport
Naugatuck Valley Project	Jay Klemundt	Waterbury

Organization, by State	Lead Staff Organizer	City
Delaware:		
Wilmington Interfaith Network	Peggy Heins	Wilmington
District of Columbia:		
Washington Interfaith Network	Martin Trimble	Washington
Florida:		
Federation of DART Organizations in Florida	Rev. Aleem Fakir	Miami
Fighting against Injustice and toward Hope	Haley Grossman	Daytona Beach
Greater Pensacola Community	Richard Papantonio	Pensacola
Hillsborough Organization for Progress and Equality (HOPE)	Rev. Sharon Streater	Tampa
Interchurch Coalition for Action, Reconciliation, and Empowerment	Rev. Paul Cromwell	Jacksonville
Justice for All in Broward	Rev. Johnny Chestnut	Fort Lauderdale
Miami Workers Center†	Gihan Porera	Miami
Orlando Area Interfaith Sponsoring	Peter Phillips	Orlando
People Acting in Community Together	Aaron Dorfman	Miami
People Engaged in Active Community Efforts (PEACE)	Aleem Fakir	West Palm Beach
Polk Ecumenical Action Council for Empowerment	Laura Cooper	Lakeland
Sarasotans United for Responsibility and Equity	Steve Thomas	Sarasota
Georgia:		
Atlantans Building Leadership for Empowerment	Gwen Robinson	Atlanta
Hawaii:		
Faith Action for Community Equity	Pele Soakai	Honolulu

Organization, by State	Lead Staff Organizer	City
Illinois:		
Alliance of Congregations Transforming the South-side	John Eason	Chicago
Central Illinois Organizing Project	Don Danenbring-Carlson	Bloomington
Community Action Group	Joe Ann Bradley	Chicago
Isaiah	David Hatch	Chicago
JACOB	George Hemberger	Joliet
Metropolitan Alliance of Con-gregations	Mary Gonzales	Chicago
Pilsen Neighbors Community Council	Juan Soto	Chicago
South Suburban Action Council	John Heiss	Hazel Crest
Southwest Youth Collabora-tive (SWYC)†	Corina Pedraza	Chicago
United Power for Action and Justice	Stephen Roberson	Chicago
Indiana:		
Interfaith Federation	Cindy Bush	Gary
Iowa:		
Des Moines Area Sponsoring Committee	Tom Holler	Des Moines
Quad Cities Interfaith Spon-soring	Tom Boswell	Davenport
Kansas:		
Wyandotte County Interfaith Sponsoring Council (WISC)	Warren Adams-Leavitt	Kansas City
Kentucky:		
Citizens of Louisville Orga-nized and United Together (CLOUT)	Rev. Robert Owens	Louisville

Organization, by State	Lead Staff Organizer	City
Louisiana:		
All Congregations Together	Joe Givens	New Orleans
Bayou Interfaith Sponsoring Committee (BISCO)	Sharon Gauthe	Houma/Thibodeaux
Congregations Organizing People for Empowerment	Angela Dupris-Givens	Lafayette/New Iberia
East Carroll Interfaith Sponsoring Committee	Sr. Angela Cools-Lartique	Lake Providence
Jeremiah Group Northshore	Van Jones	New Orleans
Louisiana Interfaith Together	Joe Givens	New Orleans
Working Interfaith Network	Rev. Jennifer Jones	Baton Rouge
Maryland:		
Action in Montgomery	Mark Fraley	Silver Spring
Baltimoreans United in Leadership	Jonathan Lange	Baltimore
Interfaith Action Communities	Robert Clemenson	Capitol Heights
Massachusetts:		
Brockton Interfaith Community	Meyer Laken	Brockton
Essex County Community Organization	Luke Hill	Lynn
Greater Boston Interfaith Organization	Lew Finfer	Dorchester
InterValley Project	Ken Galdston	Newton
Merrimack Valley Project	Danny LeBlanc	Lawrence
Pioneer Valley Project	Fred Rose	Springfield
United Interfaith Action	Ray Gagne	Fall River
Worcester Interfaith	Frank Kartheiser	Worcester
Michigan:		
EZEKIEL	Renee Lundgren	Saginaw
Greater Lansing Association for Development and Education (GLADE)	Rev. Walter Reid	Lansing
Michigan Organizing Project	Dwayne Watkins	Grand Rapids
Michigan Organizing Project	Diane Rundquist	Muskegon
Michigan Project	Sr. Cheryl Liske	Detroit
MOSES	Ponsella Hardaway	Detroit

Organization, by State	Lead Staff Organizer	City
Michigan:		
United Now in Serving Our Neighborhoods	Tad Wysor	Ypsilanti
Minnesota:		
Interfaith Action Organization	Jay Schmidt	Minneapolis
Isaiah	Paul Marincel	Minneapolis
Mississippi:		
Amos Network	Carol Stewart	Jackson
Missouri:		
Churches Allied for Community	Kevin Jokisch	Saint Louis
Churches United for Community Action	Sr. Gail Guelker	Saint Louis
Kansas City Church-Community	Warren Adams-Leavitt	Kansas City
Nebraska:		
Community Organizing in Nebraska	Steven Boes	Winnebago
Omaha Temporary Organizing Committee	Damien Zuerlein	Omaha
Omaha Together One Community	Paul Turner	Omaha
New Jersey:		
Camden Churches Organized for People	Joe Fleming	Camden
Interfaith Community Organization	Rev. Geoff Curtiss	Hoboken
New Mexico:		
Albuquerque Interfaith	Sr. Consuelo Tovar	Albuquerque
Southwest Organizing Project†	Michael Guerrero	Albuquerque
New York:		
Central Brooklyn Churches	Rev. Le'roi Gill	Brooklyn

Organization, by State	Lead Staff Organizer	City
New York:		
Community Action Project	Francois Pierre-Louis	Brooklyn
East Brooklyn Congregations	Cathy Maier	Brooklyn
East Harlem Partnership for Change	Robert Moriarity	New York
Families United for Racial and Economic Equality†	Ilana Berger	Brooklyn
Interfaith Action	Brian Kane	Rochester
Long Island CAN	Steve O'Neil	Valley Stream
Lower Manhattan Together	Joe Morris	New York
Make the Road by Walking†	Andrew Friedman	Brooklyn
Mothers on the Move (MOM)°	Helen Schaub	Bronx
Queens Citizens Organizations	Vanessa Dixon	Rego Park
South Bronx Churches	Kim Zalent	Bronx
Voice Buffalo	Nancy Freeland	Buffalo
West Siders Together	Louise Green	New York
North Carolina:		
Helping Empower Local People	Chris Braumann	Charlotte
Ohio:		
ACTION	Michael Stepp	Youngstown
AMOS Project	Kevin Sarsok	Cincinatti
Building Resposibility, Equality, and Dignity (BREAD)	John Aeschbury	Columbus
Interfaith Suburban Action Coalition	Dawn Pella	Euclid
Leaders for Equality and Action in Dayton	Angela Havens	Dayton
Toledoans United for Social Action	Fr. Richard Notter	Toledo
Westside Eastside Congregations Acting Now (We-Can)	Sue Lacy	Cleveland
WIN Action Organizing Project	Dave Scharfenberger	Cincinnati

Organization, by State	Lead Staff Organizer	City
Oregon:		
Portland Organizing Project	Dick Harmon	Portland
Pennsylvania:		
Congregational Action to Lift by Love	Rev. T. Hilbert	Erie
Congregations United for Neighborhood Actions	Monica Sommerville	Allentown
Eastern Pennsylvania Organizing Project	Steve Honeyman	Philadelphia
Philadelphia Interfaith Action	Ceci Schikle	Philadelphia
Shenango Valley Initiative	Peter da Silva	Sharon
United Congregations of Chester County	Robert Davis	Coatesville
Rhode Island:		
Direct Action for Rights and Equality (DARE)†	Sara Mersha	Providence
Rhode Island Organizing Project	Duane Clinker	Providence
South Carolina:		
Tri-County United Action†	Corry Stevenson	Orangeburg
Tennessee:		
Knoxville Interfaith Network	Vivian Manigat	Knoxville
Shelby County Interfaith Sponsoring Committee	Moriba Karamoko	Memphis
Tying Nashville Together	Angela Cowser	Nashville
Texas:		
Allied Communities of Tarrant	Willie Bennett	Fort Worth
Austin Interfaith Sponsoring Committee	Allen Cooper	Austin
Dallas Area Interfaith	Sr. Pearl Ceasar	Eagle Pass
El Paso Interreligious Sponsoring Organization (EPISO)	Joe Rubio	El Paso
Fort Bend Interfaith Council	John Rubenstein	Houston

Organization, by State	Lead Staff Organizer	City
Texas:		
San Antonio Communities Organized for Public Service (COPS)	Elizabeth Valdez	San Antonio
The Metropolitan Organization (TMO)	Joe Higgs	Houston
Triangle Interfaith Project	Sr. Mignonn Koneeny	Nederland
Valley Interfaith	Sr. Judy Donovan	Mercedes
West Texas Organizing Strategy	Ramon Duran	Lubbock
Washington:		
Parent Organizing Project	Joe Chrastil	Spokane
Puget Sound Org. Project	Gary McNeil	Seattle
Wisconsin:		
Hope Offered through Shared Ecumenical Action (HOSEA)	Frank Klein	Milwaukee
Milwaukee Innercity Congregations Allied for Hope (MICAH)	David Liners	Milwaukee
Racine Interfaith Coalition	Ana Garcia-Ashley	Racine

History and Development of PICO

The PICO network expanded greatly following its conversion from a neighborhood-based model to a more explicitly faith-based model and as a more explicitly religious cultural strategy gradually took shape. In the transition to a new cultural strategy, PICO's core staff of the early 1980s was by no means fully aware of where the model would lead them. In particular, they did not clearly see the potential for the kind of symbiotic relationship between democratic organizing efforts and traditional religious institutions that would gradually develop. Indeed, up until the faith-based model actually began to be implemented, many organizers saw churches as just another of the "official institutions" they had rejected as irrelevant or "part of the problem" during the ferment of the 1960s and early 1970s.[1]

The faith-based model was the product, part serendipitous and part strategic, of several factors coming together and gradually reinforcing each other.[2] First, the neighborhood-based model of organizing, in PICO and elsewhere, had stagnated badly and faced a crisis; in director John Baumann's words, "we realized we had to do something differently or we might as well fold up shop." Thus, the PICO staff and leadership were open to change.

Second, the longstanding commitment of religious institutions to funding inner-city community organizing had ultimately made participants open to closer collaboration with churches, in spite of their misgivings at the time regarding institutionalized religion. This longstanding commitment of religious institutions to community organizing represents a story that remains to be told in its full depth. Here I simply note that according to all staff people I interviewed, the primary funders of community organizing over the last three decades have been the Catholic bishops' Campaign for Human Development and, to a lesser extent, various Protestant funding agencies. Essentially all federal funding of community organizing was eliminated in the late 1970s and early 1980s; CHD funding has been particularly essential since that time, with $27,917,500 having been disbursed to the four faith-based organizing networks in 755 grants since 1981.[3] Today, secular foundations, member institutions' dues, and some corporate contributions all play a significant role, but a proper understanding of the genesis of faith-based organizing must recognize the role of national denominational structures as incubators of this movement over many years.[4]

Third, the bald instrumentalization of human relationships common in the older model and in many other forms of political organizing had become troubling to some PICO staff, who were looking for ways to be effective organizers without violating their sense of relational ethics. These factors came together to produce an implicit "search process" as the organization sought alternative models. Once that search process was under way, at least three partial solutions were already available from PICO's internal and external environments.[5]

First, when the staff sought to make ethical sense of the dilemmas of political organizing, religious culture provided the primary shared language through which they could do so. A staff retreat in the midst of the organization's crisis in 1984 encouraged organizers to reflect on the values that motivated their work, and many found that the only language they had to express those values was implicitly or explicitly religious. Likewise, when they tried to articulate why they were uncomfortable with the instrumental approach to organizing, notions of relational integrity rooted in religious traditions provided their main way of doing so.

Second, Dr. José Carrasco, who served as the facilitator of that retreat and remains a key intellectual strategist and visionary within PICO, previously had contact with the Industrial Areas Foundation, which had begun to elaborate on a model for closer collaboration with churches, based on the 1970s experience of COPS, its federation in San Antonio, Texas.[6] Thus, some precedent existed for moving in this direction, and PICO learned from the IAF's experience.

Third, PICO staff had previously been able to mobilize extensive relational networks within the community. Gradually, they realized that the organizational stagnation they were experiencing resulted from the erosion of those networks, as civic institutions and civic ties among poorer urban residents were eviscerated by the social disorganization following economic restructuring in the late 1970s and early 1980s. Thus, by the early 1980s, they were increasingly having to mobilize small family networks and isolated individuals—which required hiring many organizers to blanket the community, and even then was less successful than their earlier efforts. PICO staff recall looking around to consider what civic organizations might provide some institutional base in these communities and realizing that "the only institutions that still thrived at all, besides gangs, were churches."

Each of these three factors—religious culture as a source of meaning and integrity, elements of a model already in existence, and churches as the only institutional base available—represented potential, partial solutions to the dilemmas PICO was facing. They were combined to produce the first tentative forays that eventually led to a model that at its best is relationally based, ethically reflective, and institutionally collaborative. Those forays occurred in part strategically, as staff members sought to solve the problem faced by their organizations, and in part serendipitously, as "found objects" from the cultural milieu around and within PICO. The central element was a cultural strategy: a more direct appeal to religious culture as the basis for organizing, working through churches to reach those who shared that culture.

One clarification is in order here. In a sense, PICO's cultural strategy might be better termed (at least in its initial stages) an institutional strategy that implied a cultural strategy. Within the menagerie of factors leading PICO to seek a new model, the primary factor was PICO's need for a more stable institutional base from which to organize. The cultural factors were also clearly in play, as participants strove to instill meaning into their work in the face of crisis and preserve the integrity of relationships they had forged during the organizing work. Both factors led PICO staff to reclaim religious cultural elements for understanding what they were doing. But initially the key imperative on participants' minds was the need to forge alliances with church institutions; the cultural strategy was thus predominantly institutional and strategic at its origins. That is, it was a PICO-church partnership meant to benefit PICO—more of a strategy than a partnership. Drawing on religious culture was a way to make that strategy more effective.

However, the dynamics of the relationship would soon transform the basis on which it was established, making PICO's turn to religious culture far more substantial, and PICO's sense of partnership far more profound. Prior to its first organizing efforts under the new cultural strategy, PICO's political capacity can be summarized as follows: PICO worked through five neighborhood-based organizations, turned out a maximum of a few hundred participants for citywide actions, and had lost badly on its last major initiative (a moderate reform of city hiring practices). PICO began implementing the new cultural-cum-institutional strategy in Oakland in 1985, following a 1984 staff retreat and extensive consultations with its leadership base. It launched the new effort in the same few neighborhoods, but did so by working directly through one or two key churches in each area.

The institutional effects of this change were immediately evident. In early 1987, after a year and a half of organizing with the express support of church institutions and drawing to some extent on the religious self-understanding of church members, PICO turned out two thousand members to an action with then-mayor Lionel Wilson.[7] His refusal to collaborate with the local PICO federation and his haughty treatment of the low-income and middle-class residents at the meeting earned him the nickname "King Lionel" from the local newspaper. Along with other factors, this event led to his eventual decision not to seek reelection.

Organizers see the shift to this new status, from being a relatively weak organization and a marginal player in city politics to getting the first taste of what would become significant clout at city hall, as resulting directly from the shift in strategy chronicled above; they speak of "new openness" and "new relationships" in people, as well as "a new level of power" that came with the switch. This shift in strategy may or may not in fact alone explain PICO's new success. In a sense, it hardly matters; the situation could reasonably be interpreted in this way, and this gave organizers new confidence in their potential impact.

Though difficult to document, an additional factor no doubt contributed to PICO's success in parlaying religiously linked social capital into political reform efforts: access to sophisticated theological and scriptural expertise. Key PICO personnel in the early 1980s were themselves either strongly religiously committed or explicitly theologically trained, including strategists José Carrasco and Scott Reed; the PICO cofounder and director, Catholic priest John Baumann SJ; and key lead organizers Stephanie Gut and Ron Snyder. PICO's headquarters in Oakland gave it access to the theological and scriptural resources of the Graduate Theological Union in Berkeley, from which it has drawn both articulate spokespersons and new organizers, most prominently Jim Keddy, a key proponent of more explicitly linking the work of organizing to participants' diverse faith commitments and now director of the PICO California Project. That geographical location also gave PICO access to the rich resources of scriptural interpretation and religious oratory of the African American church tradition—which the organization increasingly came to draw on through the 1990s.

Likewise, PICO's strong presence in California meant that its strengthening religious linkages would keep it from being beholden to any one denominational tradition, for those linkages included the social Christianity of the historic black churches, the social gospel and Christian realist perspectives in liberal and moderate Protestantism, the strongly evangelical but socially responsible orientation of the Church of God in Christ, and the intellectual resources, working-class commitments, and Hispanic cultural ties of Roman Catholicism.

Together, these factors pushed PICO's development in the 1990s to the point that it converged in a characteristic local structure for PICO federations, termed here "structural dualism."

Roots of Church-PICO Structural Symbiosis

The symbiotic relationship between PICO and its sponsoring churches developed gradually, as PICO's cultural strategy came to center more clearly on religious culture. Key participants on both sides of the PICO-church collaboration gradually committed themselves to deepening a mutually beneficial relationship. That commitment was dependent upon each side consciously recognizing benefits to be gained from the relationship and a slow process of establishing ties of trust across the PICO-church divide. This has happened unevenly across the PICO network. Where it has occurred, the events follow the same pattern.

The benefits that PICO gains from the relationship are by now clear: above all, relatively unhindered access to the cultural resources and social capital embedded in church congregations. Also significant, in those congregations where the pastor fully endorses and participates in the organizing process, is the pastor's role in "calling out the troops," as one organizer put it, that is, encouraging members to attend actions and other meetings. To a lesser extent, PICO gains some level of legitimacy both among local residents who are not church members and in the wider social world of the city, in which churches are perceived as legitimate institutions. This is true "to a lesser extent" because neither kind of legitimacy is unmixed; some sectors of American political culture—and in particular many political elites—see religion as an illegitimate participant in the public realm (Carter 1993). Also, some neighborhood residents see the local church as an alienating presence rather than as a source of legitimate authority. But on balance, PICO gains legitimacy from this relationship.

PICO also gains motivational benefit from being able to speak of its work in the language that many Americans hold as fundamental to their sense of self. The moral language and symbolism of religion moves from being a "second language" that remains in the background for people to draw on privately, to being a "first language" of shared commitment, solidarity, and calling (Bellah et al. 1985).

For their part, what do religious congregations gain from collaboration with community organizing efforts? Pastors generally identified two primary benefits. First, most pastors consistently identified "leadership development," the formation of individual leaders, as a benefit to their congregations.[8] Most believed their members' leadership experience in faith-based organizing translated effectively into leadership roles in church affairs; for example, Father Joseph Justice of Orange County, California, watched his PICO-trained leaders organize on their own initiative to pay off the parish debt—successfully. This perception of the transferability of leadership skills was strongest among pastors who valued lay decision-making authority and did not already feel their own authority challenged by lay participation. PICO's leadership formation appears to be appreciated most by pastors who value both lay initiative and retain sufficient autonomy to feel effective as leaders themselves.

Second, pastors spoke of deriving great satisfaction from seeing their members active in transforming society, in keeping with the social ethical teachings of their tradition. They expressed this in various ways, such as "implementing the gospel vision in the world," "building the Kingdom of God," "making the world the place God wants it to be," or, more ambiguously, "taking the city for our Lord Jesus Christ." Many noted the frustration of trying to transform the world from the pulpit, and saw it as a calling specific to laypeople to "carry the message from the church community into the political world," in the words of one Episcopalian priest.

There may also be significant benefits to churches rarely recognized by pastors themselves. First, since they are part of and dependent on the wider social fabric of

American society, churches stand to benefit from whatever success a federation has in improving life in its community. Second, *if* it is not abused, the church-constituted social capital on which faith-based organizing draws is not used up in the process of organizing; indeed, as noted above the whole notion of social capital conceives of trust and networks as "moral resources" whose mobilization actually deepens the reservoir of trust and relationship. Third, extensive involvement in community affairs can strengthen churches by keeping worship from becoming so otherworldly as to be meaningless to some members. That is, it can anchor the worship-based experience of transcendence—at its best, the heart of the spiritual experience fostered by religious communities, as I argue in chapter 6—in the everyday lives and struggles of churchgoers. Fourth, lay-led community organizing sponsored by religious institutions may bring heightened public authority to religious leaders. This may be particularly attractive to some clergy, in that the therapy-based model of the role of pastors popularized in American seminaries in the last two decades appears to have contributed to the declining social prestige accorded to pastors in American society. High-profile engagement with successful organizing projects may be quite satisfying to pastors uncomfortable with this weakening of the pastorate—which, though sometimes derisively called the effeminization of the pastor's office, can be constraining to female and male religious leaders alike.

Lay leaders also benefit from the deepening symbiosis between PICO and their churches. As religious discourse has moved from being a private second language to a public first language of PICO's political culture, they gain a deeper sense of integration between their "spiritual lives" and their "civic lives." The lay believers who lead the organizing effort have come to experience civic engagement as an integral dimension of their religious commitment rather than as extraneous or, at best, only vaguely related to it. Though of course not all participants experience this work in this way, multiple respondents echoed the sentiment of leader Willie Mae Randerson: "I find God in this work. I find God in church on Sunday mornin', but I sure find God in the people I do this work with. And, whew, do I find God when we've got two hundred people in a room, makin' our leaders lead." Finally, as the faith-based organizations have grown more effective, lay leaders and their churches benefit from government policies that better sustain the neighborhoods in which they live, the schools their children attend, the medical systems on which they depend, and more equitable labor markets in which they work.

The symbiosis between churches and contemporary faith-based organizing also means that political tactics once acceptable in the traditional models of community organizing more loosely affiliated with churches are now rendered dubious or unacceptable: embedding the organizing work within religious language makes that work more vulnerable to ethical critique based on religious moral traditions. We saw this in previous chapters, when pastors cautioned their members against treating political officials unfairly. While this ethical moderation of the tone of community organizing constrains political tactics, in the long run it has politically *strengthened* the organizations by making them acceptable interlocutors in political negotiations.

Some organizers recognize the implications of both the integration of the spiritual and political dimension of leaders' lives and the ethical frame in which this places their work. Founder John Baumann compared the older model to PICO's current work:

> I would say that in the old model we *used* the church. . . . And we had no systematic way of developing leadership. People were often uncomfortable with tactics we used. . . . If we're going to empower people, we need to empower them both spiritually and physically. The old Alinsky model is much more into power, go after them, beat them up . . . it tends to use the church, while I see the church as central, important, a building block for everything we do. It's not just a source of people. [Integrating the spiritual and civic] lets us work with leaders over the long term, gradually develop them as leaders. Pastors and churches do the personal formation, and we form them as leaders.

Thus faith-based organizing has moved from an arguably parasitic relationship with local faith communities toward a potentially rich, symbiotic relationship. In a sense, this symbiosis has transformed PICO in the same way that PICO's work has transformed the lives of some of its leaders; both PICO and its leaders affirm pragmatically that they have interests (organizational interests and self-interests) that they seek to further, and assume that their collaborators (churches and other leaders) also legitimately strive to further their own interests. But in both cases their reciprocal collaboration has moved them beyond an instrumental quid pro quo arrangement, a bartering for services and benefits in pursuit of self-interest. Rather, the most advanced leaders, organizers, and pastors have come to live in sufficiently shared symbolic worlds that the "self" at the heart of the self-interest calculation has expanded; the organizational and personal "selves" involved in this work experience themselves as embedded in a wider social world within which they share common interests.

Notes

Introduction

1. PICO relied extensively on research by the Health Insurance Policy Program, based at the Center for Health and Public Policy Studies at UC-Berkeley and the Center for Health Policy Research at UCLA; and the Insure the Uninsured Project based in Santa Monica. The data quoted in this political event came from "The State of Health Insurance in California, 1999" report by the UCB-UCLA group (Schauffler and Brown 2000).

2. I was not in the vicinity when these politicians entered the hall, and thus did not observe this. It was the object of much mirth after the event, with PICO leaders reenacting the looks on politicians' faces as they walked in and saw the crowd.

3. The closing lines from Amos also, of course, evoke the American civil rights movement and the legacy of Dr. Martin Luther King, Jr., who used them frequently in his work—most memorably in his 1964 "I have a dream" speech at the March on Washington.

4. Here and elsewhere, speeches and prayers at large actions are quoted as reconstructed from the author's notes, recorded simultaneously with the events reported.

5. See *Inequality by Design* by Claude Fischer et al. (1996) for one account of this heightened polarization in America—already one of the most inegalitarian advanced industrial societies in the world. Recent increases in the minimum wage and tight labor markets have marginally improved the situation of the working poor, but have barely dented the polarization between rich and poor.

6. This in contrast to an older literature on political culture, originating in the work of Gabriel Almond and Sidney Verba (1963).

7. The best source on Alinsky's career is Horwitt 1989; see also Alinsky's own statements (1969; 1971). For an excellent brief analysis of how his version of radical democracy influenced faith-based organizing, see Hart 2001.

8. Boyte 1989, Boyte and Kari 1996, and Greider 1992 include some analysis of faith-based community organizing. Rogers 1990 provides a popular account of this work. More recently, excellent scholarly analyses have appeared; see Hart 2001 and Warren 2001.

9. Several factors explain the rather invisible nature of faith-based organizing. First, although they indeed make up a coherent field of similar organizations, the 133 federations go by a diverse set of names so that one might move from one city to another and never know that the same organizing model is at work. See appendix 1 for a full list of all 133 federations. Second, a large portion of the national-level publicity on the field has focused on the Industrial Areas Foundation, thus blurring the perception of the wider field. Third, though faith-based organizing groups have been mentioned frequently as practitioners of civic engagement, until recently little scholarly work has focused on the field. Finally, faith-based organizing has escaped the attention of national political observers because until recently none of the networks were capable of operating in arenas of political power beyond local or county governments; see the discussion in chapter 2.

10. These and the following data are from a study sponsored by Interfaith Funders, the first study to gather data on the entire field of faith-based community organizing (Warren and Wood 2001). The two million figure is the midpoint between high and low estimates of total members of congregations sponsoring this organizing. All numbers listed in the text are projections. The study interviewed the directors of three-quarters of the organizing federations around the country that could be identified (network-affiliated or independent, with the criteria for inclusion being that they practice a form of organizing recognizable as faith-based community organizing and have an office and at least one full-time staff member on the payroll at the time of the study). Data were then projected from the 100 responding federations to reflect the full universe of 133 federations nationwide, with the projection weighted by network to reflect differential participation. Numbers are rounded off, in keeping with methodological uncertainties and the projected nature of the data. See also Wood 1997, 2002.

11. I use the term "federation" here to describe the typical organizations that carry out faith-based organizing in a single location (usually a city, though in some instances in one part of a city or in an entire metropolitan area). Some of the networks would not use this terminology, instead referring to their typical citywide units as "broad-based organizations" or just "organizations," for example.

12. Because the staff of the Center for Third World Organizing (CTWO) prefer the term "multiracial organizing" to describe their work, I will use it except in contexts where it will create confusion. Primarily, this is where I compare the constituencies of CTWO and PICO: since both are highly multiracial (in different ways), I use the term "race-based organizing" to describe CTWO's work.

13. See Anner 1996 for the only available book-length account of multiracial organizing. See also Delgado [1993a?] for a leading insider's account of multiracial organizing and its contrast with the Alinsky tradition.

14. The most influential of the social movements work has been done by Sidney Tarrow, Doug McAdam, Charles Tilly, David Snow, and their students. Core concepts in much of this literature include political opportunity structure, mobilizing structures, collective action frames, strategy, and action repertoires. See Tarrow 1994 for an excellent summary of this work. My focus on institutional and cultural dynamics overlaps with these approaches but links them to the overall institutional and cultural dilemmas of democracy. My approach is closely akin to the rethinking of social movement studies outlined in McAdam, Tarrow, and Tilly 2001, which centers attention on

the flow of relations within and across movements. On strategy in social movements, see Ganz 2000b.

15. On the role of political opportunity structures in shaping social movements, see Tarrow 1994 and McAdam 1982. For a critique of this concept, see Goodwin and Jasper 1999.

16. The budget figures cited are for CTWO's and PICO's projects in Oakland only, called People United for a Better Oakland (PUEBLO) and Oakland Community Organizations (OCO) respectively; i.e., they do not include the central office budgets of CTWO and PICO, both of which are based in Oakland. Note too that by the year 2000 OCO's budget had grown significantly to about $447,000. PUEBLO's budget had remained about the same. In-kind support to both organizations is limited to occasional donations, plus space for meetings when they are held away from the central offices. Both organizations draw on the latter, but PICO more substantially: organizing committees typically meet once a month at their sponsoring churches (more often immediately before actions), whereas CTWO held meetings at social service agencies only a few times a year.

17. Both the lead contamination project and the Beat Health project, initiated under pressure from CTWO and PICO respectively, have reportedly been used as models for similar projects nationwide. The term "community policing" covers a range of models that focus on police having a stable presence and problem-solving orientation in high-crime neighborhoods, rather than primarily pursuing a reactive crime-response model of policing. See Skogan and Hartnett 1997 and various publications available from the web site of the National Institute of Justice.

18. One partial exception to the similarity in the two groups' political orientations can be seen in occasional PICO support for increased police presence in high-crime neighborhoods, whereas CTWO wants to reduce that presence. Some participants see this as evidence that CTWO represents a more "radical" political stance, and PICO a more "mainstream" stance. There is some truth in this, but more striking is the similarity between the two groups' actual relations with the police department: both sought specific concessions, including measures (asset forfeiture, Beat Health, community policing) opposed initially by the department or the police officers' union. Their negotiations regarding these matters were at times confrontational and at times rather friendly; and both ultimately won limited concessions that impinged somewhat on police autonomy but largely left intact the political power of the law enforcement lobby on local American politics.

19. The four core leaders in PUEBLO (CTWO) during most of this study were all women, as were eleven of the fourteen people in a broader group of those attending organizing meetings more or less regularly. Of the twenty-two leaders who attended OCO executive board (PICO) and organizing meetings more or less regularly, ten were men and twelve women.

20. Other participants in PICO and CTWO were informed that I was writing a study of the organizations, and I regularly identified myself in that way.

21. "Participants" as I use it here includes the three groups playing key roles within these organizations: (1) leaders, i.e., the participating residents in neighborhoods and members of congregations or other institutions (and, more ambiguously, the clients of social service agencies that attend political events); (2) pastors and social

agency staff who provide entree to their congregations or agencies and sometimes are active in the organizing process; and (3) paid organizing staff in each organization.

22. Burawoy 1991 and Whyte 1991a, 1999b, provide further description of ethnographic and participatory action research.

23. See especially Putnam 2000; Verba, Schlozman, and Brady 1995; Casanova 1994; Habermas 1989; Calhoun 1992; Coleman 1996; Benhabib 1992; and Cohen and Arato 1992.

Part One

1. I do not do so, however, in the vein they recommend, which is to identify the "mechanisms" that concatenate up into larger "processes" of contention—at least, I do not do so explicitly. My orientation is instead toward the relational processes themselves, both within these organizations and in their relationships with outside actors and political elites. As a result, this study will no doubt have a different tenor than one more explicitly anchored in the conceptual categories of *Dynamics of Contention*, but it carries a parallel analytic thrust.

Chapter 1

1. My "culture in action" perspective owes a great deal to Ann Swidler's seminal article (1984). This analysis shares Swidler's stance that we can understand culture most fully by seeing it dynamically at work in specific situations, but only partially adopts her orientation toward focusing on the strategic uses of cultural skills. Attention in later parts of this book will be on how culture shapes action despite people's strategic intentions.

2. This anticipates the later analysis of the importance of information sharing and strategy development across the PICO network. That is, while concerns and issues are identified through wide consultation with the organization's constituents, the latter are not assumed to be familiar with all the potential solutions to those concerns. Strategies for addressing issues are formed through consultations with participants, other local experts, the national PICO network, and outside academic and political experts.

3. Though the citywide PICO organizing effort is markedly multiracial, the Saint Elizabeth committee is heavily Latino, reflecting the parish as a whole.

4. Most names used throughout this book are real. Participants in public events already had made their involvement public; I offered to use pseudonyms for all interviewees, but most signed releases saying they preferred to have their real names used. In a few instances, names have been changed or deleted at the interviewee's request.

5. At this point someone suggested, "Or maybe we should just go take over his offices, sit in there until he meets with us!" This drew laughter and appeared to have been suggested in jest, although it also clearly represented real frustration among the participants. Note the contrast with the culture of CTWO's model of multiracial organizing, in which "direct action" such as this plays a central role.

6. Here and throughout the book, unless otherwise noted italics in the quotations indicate verbal emphasis present in the speaker's original diction.

7. The citywide OCO campaign the previous spring had focused on getting the city to improve street lighting in high-crime areas of town; the lighting had been turned down as a budget-reduction measure. The OCO campaign eventually succeeded

in diverting city money from a parking garage desired in a wealthy area of the Oakland hills toward an extensive street lighting improvement project.

8. See McAdam 1982 and Tarrow 1994. In three years of participant observation within PICO, I never heard organizers or leaders refer to PICO as a "social movement"; they understand their work as permanent and grounded in participants' everyday lives in a way they believe is not reflected in the term "social movement"—which they associate with "mobilizing" people rather than "organizing" them. Analytically, of course, faith-based organizing does amount to a "social movement," albeit one in some ways different from more familiar examples. I will follow the participants' own usage, except where a more analytical term is appropriate.

9. In at least some federations of one national network, gatherings of five to fifteen acquaintances in "house meetings" complement and sometimes largely supplant one-on-one meetings as the relational basis of organizing. The house meeting appears to have entered faith-based organizing through the influence of the United Farm Workers.

10. I attended this five-day national training for PICO leaders outside San Jose, California, in July 1993. More details of the retreat are included in chapter 5 below. The staff person leading this session was PICO associate director Scott Reed.

11. As Mark Warren (1995) argues, the match between "participative hierarchy" in faith-based organizing and some church settings partly explains the success of this model: pastoral authority facilitates the organizing process, but only in combination with a participatory organizing process does it lead to the dynamic democratic potential of faith-based organizing. Otherwise, it can amount to the vertical social networks that Putnam (1993) correlated with less effective democratic institutions in Italy.

12. Prayer plays some role in all the faith-based organizing networks and independent efforts, but the fuller incorporation of public prayer into the work is an uneven (and probably contested) trend within the field. The discussion here summarizes the situation in those federations that are working to incorporate religious elements more fully into the organizing process.

13. The seventeen actions include three OCO citywide actions, two PICO statewide actions, and seven local actions by OCO congregations—plus actions in three other PICO federations and two in another network.

14. Both examples are actual scenarios I witnessed. Note that the challenge from an organizer to a pastor is atypical, the product of the pastor's clear commitment to faith-based organizing and the organizer's perception that her relationship with the pastor was strong enough to allow her to take this role. More typically, leaders from the pastor's own congregation would be asked to take this role.

15. Anecdotes from organizers suggest that such organizational collapse occurred regularly under older models of organizing. Apparently, a similar collapse occurred more recently in Los Angeles under a faith-based organizing effort that, while initially successful, failed to continuously cultivate these local roots. See Skerry 1993 for an account of the early years of this effort; I am unaware of any published analyses of its near-collapse. That effort is now being rebuilt.

16. For critiques of this parochial tendency in community organizing, see Kling and Posner 1990 and Delgado [1993a?].

17. On strategy, leadership, and professional organizers, see especially Ganz 2000a, 2000b. On resources, networks, and political opportunities, see Tarrow 1994. For a recent theoretical rethinking of the social movements and democratization literatures along lines consistent with my emphasis on relational and cultural flows, see McAdam, Tarrow, and Tilly 2001.

18. In noting this history, I do not wish to caricature the earlier years of community organizing. A great deal of creative democratic organizing went on in the earlier stages of Alinsky-inspired organizing that eventually gave rise to the faith-based and multiracial organizing models developed here. Its best practitioners sustained that creativity and democratic focus, in the work of independent organizers and groups like the Association of Community Organizations for Reform Now (ACORN) and National People's Alliance. But the broad pattern identified here captures the spirit of much of the later period. Mike Miller of the Organize! Training Center in San Francisco has taught me much about these complexities in the organizing tradition.

Chapter Two

1. The Interfaith Funders study is described more fully in the introduction. See Warren and Wood 2001 for the full report.

2. Based on the criteria cited above, the total number of projects affiliated with each network in 1999 were as follows: IAF (48); PICO (30); Gamaliel (27); DART (12); smaller networks (Regional Council of Neighborhood Organizations [RCNO], Organizing Leadership and Training Center [OLTC], InterValley Project [IVP]: 10 total); and independent federations (6). Strong concentrations exist in California, Texas, New York, Illinois, and Florida. Full disclosure: my own research has been within PICO and the IAF, nearly all of which has been done through funding from foundations or academic sources. I have had costs of one two-day research trip partially subsidized by each organization, but have received financial compensation from neither.

3. By 1999, OCO had grown to include thirty-six member organizations, of which thirty-four were religious congregations, and by 2000 it included forty member organizations—all of which were religious congregations. The sixteen congregations that joined OCO between 1995 and 1999 (three former member congregation no longer participated) were predominately historic black Protestant churches, though they included an outreach ministry to the homeless, a Pentecostal congregation, two "mainline" congregations (Methodist and Presbyterian), and a Disciples of Christ congregation. I concentrate here on the 1995 member organizations, as they constituted OCO at the time of my most intense fieldwork and continue to provide the bulk of participants and because the congregations that recently joined OCO may or may not endure for the long term. The 1995 numbers thus provide the most solid profile of the organization, though of course the congregations that joined more recently may ultimately prove equally or more important.

4. From the 1998 Annual Report of Oakland Community Organizations, 2.

5. On African American religious forms and social ministries, see Lincoln and Mamiya 1990; Pattillo-McCoy 1998, 1999; and McRoberts 2000.

6. At this time Reyes was a local leader whithin an OCO member church. She later became a staff person for the PICO California Project. Likewise, Reverend James Abner later became a PICO organizer in Florida.

7. From an undated OCO flier distributed in early 1994.

8. "Charter schools" are part of an experiment in school reform based on giving on-site administrators, teachers, and parents direct control over their school. Though financed publicly, they operate largely independent of school district supervision.

9. Nationally, in 1999 13 percent of faith-based organizing federations had at least one labor union local as a member institution, and the latter made up 15 percent of the noncongregational institutions that participated as members (Warren and Wood 2001, tables 3 and 4).

10. See prominent coverage throughout this period in local newspapers, including the *San Francisco Chronicle* (e.g., November 9, 1999) and the *Oakland Tribune* (e.g., August 15, 1999, and March 5, 2001).

11. See, for example, Skerry's (1993) account of organizing in Los Angeles.

12. Interestingly, the one occasion of a pastoral veto on access by a federation to his congregation did not involve disagreement over a particular issue in which the federation was involved. Rather, it concerned a disagreement over the *style* of organizing, particularly the use of conflict as an organizing tool. The pastor objected to any public confrontation with elected officials under any circumstances. This underscores the importance of cultural work on the issue of conflict within faith-based organizing, which was touched upon earlier and to which we return in chapter 5.

13. For the best discussion of moral communities as "communities of memory and hope," see Bellah et al. 1985.

14. These elements of course vary across congregations tied to differing religious traditions, and even differing denominations within the same broad religious tradition. But the important recent work by Becker (1999) shows how they vary dramatically within denominations as well.

15. McRoberts (forthcoming) depicts the remarkable diversity of religious practice and moral-political vision even within one segment of American life often depicted as monolithic: urban African American Christianity.

16. Of course, not all symbols and meanings are appropriate in this way; we will see in chapter 5 how participants in PICO highlight some religious meanings over others.

17. "Symbiosis" is defined by *Merriam-Webster's Collegiate Dictionary*, 10th ed., as "the intimate living together of two dissimilar organisms in a mutually beneficial relationship." The classic example of symbiosis is the relationship between nitrogen-fixing bacteria and plants that cannot obtain necessary nitrogen on their own. Their symbiotic relationship allows both organisms to thrive, each drawing benefit from the other.

18. Wuthnow (1988) provides the best account of the recent shift in American religious life to para-denominational forms of organization—i.e., religious organizations that transcend local congregations but operate outside of denominational structures. Coleman (forthcoming) looks in detail at the contemporary ministries of such para-denominational groups, including Bread for the World, Pax Christi, Focus on the Family, Habitat for Humanity, PICO, and the social ministries of black megachurches.

19. I gloss over here, for the sake of brevity, another important constituent ingredient in the recipe for symbiotic, ethically rooted organizing. Key personnel in several foundations play crucial roles in fostering faith-based organizing generally and deepen-

ing pastor-organizer understanding particularly. Among the key players in this regard are the Irvine Foundation in California; a multitude of local and national program officers in the Catholic Campaign for Human Development, the Jewish Fund for Justice, and denominational funding agencies of the Methodist, Presbyterian, Lutheran, and other Protestant traditions; Interfaith Funders and the Neighborhood Funders Group; and the Raskob, Mott, Discount, Needmor, and Veatch foundations, as well as a variety of regional foundations. The major religious funders nationally, the Lilly Endowment and Pew Charitable Trusts, as well as the Ford Foundation, have up until now funded *studies* of faith-based organizing and/or the continuing formation of professional organizers, but not faith-based organizing per se. Any of the three might move in this direction in the future. Doing so would allow these major foundations to promote the coordination, professional and congregational development, evaluation of best practices, and ethical reflection that would strengthen faith-based organizing.

20. Of course a pastor's understanding of this "proper relationship" may reflect sophisticated understanding of the relationship of faith traditions to politics and of religious institutions to the wider civil society, political world, and economic system—or may reflect a desire for an unhealthy degree of control over church members' political views and activities.

21. Other significant statewide or regional organizing efforts include the Arizona IAF, PICO in Colorado, Gamaliel in several locations in the upper Midwest, DART in Florida, separate initiatives by PICO and the IAF in Louisiana, and an important collaborative effort in New England involving the IVP, OLTC, and the IAF.

22. *Sacramento Bee*, September 2, 2000, 1. A conspiracy theorist might suggest such an outcome could only be the result of behind-the-scenes machinations by the political leadership. I can find no evidence to support that interpretation: it appears to have been a case of last-minute catastrophe under the pressure of multiple deadlines. Indeed, at a press conference the following day, Senator Burton was intensively questioned by reporters regarding the death of this bill, and is reported by those present to have raised his arms to his sides and said, "Hey, just fucking shoot me!"

23. See especially Brown, Ponce, and Rice 2001.

24. PICO's strong political capacity in California is further evidenced by the fact that even as the legislative endgame regarding health care was developing, the network moved to address the California housing crisis—particularly the dearth of affordable housing for working families in high-rent areas—with another statewide action with three thousand people present (*San Francisco Chronicle*, February 26, 2001). Key demands included one billion dollars in one-time funding from the state's large surplus, to be used for affordable housing development, including rental, home ownership, and farmworker housing programs (this bill died under the fiscal pressure of the energy crisis, at least for 2001); and a supplemental twenty million dollars per year (a 40 percent increase) in ongoing money for California's key tax credit for low-income rental housing (this bill was still under consideration in September 2001). The legislature did pass fifteen million dollars in continuing funding for the parent-teacher home visit program that PICO was instrumental in founding.

25. The political opinion data come from "California Statewide Tobacco Settlement Priorities," the report from an August 2000 poll by Fairbank, Maslin, Maullin & Associates, commissioned by the Health Committee of the California State Senate.

Chapter Three

1. At the time of this research, PUEBLO was one of five community organizing projects directly affiliated with or closely coordinated by CTWO (see appendix 1 for list). CTWO also trains organizers from many other organizations focused on working in minority communities, and publishes *Third Force,* a magazine on organizing respected among promulticulturalism grassroots activists. CTWO is also informally affiliated with the Applied Research Center in Oakland, run by CTWO founder Gary Delgado.

2. In 1995 several federal appeals courts ruled that such seizures of cash and/or property, in combination with criminal charges, constituted double jeopardy and were thus unconstitutional. As of 2001, asset forfeiture continues, but on a much-restricted basis, in that assets can be forfeited only following conviction.

3. See Alinsky 1969, 1971, for the key strategic statements informing this model of organizing; see Boyte 1980, 1989, and Horwitt 1989 for good assessments of Alinsky's work.

4. Delgado [1993a?], 20–21. Delgado was among the founders of CTWO and now directs the Applied Research Center, an independent but closely affiliated institution resembling a kind of grassroots think tank. He characterizes contemporary faith-based organizing in these same terms. As will become clear in later chapters, I think this mischaracterizes the faith-based model.

5. Because I frequently served as a translator during PUEBLO organizing meetings, it was at times impossible to take extensive notes. These summaries are reconstructions from limited quotations recorded during meetings and extensive notes recorded immediately thereafter.

6. OCO/PICO was not among those listed. It was mentioned at least twice, but never written on the list by the staff person serving as recorder. At this time, neither OCO nor PUEBLO pursued alliances with the other. Though counterintuitive, non-collaboration between faith-based and race-based groups is typical. It arises from both their similarities and their differences: their similarities make them competitors, and their divergent organizing styles make merging efforts difficult. Much less typical is the collaboration of the two organizations in the late 1990s on a campaign called Kids First!, which successfully fought to set aside a portion of the Oakland city budget for programs serving children.

7. See Lichterman's (1996) rich analysis of similar forms of "personalist" political culture in mostly white environmental groups.

8. By "reinforced" here, I refer to what sociologists call "institutionalization"— the process by which shared symbols, commitments, and social ties become routine, taken-for-granted aspects of people's social worlds. For key insights into the role of cultural elements in stabilizing interpersonal ties, see Zucker 1977, 1988, Wood 1999, and chapter 6 below.

9. The arrangement affected only *federal* asset forfeiture funds: 15 percent of any such funds over ten thousand dollars were made available for disbursement. It did not touch smaller amounts from the federal process nor the much larger state asset forfeiture funds. While certainly short of the goal of a fifty-fifty split, this represented significant success coming as it did at a time of increasing concentration of city funds in law enforcement agencies.

10. This of course oversimplifies the relationship among the SCLC, SNCC, and the Nation of Islam, as well as organizations such as the NAACP and CORE. The key point here is CTWO's closer affinity to the later trends in that movement, in which racial identity with its particularizing appeal became more salient within the movement than the earlier, more universalizing appeal to human dignity and civil rights. This transition coincides with and partly resulted from the shift in geographical focus of the movement out of the South, with its highly personalized racism in all areas of social life, and into the northern and western cities, where the early forms of identity politics took shape in confronting the impersonal, more bureaucratic forms of racism found there. That broad transition affected all branches of the civil rights struggle, including the SCLC. These issues have been discussed extensively elsewhere, and lie well beyond the purposes of this book. Morris (1984) offers a good entry point to that discussion.

11. Here and in chapters 5 and 6, I simply use practices, beliefs, and ethos as a way of framing the description of the internal cultures of CTWO, PICO, and individual local organizing units within a PICO federation. Within this description, I use insights from more recent work in cultural analysis to better illuminate the cultures of community organizing.

12. For the sake of brevity, this description of CTWO's social analysis distills into a paragraph the content of several "political education" sessions, the written materials used in those session, conversations and interviews with organizers in CTWO and PUEBLO, and multiple issues of CTWO's publication *Third Force*.

13. In chapter 6, I draw on the "new institutionalism" in the study of organizations for insight into the role of rituals in stabilizing organizational solidarity. See, for example, Zucker 1977, 1988.

14. In recent years, some PICO organizations have cultivated prominent roles for youth leaders. The PICO federations in San Francisco and New Orleans have been especially active in this regard.

15. The attendance goal of 250 was expressed repeatedly during the organizing campaign. At least one newspaper account of the session said that 125 people attended, but this definitely was an overcount.

16. This discussion reflects Pedersen and Sorensen's (1989) argument for the analytic advantages to identifying cultural *contradictions* within organizations, rather than assuming such contradictions are reconciled through underlying organizational assumptions. They argue that, though scholarly analysts often believe they have "identified" such reconciling assumptions, more typically these reconciliations are *constructed* by the scholars in their search for rational explanations of organizational life when in fact significant irrationalities pervade most organizations.

17. At times in both interviews and official organizational statements, sexual preference was also included as a key category. But this was not done consistently.

18. It is worth noting here that "family" as the basis of CTWO's organizing entered into the interviews fairly frequently, mostly with leaders but also occasionally with staff. Thus, for example, Rinku Sen's opening description of CTWO was as "a multiracial, family-membership organization, with direct action as the linchpin of organizing for policy change that is replicable."

19. Personal correspondence to the author, January 27, 2000. This comment came

in response to HoSang's reading of an initial draft of this chapter, when I solicited his reactions and feedback to the analysis here. He introduced this feedback by writing "I thought your treatment of the internal culture of PUEBLO was excellent."

20. See Taylor 1991 for an insightful discussion of the philosophical underpinnings of these currents.

21. Note the heavy reliance throughout CTWO's organizational culture on the notion of the dominant culture. On one hand, this denotes anything embodied in dominant institutions; with this meaning, it is a powerful rhetorical tool for effective organizing. It creates a dividing line between organizing participants and institutions of oppression in the wider society, which lends cultural force to organizing against "them." On the other hand, the dominant culture in contemporary America is a mass consumer culture that takes different forms in different social settings, but deeply pervades not only the lives of whites, but all minority communities as well (except perhaps first-generation immigrants). But in this second meaning, the concept loses its rhetorical power for us-versus-them organizing. The second meaning thus receives little or no attention in the organizational culture.

22. See Barber 1984 for one discussion of "strong democracy."

23. I do not suggest that the direct action strategy results only from this dynamic—clearly it represents both a conscious calculation on the part of staff about what strategies most effectively mobilize and educate constituents and an outgrowth of the organization's experience of being ignored except when such disruption looms. Indeed, I suspect these latter factors are more important influences, as discussed earlier. But I do suggest that the dynamics of trust necessarily play a role whenever some participants are to represent others in negotiation settings.

24. I do not analyze the Kids First! campaign in detail here, as it occurred after my fieldwork was completed and in collaboration with OCO; both factors make it difficult to adequately analyze the cultural and political dynamics within this campaign. Worth noting, however, is that it did not generate any greater sustained collaboration between the two organizations.

25. Calpotura and Fellner 1996, 1; this paper was part of a debate within organizing circles concerning what I call here faith-based and race-based organizing.

26. Calpotura and Fellner 1996, 6.

27. These powers make Oakland's board a relatively strong model for civilian police review (Walker and Kreisel 2001). This initial victory may become a basis for key CTWO leverage in other areas of the CCSPA campaign.

Chapter Four

1. In addition to the sources cited, the ensuing discussion is shaped by Tocqueville's pioneering account in *Democracy in America* ([1835–40] 1956) of the importance of voluntary associations in sustaining democracy; the attention of Bellah et al. (1985, 1991) to the moral languages and social institutions that sustain a democratic culture; Foley and Edwards's (Foley and Edwards 1998; Edwards and Foley 1997) critical discussions of the social capital theoretical framework; and Bent Flyvbjerg's (2001) argument for "making social science matter."

2. A broad recent literature focuses on the public sphere. Among the seminal works are Habermas 1984, 1987, 1989; Cohen and Arato 1992; Stepan 1988; Calhoun 1992; and Casanova 1994.

3. My use of the concepts of political society and government draws heavily from the theoretical framework developed by Alfred Stepan (1988). Though there and elsewhere in political science the terms "government" and "state" are distinguished, I here use them interchangeably for the sake of simplicity.

4. Aldrich 1995, Coleman 1996, and Wattenberg 1998 provide the best recent analyses of the current status of American political parties.

5. Seligman (1995) provides a fine overview of the rich but confused literature on the concept of civil society. I emphasize here the organizational and associational element of civil society. Though historically the concept of civil society developed in contrast to the realm of government, I use it in contrast to both government and economic activity—that is, in contrast to what Habermas calls "the Systems." Civil society thus represents the organizational and associational component of the life-world.

6. For further discussion of these competing and complementary understandings of the public realm, see Benhabib 1992; Arendt 1958, 1990; and Cohen and Arato 1992.

7. I am unable to trace the origins of the phrase; the earliest usage I can document was by Ernesto Cortes of the IAF network.

8. I draw particularly from Putnam 1993, which combines detailed empirical evidence and strong theoretical insight. Though his more recent work on the United States (2000), provides compelling evidence of a broad and steep decline in social capital in American society since the 1950s, his emphasis on this as the "cause" of our society's ills and lack of critical focus on the institutional, political, and economic forces and decisions that have led to this decline directs attention away from the core concerns of this book. Thus, for my core concerns here—the cultural and institutional underpinnings of democratic accountability—Putnam's work on Italy is far more relevant.

9. See Almond and Verba 1963 for a classic international comparative study of "civic culture"—albeit one that thinks of political culture in a less than satisfactory way. The classic statement of the role of civic ties in the United States came from Tocqueville 1956.

10. The recent debate on the concept of social capital has sometimes been bitter. I draw on Putnam's work here despite disagreeing with aspects of the narrow causal framework in which he places social capital dynamics due to his extensive empirical data on the United States and Italy and because his conceptual difficulties do not undermine the key aspects of his work relevant here. The early conceptualizations of social capital are in Loury 1977; Coleman 1988, 1990; and Bourdieu 1983. For the best overviews of the recent social capital discussions, see Woolcock 1998, Paxton 1999, Portes 1998, Foley and Edwards 1998, Edwards and Foley 1997, and a review symposium of *Bowling Alone* in *Contemporary Sociology* (May 2001).

11. On the concept of "deepening democracy," see the excellent discussion in Roberts 1998, 3–7, 25–33.

12. Verba, Schlozman, and Brady (1995) study democratic skills acquisition by tracking such things as the ability to write a letter to a political representative, make a public speech, plan and lead a meeting, and attend a meeting. Though this book looks at democratic skills more broadly, their point holds.

13. Among the important voluntary organizations are paradenominational reli-

gious organizations that function alongside congregations and denominations. See Wuthnow 1988, 1994; Coleman forthcoming; and Baggett 2001.

14. Only among Latinos does this pattern break down: religious organizations do not provide democratic skills as extensively to Latinos as they do to whites or blacks. Verba, Schlozman, and Brady (1995) trace this to the fact that Latinos are heavily Catholic, and the Catholic Church appears to provide fewer opportunities for skills acquisition than other major American religious institutions even following the Vatican II reforms (Verba, Schlozman, and Brady 1995, 245–47). The finding that religious institutions provide relatively equal opportunities for democratic skills building of course has important implications for faith-based organizing, to which I return in chapter 5.

15. On the erosion of political parties in the United States, see Coleman 1996, Aldrich 1995, and Pomper 1992.

16. Though he does not use this term, Casanova (1994) assumes something akin to this concept in considering the public role of religion in four modern societies.

17. On the need to refashion American popular political culture, see Eliasoph's (1998) engaging analysis of how it actively constructs political apathy.

18. Indeed, some PICO organizers refer to their work in the pre-1984 period as "neighborhood-based organizing" to contrast it with their current work. It is noteworthy that some PICO staff see CTWO's work as quite similar to PICO's own work during this period; they describe both as "issues-based." I cannot assess this alleged similarity, since my study began after PICO's transition to the newer model.

19. Parallel dynamics occurred in the field as a whole. Today, 50 percent of professional faith-based organizers are white, 29 percent are African American, 16 percent are Hispanic, and 3 percent are Asian American or Native American (Warren and Wood 2001, table 6).

20. For example see *Sacramento Bee,* May 3, 2000, A1, A14, and June 8, 2000, A4; *San Jose Mercury News,* June 8, 2000, 1B; and *Los Angeles Times* coverage on May 3 and June 8, 2000, and *San Francisco Examiner* coverage on February 26, 2001.

21. I cannot document this interpretation very extensively. Information on which it is based comes from the *New York Times* and *New Orleans Times-Picayune* throughout 1994–95, an interview with a city council member, and the quoted interview. All these may be presumed to be self-interested accounts and thus need verification; the interpretation offered here appears plausible, at least from the outside and on the basis of limited information.

22. See Warren and Wood 2001 or Wood and Warren forthcoming for a fuller discussion of the cross-racial and cross-denominational social capital fostered by faith-based organizing.

23. Also see Warren 2001 for an excellent analysis of how faith-based organizing generates cross-racial "bridging social capital," using the Texas Industrial Areas Foundation as a case study.

24. The linguistic similarity of the concepts of "bridging institutions"—used here and in previous work (Wood 1994)—and "bridging social capital" masks a key analytic difference: whereas "bridging social capital" emphasizes the emergent quality of new horizontal linkages among previously isolated groups, "bridging institutions" emphasizes the more established ("institutionalized") character of faith-based organizing federations *vertically* linking civil, political society, and state levels of the public realm.

25. I would caution against too easily writing off the Seattle WTO protests as the work of hooligans, as they were portrayed in many press accounts at the time. As of this writing, scholarly analyses of the Seattle WTO events have yet to appear, but despite press portrayals, the property destruction and violence in Seattle appear to have been the work of a small minority of demonstrators; most engaged in the standard repertoire of nonviolent civil disobedience (Finnegan 2000). In any case, the point here is that nonviolent direct action tactics built around a strategy of disruption can be effective, at least in the short term.

26. This is not to say that race-based organizing engages more individuals from marginalized social sectors in the sense of absolute numbers, however. Given the substantially larger numbers mobilized by faith-based organizing and the fact that a significant portion of them are from very low socioeconomic groups, poor immigrants, etc., it may well be the case that faith-based organizing engages more such individuals. But the tenor of organizational life does not center on them.

27. Indeed, CTWO's autonomy to engage in confrontational tactics even with its own sponsors was demonstrated during summer 2000, when the organization took out prominent advertisements denouncing one of its religiously based funders for enforcing criteria prohibiting its recipients from taking public stands in favor of abortion rights.

28. PICO, the IAF, and probably all the faith-based organizing networks have for years used the phrase "working families" as shorthand for their working-class and lower-middle-class constituencies. It appears to be used to signal a class commitment while avoiding the rhetoric of class analysis, with its risk of alienating more elite supporters. For an excellent recent analysis of the term, see Skocpol 2000.

29. For an illuminating account of how organizations generate a culture of political engagement, albeit one that is less intentional in focusing on the cultural process of organizing, see Fantasia 1988. Gould 1995 provides a fine, theoretically sophisticated historical account of how organizationally sanctioned culture and networks shape social movements.

Part Two

1. The seminal work of Jürgen Habermas (1984, 1987) has shaped this understanding of meaning as a resource for human action. In his analytic framework, three dimensions compose the life-world of human communities; each dimension provides specific kinds of resources for social action. The societal dimension of the life-world provides *solidarity* within human communities. The psychological dimension provides *ego strength* or what might also be called *identity* for individuals within those communities. And the cultural dimension provides *meaning* that orients people and communities as they take action in the world. This book has focused on solidarity through the analysis of social capital; it focuses on meaning through the coming analysis of cultural dynamics. An analysis of ego strength would entail an in-depth study of its own of the leadership development process and the training of organizers within faith-based organizing.

2. Somers (1995a, 1995b) provides a historical discussion of the concept of political culture that shapes the use of the term here. For her use of the term in analyzing the rise of citizenship and the public realm in England see Somers 1993.

3. In isolating the cultural influences on political effectiveness of challenger

groups, I of course recognize that other factors are also crucial—such factors as the structure of political opportunities, access to resources, powerful allies, strategy and tactics, mobilization networks, the broad socioeconomic processes that create movement grievances, etc., all matter greatly. But culture plays its own role, both as discussed here and in shaping many of these other factors.

4. My thinking about cultural work was influenced by Hobsbawm (1984) and a talk by Stephen Hart in 1994. The latter informs his recent book (Hart 2001), which uses faith-based organizing as a case study of progressive organizations that are relatively sophisticated in doing cultural work. Perhaps no other scholar has paid as careful attention to this kind of work within social movements as has Hart.

5. Key works in the sociology of culture and political sociology that have shaped my thinking include Becker 1999; Eliasoph 1998; Fraser 1992; Griswold 1992; Hart 2001; Laitin 1986; Lichterman 1996; Pred 1990; Smith 1996b; Somers 1993, 1995a, 1995b; Swidler 1984; Williams 1999a; Wolfe 1989; and Wuthnow et al. 1984. Also helpful was the cultural and institutional orientation of Bellah et al. 1985, 1991, and Douglas 1986. In the sociology of religion, key sources include Ammerman and Farnsley 1997; Bellah 1970; Durkheim 1965, 1973; Geertz 1968, [1973] 2000; Pattillo-McCoy 1998, 1999; Roozen, McKinney, and Carroll 1984; Troeltsch 1981; Weber [1930] 1998; and Williams 1999b. Studies of the role of culture in social movements have deepened our insight into how collective politics emerge, take shape, and succeed or decline (Gould 1995; Jasper 1996; Johnston and Klandermans 1995; Klandermans, Kriesi, and Tarrow 1988; Morris 1984; Morris and Mueller 1992; Smith 1996a; Williams 1995, 1996). But as some have noted (e.g., Gould 1995; Hart 2001), culture not only enables social action, it also constrains it; the following chapters strive to focus on both these dimensions of culture in action.

Chapter Five

1. The epigraph is quoted from a presentation at the PICO national training for leaders in 1994. Dr. José Carrasco was a key figure in PICO's development of a more faith-based organizing model in the early 1980s, following the stagnation in the organization's earlier "neighborhood-based" model after ten years of significant success (see appendix 2). He continues to be a key visionary and strategist within the organization, and is a faculty member at San Jose State University in California.

2. Though the internal public sphere in faith-based organizing functions in a more multidimensional way than the highly oppositional subaltern counter-publics discussed by Fraser (1992), her concept helps illuminate the dynamics found there.

3. Effective organizing in fact involves a remarkable multiplicity of roles, including fund raising, political strategizing, what organizers call "relational ability," public speaking, adult pedagogy, etc. I focus here on their roles in developing the internal organizational culture of faith-based organizing.

4. Within the organizing process, organizers regularly cited Alinsky's adage that effective political work must address "the world as it is" rather than "the world as it should be"—Alinsky's way of forcing political realism on those inclined toward religiously driven idealism. In fact, however, effective organizations operate not on one side of this dichotomy, but rather at the tension between the poles; they operate on political terrain as it is, while articulating a vision of the way things should be to generate political support. Only by properly understanding this tension can we adequately

explain the successes and limitations of faith-based organizing. For example, some of its limitations result from the tendency to collapse organizing into a pure technique of confronting the world as it is.

5. On the concept of religiously generated leverage for criticizing and reforming the status quo of social relations, see Bellah 1970. The key insight is that if one is completely embedded within a given cultural worldview and its associated social relations (with its hegemonically imposed acceptance of the status quo), it is not simply impossible to change society, it is impossible even to imagine the transformation of those relations (or at least to imagine them in socially relevant ways). Thus, social action to transform society is dependent upon the elaboration of alternative cultural worldviews to motivate such action, shape actors capable of engaging in it, and guide it as it moves forward. See Flyvbjerg 2001 for an excellent analysis of the role of the social sciences in fostering such worldviews.

6. For important recent work on the importance of the affective dimension of social movements for understanding their dynamics, see Goodwin, Jasper, and Polletta 2001.

7. See Hart 2001 for the best analysis of the various cultural traditions shaping faith-based organizing today.

8. Boyte (1980, 1989) and Evans and Boyte (1986) document some of this erosion of democratic radicalism after the 1970s. Of course, it has been reborn in altered form in movements like the antiglobalization phenomenon of recent years.

9. Whether a broad organizational culture underlies the whole field of faith-based organizing—that is, across PICO, IAF, Gamaliel, DART, and the smaller networks and independent organizing efforts—is debated. But it is debated primarily by organizers themselves, who have a vested interest in seeing their own network's model as unique. Among scholars and funders, the prevailing view is that they indeed share a very substantial portion of their organizational cultures. However, my account of the religious grounding of the ethos of faith-based organizing emerges from fieldwork within the PICO network; this aspect of the organizational culture does appear to vary across networks.

10. By itself, this chapter's cultural analysis allows power relations within the organization to recede into the background, unexamined, in order to focus on the intersection of religious commitment and democratic organizing. So this chapter should be read recalling chapter 2's discussion of power dynamics within faith-based federations (among staff, leaders, and pastors; and across racial, class, and gender lines); here, those power dynamics will be very much present, but not the focus of attention.

11. It is interesting to note that never during three years of ethnographic work was either trust building or using religious language made an explicit part of trainings for doing one-to-ones. The idea that trust building is central to one-to-ones is thus my own analytic gloss, not a theme in PICO culture—but it seems too obvious to miss. Religious language seems to enter the one-to-one process at the initiative of leaders, without coaching from organizing staff. In any case, for organizers to insert this kind of language into the one-to-one process would appear manipulative.

12. In this setting, it would have been intrusive and inappropriate to take notes. This prayer is thus a later transcription from memory, and thus presumably an approximation.

13. As a practicing Catholic (albeit with a complex relationship to that tradition), this author takes prayer seriously and bristled on those occasions when it appeared to be used purely instrumentally within the organizing process. Though well beyond my focus here, this particular bit of subjectivity seems important to reveal, so readers can make their own judgments.

14. Of course, this is not without irony, given the insistence in the culture of organizing on framing nearly everything initially around a language of self-interest (see below). As I argue, this language shrouds a much richer set of cultural orientations, involving an expansion of both the notion of self and the notion of interests.

15. A one-dimensional orientation toward conflict can also undermine the public realm, especially when public officials are battered by antigovernment sentiment in much of American culture. Finding the right balance between a constructive understanding of the role of government in promoting equality and democracy and the willingness and ability to engage in conflict with government officials is key to making any kind of organizing a constructive institution, rather than simply a destructive force.

16. This training drew on the theological and scriptural work of Carlos Bravo, S.J. (1986).

17. Indeed, a priest who had been intimately involved in the earliest origins of an explicitly faith-based organizing model in San Antonio, Texas, suggested in an interview that its success was the product of precisely this kind of cultural work, and that subsequent organizing in that city has too often downplayed this dimension of faith-based organizing.

18. The text as cited appears in PICO's national 1994 strategic plan and various subsequent funding proposals; similar statements continue to be the norm.

19. This is a case of what Williams (1999a) calls the dual character of assertions of "common good" language. Such language both reflects particular interests and claims to hegemony and provides a basis for contesting that hegemony.

20. This is not to suggest that how people talk necessarily reflects their internal thinking, but rather that beliefs relevant for an analysis of the organization's internal culture are those that are either expressed in official statements or articulated in conversations. Purely private beliefs that individuals might hold are much less relevant for the cultural life of the organization. On the importance of "talk" for analyzing culture, see previously cited works by Lichterman (1996) and Eliasoph (1998), as well as Swidler (2001).

21. See E. J. Wood 2001 for an analysis of the "pleasure of agency" among Salvadoran campesinos supporting the guerrilla insurgency in the 1980s, and Goodwin, Jasper, and Polletta 2001 for important recent work on the role of emotions in social movements.

22. The primary analysis of the dynamics of the distortion of democratic communicative processes by the systems logic revolving around power and money anchored in the political and economic systems is found in Habermas 1987.

23. This broadening of the religious or spiritual dimension of faith-based organizing has occurred partly as more religiously trained individuals have become influential organizers and supervisors (both laypeople and clergy have entered these roles) in the networks, partly through the influence of clergy-led efforts independent of the net-

works, and partly through "cultural work" focused on precisely this dimension, in such settings as monthly "clergy caucuses" in local federations. For cultural work drawing on the more evangelical and Pentecostal strands of Christianity, see the important work of the Regional Council of Neighborhood Organizations in Southern California and the Ten Points Coalition in Boston (McRoberts 1999, 2000, forthcoming); the organizational work of Christians Supporting Community Organizing; and the scriptural writings of Linthicum (1991a, 1991b). On liberal Protestantism and organizing, see Jacobsen 2001.

24. This of course varies from tradition to tradition, with Roman Catholic social teaching and Jewish social ethics probably being the most systematized of the strands mentioned. Even in the Catholic tradition, however, on the level of local parish life, the church's social teaching is presented more implicitly than explicitly. On Catholic social teaching, see Coleman 1991; on the Jewish ethical tradition as it applies to organizing, see Sacks 1997.

25. This distinction of roles is not universal in PICO or elsewhere in faith-based organizing. In some places, using ministerial authority as a primary mechanism for mobilizing participants appears to be common practice.

26. In previous writing on faith-based organizing, the most evocative phrase used to describe the overall ethos of this kind of work is "cold anger" (Rogers 1990). Though a certain kind of anger is an important component of the political culture of faith-based organizing, this phrase places too great an emphasis on strategic calculation and the controlled channeling of anger for political effect. This is too one-dimensional to describe the broad ethos of faith-based organizing in its contemporary manifestation; channeled anger is one facet of that ethos, but not the only one. We understand the field better if we see its underlying ethos more fully. Note that Rogers's work focuses on the Texas Industrial Areas Foundation and is over ten years old. Some of the difference between "cold anger" and "ethical democracy" as the best description of the ethos of faith-based organizing presumably reflects different networks and changes in the field since the late 1980s.

27. I was not doing fieldwork during this period; this interpretation thus relies on the (presumably at least somewhat revisionist) retrospective reports. That being said, this account rings true to my knowledge of the organization.

28. See Habermas 1987 on the role of power in the political system and how this shapes the public realm.

29. This reflection, in a religious but highly cross-denominational setting, straddles the divide between secular and faith-based language. The tenor parallels much Catholic philosophical ethics of the natural law tradition, which strives to articulate ethical teaching in ways accessible to both believers and nonbelievers. In more religiously homogeneous settings, reflections frequently drew much more explicitly on particular faith traditions.

30. Here again we see that truly deliberative conversation about public life is rare in faith-based organizing. But it certainly occurs there more commonly than in most of contemporary American society. Given that scarcity, the fact that deliberative reflection occurs at all in faith-based organizing is evidence for its ethical vitality—at least in some settings.

31. A rough measure of how widespread exposure to such national training is comes from the Interfaith Funders study (Warren and Wood 2001, sec. 7): in 1999,

about 1,600 people participated in national trainings offered by any of the four major networks, which vary in duration from five to ten days. Their format and content appear to overlap considerably across the four networks, though the tenor in which they are conducted reportedly diverges considerably. Steve Hart has shared notes from the early 1990s Gamaliel training he observed while doing research for his recent book (2001), and I have interviewed participants in IAF national trainings; the parallels are striking.

32. The relationship between instrumental values and moral values I analyze here draws heavily from the discussion in Bellah 1957 of "goal attainment" and "integrative" values in Tokugawa, Japan.

33. The networks' national trainings range from five to ten days. Seventy-seven people from ten states, evenly divided along gender lines (thirty-eight men, thirty-nine women) and fairly ethnically diverse (approximately half white, a quarter African American, and a quarter Hispanic), attended the July 24–29, 1993, national training at Santa Clara University in California. I attended all formal sessions and many of the informal gatherings.

34. The analysis of this training may well be out-of-date by now: PICO has significantly revised its national training since this time, and I know Reed to be a reflective thinker and articulate spokesperson regarding the ethical framework of faith-based organizing. But this analysis captures the flavor of the training that dominated faith-based organizing generally for many years and still affects the work of many federations.

35. Of course, in our postmodern cultural world, this assertion of a common good in a "community" is vulnerable to a charge that it suppresses "difference" among groups whose interests do not coincide—say Christian conservatives and gay rights advocates. This is of course accurate and important. But giving up entirely on the notion of a common good across such differences only plays into the hands of more powerful groups in society. After all, by virtue of living in a single city or region, groups ineluctably share a common destiny—whatever future they construct for that city will touch their lives. Such a position can indeed be used to suppress dissent, but it can also be the basis for shared work to build a common future.

36. In his key writings about self-interest, Alinsky himself actually adopted a stance that provides some nuance to the concept—albeit in a confused way. Oddly, he cites as a Christian endorsement of self-interest words from Jesus that sound much more like altruism: "Greater love has no man than this, that a man lay down his life for his friends" ([1946] 1969, 53). He goes on to cite Machiavelli's radical assertion of self-interest at the heart of politics, but then says:

> But Machiavelli makes a mortal mistake when he rules out the "moral" factors of politics and holds purely to self-interest as he defines it. . . . The overall case must be of larger dimensions than that of self-interest narrowly defined; it must be large enough to include and provide for the shifting dimensions of self-interest. (54–55)

The "shifting dimensions of self-interest" correspond to the expanding boundaries of self discussed above. For evidence that such a broadly social understanding of the human person underlies many human societies, see Bowles et al. 2001.

37. Of course, this sits uneasily with many religious believers' discomfort with conflict—at least in middle-class Christianity. Organizers thus invest significant effort

in convincing some participants that anger is not contradictory to the Christian tradition—in my fieldwork, perhaps most effectively in the reflection noted above led by a
theologically trained PICO organizer (Jim Keddy), using Bravo's work (1986) to discuss
the role of anger and conflict in Jesus' life.

38. See Rogers 1990.

Chapter Six

1. On the nature of religious social capital, see Greeley 1997a, 1997b, and Verba,
Schlozman, and Brady 1997.

2. A fuller argument paralleling this section appears in Wood 1999.

3. The term "likelihood" here is important; I do not make the claim that internal
culture alone determines an organization's political chances. Rather, cultural dynamics
represent loose structuring tendencies that in a given instance may not by themselves
determine outcomes but over the course of time greatly shape organizational experience and therefore political development.

4. My orientation thus diverges from studies contending that simply contesting
and disrupting power is the best strategy for challenger groups in democratic polities.
See for example Piven and Cloward 1977.

5. See Swidler 2001, Hart 2001, Eliasoph 1998, and Lichterman 1996 for exemplary work adopting the talk-centered approach.

6. See Becker 1999 for an exemplary approach to applying "new institutionalist"
ideas to the organizational culture of religious congregations. See also Demerath and
Williams 1992 for an early work that considers political culture cross-institutionally;
and Williams 1995, 1996, 1999b for insightful theoretical work on the cultural dynamics behind the relationship between religion and politics.

7. Attending worship was constrained by the fact that all three held their primary
worship services on Sunday morning, making it impossible to attend more than one
"core" service in any given week.

8. See Pattillo-McCoy 1999 and Ammerman and Farnsley 1997 for excellent congregational studies that take seriously the role of worship in constructing religious culture.

9. All songs, prayers, and other aspects of the service here are translated from
Spanish by the author. On a given weekend, about half of the worship services at Saint
Elizabeth are in Spanish, and half in English. Where it was particularly awkward to
take extensive notes, quotations are rendered in single quotation marks, to indicate
they were reconstructed from brief contemporaneous notes.

10. The tabernacle contains bread for communion services when not in use; it is a
central place for prayer in some versions of traditional Catholic spirituality.

11. Later in the course of this study, when California's Proposition 187 to curtail
undocumented immigration was being debated, services more directly addressed the
political issues surrounding immigration in a tone clearly opposed to that ballot initiative. As the California Catholic Conference (the coordinating body for Catholic bishops in the state) was opposing Proposition 187, and given the ethnic makeup of this
parish and the general liberal climate of the Bay Area, this was not a very polarizing
move.

12. I am unaware of any quantitative studies on which to base this assertion; my

confidence in it rests on wide observance of Catholic services in the American Southwest and Mexico.

13. See, for example, Sanford 1987.

14. Admittedly, the modifiers used here ("moderately," "exceptionally," etc.) provide only marginal insight in the present context; they become much more meaningful in the comparative context of the following chapter.

15. Note that the universalist thrust of most Christian traditions today legitimates relations with out-groups and that racial or ethnic consciousness sometimes lacks such universalism. Though this deserves fuller treatment, I focus on the cultural dynamics through which such universalism makes a democratic difference.

Chapter Seven

1. The description of Oakland that opens this chapter reflects the situation there as of 1995, when the intensive period of my fieldwork in Oakland ended. The dot-com economic revitalization that reverberated through the Bay Area in the late 1990s led to significant economic redevelopment in these districts—though with mixed results for the residents of low-income neighborhoods described here. Also, new migration by Hispanic (mostly Mexican) and southeast Asian immigrants combined with significant out-migration by African American residents to dilute the strong concentration of black residents in some areas of East Oakland. Also during this period parts of Oakland began to gentrify. But the implosion of the high-tech economic sector in the last two years has halted these trends, and this description still captures much of the present economic reality (late 2001), though with somewhat different racial mixes.

2. Names of this church and its leaders and members are pseudonyms.

3. These streetlights have now been improved, as part OCO's improved street lighting initiative described in chapter 2.

4. See Cox 1995 for a recent interpretation of the broad Pentecostal tradition. On black churches more broadly see Freedman 1984; McRoberts 1999, 2000. See also Neitz 1987 on the broader charismatic movement, a recent cousin but not identical to Pentecostalism. Ammerman and Farnsley 1997 offers an outstanding series of portraits of religious congregations. Chapman 1991 provides an analysis of the political ministry of mainline Protestant churches; though I do not discuss such churches here, they are often involved in faith-based organizing and their patterns of engagement may fall along the lines of any of the churches discussed here.

5. This is the pattern Sanchez Jankowski (1991) finds among African American gang members. Among Latino and Irish gang members, some (at least vestigial) sense of self rooted in a communal tradition remains vis-à-vis family and some wider Latino community. But he finds that even the apparent moral solidarity of "brotherhood" among gang members is essentially a fiction and is fully instrumentalized for the pursuit of a "piece of the action" (86–87).

6. This interpretation was endemic among Gospel Church lay leaders, exposed weekly to the religious imagery described above—despite the fact that Owens himself saw city leaders somewhat differently; he maintained constructive relations with city officials including the mayor and the police chief, for example hosting them amiably on his cable TV show (Concord, Calif., United Christian Broadcasters' *Coast to Coast,* June 30, 1994).

7. "Sect" is used here in the analytical and descriptive sense intended by Troeltsch (1981) and Weber ([1930] 1998)—that is, a small religious group subscribing to the idea of a salvation that is not hierarchically mediated. Sects often have a tense relationship with outsiders. I do not use "sect" in the pejorative sense common today.

8. A current national effort strives to develop scriptural resources and a network of support for Christian congregations in the evangelical, Pentecostal, and Holiness traditions who wish to engage in faith-based organizing. See the scriptural and theological writings of Robert C. Linthicum (1991a, 1991b, 1995) and the work of Christians Supporting Community Organizing, based in Denver, Colorado.

9. The worship service reported here, though held in honor of Dr. King's birthday, was reasonably typical of regular Sunday Mass at Saint Columba. I attended perhaps two dozen worship services at this congregation during my fieldwork—more than the other churches examined in this book—in part to try to understand the complexities of a religious culture that combines a richly evocative worship life and strong social understanding of the Christian faith (the latter drawn from both Roman Catholic social teaching and African American social Christianity), and yet rather strongly embraced therapeutic understandings of religious faith. Ultimately, I joined this church as a member; because I was already Catholic, this involved no public ceremony and did not appear to significantly alter how I was perceived in my fieldwork there.

10. On the historical experience and worship lives of African American Roman Catholics, see Davis and Farajajé-Jones 1991.

11. See the rich literature on therapeutic religion originating with Bellah et al. 1985. For a much more optimistic assessment of this cultural current, see Bloom 1992. Though Bellah's team studied white Americans from the broad middle class, this analysis suggests that their findings on the centrality of expressive-therapeutic language and cultural orientations apply across other segments of American society, including African Americans, though the patterns are no doubt more complex there.

12. See O'Malley 1993 for one of the sources of this understanding of evangelism within the Roman Catholic tradition, and Deck 1989 for an application of it in contemporary Catholicism.

13. On Roman Catholic social teaching, see Coleman 1982, 1991; on the African American religious tradition, see Lincoln and Mamiya 1990.

14. I was unable to attend this action meeting. This brief description comes from conversations with Saint Columba's leaders, the pastor, and the police chief.

15. During the summer of 1994, a new organizer took over PICO's work at Saint Columba's. As he was by all accounts highly competent, I have no evidence that this change contributed to the decline of organizing at the parish.

16. In the Catholic Church, the local bishop appoints pastors to local parishes. In most of the United States, this occurs through the mediation of a diocesan personnel committee, which asks for input from the parish.

17. There are of course methodological difficulties in this paragraph's assessment of the intensity of cultural commitment in the four organizations on the basis of externally observable behaviors. A given individual may of course be deeply committed to and moved by a particular symbolic system without showing external signs of this, and even when expressed in external behavior, the intensity of that behavior will be mediated by the varying expectations of emotional restraint or self-expression carried

within different subcultures. But because my focus is on the role of culture in moving people to take democratic action, cultural commitment not given some degree of public expression is much less relevant. Overall, I believe these broad qualitative distinctions accurately reflect the patterns in these organizations; in any case, I do not attempt to quantify them.

18. This appears to be the case in Orange County, New Orleans, New York, Los Angeles, Chicago, Florida, and elsewhere.

19. This parallels Weber's ([1930] 1998) famous contrast between the logical and the psychological consequences of religious belief.

Chapter Eight

1. I follow Somers in emphasizing that this as an *analytic* autonomy, not a *concrete/empirical* autonomy. That is, cultural dynamics overlap with and operate within other concrete processes such as the dynamics of resource flows, political opportunities, and strategic calculation that also influence political outcomes. By designing this research to analytically isolate the cultural dynamics, I strive here to gain analytic leverage for understanding them; at the same time, in contrast to some cultural studies, I strive to locate the cultural dynamics very much within the social process of organizing and its political environment.

2. Of course, simplistic political interpretation sometimes generates powerful short-term political mobilization; the focus here is on the cultural tasks of sustaining democratic engagement over the long term.

3. See especially Casanova 1994; Smith 1996a, 1996b; and Williams 1995, 1999a, 1999b. On the role of culture in social movements more generally, see the discussion and citations in the introduction and chapter 5.

4. See Dillon 1999 for one account of contemporary believers who do so.

5. Casanova 1994, 234. I also note the cogency of Casanova's invitation in light of events in September 2001. Among the traditions raising questions about Western modernity we must count not only the religious traditions discussed here, but also worldwide Islam. By this I by no means mean the latter's extremist distortions; mainstream Islam, like Catholicism, mainline Protestantism, evangelicalism, and Judaism, raises important concerns about the nature of modernity.

6. See McAdam, Tarrow, and Tilly 2001 for a recent rethinking of the study of social movements consistent with the approach adopted here.

7. Castells 1983, 336.

Appendix Two

1. For the broader history of community organizing, see Betten and Austin 1990, Fisher 1994, and Fisher and Kling 1993.

2. The pattern will be familiar to readers of the literature on the sociology of organizations as the dynamic of solutions searching for problems to solve and the "garbage can" model of decision making. See March and Olsen 1979; DiMaggio and Powell 1991; Scott 1981.

3. Internal 1981–99 data from the CHD, now officially designated the Catholic Campaign for Human Development. The table below breaks down by network the to-

tals for 1981–99 and for the most recent year available, 1999 ($3,044,000 in total 1999 disbursements to four faith-based organizing networks).

	1981–99	1999
Pacific Institute for Community Organization	17.7%	23.8%
Industrial Areas Foundation	57.3%	50.4%
Gamaliel	15.5%	15.1%
Direct Action, Research and Training	9.5%	10.7%

4. A key part of this story is the role played by Monsignor Jack Egan and Tom Gaudette, both key Alinsky collaborators. They were central players in community organizing from the early days in Chicago to the spread under church auspices of Alinsky's model throughout the United States and during later transition and promotion of the faith-based model by the CHD through the work of the IAF, PICO, Gamaliel, and DART. It is a story worthy of significant scholarly attention, and extensive archives for reconstructing it are now available, as Gaudette saved correspondence, meeting notes, and other written artifacts of some forty years in organizing.

5. This process by which "answers" and "solutions" exist before the "questions" and "problems" that they are eventually called upon to resolve has been called the "garbage can model" of organizational decision making (March and Olsen 1979). It of course reverses the usual way we think of solutions being developed in response to a specific problem—but organizations frequently cannot wait for new solutions to be developed and must instead draw on whatever is at hand.

6. See Warren 2001 for an excellent scholarly analysis of COPS and the Texas Industrial Areas Foundation; see Rogers 1990 for a more popular account.

7. Since the action occurred well before I began this study, the turnout cited here is not my own count and may well be inflated. Serendipitously, I actually was in attendance due to general interest in the Oakland politics of the time, but took no count of attendance. My memory would place attendance in the fifteen hundred range, but it may have been larger.

8. In interviews, not all pastors expressed confidence that such leadership development occurs or believe that it translates into other areas of congregational life. Indeed, two (out of almost two dozen pastors interviewed in six cities) said they saw little contribution that the community organizing makes to their churches. The more typical response, however, was as described above; I am unable to judge whether the contrast reflects real differences in how well various PICO organizations form leaders, differences in pastors' appreciation of lay leadership, or other factors. I am now further exploring this topic, in collaboration with Interfaith Funders.

References

Aldrich, John A. 1995. *Why Parties? The Origin and Transformation of Political Parties in America*. Chicago: University of Chicago Press.

Alinsky, Saul D. [1946] 1969. *Reveille for Radicals*. New York: Vintage.

———. 1971. *Rules for Radicals: A Pragmatic Primer for Realistic Radicals*. New York: Random House.

Almond, Gabriel Abraham, and Sidney Verba. 1963. *The Civic Culture: Political Attitudes and Democracy in Five Nations*. Princeton: Princeton University Press.

Ammerman, Nancy T., and Arthur E. Farnsley. 1997. *Congregation and Community*. New Brunswick: Rutgers University Press.

Anner, John, ed. 1996. *Beyond Identity Politics: Emerging Social Justice Movements in Communities of Color*. Boston: South End.

Arendt, Hannah. 1958. *The Human Condition*. Chicago: University of Chicago Press.

———. 1990. "Philosophy and Politics." *Social Research* 57(1): 73–105.

Baggett, Jerome P. 2001. *Habitat for Humanity: Building Private Homes, Building Public Religion*. Philadelphia: Temple University Press.

Banfield, Edward C. [1958] 1967. *The Moral Basis of a Backward Society*. New York: Free Press.

Barber, Benjamin. 1984. *Strong Democracy: Participatory Politics for a New Age*. Berkeley and Los Angeles: University of California Press.

Becker, Penny Edgell. 1999. *Congregations in Conflict: Cultural Models of Local Religious Life*. Cambridge and New York: Cambridge University Press.

Bellah, Robert N. 1957. *Tokugawa Religion: The Values of Pre-industrial Japan*. Glencoe, Ill.: Free Press.

———. 1970. *Beyond Belief: Essays on Religion in a Post-traditional World*. New York: Harper and Row.

Bellah, Robert N., Richard Madsen, William M. Sullivan, Ann Swidler, and Steven M. Tipton. 1985. *Habits of the Heart: Individualism and Commitment in American Life.* Berkeley and Los Angeles: University of California Press.

————. 1991. *The Good Society.* New York: Knopf.

Benhabib, Seyla. 1992. "Models of Public Space: Hannah Arendt, the Liberal Tradition and Jürgen Habermas." In *Habermas and the Public Sphere,* edited by Craig Calhoun. Cambridge: MIT Press.

Betten, Neil, and Michael J. Austin. 1990. *The Roots of Community Organizing, 1917–1939.* Philadelphia: Temple University Press.

Bloom, Harold. 1992. *The American Religion: The Emergence of the Post-Christian Nation.* New York: Simon and Schuster.

Borg, Marcus J. 1984. *Conflict, Holiness, and Politics in the Teachings of Jesus.* New York: Mellen.

Bourdieu, Pierre. 1983. "Forms of Capital." In *Handbook of Theory and Research for the Sociology of Education,* edited by J. G. Richardson, 241–58. New York: Greenwood.

Bowles, Samuel, R. Boyd, C. Camerer, E. Fehr, H. Gintis, J. Henrich, and R. McElreath. 2001. "In Search of *Homo Economicus:* Behavioral Experiments in 15 Simple Societies." *American Economic Review* 91:73–78.

Boyte, Harry C. 1980. *The Backyard Revolution: Understanding the New Citizen Movement.* Philadelphia: Temple University Press.

————. 1989. *Commonwealth: A Return to Citizen Politics.* New York: Free Press.

Boyte, Harry C., and Nancy N. Kari. 1996. *Building America: The Democratic Promise of Public Work.* Philadelphia: Temple University Press.

Bravo, Carlos, S.J. 1986. *Jesús Hombre en Conflicto.* Coyoacan, Mexico: Centro de Reflexión Teológica.

Brown, E. Richard, Ninez Ponce, and Thomas Rice. 2001. "The State of Health Insurance in California: Recent Trends, Future Prospects." UCLA Center for Health Policy Research.

Burawoy, Michael. 1991. *Ethnography Unbound: Power and Resistance in the Modern Metropolis.* Berkeley and Los Angeles: University of California Press.

Butler, Jon. 1990. *Awash in a Sea of Faith: Christianizing the American People.* Cambridge: Harvard University Press.

Calhoun, Craig, ed. 1992. *Habermas and the Public Sphere.* Cambridge: MIT Press.

Calpotura, Francis, and Kim Fellner. 1996. "The Square Pegs Find Their Groove: Reshaping the Organizing Circle," available as of 2001 at http://comm-org.utoledo.edu//papers96/square.html.

Carter, Stephen L. 1993. *The Culture of Disbelief: How American Law and Politics Trivialize Religious Devotion.* New York: Basic.

Casanova, José. 1994. *Public Religions in the Modern World.* Chicago: University of Chicago Press.

Cassidy, Richard J. 1978. *Jesus, Politics, and Society: A Study of Luke's Gospel.* Maryknoll, N.Y.: Orbis.

Castells, Manuel. 1983. *The City and the Grassroots: A Cross-Cultural Theory of Urban Social Movements.* Berkeley and Los Angeles: University of California Press.

Chapman, Audrey R. 1991. *Faith, Power, and Politics: Political Ministry in Mainline Churches*. New York: Pilgrim.

Cohen, Jean L., and Andrew Arato. 1992. *Civil Society and Political Theory*. Cambridge: MIT Press.

Cole, Robert E. 1989. *Strategies for Learning: Small-Group Activities in American, Japanese, and Swedish Industry*. Berkeley and Los Angeles: University of California Press.

Coleman, James S. 1988. "Social Capital in the Creation of Human Capital." *American Journal of Sociology* 94 (supplement): S95–S120.

Coleman, James S. 1990. *Foundations of Social Theory*. Cambridge: Harvard University Press.

Coleman, John A. 1982. *An American Strategic Theology*. New York: Paulist.

Coleman, John A. 1991. *One Hundred Years of Catholic Social Thought: Celebration and Challenge*. Maryknoll, N.Y.: Orbis.

Coleman, John A. Forthcoming. *Public Discipleship in the Modern World*. Champaign-Urbana: University of Illinois Press.

Coleman, John J. 1996. *Party Decline in America: Policy, Politics, and the Fiscal State*. Princeton: Princeton University Press.

Contemporary Sociology. 2001. Review symposium of Robert Putnam's *Bowling Alone*. *Contemporary Sociology* 30:223–30.

Cox, Harvey Gallagher. 1995. *Fire from Heaven: The Rise of Pentecostal Spirituality and the Reshaping of Religion in the Twenty-First Century*. Reading, Mass.: Addison-Wesley.

Davis, Kortright, and Elias Farajajé-Jones. 1991. *African Creative Expressions of the Divine*. Washington: Howard University School of Divinity.

Deck, Allan Figueroa. 1989. *The Second Wave: Hispanic Ministry and the Evangelization of Cultures*. New York: Paulist.

Delgado, Gary. 1986. *Organizing the Movement: The Roots and Growth of ACORN*. Philadelphia: Temple University Press.

Delgado, Gary. [1993a?]. *Beyond the Politics of Place: New Directions in Community Organizing in the 1990s*. Oakland, Calif.: Applied Research Center.

Delgado, Gary. 1993b. "Building Multiracial Alliances: The Case of People United for a Better Oakland." In *Mobilizing the Community: Local Politics in the Era of the Global City*, edited by Robert Fisher and Joseph Kling. *Urban Affairs Annual Review*, no. 41. Newbury Park, Calif.: Sage.

Demerath, N. J., and Rhys H. Williams. 1992. *A Bridging of Faiths: Religion and Politics in a New England City*. Princeton: Princeton University Press.

Dillon, Michele. 1999. *Catholic Identity: Balancing Reason, Faith, and Power*. Cambridge and New York: Cambridge University Press.

DiMaggio, Paul J., and Walter W. Powell. 1991. *The New Institutionalism in Organizational Analysis*. Chicago: University of Chicago Press.

Douglas, Mary. 1986. *How Institutions Think*. Syracuse: Syracuse University Press.

Douglas, Mary. [1973] 1996. *Natural Symbols: Explorations in Cosmology*. London: Barrie and Rockliff the Cresset; New York: Routledge.

Durkheim, Emile. 1965. *The Elementary Forms of the Religious Life*. New York: Free Press.

Durkheim, Emile. 1973. *On Morality and Society: Selected Writings*. Edited and with an introduction by Robert N. Bellah. Chicago: University of Chicago Press.

Edwards, Bob, and Michael W. Foley. 1997. "Social Capital, Civil Society, and Contemporary Democracy." *American Behavioral Scientist* 40 (6): 5–21.

Eliasoph, Nina. 1998. *Avoiding Politics: How Americans Produce Apathy in Everyday Life*. Cambridge and New York: Cambridge University Press.

Evans, Sara M., and Harry C. Boyte. 1986. *Free Spaces: The Sources of Democratic Change in America*. New York: Harper and Row.

Fanon, Frantz. 1965. *The Wretched of the Earth*. New York: Grove.

Fantasia, Rick. 1988. *Cultures of Solidarity: Consciousness, Action, and Contemporary American Workers*. Berkeley and Los Angeles: University of California Press.

Finke, Roger, and Rodney Stark. 1992. *The Churching of America 1776–1990: Winners and Losers in Our Religious Economy*. New Brunswick: Rutgers University Press.

Finnegan, William. 2000. "After Seattle." *New Yorker*, 17 April, 40–51.

Fischer, Claude S., Michael Hout, Martín Sánchez Jankowski, Samuel R. Lucas, Ann Swidler, and Kim Voss. 1996. *Inequality by Design: Cracking the Bell Curve Myth*. Princeton: Princeton University Press.

Fisher, Robert. 1994. *Let the People Decide: Neighborhood Organizing in America*. New York: Twayne.

Fisher, Robert, and Joseph Kling, eds. 1993. "Mobilizing the Community: Local Politics in the Era of the Global City." *Urban Affairs Annual Review*. Newbury Park, Calif.: Sage.

Flyvbjerg, Bent. 2001. *Making Social Science Matter: Why Social Inquiry Fails and How It Can Succeed Again*. Cambridge and New York: Cambridge University Press.

Foley, Michael W., and Bob Edwards. 1998. "Beyond Putnam: Civil Society and Social Capital." *American Behavioral Scientist* 42 (1): 129–39.

Fraser, Nancy. 1992. "Rethinking the Public Sphere: A Contribution to the Critique of Actually Existing Democracy." In *Habermas and the Public Sphere*, edited by Craig Calhoun. Cambridge: MIT Press.

Freedman, Samuel G. 1984. *Upon This Rock: The Miracles of a Black Church*. New York: HarperCollins.

Freire, Paulo. 1970. *Pedagogy of the Oppressed*. Translated by Myra Bergman Ramos. New York: Seabury.

———. 1973. *Education for Critical Consciousness*. New York: Seabury.

Gamson, William A. 1975. *The Strategy of Social Protest*. Homewood, Ill.: Dorsey.

———. 1980. "Understanding the Careers of Challenging Groups: A Commentary on Goldstone." *American Journal of Sociology* 85 (5): 1042–44.

Ganz, Marshall. 2000a. "Five Smooth Stones." Ph.D. diss., Harvard University.

———. 2000b. "Resources and Resourcefulness: Strategic Capacity in the Unionization of California Agriculture, 1959–1966." *American Journal of Sociology* 105:1003–63.

Geertz, Clifford. 1968. *Islam Observed: Religious Development in Morocco and Indonesia*. New Haven: Yale University Press.

———. [1973] 2000. *The Interpretation of Cultures: Selected Essays*. New York: Basic.

Gitlin, Todd. 1995. *The Twilight of Common Dreams: Why America Is Wracked by Culture Wars.* New York: Metropolitan.

Gittell, Ross J., and Avis Vidal. 1998. *Community Organizing: Building Social Capital as a Development Strategy.* Thousand Oaks, Calif.: Sage.

Goldstone, Jack A. 1980. "The Weakness of Organization: A New Look at Gamson's 'The Strategy of Social Protest.' " *American Journal of Sociology* 85 (5): 1017–42.

Goodwin, Jeffrey, and James M. Jasper. 1999. "Caught in a Winding, Snarling Vine: A Critique of Political Process Theory." *Sociological Forum* 14 (1): 27–54.

Goodwin, Jeff, James M. Jasper, and Francesca Polletta, eds. 2001. *Passionate Politics: Emotions and Social Movements.* Chicago: University of Chicago Press.

Gould, Roger V. 1995. *Insurgent Identities: Class, Community, and Protest in Paris from 1848 to the Commune.* Chicago: University of Chicago Press.

Granovetter, Mark. 1983. "The Strength of Weak Ties: A Network Theory Revisited." *Sociological Theory* 1:201–33.

———. 1985. "Economic Action and Social Structure: The Problem of Embeddedness." *American Journal of Sociology* 91:481–510.

Greeley, Andrew. 1997a. "The Other Civic America: Religion and Social Capital." *American Prospect* 32 (May–June): 68–73.

———. 1997b. "Coleman Revisited: Religious Structures as a Source of Social Capital." *American Behavioral Scientist* 40:595–605.

Greider, William. 1992. *Who Will Tell the People? The Betrayal of American Democracy.* New York: Simon and Schuster.

Griswold, Wendy. 1992. "The Writing on the Mud Wall: Nigerian Novels and the Imaginary Village." *American Sociological Review* 57:709–24.

Habermas, Jürgen. 1984. *The Theory of Communicative Action.* Vol. 1: *Reason and the Rationalization of Society.* Translated by Thomas McCarthy. Boston: Beacon.

———. 1987. *The Theory of Communicative Action.* Vol. 2: *Lifeworld and System: A Critique of Functionalist Reason.* Boston: Beacon.

———. 1989. *The Structural Transformation of the Public Sphere: An Inquiry into a Category of Bourgeois Society.* Translated by Thomas Burger with Frederick Lawrence. Cambridge: MIT Press.

Hannan, Michael T., and John Freeman. 1989. *Organizational Ecology.* Cambridge: Harvard University Press.

Hart, Stephen. 2001. *Cultural Dilemmas of Progressive Politics: Styles of Engagement among Grassroots Activists.* Chicago: University of Chicago Press.

Hobsbawm, Eric. 1984. *Workers: Worlds of Labor.* New York: Pantheon.

Horwitt, Sanford D. 1989. *Let Them Call Me Rebel: Saul Alinsky, His Life and Legacy.* New York: Knopf.

Hunter, James Davison. 1991. *Culture Wars: The Struggle to Define America.* New York: Basic.

Iannacone, Laurence R. 1994. "Why Strict Churches Are Strong." *American Journal of Sociology* 99:1180–1211.

Inglehart, Ronald. 1988. "The Renaissance of Political Culture." *American Political Science Review* 82:1203–30.

Jacobsen, Dennis A. 2001. *Doing Justice: Congregations and Community Organizing.* Minneapolis: Fortress.

Jasper, James M. 1996. *The Art of Moral Protest.* Chicago: University of Chicago Press.

Johnston, Hank, and Bert Klandermans, eds. 1995. *Social Movements and Culture.* Social Movements, Protest, and Contention Series, vol. 4. Minneapolis: University of Minnesota Press.

Kanter, Rosabeth Moss. 1972. *Commitment and Community: Communes and Utopias in Sociological Perspective.* Cambridge: Harvard University Press.

Klandermans, Bert, Hanspeter Kriesi, and Sidney Tarrow. 1988. "From Structure to Action: Comparing Social Movement Research across Cultures." In *International Social Movement Research* vol. 1, ed. Bert Klandermans, Hanspeter Kriesi, and Sidney Tarrow. Greenwich, Conn.: JAI Press.

Kling, Joseph M., and Prudence S. Posner. 1990. *Dilemmas of Activism: Class, Community, and the Politics of Local Mobilization.* Philadelphia: Temple University Press.

Krackhardt, David. 1992. "The Strength of Strong Ties: The Importance of Philos in Organizations." In *Networks and Organizations: Structure, Form, and Action,* edited by Nitin Nohria and Robert G. Eccles. Boston: Harvard Business School Press.

Laitin, David D. 1986. *Hegemony and Culture: Politics and Religious Change among the Yoruba.* Chicago: University of Chicago Press.

Lichterman, Paul Roger. 1996. *The Search for Political Community: American Political Activists Reinventing Commitment.* Cambridge and New York: Cambridge University Press.

Lincoln, C. E., and L. H. Mamiya. 1990. *The Black Church in the African American Experience.* Durham: Duke University Press.

Linthicum, Robert C. 1991a. *City of God, City of Satan : A Biblical Theology for the Urban Church.* Grand Rapids: Zondervan.

———. 1991b. *Empowering the Poor.* Monrovia, Calif.: Marc.

———. 1995. *Signs of Hope in the City.* Monrovia, Calif.: Marc.

Loury, Glen. 1977. "A Dynamic Theory of Racial Income Differences." In *Women, Minorities, and Employment Discrimination,* edited by P. A. Wallace and A. LeMund, 153–88. Lexington, Mass.: Lexington.

March, James G., and John P. Olsen. 1979. *Ambiguity and Choice in Organizations.* Bergen, Norway: Universitetsforlaget.

McAdam, Doug. 1982. *Political Process and the Development of Black Insurgency, 1930–1970.* Chicago: University of Chicago Press.

———. 1988. *Freedom Summer.* New York: Oxford University Press.

McAdam, Doug, Sidney Tarrow, and Charles Tilly. 2001. *Dynamics of Contention.* Cambridge and New York: Cambridge University Press.

McRoberts, Omar. 1999. "Understanding the 'New' Black Pentecostal Activism: Lessons from Ecumenical Urban Ministries in Boston." *Sociology of Religion* 60:47–70.

———. 2000. "Saving Four Corners: Religion and Revitalization in a Depressed Neighborhood." Ph.D. diss., Harvard University.

———. Forthcoming. *Saving Four Corners: Faith and Revitalization in a Religious District.* Chicago: University of Chicago Press.

Michels, Robert. 1915. *Political Parties: A Sociological Study of the Oligarchical Tendencies of Modern Democracy*. Translated by Eden and Cedar Paul. New York: Hearst's.

Morris, Aldon. 1984. *The Origins of the Civil Rights Movement: Black Communities Organizing for Change*. New York: Free Press.

Morris, Aldon, and Carole Mueller, eds. 1992. *Frontiers in Social Movement Theory*. New Haven: Yale University Press.

Neitz, Mary Jo. 1987. *Charisma and Community: A Study of Religious Commitment within the Charismatic Renewal*. New Brunswick: Transaction.

Nohria, Nitin, and Robert G. Eccles, eds. 1992. *Networks and Organizations: Structure, Form, and Action*. Boston: Harvard Business School Press.

O'Malley, John W. 1993. *The First Jesuits*. Cambridge: Harvard University Press.

Ott, J. Steven. 1989. *The Organizational Culture Perspective*. Chicago: Dorsey.

Pattillo-McCoy, Mary. 1998. "Church Culture as a Strategy of Action in the Black Community." *American Sociological Review* 63:767–84.

———. 1999. *Black Picket Fences: Privilege and Peril among the Black Middle Class*. Chicago: University of Chicago Press.

Paxton, Pamela. 1999. "Is Social Capital Declining in the United States? A Multiple Indicator Assessment." *American Journal of Sociology* 105:88–127.

Pedersen, Jesper S., and Jesper S. S<oslash>rensen. 1989. *Organisational Cultures in Theory and Practice*. Brookfield, Mass.: Avebury.

Piven, Frances Fox, and Richard A. Cloward. 1977. *Poor People's Movements: Why They Succeed, How They Fail*. New York: Vintage.

Pomper, Gerald M. 1992. *Passions and Interests: Political Party Concepts of American Democracy*. Lawrence: University of Kansas Press.

Portes, Alejandro. 1998. "Social Capital: Its Origins and Applications in Modern Sociology." *Annual Review of Sociology* 24:1–24.

Pred, Allan. 1990. *Lost Words and Lost Worlds: Modernity and the Language of Everyday Life in Late Nineteenth-Century Stockholm*. Cambridge and New York: Cambridge University Press.

Putnam, Robert D., with Robert Leonardi and Raffaella Y. Nanetti. 1993. *Making Democracy Work: Civic Traditions in Modern Italy*. Princeton: Princeton University Press.

Putnam, Robert D. 2000. *Bowling Alone: The Collapse and Revival of American Community*. New York: Simon and Schuster.

Roberts, Kenneth M. 1998. *Deepening Democracy? The Modern Left and Social Movements in Chile and Peru*. Palo Alto: Stanford University Press.

Rogers, Mary Beth. 1990. *Cold Anger: A Story of Faith and Power Relations*. Denton: University of North Texas.

Roozen, David A., William McKinney, and Jackson W. Carroll. 1984. *Varieties of Religious Presence: Mission in Public Life*. New York: Pilgrim.

Sacks, Jonathan. 1997. *Faith in the Future: The Ecology of Hope and the Restoration of Family, Community, and Faith*. Macon, Ga.: Mercer University Press.

Sanchez Jankowski, Martin. 1991. *Islands in the Street: Gangs and American Urban Society*. Berkeley and Los Angeles: University of California Press.

Sanford, John A. 1987. *The Kingdom Within: The Inner Meaning of Jesus' Sayings.* San Francisco: Harper and Row.

Schauffler, H. H., and E. R. Brown. 2000. "The State of Health Insurance in California, 1999." Regents of the University of California.

Schneider, Benjamin, ed. 1990. *Organizational Climate and Culture.* San Francisco: Jossey-Bass.

Schrag, Peter. 1998. *Paradise Lost: California's Past, America's Future.* New York: New Press.

Scott, W. Richard. 1981. *Organizations: Rational, Natural, and Open Systems.* Englewood Cliffs, N.J.: Prentice-Hall.

Seligman, Adam B. 1995. *The Idea of Civil Society.* Princeton: Princeton University Press.

Skerry, Peter. 1993. *Mexican Americans: The Ambivalent Minority.* New York: Free Press.

Skocpol, Theda. 2000. *The Missing Middle: Working Families and the Future of American Social Policy.* New York: Norton.

Skogan, Wesley G., and Susan M. Hartnett. 1997. *Community Policing, Chicago Style.* New York: Oxford University Press.

Smith, Christian. 1996a. *Disruptive Religion: The Force of Faith in Social-Movement Activism.* New York: Routledge.

———. 1996b. *Resisting Reagan: The U.S. Central America Peace Movement.* Chicago: University of Chicago Press.

Snow, David A., and Robert D. Benford. 1988. "Ideology, Frame Resonance, and Participant Mobilization." *International Social Movement Research* 1:197–217.

———. 1992. "Master Frames and Cycles of Protest." In *Frontiers in Social Movement Theory,* edited by A. Morris and C. Mueller. New Haven: Yale University Press.

Somers, Margaret R. 1993. "Citizenship and the Place of the Public Sphere: Law, Community, and Political Culture in the Transition to Democracy." *American Sociological Review* 58:587–620.

———. 1995a. "Narrating and Naturalizing Civil Society and Citizenship Theory: The Place of Political Culture and the Public Sphere." *Sociological Theory* 13:229–74.

———. 1995b. "What's Political or Cultural about Political Culture and the Public Sphere? Toward an Historical Sociology of Concept Formation." *Sociological Theory* 13:113–44.

Stepan, Alfred. 1988. *Rethinking Military Politics.* Princeton: Princeton University Press.

Swarts, Heidi. 2001. "Moving without a Movement: Organized Churches and Neighborhoods in American Politics." Ph.D. diss., Cornell University.

Swidler, Ann. 1984. "Culture in Action." *American Sociological Review* 51:273–86.

———. 2001. *Talk of Love: How Culture Matters.* Chicago: University of Chicago Press.

Tarrow, Sidney. 1994. *Power in Movement: Social Movements, Collective Action, and Politics.* Cambridge and New York: Cambridge University Press.

Taylor, Charles. 1991. *Multiculturalism and "The Politics of Recognition."* Princeton: Princeton University Press.

Thompson, James D. 1967. *Organizations in Action: Social Science Bases of Administrative Behavior*. New York: McGraw-Hill.

Tipton, Steven M. 1982. *Getting Saved from the Sixties: Moral Meaning in Conversion and Cultural Change*. Berkeley and Los Angeles: University of California Press.

Tocqueville, Alexis de. [1835–40] 1956. *Democracy in America*. New York: New American Library.

Troeltsch, Ernst. 1981. *The Social Teaching of the Christian Churches*. Translated by Olive Wyon. Chicago: University of Chicago Press.

Verba, Sidney, Kay Lehman Schlozman, and Henry E. Brady. 1995. *Voice and Equality: Civic Voluntarism in American Politics*. Cambridge: Harvard University Press.

———. 1997. "The Big Tilt: Participatory Inequality in America." *American Prospect* 32 (May–June): 74–80. Also available at http://epn.org/prospect/32/32verbfs.html.

Walker, Samuel, and Betsy Wright Kreisel. 2001. "Varieties of Citizen Review: The Relationship of Mission, Structure, and Procedures to Police Accountability." In *Critical Issues in Policing*, 4th ed., edited by Roger G. Dunham and Geoffrey P. Alpert. Prospect Heights, Ill.: Waveland.

Warner, S. 1993. "Towards a New Paradigm for the Sociology of Religion in American Society." *American Sociological Review* 58:1044–93.

Warren, Mark R. 1995. "Social Capital and Community Empowerment: Religion and Political Organization in the Texas Industrial Areas Foundation." Ph.D. diss., Harvard University.

———. 2001. *Dry Bones Rattling: Community Building to Revitalize American Democracy*. Princeton: Princeton University Press.

Warren, Mark R., J. Phillip Thompson, and Susan Saegert. 2001. "Social Capital and Poor Communities: Assets, Barriers, and Challenges." In *Social Capital and Poor Communities*, edited by Susan Saegert, J. Phillip Thompson, and Mark R. Warren. New York: Sage.

Warren, Mark R., and Richard L. Wood. 2001. "Faith-Based Community Organizing: The State of the Field." Jericho, N.Y.: Interfaith Funders.

Wattenberg, Martin P. 1998. *The Decline of American Political Parties, 1952–1996*. Cambridge: Harvard University Press.

Weber, Max. [1930] 1998. *The Protestant Ethic and the Spirit of Capitalism*. Los Angeles: Roxbury.

Weick, Karl E. [1969] 1979. *The Social Psychology of Organizing*. 2d ed. Reading, Mass.: Addison-Wesley.

———. 1995. *Sensemaking in Organizations*. Thousand Oaks, Calif.: Sage.

West, Darrel M., and B. A. Loomis. 1998. *The Sound of Money: How Political Interests Get What They Want*. New York: Norton.

Whyte, William Foote, ed. 1991a. *Participatory Action Research*. Newbury Park, Calif.: Sage.

———. 1991b. *Social Theory for Action: How Individuals and Organizations Learn to Change*. Newbury Park, Calif.: Sage.

Williams, Rhys H. 1995. "Constructing the Public Good: Social Movements and Cultural Resources." *Social Problems* 42:124–44.

———. 1996. "Politics, Religion, and the Analysis of Culture." *Theory and Society* 25: 883–900.

———. 1999a. "Public Religion and Hegemony: Contesting the Language of the Common Good." In *The Power of Religious Publics,* edited by William H. Swatos Jr. and James K. Wellman Jr. Westport, Conn.: Praeger.

———. 1999b. "Visions of the Good Society and the Religious Roots of American Political Culture." *Sociology of Religion* 60:1–34.

Wolfe, Alan. 1989. *Whose Keeper? Social Science and Moral Obligation.* Berkeley and Los Angeles: University of California Press. ·

Wood, Elisabeth J. 2001. *Insurgent Collective Action and Civil War in El Salvador.* Cambridge and New York: Cambridge University Press.

Wood, Richard L. 1994. "Faith in Action: Religious Resources for Political Participation in Three Congregations." *Sociology of Religion* 55:389–97.

———. 1995. "Faith in Action: Religion, Race, and the Future of Democracy." Ph.D. diss., University of California at Berkeley.

———. 1997. "Social Capital and Political Culture: God Meets Politics in the Inner City." *American Behavioral Scientist* 40:595–605.

———. 1999. "Religious Culture and Political Action." *Sociological Theory* 17:307–32.

———. 2002. "Religion, Faith-Based Community Organizing, and the Struggle for Justice." In *Cambridge Handbook of Sociology,* edited by Michele Dillon. Cambridge and New York: Cambridge University Press.

Wood, Richard L., and Mark R. Warren. Forthcoming. "Building Bridges in the Public Sphere: A Different Face of Faith-Based Politics."

Woolcock, James. 1998. "Social Capital and Economic Development: Toward a Theoretical Synthesis and Policy Framework." *Theory and Society* 27:151–208.

Wuthnow, Robert. 1988. *The Restructuring of American Religion: Society and Faith since World War II.* Princeton: Princeton University Press.

———. 1994. *Sharing the Journey: Support Groups and America's New Quest for Community.* New York: Free Press.

Wuthnow, Robert, James Davison Hunter, Albert Bergesen, and Edith Kurzweil. 1984. *Cultural Analysis: The Work of Peter L. Berger, Mary Douglas, Michel Foucault, and Jürgen Habermas.* Boston: Routledge.

Yarnold, Barbara M., ed. 1991. *The Role of Religious Organizations in Social Movements.* Westport, Conn.: Praeger.

Zucker, Lynne G. 1977. "The Role of Institutionalization in Cultural Persistence." *American Sociological Review* 42:726–43.

———. 1988. *Institutional Patterns and Organizations: Culture and Environment.* Cambridge, Mass.: Ballinger.

Index

visibility of, 300n. 9; lack of race-based groups' collaboration with, 307n. 6; list of, 282–90; as model for democratic renewal, 6–7; national profile of, 56–57; potential of, 132, 266; race/religion/politics' implications for, 267–71, 273–75; racial diversity in, *145;* religious diversity in, *146;* state-level influence of, 82–87, 306n. 21; strengths and limits of, 81–82, 148–51, 163–64, 273–75, 313–14n. 4; structure of, 68–76; study of, 78–81, 300n. 10; success of, 50–52, 259–60; terminology of, 149, 300n. 11. *See also* beliefs; ethos; federations; organizing practices; Pacific Institute for Community Organization (PICO); pastors and pastoral support; power; self-interest; structural symbiosis
Fantasia, Rick, 134
federations: as bridging social capital, 144–47; competition for resources among, 150; differences in, 75–76, 164, 314n. 9; foundation staff's role in, 305–6n. 19; institutions as members of, 56–58, 68; religious/political/civil joined in, 141–44; strengths and limits of, 273–75; structure of, 68–76; use of term, 300n. 11. *See also* structural symbiosis; *specific federations* (e.g., Pacific Institute for Community Organization [PICO])
feminist movement, as model, 163
Figueroa, Fr. Marco Antonio, *196*
Filipinos, outreach to, 30
Fischer, Claude, 299n. 5
Flaherty, Mary Ann, 281
Florida: DART project in, 45, 306n. 21; joy in collective action in, 176; organizations in, 6, 284
Ford Foundation, 305–6n. 19
foundations, staff and role of, 305–6n. 19
Fraser, Nancy, 161, 313n. 2
Freire, Paulo, 169
Full Gospel Church. *See* Gospel Church

Gamaliel Network: funding for, 321–22n. 3; national profile of, 56; number of projects of, 304n. 2; state-level influence of, 306n. 21; training of, 316–17n. 31
gambling, responses to, 75
Gamson, William A., 199, 200
gang members, character traits of, 224, 319n. 5
"garbage can model," 321n. 2, 322n. 5
Gateway Foods, 49
Gaudette, Tom, 322n. 4
gender: beliefs and, 113–14; in organizations' demographics, 12, 301n. 19; in PUEBLO's focus, 95
Georgia, organizations in, 284
God: focus on individual and, 227–28, 241; in historical context, 241–42; power and authority of, 212
Gore, Rev. Willie, 180
Gospel Church: cultural dynamics of, 216, 224–30; description of worship at, 221–24; as inwardly, individually focused, 227–29, 233–34; locale of, 219, 220; Saint Columba compared to, 240–41, 242
Gospel Church Civic Committee: concerns of, 229–30; difficulties of, 230–34; meetings of, 222, 230–31; other organizations compared to, 250–57
government: as component of public sphere, 126, 131–32; constructive role for, 275–76; religion's role and, 4; use of term, 310n. 3. *See also* public officials; public policy; public sphere
Graduate Theological Union (Berkeley), 294
Groot, Fr. Ignatius de: criticism of, 26–27, 302n. 5; ethical reflection of, 187–88; letter from, 27–28; Montgomery Ward site political action and, 33; worship led by, 206–10, 212–13
Gut, Stephanie, 73, 294

Habermas, Jürgen, 310n. 5, 312n. 1
Hamer, Fanny Lou, 236
Hardy, Gwen, 97, 106–7, 114
Harris, Elihu: criminal justice issues and, 90, 91–93; economic development

social capital: bridging of, 144–47, 311n. 24; building of, 35; cultural strategies' impact on, 125–26; debate on, 310n. 10; decline of, 129, 266–67, 310n. 8; in democratic life, 128–30, 132–33; different uses of, 198; as factor, 157, 262; OCO and PUEBLO compared, 135; of PICO, 137, 138–41; of race-based organization, 133–35; of religious culture, 138–41, 204–5, 263, 296; trust in, 118, 129, 133–35, 309n. 23; of working poor, 267, 269

social movements: democratic aspirations of, 16–17; organizational collapse in local, 303n. 15; pessimism about, 55–56, 86–87, 137, 259–60, 269; political contestation and, 19–20; political opportunity structure for, 9; potential of, 268; racial identity as basis for, 103–5, 133; recruitment techniques in, 29; research on, 300–301n. 14; stability in, 199–200; transition in, 308n. 10; use of term, 172, 303n. 8. See also community organizing; cultural dynamics and strategies; resources; social capital

social services: as critical issue, 80; funding for, 96; OCO/PUEBLO campaign focused on, 120, 307n. 6, 309n. 24; personnel of, 118–19, 135. See also health care

socioeconomic status: beliefs and, 113–14; consumer culture and, 224–25; democratic skills linked to, 130; in organizations' demographics, 12, 147, 277–78. See also subaltern groups; working and low-income families

Soltero, Lupe, 32–33, 42

Somers, Margaret R., 261–62, 263, 312n. 2, 321n. 1

South Carolina, organizations in, 289

Southern Christian Leadership Conference (SCLC), 105, 308n. 10

Southwest Network for Environmental and Economic Justice, 7

Spread the Word Around Town (SWAT) teams, 228

stability: church's role in, 225–26; factors to bolster, 252–53; limitations on, 225; maintenance of, 199–201

staff. See organizers

state. See government

Stepan, Alfred, 310n. 3

strategy, as organizers' key word, 94–95. See also organizing practices

street lighting: campaign for, 65, 302–3n. 7, 319n. 3; inadequate amount of, 220; support for, 29

structural position in public life: concept of, 126–32; of CTWO, 133–37; of PICO, 137–38, 141–47

structural symbiosis: benefits of, 295–97; concept of, 73–75; cultural strategy's success and, 138–41, 257; origins of, 294–95; strengths and limits of, 276–79; sustaining of, 76–82, 194

Student Nonviolent Coordinating Committee (SNCC), 104–5, 308n. 10

subaltern groups: as agents, 176; counterpublic for, 161, 313n. 2; oppression of, 115, 116–19, 134, 309n. 21; organizations based in concerns of, 147, 174, 214–17, 268; political contestation and, 19–20, 98, 254, 255; political interpretations and, 201–2; power and, 192–93; in public realm, 128; social capital as resource of, 129–30; sustaining inclusion of, 277–78. See also multiracial culture; working and low-income families

SWAT (Spread the Word Around Town) teams, 228

Swidler, Ann, 302n. 1

symbiosis, definition of, 305n. 17. See also structural symbiosis

target: as organizers' key word, 94–95; use of term, 41–42, 185

Tarrow, Sidney, 20, 300–301n. 14

Taylor, Joyce, 92

Taylor, Maria de Porres, 236

Tennessee, organizations in, 289

Ten Points Coalition (Boston), 315–16n. 23

terrorist attacks, implications of, 260